Twice upon a Time

SELECTED STORIES, 1898–1939

Although L.M. Montgomery (1874–1942) is best remembered for the twenty-two book-length works of fiction that she published in her lifetime, from *Anne of Green Gables* (1908) to *Anne of Ingleside* (1939), she also contributed some five hundred short stories and serials to a wide range of North American and British periodicals from 1895 to 1940. While most of these stories demonstrate her ability to produce material that would fit the mainstream periodical fiction market as it evolved across almost half a century, many of them also contain early incarnations of characters, storylines, conversations, and settings that she would rework for inclusion in her novels and collections of linked short stories.

In *Twice upon a Time*, the third volume in The L.M. Montgomery Library, Benjamin Lefebvre collects and discusses over two dozen stories from across Montgomery's career as a short fiction writer, many of them available in book form for the first time. The volume offers a rare glimpse into Montgomery's creative process in adapting her periodical work for her books, which continue to fascinate readers all over the world.

(THE L.M. MONTGOMERY LIBRARY)

BENJAMIN LEFEBVRE, editor of The L.M. Montgomery Library, is director of L.M. Montgomery Online. His publications include an edition of Montgomery's rediscovered final book, *The Blythes Are Quoted*, and the three-volume critical anthology *The L.M. Montgomery Reader*, which won the 2016 PROSE Award for Literature from the Association of American Publishers. He lives in Kitchener, Ontario.

T0283226

THE L.M. MONTGOMERY LIBRARY
Edited by Benjamin Lefebvre

A Name for Herself: Selected Writings, 1891–1917
A World of Songs: Selected Poems, 1894–1921
Twice upon a Time: Selected Stories, 1898–1939

L.M. MONTGOMERY

Twice upon a Time

SELECTED STORIES, 1898–1939

Edited by BENJAMIN LEFEBVRE

UNIVERSITY OF TORONTO PRESS
Toronto Buffalo London

© University of Toronto Press 2022
Toronto Buffalo London
utorontopress.com

ISBN 978-1-4875-4415-7 (cloth)   ISBN 978-1-4875-4413-3 (EPUB)
ISBN 978-1-4875-4412-6 (paper)   ISBN 978-1-4875-4414-0 (PDF)

Library and Archives Canada Cataloguing in Publication
Title: Twice upon a time : selected stories, 1898–1939 / L.M. Montgomery ;
edited by Benjamin Lefebvre.
Other titles: Short stories. Selections
Names: Montgomery, L.M. (Lucy Maud), 1874–1942, author. | Lefebvre,
Benjamin, editor.
Series: Montgomery, L.M. (Lucy Maud), 1874–1942. L.M. Montgomery
library.
Description: Series statement: The L.M. Montgomery library | Includes
bibliographical references.
Identifiers: Canadiana (print) 20220132445 | Canadiana (ebook)
20220132488 | ISBN 9781487544126 (softcover) | ISBN 9781487544157
(hardcover) | ISBN 9781487544133 (EPUB) | ISBN 9781487544140 (PDF)
Subjects: LCSH: Montgomery, L.M. (Lucy Maud), 1874–1942—History and
criticism. | LCGFT: Short stories.
Classification: LCC PS8526.O55 A6 2022 | DDC C813/.52—dc23

This book has been published with the help of a grant from
the Federation for the Humanities and Social Sciences, through
the Awards to Scholarly Publications Program, using funds provided by
the Social Sciences and Humanities Research Council of Canada.

We wish to acknowledge the land on which the University of Toronto
Press operates. This land is the traditional territory of the Wendat,
the Anishnaabeg, the Haudenosaunee, the Métis, and
the Mississaugas of the Credit First Nation.

University of Toronto Press acknowledges the financial support of
the Government of Canada and the Ontario Arts Council, an agency of
the Government of Ontario, for its publishing activities.

Canada Council   Conseil des Arts
for the Arts   du Canada

ONTARIO ARTS COUNCIL
CONSEIL DES ARTS DE L'ONTARIO
an Ontario government agency
un organisme du gouvernement de l'Ontario

Funded by the   Financé par le
Government   gouvernement
of Canada   du Canada

Contents

CONTENTS

A Note on the Author

L.M. Montgomery is now widely recognized as a major twentieth-century author, one whose bestselling books remain hugely popular and influential all over the world more than three-quarters of a century after her death. Born in Clifton (now New London), Prince Edward Island, in 1874, into a family whose ancestors had immigrated to Canada from Scotland and England, she was raised in nearby Cavendish by her maternal grandparents following the death of her mother and spent a year during her adolescence with her father and his new family in Saskatchewan. Raised in a household that distrusted novels but prized poetry and oral storytelling, she began to write during childhood, although few examples of her juvenilia survive. She received a teaching certificate from Prince of Wales College (Charlottetown) and, after one year of teaching school, took undergraduate courses in English literature for a year at Dalhousie University (Halifax), but she did not have the financial resources to complete her degree. During this time, she began publishing essays, short fiction, and poems in North American periodicals. In 1898, after two more years of teaching school, she returned to Cavendish to take care of her widowed grandmother and to write full-time, soon earning more from her pen than she had teaching school. With the exception of a nine-month stint on the staff of the *Halifax Daily Echo*, where her duties included writing a weekly column entitled "Around the Table," Montgomery remained in Cavendish until 1911, when the death of her grandmother freed her to marry a Presbyterian minister. After a honeymoon in England and Scotland, she and her husband moved to southern Ontario, where she divided her time between writing, motherhood, and the responsibilities that came with her position as a minister's wife.

Her first novel, *Anne of Green Gables* (1908), the benchmark against which her remaining body of work is measured, was followed by twenty-three additional books, including ten featuring Anne Shirley: *Anne of Avonlea* (1909), *Chronicles of Avonlea* (1912), *Anne of the Island* (1915), *Anne's House of Dreams* (1917), *Rainbow Valley* (1919), *Further Chronicles of Avonlea* (1920), *Rilla of Ingleside* (1921), *Anne of Windy Poplars* (1936), *Anne of Ingleside* (1939), and *The Blythes Are Quoted*, completed shortly before her death but not published in its entirety until 2009. During her distinguished career, she was made a Fellow of the British Royal Society of Arts, was named one of the twelve greatest women in Canada by the *Toronto Star*, and became an Officer of the Order of the British Empire. When she died in 1942, apparently by her own hand, her obituary in the *Globe and Mail* declared that her body of work "showed no lessening of that freshness and simplicity of style that characterized *Anne of Green Gables*." Since her death, several collections of her periodical pieces have been published, as have more than a dozen volumes of her journals, letters, essays, and scrapbooks. Ontario and Prince Edward Island are home to many tourist sites and archival collections devoted to her, and her books continue to be adapted for stage and screen.

Abbreviations

EQ	*Emily's Quest*
FCA	*Further Chronicles of Avonlea*
GGL	*The Green Gables Letters from L.M. Montgomery to Ephraim Weber, 1905–1909*
GR	*The Golden Road*
JLH	*Jane of Lantern Hill*
KO	*Kilmeny of the Orchard*
LMMCJ, 1	*L.M. Montgomery's Complete Journals: The Ontario Years, 1911–1917*
LMMCJ, 2	*L.M. Montgomery's Complete Journals: The Ontario Years, 1918–1921*
LMMCJ, 5	*L.M. Montgomery's Complete Journals: The Ontario Years, 1930–1933*
MDMM	*My Dear Mr. M: Letters to G.B. MacMillan from L.M. Montgomery*
MM	*Magic for Marigold*
MP	*Mistress Pat: A Novel of Silver Bush*
NH	*A Name for Herself: Selected Writings, 1891–1917*
RI	*Rilla of Ingleside*
RV	*Rainbow Valley*
SG	*The Story Girl*
SJLMM	*The Selected Journals of L.M. Montgomery*, Volume 4: 1929–1935; Volume 5: 1935–1942
TW	*A Tangled Web*
WOP	*The Watchman and Other Poems*
WS	*A World of Songs: Selected Poems, 1894–1921*

Preface

IN HER 1995 ARTICLE ON L.M. MONTGOMERY'S PROCESS
of writing and revision, Elizabeth Epperly suggests that "anyone who has studied manuscripts knows the excitement of
finding out something intimate about the writer in the changes
of ink and slant of the words, in the crossings out and the addi-
tions, in the marginal notations and in the quality and care of
the papers themselves."[1] In the years since Epperly's pioneering
research in this area, readers have had the opportunity to see
Montgomery's writing process in action, thanks to the recent
publication of *Readying Rilla* (2016), edited by Elizabeth
Waterston and Kate Waterston, and of *Anne of Green Gables:
The Original Manuscript* (2019), edited by Carolyn Strom
Collins. As Elizabeth Waterston notes, the manuscript of *Rilla of
Ingleside* shows "Montgomery's scrupulous self-editing," both in
"the first rush of writing" and throughout the process of revising.
In short, studying the manuscript gives readers access to "the log
of [Montgomery's] creative voyage." Extending this idea further,
Collins suggests that "it should be comforting to those who wish
to gain inspiration and insight into the construction of a classic
novel such as *Anne of Green Gables* that it did not spring fully
formed from the pen of the author, but had to be 'pruned down
and branched out,' as Anne said about herself, before it made its
entry into the world of exceptional literature."[2] Although cover
art on recent trade editions of Montgomery's novels tends to opt
for a vaguely turn-of-the-twentieth-century aesthetic, regardless of when each book was written or is set, these particular
editions of *Anne* and *Rilla* emphasize the process of creation and

revision as rooted in time and place—Cavendish, Prince Edward Island, around 1905; Leaskdale, Ontario, between 1919 and 1920—and in the materiality of pen and paper.

Twice upon a Time, the third volume in The L.M. Montgomery Library, likewise gives readers a chance to look under the hood, so to speak, of some of Montgomery's best-known books in order to gain a more nuanced understanding of the process of inspiration, creation, reconsideration, and revision that led to book-length fiction that has remained in print for decades since her death. As the first volume in this series to centre on Montgomery's fiction, preceded by a volume of her selected miscellaneous pieces (*A Name for Herself*) and a volume of her selected poems (*A World of Songs*),[3] it offers readers a selection of her short stories that, with a few exceptions, were first published in periodicals between 1898 and 1939 and that consist of early versions of well-known characters, plot points, conversations, and settings in her books. As such, this volume of short fiction, like those that will follow in this series, seeks not only to add to the canon of known Montgomery texts but also to trouble the notion of a canon, showing the complex relationship Montgomery saw between periodical work (fleeting, given the frequency of publication, but with the potential to reach a large number of new readers) and book publication (given that a book could be reprinted indefinitely depending on public demand).[4] In a study that juxtaposes Montgomery with four contemporaneous Canadian authors who also wrote bestselling fiction, Clarence Karr notes that "after a long apprenticeship, she managed, with *Anne of Green Gables*, to find the proper mix of good writing, satire, wit, and character portrayal to synchronize with the popular market for fiction."[5] Although Montgomery downplayed the scope of this "long apprenticeship" in several autobiographical essays published after she had become a bestselling novelist,[6] her strategic use of the periodical story as a place to test out characters and storylines was considerable.

Earlier scholars who have looked at some of these stories have referred to them as "practice exercises" in the case of Elizabeth Waterston, "prequels" in the case of Irene Gammel, and "brief periodical warm-ups" in the case of Wendy Roy. Yet examining the material included in this volume shows that Montgomery's use of the periodical story as a prelude to the novel—or as what

Cecily Devereux calls an "early working-out in narrative"—is far more complex than it first seems.[7] While stories such as "A Garden of Old Delights," "Aunt Philippa and the Men," "Abel and His Great Adventure," and "Tomorrow Comes" were published a few years prior to their revised reappearance in book form, adding weight to the speculation that Montgomery wrote these stories with the intention of using them in a book that was already in progress, others like "Our Uncle Wheeler," "A New-Fashioned Flavoring," "Miss Marietta's Jersey," "The Little Fellow's Photograph," and "The Matchmaker" appeared in revised form in a novel a decade or longer after their appearance in periodical form, making for a different kind of creative process. Also in this collection is evidence of two more kinds of creative revision: "Retribution," found in Montgomery's papers in the form of a typescript that evidently precedes her expansion of the story for her final book, *The Blythes Are Quoted* (2009), but not, apparently, ever published in this form; and, as an appendix, "Dog Monday's Vigil," which was reworked from *Rilla of Ingleside* for inclusion in the third edition of *Our Canadian Literature: Representative Prose and Verse* (1923).

It is important to point out that, although Montgomery acknowledged in her book *The Watchman and Other Poems* (1916) the several periodicals that had first published some of the poems reprinted therein, she did not do likewise in any of her books of fiction.[8] This includes *Chronicles of Avonlea*, a collection of linked short stories previously published separately in different form ("The Hurrying of Ludovic," in this present volume, is a representative sample of a short story reworked for the *Chronicles* collection). Moreover, except for occasional remarks in her surviving life writing, she left no record of her rationale for selecting certain pieces as worthy of repurposing over others, nor did she comment on the timing of these publications. What fascinates me especially is that Montgomery published "The Schoolmaster's Bride" and republished "A Pioneer Wooing" and "The Indecision of Margaret" in periodicals just before the publication of the novel in which a revised version appeared, almost as an attempt to whet the reading appetites of prospective book buyers, for whom the periodical story would be an unstated advertisement for a forthcoming novel. In so doing, Montgomery gave interested readers the "log" of her creative process, to return to Elizabeth Waterston's phrase, but left much open to speculation based on the evidence she left behind.

Indeed, connecting the dots between Montgomery's stated intentions and the clues scattered in hundreds of periodicals around the world has involved the time and expertise of several dedicated people. I am grateful to friends and colleagues in the L.M. Montgomery community—particularly Vanessa Brown, Mary Beth Cavert, Donna J. Campbell, Carolyn Strom Collins, Elizabeth Rollins Epperly, Melanie J. Fishbane, Carole Gerson, Caroline E. Jones, Yuka Kajihara, Joanne Lebold, Jennifer H. Litster, Simon Lloyd, Andrea McKenzie, Kate Sutherland, and the late Christy Woster—for several years of conversation and collaboration about Montgomery's publishing history. Thanks as well to Mark Thompson, Christine Robertson, and their colleagues at University of Toronto Press for shepherding this book through the production process; to two anonymous referees whose helpful feedback on a draft of this book's manuscript gave me much to think about; to a James F. Harvey and Helen S. Harvey Travel Scholarship at McMaster University that made possible a research trip in 2006 (near the end of my doctoral studies) to Charlottetown, where I spent some time with Montgomery's handwritten manuscripts; to staff at the Confederation Centre Art Gallery (Charlottetown), Archival and Special Collections at the University of Guelph Library, and University Archives and Special Collections at the University of Prince Edward Island Library, all of which house many Montgomery materials; to staff at the interlibrary loan departments at several university libraries, including Guelph, Laurier, Ryerson, Waterloo, and Winnipeg; and to Jacob Letkemann for his continued support and encouragement.

Once again, my editorial work on Montgomery's periodical publications owes a particular debt to the late Rea Wilmshurst (1941–1996), to whose memory this volume is dedicated. Rea was an indefatigable researcher whose contributions to the field of Montgomery studies include co-authoring *Lucy Maud Montgomery: A Preliminary Bibliography* (1986), editing eight trade collections of Montgomery's short fiction, and compiling two exhaustive bibliographies of literary allusions in Montgomery's novels.[9] I never met Rea, but there have been many times during my own research in libraries and online that I have felt a professional kinship with her and her work. What is especially noteworthy about her contributions to the field is that she completed them prior to the digital age, which has revolutionized humanities research by making early print materials far more accessible than before, to the great benefit of Montgomery's global reading community. As she noted in an essay about her work on Montgomery's short stories, "There are depths to Montgomery, as scholars, critics, and readers are increasingly coming to discover."[10] Hopefully, this new volume of Montgomery's short fiction, organized around the creative process of writing and revision, will extend Wilmshurst's observation in compelling new ways.

BENJAMIN LEFEBVRE

NOTES

1 Epperly, "L.M. Montgomery's Manuscript Revisions," 228–29. This article focuses on the handwritten manuscripts of *Anne of Green Gables* and *Emily of New Moon*. For a study of all fifteen handwritten book-length manuscripts by Montgomery housed at the Confederation Centre Art Gallery in Charlottetown, see Epperly, "Approaching the Montgomery Manuscripts."

2 Waterston, "L.M. Montgomery's Creative Path to Publication," vi, viii, xiv; Collins, Introduction, 9; see also *AGG*, 384.

3 *A Name for Herself* does include a newspaper column about fictional characters ("Around the Table," signed Cynthia and published in the *Halifax Daily Echo* between 1901 and 1902) and one short story (the undated "Two Sides of a Life Story," signed J.C. Neville and presumed to have been published sometime after Montgomery's marriage in 1911). See *NH*, 75–191, 223–30.

4 The discrepancy between periodical publication and book publication extended to remuneration as well: as per standard publishing practices, Montgomery received a one-time fee (sometimes per word) for an item published in a periodical and a royalty for book publication based on a percentage of earnings from the number of copies sold. Given that Montgomery's novels sold well in multiple countries, the gap between a flat fee for a short story or a poem and a royalty payment for a book was considerable: as

I mentioned before, when Montgomery did a tally of her earnings in February 1921, she noted that she had received an average of $3.45 per poem and an average of $13.14 per story since the mid-1890s, whereas she had received $16,456.26 so far in royalties for *Anne's House of Dreams*, published just four years earlier (Lefebvre, Afterword to *A World of Songs*, 106, 108).

5 Karr, *Authors and Audiences*, 125.

6 See, for instance, her essays "How I Began to Write," "How I Began," "Novel Writing Notes," and "An Autobiographical Sketch." Montgomery offered more details about her early writing in "The Alpine Path: The Story of My Career" (*NH*, 272–89), but few examples of her juvenilia survive.

7 Waterston, *Magic Island*, 12; Gammel, *Looking for Anne*, 66; Roy, *The Next Instalment*, 113; Devereux, Headnote to "Our Uncle Wheeler," 335.

8 Montgomery's acknowledgment in *Watchman* may have been more a legal requirement than a courtesy, given that she acknowledged the right "to use the poems of which [the periodicals] own the copyright" (*WOP*, n.pag.). Still, the mere fact of listing nineteen periodicals from *The Smart Set* to *Everybody's Magazine* also served to showcase the prominent markets in which Montgomery had circulated some of this work previously.

9 Wilmshurst's lists of Montgomery's short stories, poems, and miscellaneous pieces included in *Lucy Maud Montgomery: A Preliminary Bibliography* were the starting point for my own extensive research in this area; Carolyn Strom Collins's updated version of Wilmshurst's bibliography reflects recent findings by several Montgomery collectors. Wilmshurst's collections of Montgomery's short fiction, grouped thematically, included *Akin to Anne: Tales of Other Orphans* (1988), *Along the Shore: Tales by the Sea* (1989), *Among the Shadows: Tales from the Darker Side* (1990), *After Many Days: Tales of Time Passed* (1991), *Against the Odds: Tales of Achievement* (1993), *At the Altar: Matrimonial Tales* (1994), *Across the Miles: Tales of Correspondence* (1995), and *Christmas with Anne and Other Holiday Stories* (1995). All but the last title have long been out of print. Wilmshurst's final collection of Montgomery's stories, completed by Joanne Lebold, appears as *Around the Hearth: Tales of Home and Family* (2022).

10 Wilmshurst, "Finding L.M. Montgomery's Short Stories," 227.

A Note on the Text

The items included in this volume in chronological order were published separately in a wide range of Canadian, American, and British periodicals over a period of three decades and appeared under the byline "L.M. Montgomery." Exceptions are "Retribution," which survives in typescript form only, and "Dog Monday's Vigil," signed "Lucy Maud Montgomery" and anthologized two years after this material appeared in *Rilla of Ingleside.* While some of these stories have been collected previously (in a critical edition of *Anne of Green Gables* edited by Cecily Devereux and in trade collections of short stories edited by Catherine McLay, by Rea Wilmshurst, and by Carolyn Strom Collins and Christy Woster), in this edition I use the original periodical publications as my copy-texts, collating them against copies of these stories in Montgomery's scrapbooks when they are found there and treating her handwritten corrections as authoritative. While I have not attempted to regularize or modernize the stylistic conventions (in terms of spelling, hyphenation, and punctuation) that the original publications followed, for ease of reading I have silently regularized some inconsistencies in terms of the placement of commas and periods within quotation marks and other idiosyncratic forms of usage (the published version of "Aunt Philippa and the Men," as one example, consistently drops the apostrophe in the words "ain't" and "won't" for some reason).

I have also made the following substantive corrections (keyed here to page and line numbers), following Montgomery's handwritten amendments in her scrapbooks:

6.13	so we didn't] if we didn't
9.4	glanced at us] glared at us
23.34	will impress you.] will surprise you.
85.18–19	All women are lovely] All women were lovely
91.22	horrors of thousands.] horror of thousands.
91.32	must be there] must be here

I have resisted making substantive corrections of my own to Montgomery's text, including one case in which a verb is clearly missing from the original (when Miss Marietta "watched him down the steps and across the yard") and one case of a name change involving Mrs. Churchill's late sister in "The Matchmaker." Instead, my own corrections (again keyed to page and line numbers) are as follows:

16.30	Reeve and Robby] Reeve and Bobby
19.15	flower-scoop] flour-scoop
22.36	should have tasted] should not have tasted
27.17	fashion a hot day] fashion on a hot day
31.9	Five minutes latter] Five minutes later
36.5	attended grandmother] attend grandmother
40.19	your great-grandfather] your great-grandmother
42.18	I suppose they were] I supposed they were
46.1	anybody's else] anybody else's
84.20	deeply line] deeply lined
87.3	terrible." and] terrible."—and
93.29	doubtedly sadly] doubted sadly
105.10	curtesy] curtsy
108.31	came a-wooing,] come a-wooing,
109.22	We got out] He got out
114.22	misty misty white] misty white
134.13	given me to do it;] given me to do;
155.17	she explained.] she exclaimed.
165.37	woke up along] woke up alone
169.29	me the dappled] me on the dappled
174.32	pour of its] pour off its
186.12	you every try] you ever try
186.23	as anything] was anything
216.4	dare not] dared not

218.37   Who was "he".] Who was "he"?
221.19   than it was] than if it was

My notes at the end of the volume are keyed to page numbers within the text rather than to superscript note numbers. They provide bibliographical details about the items included in this volume and identify literary allusions, archaic terminology, historical references, and connections between these stories and Montgomery's life writing and book-length fiction. In the notes, I have adjusted currencies for inflation using the inflation calculator on the Bank of Canada website, found at https://bankofcanada.ca/rates/related/inflation-calculator; this consumer price index goes only as far back as 1914, but it helps put currency figures into context and explains, for instance, the astonishment of two teenage boys after each of them receives a $20 bill from their uncle.

Scans of many of these stories from their original publications are available on the Kindred Spaces website, an initiative of the L.M. Montgomery Institute at the University of Prince Edward Island, available at https://kindredspaces.ca. Additional information about Montgomery's periodical publications and about her life, her work, and her legacy more broadly can be found at the website of L.M. Montgomery Online (which I direct) at https://lmmonline.org.

B.L.

Twice upon a Time
SELECTED STORIES, 1898–1939

Our Uncle Wheeler

The first story in this volume precedes by a decade the episode in *Anne of Green Gables* (1908) in which Anne Shirley and Diana Barry, overly excited after attending a concert hosted by Avonlea's Debating Club on Diana's twelfth birthday, race to the Barrys' spare room and jump onto the bed—only to discover, to their horror, that Diana's elderly great-aunt Josephine is already asleep in it. In this initial version, published in *Golden Days for Boys and Girls* (a popular weekly paper from Philadelphia) in January 1898, Montgomery writes this story as one in which the perpetrators of the race and its victim are male, which is not surprising given that, according to her journals, this chapter from the novel had been "suggested to me by a story father told me of how he and two other boys had jumped into bed on an old minister in the spare room at Uncle John Montgomery's long ago." For Cecily Devereux, who included this story in her Broadview critical edition of *Anne of Green Gables*, "This early working-out in narrative is a compelling indication of Montgomery's writing practices of revising and reworking material and of negotiating particular domestic genres. While this version is arguably more concerned with administering moral advice to its readers about telling the truth than is the case in [the novel], in both cases the story has to do with learning to take responsibility for one's actions." Also significant are the ways Montgomery imagines separate motivations, deliberations, and outcomes depending on the gender of the participants.

I N REALITY HE WAS OUR GREAT-UNCLE, AND WE WERE very much in awe of him.

The rare times when he came to visit us—usually popping down unexpectedly at some particularly inconvenient moment—were periods of misery for us lively boys, for Uncle Wheeler was a very precise old gentleman, fidgety when boys were around, and with all an old bachelor's decided opinions as to the training and behavior of those unavoidable evils.

Consequently, as Rod used to say, we were "as unhappy as a cat on hot bricks" when Uncle Wheeler came.

He had befriended and aided father more than once in troublous times, for he was really kind-hearted at the core, and hence we were instructed to regard him with gratitude and respect. He was always "Uncle Wheeler" to us. Our other uncles were Uncle Tom, Dick or Harry, but we would as soon have thought of calling Uncle Wheeler "Uncle James" as of saying "hello" to the minister.

Rod and I were the oldest of our family, being fifteen and fourteen respectively. We were hearty, growing boys, and found it very hard to "tone down" during Uncle Wheeler's sojourn.

Nevertheless, we tried our best, for we really liked the old man, in spite of our fear of him. When it was decided that Rod should go to college if it could be managed, Uncle Wheeler wrote to father and mother a letter in which he denounced the project as "absurd nonsense," and railed at it for three pages. On the fourth he announced his intention of paying Rod's way through college if he were really bent upon going, and hoped he wouldn't disgrace the family.

Rod was jubilant; but it behooved him to be very careful, for Uncle Wheeler was extremely touchy, and sometimes got offended at very trifling things. Therefore we made up our minds to be more than usually sedate and proper on the occasion of his next visit.

About two months after this letter, Rod and I received an invitation to a party at the house of one of our schoolmates. During the afternoon Sydney Hatfield, a cousin of ours, arrived and decided to stay over night, as he was going to Tracy's, too.

Mother intended to put him in the spare room to sleep; but about dusk a cutter drove up to the door, and in it were the three Winsloe boys from Bracebridge, who came in and said they were also bound for the party and would afterwards remain with us until the next day.

We were a big family, all told, so that mother said to us, just before we left:

"I think, boys, you'd better take Sydney up to your room to-night and let the Winsloe boys have the spare room. We can accommodate you all if you won't mind a little crowding."

Lou Winsloe said uninvited guests ought to be thankful to be taken in at all, and for his part he thought it jolly to sleep three in a bed, if it was a big one, and we all drove off to the party in high spirits.

It was late when we returned, and of course everybody was in bed. Mother had left a light burning for us, and we tip-toed in cautiously, so as not to disturb the sleepers.

While we were putting away our coats I noticed Rod and Dave Winsloe talking earnestly, and when I went out to lock the back porch door Rod followed me.

"Say, Art, Dave's nervous; he's afraid of the ghost and doesn't want to sleep in the spare room. Of course he's a ninny, but arguing won't do any good. What's to be done?"

Dave Winsloe was a delicate boy of nearly fifteen, and we always regarded him as "babyish." He was extremely sensitive, and his nervous whims had to be indulged.

I don't know how he'd got wind of "our ghost," but he had. I may here remark that our spare room had the reputation of being haunted during the sojourn of the family who had preceded us. None of us had ever seen or heard anything worse than ourselves in it, and never felt in the least disturbed. We had good, healthy nerves and didn't worry about spooks.

But I knew Dave couldn't help his terror, so, feeling sorry, I said,

"Well, the three Winsloes had better go up stairs to our room and you and Syd and I will take the spare room. We're equal to any ghost who may be on the hunting trail to-night."

This arrangement suited all hands, so we showed the Winsloes up stairs and separated.

Our house was an old-fashioned one, and the spare room opened off the end of the parlor. The parlor was a long, narrow room, and the bedroom was also long and narrow, so that from the parlor door to the extreme end of the bedroom, where the bed was, was quite a distance.

Syd, Rod and I went into the parlor and found it deliciously warm, as there had been a fire in the stove. We supposed mother had lit it to warm the spare room for the Winsloes, and we thought it rather a good joke that Dave's ghostly terrors should have put him out of a warm sleeping room.

We undressed by the fire quietly enough, for we were tired; but when we were ready for bed, Syd, who was always up to mischief, had a brilliant idea.

"Say, you chaps, let's start from the hall door and see which will get into bed first."

Rod and I thought it would be good fun, if we didn't make a noise. So, having taken a vow of silence, we put out the candle, for the moonlight was streaming in at the windows, ranged ourselves by the hall door, and Syd gave the word, "Go!"

The bedroom door was open, so we flew down the parlor, shot through the door and the spare room, and the whole three of us, with one spring, bounded on the bed at the same instant.

There was one awful moment in which we realized what had happened, and then a wheezy, sleepy, well-known voice puffed out:

"Why, bless my soul, what's the matter?"

It was Uncle Wheeler!

We had jumped upon that bed pretty quick, but we jumped off three times quicker, dashed out of the room and scuttled through the parlor, never stopping for breath until we reached the kitchen.

Rod and I wished the floor would open and quietly let us into the cellar. Syd, being a stranger, of course didn't appreciate the situation so keenly.

"Say, you chaps, that old duffer must have got his breath most lammed out of him. Who is it?"

"Uncle Wheeler," groaned Rod. "And, oh! what *will* he say? How ever did he come to be there, and *why* didn't mother leave some way for us to know?"

Just then we heard a gasp and sigh and a sort of groan in the little breakfast-room off the kitchen.

We all jumped.

"Great Scott! Is that one of Dave Winsloe's ghosts?" exclaimed Syd.

But I had got a lamp lit, and by its light we saw our eleven-year-old brother, Tad, come shuffling out of the breakfast-room, rubbing his eyes.

"Say, you fellows, have you got back? Mother told me to sit up and tell you—"

"Tell us what?"

"That Uncle Wheeler'd come, and she'd put him in the spare room, and that the Winsloe boys must have your room, and you chaps would have to sleep in the kitchen loft. I meant to keep awake—honest, I did—but I got so tired, I went in there and lay down on the lounge. I guess I went to sleep."

"I guess you did," growled Rod. "You've done for us now."

And after each of us had rated the still stupid and half asleep Tad soundly by way of venting our ill humor, we crept off, shiveringly, to the kitchen loft.

We were too tired and cold and cross to talk it over then, but by dawn Rod and I were sitting up in bed, discussing our mishap in whispers, so as not to waken Syd.

"Nothing worse *could* have happened," lamented Rod. "Uncle Wheeler will be piping mad; you could hardly blame him, I suppose. What a rousing scare he must have got! But he won't listen to any excuse, and not a blessed cent need I expect for college if he finds out. Some men would just look on it as a joke, but Uncle Wheeler isn't that sort."

After forlornly admitting that we'd got into a scrape beyond doubt, we got up, put on some old clothes and went down to sneak Syd's suit out of the parlor for him, for, needless to say, we hadn't stopped to get our clothes in our stampede of the night before.

On our way through the hall, we met the Winsloe boys tiptoeing down stairs, much to our surprise, for it was barely daylight.

"What's the rush?" asked Rod, with an attempt at hilarity. "Been seeing any ghosts, Dave?"

"It's beginning to rain," announced Lou, "and it's setting in for a big thaw, so we decided to get up, rouse you out if we could and start just as soon as possible. You know it's a long drive home, and a wretched road at the best of times. It'll hardly be passable in a thaw."

They passed on out to the stables. Rod and I looked at each other, both struck by the same idea.

"Nobody else will be stirring for an hour yet," said Rod, voicing my thoughts rather shamefacedly. "We'll light a fire and get some grub for the boys, and they'll be gone before mother or Uncle Wheeler come on the scene. They were supposed to be going to the spare room, and if we just hold our tongues, and get Syd to do the same, Uncle Wheeler will think it was the Winsloes."

"But Tad?"

"Tad didn't appear till too late, so that won't give us away; and he was half-asleep, and I'll bet a cent he'll never remember how many of us were there or that we hadn't our clothes on. It hardly seems fair, though, to put it on the Winsloes."

"That won't hurt. They're nothing to Uncle Wheeler, and he doesn't even know them, so it won't do them any harm, while it would do us whole heaps."

We talked it over and decided to go ahead. I left Rod to light the fire, while I went up, wakened Syd, explained the whole affair and easily got him to promise silence.

"We're not going to tell any fibs, of course!" I said, virtuously. "If anybody asks us who it was, we'll have to tell straight out; but not likely any one will, and we'll just keep quiet. See?"

Syd thought it a good joke, and agreed to keep mum. The Winsloes came in; Rod and I got them a cold breakfast and they started off.

Just as they drove away, mother came out at the hall door, and Uncle Wheeler, in dressing gown and slippers, emerged from the sitting room. He just looked as grumpy as Uncle Wheeler could look—and that is saying a good deal.

Mother didn't see him at first, and merely asked us why we were up so early and where the Winsloe boys were. We explained, and then mother saw Uncle Wheeler, and said she hoped he'd slept well and found his pillows high enough for him.

"Slept well!" growled Uncle Wheeler. "I wonder if you, or any one else, Amelia June Millar, could sleep well, if, just when you had dropped off to sleep, after a long and arduous journey, you were suddenly awakened by half a dozen great, lubbering louts of boys coming down on you, like an avalanche, in the dead of night? I ask you how anybody could sleep well under such circumstances, madam?"

And Uncle Wheeler glared at us boys, as if he knew we were the guilty ones. Mother was greatly distressed.

"Oh, dear me! The Winsloe boys went in, after all. *Didn't* Tad tell you that Uncle was there?"

"Tad went to sleep," said Rod, promptly, nudging me with his elbow, for fear I'd put in a word too many and complicate matters, "and didn't wake up till too late. When he appeared, the mischief was done. You might have known he couldn't keep awake, mother."

"There was no one else to leave," replied mother; "and I warned him not to go to sleep. I'm *very* sorry this should have happened, Uncle Wheeler."

Uncle Wheeler barely answered.

The Winsloe boys had gone, so he couldn't come down on them, and he had no excuse for blaming any one, except Tad—who kept religiously out of the way that morning—so he felt defrauded of his rights.

He was as snappish and crusty as he could be all through breakfast, and kept making remarks about boys being out late at nights and gadding about to parties and coming home to disturb respectable folks at unseemly hours. *He* was never guilty of it, in his young days, and he felt very sorry to see that his nephews were: and, as for those three fools that had wakened him up, he'd like to teach a lesson to boys who hadn't enough sense to get into bed properly, but must race and tear like a pack of wild cubs.

There was no doubt that Uncle Wheeler was in a fearful humor, and Rod and I realized that we had had a narrow escape.

Syd Hatfield, having no particular interest at stake, enjoyed the whole performance immensely, and afterwards remarked, in the seclusion of the kitchen loft:

"It's a jolly good thing for you chaps that your respected uncle doesn't know that it was you who disturbed his peaceful slumbers. He doesn't seem particularly amiable this morning."

But, for all our success, I really didn't feel comfortable, and Rod looked awfully glum. Pretty soon he came out with it.

"I feel like an out and out sneak, Art," he confessed. "I never did anything like this before, and I never will again. We've deceived mother and Uncle Wheeler, and all I wish is that we hadn't."

"Same here, Rod," I said, heartily, for Rod had just put my own disquieting reflections into words.

Syd stared at us.

"You're a pair of geese! *I* think it is all a capital joke. Why, you didn't *say* a thing—never even stretched the truth itself; and it can't hurt the Winsloe boys one single mite."

"That isn't the question," replied Rod. "It's what *we've* done. I feel kind of dishonorable, but I suppose there's nothing more to be said now."

Still, we did feel mean. Uncle Wheeler got over his ill-humor by next day, and was as good as gold. Everything went well for a week outwardly, but Rod went about kind of grim and sulky, and as for me, I felt somehow or other that I was a pretty mean, sneaking sort of chap.

Rod and I had both been brought up to be strictly truthful and above board in everything, and we felt that we had come short of mother's standard. It wasn't that our evasion was going to harm any one else, but we had simply lost our self-respect. Syd had gone home, so we hadn't him to bolster up our consciences, and we got regularly blue and moody.

One night Uncle Wheeler had another cranky fit on. The wind was northeast and his rheumatism was always bad in a northeast wind. Finally, he remarked to mother:

"I'd a letter to-day from Henry Winsloe, the father of those rascals. He wants me to accommodate him with a loan for a short time. I shan't; I've worked hard for my money, and I'm not going to risk it in doubtful loans—not if he is honest and hard up. I don't propose to help a man that can't bring his boys up better than he's done."

And Uncle Wheeler poked the fire viciously. The memory of the tousing-up he'd got that unlucky night was still vividly present with him.

Rod and I went softly out, leaving mother trying to intercede for Henry Winsloe, with no very good success, and went to our favorite roost in the kitchen loft.

"Here's a mess," said Rod.

"A bad one," said I. "What's to be done?"

"Done? Make a clean breast of it to Uncle Wheeler, of course. It'll ruin my chances with him, but I'm not going to have other people suffer for what isn't their fault."

"If we'd only told him at first!" I said, mournfully. "But even if he could forgive us for jumping over him, he never will for bluffing him about it. He'll think we were just fooling him for pure fun."

"It's a blue show," said Rod, gloomily, "but we deserve it—so I'm not going to flinch. After all, I don't know that I'm sorry we have to. I've felt like a regular sneak this week. Uncle Wheeler will be in a fury, of course, but I think worse of how mother will feel. She hates any crawly business."

We made up our minds to beard the lion in his den as soon as possible. The afternoon of the next day we screwed up our courage and marched straight into the parlor, where Uncle Wheeler was writing letters before the table.

He shoved up his specs and looked at us sourly.

"What do you youngsters want?" he demanded, gruffly.

We both knew by experience that it doesn't do to beat about the bush with Uncle Wheeler. You have to come straight to the point and say what you've got to say.

Rod took a header right in.

"We've come, Uncle Wheeler, to tell you what we should have told you before. It wasn't the Winsloe boys who woke you up the other night. It was Syd Hatfield and Art and I."

Then we waited for the outburst. Uncle Wheeler gazed at us over his specs quite calmly. We knew he had a dozen different ways of getting mad, and this might be one; but, if so, it was brand new.

"It was you, was it?" he said, at last. "You young scamps—and you've the face to come and tell me so! And why did you say it was the other boys?"

"Please, sir, we didn't," I ventured to say. "Mother just thought it was, because she had told them to go there. But Dave was scared of the ghost; so we changed rooms. Syd wanted us to race and see who'd get into bed first—that's all. We didn't know anybody was there, and we are awfully sorry. We were kind of scared, too; so we thought it wouldn't be any harm to let you all think it was the Winsloes. But it wasn't right, and we've felt mean ever since."

Uncle Wheeler glared quite fiercely.

"What do you think you deserve?" he asked.

And Rod spoke up manfully:

"Uncle Wheeler, we deserve a sound scolding for deceiving you, and we will get it when mother finds out. But as for the rest, it was only in fun, and I don't think any one ought to regard it as a serious crime, although it was very silly of us. Most people would merely look upon it as a joke."

"Oh, they would, would they?" said uncle, grimly. "Perhaps, when you get to be my age, young man, and don't find it so easy to get to sleep as you do now, you won't consider it much of a joke to have three great boys come sprawling over you in your first doze."

"We're sorry we disturbed you, uncle," said Rod, firmly, but respectfully, "and we apologize for not owning it up right off like men. That's all we can do, and I hope you'll forgive us."

"Humph! Go out, and tell your mother I want her."

That was all the satisfaction we got, but we went gladly, for we had escaped wonderfully well.

Mother went in, and was closeted with Uncle Wheeler for half an hour. When she came out, she looked amused over something, and though she tried to be severe, it was a failure.

"You deserve a scolding, boys, but I promised your uncle I'd let you off this time. He really seems in a good humor over it all, but I wouldn't advise you to repeat the experiment."

"What's he going to do about Mr. Winsloe?" broke in Rod, anxiously.

"He's going to help him, I think, since he found out the boys are not such 'louts' as he thought them."

Rod and I felt a good deal better then, you may be sure. Uncle Wheeler went home the next day, but he parted from us kindly, told Rod to be ready for college in the fall, and to remember mother's training in straightforwardness, and finally left an envelope in our respective hands. We found a twenty-dollar bill in each of them.

"Hurrah for Uncle Wheeler!" said Rod. "He's a brick!"

(1898)

A New-Fashioned Flavoring

This second story, published in *Golden Days for Boys and Girls* seven months after "Our Uncle Wheeler," anticipates the episode in *Anne of Green Gables* in which Anne, keen to make a good impression on the new minister's wife, inadvertently flavours a cake with anodyne liniment—an episode that reportedly originated in a similar mistake Montgomery had witnessed during her teaching year in Bideford in 1894–1895, except in that case it was the minister's wife herself who had flavoured a cake with anodyne liniment. This story is the earliest of five by Montgomery that Rea Wilmshurst identifies as those that "deal with mistakes in cooking [and that] also contain the idea of reward for recognition and worth." The agony of a fearful older relative descending on a houseful of young people without parental supervision would also appear in chapter 6 of Montgomery's later novel *The Golden Road* (1913), entitled "Great Aunt Eliza's Visit," in which a cooking mishap also occurs.

WHEN MRS. CLAY WENT TO PAY A LONG-PROMISED visit to her sister it was not without some misgivings that she left her household in charge of Edmund and Ivy.

To be sure, Ivy could be trusted; she was fifteen, and had been her mother's right hand for years. But Edmund, who was sixteen and ought to have had more sense than Ivy, but hadn't, was prone to tricks and nonsense; and all the rest of the little Clays, a round half dozen in number, were noted for the numerous scrapes they contrived to get into daily.

Nevertheless, Mrs. Clay stifled her doubts and went away for a week, burdening Edmund and Ivy with so many charges and reminders that they forgot half of them before she was fairly out of the gate.

Edmund was deputed to kindle fires, chop wood, feed the pig, bring in water, and, last-but-not-least, he was to look after the youthful Clays and keep them in order.

Ivy was to do the housework and see that the children were kept comparatively clean and mended and keep a wary eye on things in general.

"And if anything dreadful should happen," warned their mother, "be sure to send for me at once. Be careful of the fires, Ivy, and, Edmund, never you try to light one with kerosene. I expect in the end to come home and find the house burned to the ground or half the children killed."

"That isn't the right spirit to go on a visit in, mother," said Edmund. He was sitting on the edge of the wood-box, whittling over the floor. "Just make up your mind to enjoy yourself. Don't worry about us. We'll be all right. I give you my word everything will go swimmingly. I'll keep the kids straight—and Ivy, too, if she gets fighting. You can depend on me, mother."

"I know just how much dependence is to be placed on you, Edmund," replied his mother, severely; "now, do behave yourself while I'm away, and don't call your brothers and sisters 'kids.'"

"Well, I'm sure I can't call them lambs, anyhow. Just listen to that"—as a crash and a scream sounded in an adjoining room. "Fan and Reeve have 'gone over' on the rocking chair again. There won't be a whole piece of furniture left in this establishment by another month."

Altogether, as has been said, Mrs. Clay did not leave home in a very easy state of mind. Nevertheless the Clay household got on wonderfully well. Edmund behaved himself tolerably well and attended to his man-of-the-house duties with praiseworthy diligence. Moreover, he kept the younger Clays within reasonable bounds and refused to aid or abet them in making nuisances of themselves.

He studied hard in the long evenings after Fan and Reeve and Kitty and Jo and Frank and Bobby had been tucked away in their beds and Ivy had taken her knitting and sat down in the little sitting-room.

"I'd put more heart into it if I thought it would come to anything," he said mournfully; "but it won't. No college for me! I'll have to leave school in the spring and pitch into earning my own living and helping you folks along. It's tough on a fellow to be poor. Don't I envy Scott Dawson! He's going to college next fall."

"It's too bad you can't go, Ed," said Ivy, sympathizingly. "You're ever so much smarter than Scott Dawson. But I don't suppose we could ever manage it."

"I know that well enough. Let a fellow complain a bit, will you? It eases me. No. I won't whine when it comes to the point. I'll get all that done beforehand, and you'll see me grinning over the counter as if I were the happiest fellow in the world. If we were not so awfully poor, Ivy, or if the good old days of fairies and three wishes hadn't gone by, what would you go in for?"

"Music," answered Ivy, with a little sigh. "Oh, dear me! I'd just love to be a good violinist. But that costs money, too; so I needn't think of it."

"If that blessed Uncle Eugene of ours wasn't such a miserly old crank," continued Edmund, "he might help us along a bit. He isn't much like a story-book uncle, is he, Ivy? I'd like to meet him just to see what he's like."

"I wouldn't," said Ivy, emphatically, "if he's as cranky and particular as mother says he is. And he behaved abominably to father when they had that dispute over the property. No, I don't want to see Uncle Eugene. If I did I should be apt to flare out and tell him what I thought of him. It's a mercy there's no fear of us seeing him. He wouldn't come here for anything."

"You don't know. It's always the unexpected that happens," replied Edmund, oracularly. "Wouldn't it be a joke if he were to come now, when mother is away. If the kids—I beg your pardon! I mean my hopeful brothers and sisters—behave as they usually do when we have company, how it would horrify him. Old bachelors generally know all about how children should be trained, and I've no doubt Uncle Eugene's an aggravated specimen."

The Clays were undeniably poor. Mr. Clay had died some five years before, leaving his family but scantily provided for. Mrs. Clay had hard work to make both ends meet. Being a woman of resource and thrift, she accomplished it, but luxuries were unknown in the little household. Yet they were happy in spite of their poverty. Edmund's college course had to be given up. He was to take a position as clerk in a dry goods store in the spring. Ivy had her own deprivations, of which she said little. She buried music dreams in the recesses of her heart, and made over her dresses and wore her hats three seasons with smiling sweetness.

I think, on the whole, they enjoyed life quite as well as richer people; only, as Edmund said, a little more cash would not have been an overwhelming inconvenience.

"I tell you what, Ivy," said Edmund, on Saturday afternoon, as he banged down a load of wood with a deafening crash, and sent a shower of dust over the dishes Ivy had so carefully wiped, "I'm glad mother's coming home Monday, when all's said and done. We've got along tip-top, to be sure, but the cares of being at the head of family affairs have weighed me down so heavily this week that I feel like an old man. We've been fortunate so far in that we've had no visitors. But they'll be sure to come to-day— just our Saturday luck!"

"Mercy! I hope not. I'm so busy. I'm determined that mother shall find this house in spic and span order when she comes home, so I'm having a grand rummage. This cupboard has to be put to rights, and I've fifty other things to do. And I've got the most dreadful cold in the head. I can scarcely breathe. Goodness, Ed! That's never a knock at the door."

"But it is! Ten to one it's Aunt Lucinda Perkins come to stay over Sunday."

"Ed, you must go to the door," said Ivy, with dismayed remembrance of her wet apron and generally disorderly appearance. "And whoever it is show them to the sitting-room. Don't dare to take anyone into the parlor, for Reeve and Bobby got in there this morning to play shop before I discovered them, and it's in an awful mess."

Ivy listened anxiously as Edmund went to the door. The visitor's tones were masculine, and she breathed a sigh of relief that it was not Aunt Perkins, anyhow; but her complacency was of short duration.

When Edmund had shown the caller into the sitting-room and returned to the kitchen, Ivy divined that the "something dreadful" had happened at last.

"Ivy, the Philistines be upon thee," said Edmund, with a solemnity belied by his dancing eyes—eyes that plainly indicated his enjoyment of the whole situation.

"Is it Aunt Perkins, after all?"

"It's worse than ten Aunt Perkinses. Ivy Clay, in that room, at this very minute, sits our respected Uncle Eugene."

"Mercy on us," exclaimed Ivy; and then collapsed, sitting down on the wood-box.

"Don't take a fit, sis. When I opened the door there he stood as grim as you please. 'Is your mother at home, boy?' he asked. 'No, sir; she isn't,' I replied. 'Well, I'm her brother-in-law, Eugene Clay,' he said, and 'I've come to see her as I have to wait a few hours here for my train.' Whereat I gasped out, 'Oh!' and towed him into the room, feeling decidedly faint. My part's done. Now, Ivy, it's your turn. Sail in gracefully and bid him welcome to the house of Clay."

"In this mess? I can't," declared Ivy.

"Well, no; you'll have to fix up a bit—brush your hair, and so forth. Do the thing up in good style, Ivy. I'm going to peek through the crack and watch the interview."

"Edmund," implored Ivy, beginning to recover her equanimity, "don't do anything dreadful now, will you? Don't make me laugh or anything like that?"

"Bless you, no! I'll be a model nephew. I'm properly scared, I tell you. Don't I look pale? All I'm afraid of, Ivy, is that Uncle Eugene will get alarmed and run, for all the kids are in the room above his head, and are making a most unearthly racket. If some of them come crashing through the ceiling, it's no more than I expect."

"Oh, Ed, do go and make them stop. My head is just in a whirl. Oh, if mother were only home! Do help me out of this scrape like a dear boy. What does he look like?"

"Who? Uncle Eugene? Oh, he's not too savage—more civilized looking than I had expected. Well, I'll go and make those little Clays up there tone down before his nervous system is utterly wrecked. You 'pretty' yourself up, Ivy, and beard the lion in his den as if you liked it. Don't let him suspect what a martyr you are to family ties."

Poor Ivy hurriedly brushed her rebellious curls into place,

replaced her soiled apron by an immaculate white one, and, with her heart in her mouth, but looking very pretty and housewifely, nevertheless, contrived, she never knew how, to get into the sitting-room and say:

"How do you do, Uncle Eugene? I am glad to see you," hoping she would be forgiven for the atrocious fib.

"Are you?" returned Uncle Eugene grimly. "So your mother isn't home, hey?"

"No; she's visiting Aunt Mary. She expects to be home on Monday."

"Was that your brother who opened the door?"

"Yes. That is Edmund, my older brother. Won't you take off your overcoat, sir? Of course, you'll stay to tea," said Ivy, devoutly hoping he wouldn't.

"Well, yes; I suppose I will, if you'll get me an early one. Train leaves at 4.30. I can't wait over. Sorry your mother is away! How many are there of you?"

"Eight."

"Humph! I should have thought there were four times eight by the noise that was going on overhead when I came in. So you're housekeeper at present? You look like your mother."

Uncle Eugene slowly divested himself of his handsome light overcoat. He was a tall man of about fifty, with grizzled hair and a clean-shaven face. He had a hard mouth and deep-set eyes.

Ivy, with a covert glance around the room, was thankful to see it was comparatively neat. A sudden calm had succeeded Edmund's entrance overhead. His measures, whatever they were, must have been sudden and effective.

"There," said Uncle Eugene, depositing himself comfortably in a rocker by the fire, "that will do. I daresay you're busy, so don't let me detain you. You needn't think you're in duty bound to entertain me; in fact, I'd prefer you wouldn't."

Thus abruptly dismissed, Ivy gladly left her grim uncle to the charms of solitude and hastened to the kitchen, where she found Edmund scrubbing the hands and faces of all the little Clays, not one of whom dared whimper under the operation, for they realized that Edmund meant business.

"Hello, Ivy! You didn't take long to dispose of him. Did he bite?"

"Oh, don't, Edmund! This is no joking matter."

"No, indeed! It's a serious case. Don't I look as if it were?"

"Ed, he's going to stay to tea, and he wants it early. What can we give him to eat?"

"What other people eat, I suppose. Or has he some abnormal appetite that craves—"

"I mean there's nothing baked in the house, only loaf bread. I was so busy this morning I thought I wouldn't make cake. And I've heard mother say what an epicure Uncle Eugene was. I'm going right to work to make a layer cake; it won't take long, but I shall have to hurry. And there is the quince preserve. That'll have to do. You'd better go in with him, Ed."

"Not I. I'll have to fly round to the grocery for butter. Do you want anything else?"

"No; don't bother me," replied Ivy, who was scurrying in and out of the pantry with a bowl and a flour-scoop. Edmund proved himself a tower of strength. He finished putting the little Clays in order and then went around to the grocery with a rush.

On his return he found Ivy whipping up her cake energetically.

"It's all ready for the flavoring, Ed. Just hand me the bottle of vanilla out of the pantry, will you? It's on the second shelf."

Edmund dived into the pantry and returned with the vanilla bottle, rushing off again to settle a noisy dispute between Frank and Bobby in the hall. Ivy measured out and stirred in a generous spoonful of vanilla, filled her pans and triumphantly banged the oven-door upon them.

"Now, I do hope it will turn out well. I'll whip up a bit of frosting for the top. What a blessing those children are behaving so well! If they only keep it up at tea-time!"

Ivy began to set the tea-table, stepping briskly in and out of the room. She saw with dismay that Jo had strayed in some how and was actually perched on Uncle Eugene's knee in earnest conversation with him.

Now, Jo Clay was six years old, and, not having arrived at years of discretion, was justly regard as the infant terrible of the family. He could not keep either his own secrets or those of other people, and Ivy was on thorns for there was no knowing what revelations Jo might be making to Uncle Eugene. She hoped devoutly that he had not overheard any of her or Edmund's remarks, for they would be fatally sure to be recounted.

In vain she surreptitiously beckoned Jo out of the room. Jo refused to heed her, and once Uncle Eugene saw her and said:

"Leave him alone. We are all right." After which she gave up in despair, although in her pilgrimages in and out she caught scraps of Jo's remarks about "moosic" and "Ed wanting to do to tollege," that made her groan.

Ivy set the table daintily, with spotless cloth and shining china, and put an apple geranium in pinkish bloom in the centre. The loaf-bread was cut in the thinnest of slices, the quince preserve was dished in an old-fashioned cut-glass bowl, and her cake came out of the oven as light and puffy as down.

"Just the best of luck, Ed," said Ivy, delightedly, as she clapped the layers together with ruby jelly, whisked the frosting over the top and sprinkled grated cocoanut on it. "Isn't that pretty? I hope it'll taste as good as it looks. Now, Ed, I'll take in the tea and you take in the children and get them settled in their places. Keep an eye on them, too. I'll have enough to attend to. And, oh, Ed! Jo's been sitting on Uncle Eugene's knee for an hour, and I know he's been telling him a fearful lot of stuff. Why couldn't you have decoyed him out?"

"Didn't dare! I'll bet Uncle Eugene knows everything about our family kinks by this time. Never mind! Come on! 'Charge, Ivy, charge! We'll win the day,' were the last words of Edmund Clay."

Edmund marshalled the little Clays soberly in and arranged them in order at the tea-table. Uncle Eugene sat down and Ivy poured out the tea with fear and trembling. But all went well at first. The tea and preserves were good and the children behaved beautifully.

Uncle Eugene said absolutely nothing. He evidently considered silence to be golden. Then Edmund, in obedience to a nod from Ivy, gravely passed the layer-cake to his Uncle, after which it went the rounds of the appreciative little Clays. Ivy took none. She was too tired and worried to eat; but Edmund helped himself to a generous slice.

When he had tasted it he laid down his fork, rolled up his eyes, and opened both his hands in exaggerated dismay for Ivy's benefit. Bobby Clay followed with "Why, Ivy, what's the matter with the layer-cake?"

Edmund silenced him with such an awful look that none of the others dared open their lips, though each, after the first mouthful, left their cake uneaten on their plates. Uncle Eugene, however, appeared to taste nothing unusual, for he gravely ate his cake with an impassive face and finished the last crumb.

Frank sat to the right of the agonized Ivy, too far away to explain, but by his pantomime he conveyed the fact that something serious was the matter.

Finally she took a peck of the triangle of cake on Reeve's plate next to her. She gave a gasp, a look at Edmund, and then, sad to relate, burst into a ringing peal of laughter, which, coming after the dead silence, was electrical in effect.

She caught herself up with a scarlet face, and in quick transition felt so much like crying that she might have done so if Uncle Eugene had not abruptly pushed back his chair and announced that he had had enough.

Ivy fled to the kitchen, whither she was followed by Edmund, with all the little Clays swarming after him.

"Ivy," demanded Edmund, tragically, "what in the world did you put in that cake? Never tasted anything like it in the cooking line before."

"Oh, Ed, how could you do such a thing?" cried poor Ivy, hysterically. "I can never forgive you. And after promising you wouldn't play any tricks, too!"

"Me!" exclaimed Edmund, too surprised to be grammatical. "Goodness, what have I done?"

"Oh, don't pretend innocence! I suppose you thought it a very smart trick to hand me out a bottle of anodyne liniment to flavor that cake with—but I call it mean."

Edmund stared at her blankly for a minute, and then flung himself on the sofa and went off into a burst of laughter that made the kitchen re-echo.

"Oh," he cried, "Ivy Adella Clay! You don't mean to say you flavored that cake with anodyne liniment? Ho, ho, ho! If that isn't an original idea! I always knew you were a genius, Ivy."

"How could you, Edmund?"

Edmund sat up.

"Ivy, I give you my word of honor I didn't do it on purpose," he said, solemnly. "I thought it was vanilla—honest, I did. Why, it was in a vanilla bottle, and it's just the same color."

"Yes; don't you remember Reeve broke the liniment bottle last week and I put what wasn't spilled into an old vanilla bottle. Oh, dear me! This is dreadful!"

"You're to blame, then? Why didn't you put it out of the way? How was a fellow to tell? And how is it you didn't smell it?"

"I couldn't, with such a cold. Oh, Edmund, what must Uncle Eugene think?"

"Dear knows," said Edmund, going off into another paroxysm. "I suppose the poor man will think we were trying to poison him, unless he happened to recognize the taste. Fortunately, the liniment is for internal as well as external application, so nobody will die. Well, this is the latest! Flavoring a cake with anodyne liniment! Well done, Ivy."

"Will we—do you think we ought to say anything to Uncle Eugene about it?"

"Goodness, no. Perhaps he didn't suspect anything amiss. He ate every crumb of it, so doubtless he imagined it was the newest thing in flavoring extracts. Your reputation as a cook would be gone forever if you let him know, Ivy."

"Well," said Ivy, disconsolately, "it's done now, and it can't be undone. Fortunately, as you say, it was harmless. But the whole thing is simply dreadful. What will mother say?"

"Accidents will happen, even in a well-regulated family like ours. Go and clear off the ruins, Ivy, and feed that liniment cake to the pig. Uncle Eugene will never be any the wiser."

Alas! When Ivy summoned up enough courage to return to the room and attack the table, what was her horror to find Jo delightedly telling all the details to Uncle Eugene!

Ivy caught the fatal word "lin'ment," and mentally collapsed. She must apologize somehow.

"Uncle Eugene," she stammered, with a scarlet face, her confusion not calmed in any degree by a glimpse of Edmund gesticulating wildly in the back hall, "I'm very sorry—that cake should not have tasted as it did—I meant to put in—vanilla, but Edmund made a mistake and—somehow—well, I put in a spoonful of anodyne liniment instead. It won't hurt anyone— you know—it's sometimes taken internally——"

"But not in cakes," came in a stage whisper from the back hall.

Ivy gave up trying to explain, and, in spite of her efforts, gave vent to something that couldn't be called anything but a snicker. As for Uncle Eugene, his eyes twinkled quite genially, but all he said was:

"Accidents will happen."

And Ivy went out, considerably mystified as to what effect the disclosure had had on him.

Soon after he looked at his watch, said it was nearly train time, and put on his coat. He shook hands with Ivy and Edmund, told them to tell their mother he was sorry not to have seen her, and relieved the Clay mansion of his unwelcome presence.

"Thank goodness!" said Edmund, emphatically, when he had seen him safely out of the gate. "The old crank has gone. I guess he won't come back in a hurry. I should say liniment-flavored cake was an excellent preventative of unwelcome guests. What an opinion he must have of us! You are always doing something brilliant, Ivy, but you've surpassed yourself in this exploit."

When Mrs. Clay returned home on Monday she listened to the tale with a curious mixture of dismay and amusement.

"I wish I had been home," she said. "I can't think what induced him to come. He once said he'd never darken our doors again. I suppose I ought to be thankful to find you all alive and sound of limb, but it's a pity Uncle Eugene should have come when I was away. I expect he's gone for good, now, Ivy, after what you gave him to eat, poor man. I know how Uncle Eugene would regard anything like that."

But she didn't! Next week a letter came from her brother-in-law—short and abrupt, as was his fashion, but the contents were satisfactory.

It ran:

"Sister Martha:

"Doubtless this will surprise you. I called at your house last week and found you away. However, your son and daughter entertained me very hospitably and I was much pleased with them both, but especially with the girl. The boy, I take it, is somewhat mischievous and likes to tease his sister. I dare say they think I'm a crusty old fellow and they are right: but

I desire to make amends for the past if you will let bygones be bygones. I am a lonely man and I want to have some interests outside myself. Edmund and Ivy did not tell me about your concerns, but I picked up an inkling from little Jo. Tell Edmund he is not to go into that store, but to prepare for college next fall and I will put him through. I have nothing else to do with my money and you must gratify me in this whim. As for Ivy, you may tell her she is to take music lessons and I will send her the best violin to be had. She is a good, housewifely girl. Tell her also that her liniment cake seems to have had an excellent effect on her cranky old uncle for it appears to have made him well all over, even to his bones and marrow. I may pay you another visit soon.

"Until then I remain yours respectfully,

"EUGENE CLAY."

"Uncle Eugene is a brick," exclaimed Edmund, breathlessly, "a regular brick! I repent in sackcloth and ashes of anything I ever said to the contrary."

"He is splendid," said Ivy, with shining eyes. "To think I am to have music lessons—and a violin. It is too good to be true."

"You may well be grateful. It's not every uncle who would behave so handsomely to a girl who gave him liniment cake to eat. What an advertisement this would be for that liniment firm if they got hold of it. A liniment warranted to cure, not only every known bodily ailment, but those of the mind and heart as well! They'd make their fortune. Mother, say something! Relieve your feelings in some way!"

"I say, 'Long live anodyne liniment!'" said Mrs. Clay, laughing. "Your experiment has turned out well this time, Ivy, but I wouldn't advise a repetition. Uncle Eugene was always kind at heart, although peculiar. And now, to prevent any further mistakes, I'll go and put that new-fashioned flavoring of yours out of the vanilla bottle into a more orthodox one. The next time Uncle Eugene comes I'll make the cake myself."

(1898)

Miss Marietta's Jersey

In the opening chapters of *Anne of Avonlea* (1909), Anne runs into difficulty with her new, "irate neighbour" from next door, Mr. Harrison, over a destructive Jersey cow. That episode originated in this 1899 story published in *The Household* of Boston and in *Farm, Field, and Fireside* of Chicago. In place of Anne and Marilla are middle-aged spinster Marietta Hunter and her cousin Cordely (short for Cordelia, no less), whose history with their next-door neighbour is far more complex than Anne's is with hers.

IT WAS TEN O'CLOCK ON A HOT JULY MORNING, AND MISS Marietta was helping Cordely shell the peas for dinner on the back veranda, which was always cool and pleasant, shaded as it was by Virginia creepers and sibilant poplars.

Miss Marietta, whose morning work was not done, was not dressed for the day. She had on her lilac wrapper, and her front hair was in curl papers. An ample white apron was tied around her trim waist and floated off in long, crisp streamers behind.

She was fair and forty, and could afford to admit it since she looked all of five years younger. Her round, plump face was flushed pinkly with the heat; she swayed easily back and forth in her rocker, holding the pan of peas in her lap, and running her fat, white fingers deftly up the green pods as she talked to Cordely.

Cordely was Miss Marietta's cousin and "stayed" with her. She was paid wages for so doing, but nobody ever thought of her as "hired help." She was much higher up in the social scale than that.

She was a thin, snapping, black-eyed woman, with angular elbows and nerves, and she shelled four peas to Miss Marietta's deliberate one. But then Miss Marietta took things easy, and Cordely never did. It wasn't her way.

"My, it's dreadfully warm, isn't it?" said Miss Marietta, making an ineffectual attempt to fan herself with a pea-pod. "I'm glad Hiram has decided not to begin haymaking until next week. I'm sure I shouldn't feel like cooking for a lot of men in such weather.

"And I do hope Mr. Randall will come this afternoon and see about buying that Jersey cow. I shall never feel easy in my mind until she's safely off the place," she concluded.

"I guess Nathaniel Griffith won't either," said Cordely, giving her chair a vicious hitch around. "I wonder if he's got over that last tantrum by now.

"My, but wasn't he mad! He knows your cow is ever so much better than his, for all they look so exactly alike, and that helps to rile him up."

"Well, it was very aggravating to find her in his best clover hay, I've no doubt," said Miss Marietta, soothingly. "I'm sure I shouldn't like to find his Jersey in my hay. But I must say I wouldn't get into such a ridiculous fluster as he did for all. And—oh, goodness me, Cordely! Look there!"

Miss Marietta pointed with a gasp across the yard. Cordely looked and saw. She sprang up, scattering peas and pods wildly over the clean veranda floor in her flight.

"Goodness gracious, Marietta! That cow has been in again. However could she have jumped out? And he's mad clear through."

Scuttling through the yard gate at a lively rate was a demure little Jersey cow, and behind her came Miss Marietta's next-door neighbor, Mr. Nathaniel Griffith, very red and puffing and angry as he bounced up the veranda steps and faced the two women.

"Now, see here, Miss Hunter," he spluttered, "this isn't going to do—I don't intend to put up with it. This is the third time, ma'am, I've found that Jersey cow of yours in my clover hay.

Think of that! I warned you last time. Now, ma'am, what do you mean by letting her in again?"

Mr. Griffith stopped, perforce, for want of breath. Miss Marietta rose in distress.

"Dear me, Mr. Griffith! I'd no idea that cow was in again. I don't know how she got out, I'm sure. I'm very sorry—"

"Sorry, ma'am! Sorry isn't going to help matters any. You'd better go and look at the havoc that animal has made in my hay—trampled it from centre to circumference. It isn't to be endured—I won't endure it!

"Oh, you needn't scowl at me back there, Miss Cordely Hunter. I'm talking to Miss Marietta. I'm a patient man, Miss Hunter."

"*Very!*" Cordely could not have helped saying it to save her life, any more than she could have kept the sarcastic inflection out of it when she did say it. "Only your patience will be the cause of your bursting a blood-vessel yet, if you go on in such a fashion on a hot day like this. If *I* was a man, Nathaniel Griffith, I would try to have a little common sense."

"Hush, Cordely," said Miss Marietta, with dignity.

"Mr. Griffith, I regret very much that my cow has been so much trouble to you. Perhaps if you had kept your fences in better order she might not have been. They are not very good, I notice."

"My fences are all right," snapped Mr. Griffith. "There weren't ever the fences built that would keep a demon of a cow like that out. Much a pair of old maids know about fences, or farming either."

Miss Marietta carefully set her pan of peas on a bench and stood up, the better to overwhelm Mr. Griffith. Her mild blue eyes were sparkling dangerously, and her cheeks were very red.

"I may be an old maid, Mr. Griffith," she said, with calm distinctness, "I've no doubt that I am; but it isn't because I've never had the chance to be anything else, and there are people not one hundred miles from here who know it, too."

Mr. Griffith grew pink all over his shiny little face to the very top of his bald head. He stepped backward awkwardly and fanned himself with his hat.

Miss Marietta was mistress of the situation after that last effective shot, and she knew it. Cordely could not repress a little chuckle of triumph as she watched him down the steps and across the yard.

When he passed out of sight up the lane, Miss Marietta sat down again with a sigh.

"Dear me, Cordely, how very unpleasant! And me to be caught in my wrapper and curl papers, too! We must certainly do something with that cow. It is quite unbearable. What a dreadful temper Mr. Griffith was in! and he has tramped those peas you spilled right into the floor."

"The old monster! I'd have liked to pitch the whole panful at his head," returned Cordely, vindictively. "Why didn't you fly at him? I'd have done it if I'd been in your place."

"Dear me, Cordely, what good would that have done? I've no doubt it was very trying to find that cow in his hay again. Of course, he need not have been quite so ridiculous."

"He can't and won't ever forgive you for refusing to marry him," said Cordely. "That's what's rankling in his mind—not Jersey cows or hay either. Didn't he get red, though? How many times did you refuse him, Marietta?"

"Twice," said Miss Marietta, with apparent satisfaction, "and the last time pretty decided, too. It doesn't become him to be casting up to me that I'm an old maid. He is an old bachelor because nobody would have him.

"I suppose it's no wonder the poor man flies into tempers. I should think it would spoil any one's temper to have to put up with a housekeeper like Mercy Fisher. I don't suppose the poor soul has a decent meal from one end of the year to the other."

"If you'd fly into a temper, too," said Cordely, who could not forgive Miss Marietta's easy-going ways, "when he comes here blustering about his hay, it would settle him."

"Law, I feel better now than if I had," laughed Miss Marietta. "You're too peppery, Cordely. Mr. Griffith does not mean half he says. You may be sure he's sorry for it already. He's always been so from a boy. But I shall certainly sell that cow. She's no milker and I don't like fracases like this. Dear me, I feel quite upset, and what a dreadful state this veranda floor is in."

The thunderstorm that came up at noon and drenched everything well did not last long, and at two o'clock Miss Marietta and her handmaid were dressed for driving, and the carriage was at the door.

Miss Marietta had harnessed the horse, her hired man being away; and, moreover, she had shut the recalcitrant Jersey up in the milking pen.

"She can't possibly get out of that unless she tears the fence down," she reflected, complacently, as she tied up the gate. "She looks pretty quiet now. I dare say she's sickened herself on that clover hay. I'm sure I wish I'd never been persuaded into buying her.

"A woman *is* apt to make mistakes in judgment when it comes to farming, after all, though I'd never admit it to Nathaniel Griffith."

And Miss Marietta sighed as she looked over the trim, well-ordered fields of her neighbor to the right; perhaps it was on account of the shortcomings of Jersey cows with jumping proclivities; or it may have been because she discovered that she had slightly draggled the skirt of her new chocolate print in crossing the yard; or it might have been for neither of these reasons.

"I do hope that cow will behave herself while we're away," said Miss Marietta, as they drove out of the gate.

It was four o'clock when they got back with a wagon full of parcels. As they drove up the lane, Cordely uttered a shrill exclamation. Miss Marietta, absorbed in a mental calculation regarding the day's expenditure, looked dreamily in the direction of Cordely's extended finger.

Before them on the right extended Mr. Griffith's broad field of clover hay, wet and odorous and luxuriant; and there, standing squarely in the middle of it, up to her broad sides in sweetness, and blinking calmly at them over the intervening blossoms, stood the Jersey cow.

Miss Marietta dropped the reins and stood up with a curious tightening of the lips. She climbed nimbly down over the wheels, whisked across the road, and over the fence before Cordely could recover her powers of speech.

"Goodness gracious, Marietta, come back," screamed the latter. "You'll ruin your dress in that wet hay—ruin it, do you hear? She doesn't hear me. The woman's gone crazy, I do believe. She'll never get that cow out by herself. I must go and help her, of course."

Miss Marietta was charging through the thick hay like a mad thing. Cordely hopped briskly down, tied the horse securely to a post, turned her neat plaid dress skirt over her shoulders, mounted the fence, and started in pursuit.

Cordely could run faster than plump Miss Marietta, and consequently overtook her before the latter had made much headway. Behind them they left a trail that would break Mr. Griffith's heart when he should see it.

"Law's sake, Marietta, hold on!" panted poor Cordely. "I'm clean out of breath and wet to the skin."

"We—must—get—that cow—out—before—Mr. Griffith— sees her," gasped Miss Marietta. "I don't—care—if I'm— drowned—if we—can—only—do that."

But the Jersey cow appeared to see no good reason for being hustled out of her luscious browsing ground. No sooner had the two breathless women got near her than she turned and bolted squarely for the opposite corner of the field. "Head her off," screamed Miss Marietta. "Run, Cordely, run."

And Cordely ran. Miss Marietta tried to, and the wicked Jersey went around the field as if she were possessed. Privately, Cordely thought she was. It was fully ten minutes before they got the cow headed off in a corner, and drove her out of a gap and down the lane into their own yard just as a buggy turned in that direction.

Miss Marietta did not often lose her temper, but at this critical moment she felt decidedly cross. Her dress was ruined, and she was in a terrible heat. Cordely, being thinner, had suffered less, but she slammed the gate behind her with a vicious emphasis.

"There's Randall and his boy now," she said. "He's heaven-sent if ever a man was. If you don't sell him that cow straight off, Marietta, I'll give warning here and now. Land sakes! I won't get over this picnic all summer."

Miss Marietta needed no urging. Her gentle nature was grievously disturbed.

"Mr. Randall," she said, "if you've come for my cow you can have her at your own price. I'll give her away before I'll keep her another hour."

In exactly twenty minutes Mr. Randall drove away, and following him went his son driving the Jersey cow. Miss Marietta counted the roll of bills in her hand complacently, and Cordely looked after the disappearing bossy with malevolent satisfaction.

"I do hope we will have some peace of our lives now," she said.

It was sunset before Miss Marietta recovered her equanimity.

"I guess I'll go out and begin milking," she said to Cordely, who was folding up the next day's ironing at the table.

"You needn't come until you've finished with the clothes. I feel flustered yet, I declare I do, but it's such a comfort to think that cow is out of the way."

Five minutes later Cordely wheeled about at sound of her own name to see Miss Marietta standing white and shaken in the doorway. She whirled across the room, and caught the latter's lilac arm.

"Marietta Hunter, what's the matter! Are you going to take a turn? You look as if you'd seen a ghost."

"So I have—or something worse," said Miss Marietta, with a hysterical little giggle, as she dropped into a chair.

"Cordely Hunter, it was Nathaniel Griffith's cow that I sold to Robert Randall this afternoon. My own is out there in the milking pen yet."

A lesser shock would have rattled Cordely's nerves completely, but this was so great that it left her perfectly calm.

"Marietta Hunter! Are you dreaming?"

"Go and look for yourself, if you don't believe me," said Miss Marietta, tragically.

Cordely needed no second bidding. She shot out over the veranda, and flew across the yard to the gate of the milking pen. There looking calmly out over the bars, and chewing the cud of placid reflection, stood Miss Marietta's Jersey cow, as she had stood, probably, ever since her incarceration therein.

"I never did in all my life," gasped Cordely, stooping for the milking-pails that Miss Marietta had dropped. When she got back to the house she found the kitchen deserted, and charged into Miss Marietta's bedroom where she found the latter putting on her best dress with nervous haste.

"Land sakes, Marietta, this is a nice scrape to be in! What are you going to do?" she asked.

"Go up to Mr. Griffith's and explain, of course; that is, unless you'd like to go in my place, Cordely."

"Heaven forbid!" said Cordely, devoutly, as she dropped limply into a chair. "I'd rather face a lion. I never did hear of such a piece of work. Mad isn't any word for what Nathaniel Griffith will be. I wonder you ain't scared to death, Marietta."

"Well, I almost am," returned Miss Marietta, tremulously, "but then you see, Cordely, it has to be done, if it's ever so humiliating. I suppose he'll say again that it's just what one would expect an old maid to do.

"There's no getting his cow back, for Randall said he meant to take her right down to Larksville and ship her on the 5.30 train. I shall offer him the money or my cow in her place, whichever he likes—and my cow is better than his, if she does jump. Oh, dear, my crimps all came out in that hurry-skurry this afternoon, and I look like a fright."

Miss Marietta started off bravely enough. Cordely watched her out of sight, and then picked up the milking-pails again. "Laws me, won't there be a scene," she sniffed.

Mr. Nathaniel Griffith was smoking a pipe on his front verandah and enjoying the view, while his housekeeper was milking. Mr. Griffith never dared to smoke a pipe inside his own house.

A henpecked husband is to be pitied, but a henpecked bachelor is the most forlorn creature on earth.

"Goodness me!" said Mr. Griffith, removing his pipe and jumping to his feet as he caught sight of Miss Marietta skimming up the lane. "If there ain't Marietta Hunter coming here as sure as a gun. She must want to see Mercy for something. I'm blessed if I want to face her after the fool I made of myself down there about that cow, darn her; but it won't never do to run, with Mercy 'way down in the yard, and she's seen me, anyhow."

Mr. Griffith did not run, but manfully stood his ground, though he got pinker and pinker until, when Miss Marietta sailed up the steps, he was crimson from chin to crown.

But Miss Marietta, in her own confusion, failed to notice this.

"Oh, Mr. Griffith," she said, desperately, without wasting time on preliminaries, "I've—I've—something dreadful to tell you."

"Bless my soul, ma'am," exclaimed Mr. Griffith, "sit down, ma'am—do sit down. Has that cow of yours got into my hay again? but it's no difference—no difference at all, ma'am—if she has. I was too hasty to-day, ma'am—far too hasty."

"Oh, it's worse than that," said poor Miss Marietta, taking no notice of the rustic seat Mr. Griffith pushed nervously towards her. "I—don't know how to tell you. I shut my cow up after you brought her home, and Cordely and I went over to Larksville after dinner, and when we came back we saw a Jersey cow in the hay again, and we chased her out, and Mr. Randall came along just then and I was so exasperated I sold her to him on the spot, and he took her away. And to-night when I went out to milk, there was my cow in the pen—and it was yours I had sold, Mr. Griffith."

And the revelation being over, Miss Marietta sat down on the rustic chair with a distinct sob.

"Bless my soul!" said Mr. Griffith. "What an extraordinary thing. Don't cry, ma'am, I beg of you. It's no difference at all—nothing to disturb yourself over, ma'am. There now, don't cry, my dear."

He stepped over and patted her shoulder nervously. Miss Marietta wiped her eyes.

"It's very good of you to say so, Mr. Griffith," she sobbed. "I do feel so dreadfully about it. Your cow is a hundred miles away by now, but I've brought the money over, or you can have my Jersey if you'd rather. She's a very good cow. I can't begin to tell you how sorry I am."

"No need to be sorry at all, ma'am," said Mr. Griffith, gently, still patting Miss Marietta's arm. "It was an accident, ma'am. One cow's the same to me as another. I'll take yours in her place, since you want to get rid of her. Now, don't think another thing about it. Bless me, I'd rather lose every cow I've got, than have your feelings harrowed up so, my dear."

Miss Marietta colored a little, and stood up. "I'm much obliged to you, Mr. Griffith. Hiram will drive the cow over in the morning. I guess I must be going now, Cordely is milking all alone."

Mr. Griffith fidgeted down two steps, and up again.

"No hurry, ma'am. Mercy will be in in a minute or two. Sit down again, won't you, and have a neighborly chat. It's—it's lonesome here by spells."

Miss Marietta sat down again. It would be very uncivil to refuse under the circumstances. Mr. Griffith had been so nice about the cow; and it must be rather lonesome for a man to be there all the time with no company but a cross old housekeeper. He looked neglected. She felt sorry for him.

Cordely had almost made up her mind to start out and see if Mr. Griffith had murdered Marietta, when she saw two figures coming up the lane in the moonlight.

"There she is now," said Cordely, peering out of the kitchen window in relief. "What on earth kept her so long? And old Griffith's with her, or my name isn't Cordelia Hunter! What can be going to happen?"

Miss Marietta and Mr. Griffith stood and talked at the gate for nearly half an hour, until Cordely thought they must both be demented. When Miss Marietta finally came in, with a very high color in her face, she found Cordely sitting blankly on a chair.

"Marietta Hunter," said Cordely, solemnly, "did I or did I not see Nathaniel Griffith kiss you out there at the gate?"

"I dare say you did," was the calm response, "especially if you happened to be peeking out of the window. We're—we're going to be—married."

"Well, I never did!" Cordely was overwhelmed. "Marietta Hunter, I've heard you say a dozen times, if you've said it once, that you wouldn't marry Nathaniel Griffith if he were the last man left alive on earth; and after your refusing him twice!"

"The third time's generally lucky, I've noticed," said Miss Marietta, loosening her bonnet strings, composedly. "Dear me what a day this has been! If you could see the state that poor man's house is in, you'd think it time somebody took pity on him; and it's a woman's privilege to change her mind, you know. To be sure, I might never have changed mine if it hadn't been for that blessed Jersey. What *could* you do, Cordelia Hunter? You couldn't say 'no' to a man when he'd just forgiven you so beautifully for selling his prize cow. *I* couldn't anyway, and I don't know that I am sorry, either."

(1899)

The Old Chest at Wyther Grange

In chapter 12 of *The Story Girl* (1911), entitled "The Blue Chest of Rachel Ward," Sara Stanley tells the story of a relative who left Prince Edward Island after her fiancé failed to show up the day of their wedding and whose trunk continues to sit undisturbed in the King kitchen half a century later. Like "Our Uncle Wheeler" and "A Pioneer Wooing" elsewhere in this volume, this story, according to Montgomery's journals, originated from an ancestor of hers—a cousin of her father's named Eliza Montgomery—at least in terms of opening and distributing the contents of the chest after her death, if not in terms of a broken heart and the circumstances that led to it. This early story about a tragic romance locked inside an old chest appeared in *Waverley Magazine* of Boston in September 1903, eight years before the publication of *The Story Girl*. Two decades later, Montgomery would reuse the name "Wyther Grange" for the home of Nancy Priest in *Emily of New Moon* (1923), whose protagonist shares a surname with a character in this story.

WHEN I WAS A CHILD I ALWAYS THOUGHT A VISIT TO Wyther Grange was a great treat. It was a big, quiet, old-fashioned house where grandmother Laurance and Mrs. DeLisle, my Aunt Winnifred, lived. I was a favorite with them, yet I could never overcome a certain awe of them both. Grandmother was a tall, dignified old lady with keen black eyes that seemed veritably to bore through one. She always wore stiffly-rustling gowns of rich silk made in the fashion of her youth. I suppose she must have changed her dress occasionally, but the impression on my mind was always the same as she went trailing about the house with a big bunch of keys at her belt—keys that opened a score of wonderful old chests and boxes and drawers. It was one of my dearest delights to attend grandmother in her peregrinations and watch the unfolding and examining of all those old treasures and heirlooms of bygone Laurances.

Of Aunt Winnifred I was less in awe, possibly because she dressed in a modern way and so looked to my small eyes more human and natural. As Winnifred Laurance she had been the beauty of the family and was a handsome woman still with brilliant dark eyes and cameo-like features. She always looked very sad, spoke in a low sweet voice, and was my childish ideal of all that was high-bred and graceful.

I had many beloved haunts at the Grange but I liked the garret best. It was a roomy old place, big enough to have comfortably housed a family in itself, and was filled with cast-off furniture and old trunks and boxes of discarded finery. I was never tired of playing there, dressing up in the old-fashioned gowns and hats and practising old-time dance steps before the high, cracked mirror that hung at one end. That old garret was a veritable fairyland to me.

There was one old chest which I could not explore and, like all forbidden things, it possessed a great attraction for me. It stood away back in a dusty, cobwebbed corner, a strong, high wooden box, painted blue. From some words which I had heard grandmother let fall I was sure it had a history; it was the one thing she never explored in her periodical overhaulings. When I grew tired of playing I liked to creep up on it and sit there, picturing out my own fancies concerning it—of which my favorite one was that some day I should solve the riddle and open the chest to find it full of gold and jewels with which I might restore the fortune of the Laurances and all the traditionary splendors of the old Grange.

I was sitting there one day when Aunt Winnifred and grandmother Laurance came up the narrow dark staircase, the latter jingling her keys and peering into the dusty corners as she came along the room. When they came to the old chest grandmother rapped the top smartly with her keys.

"I wonder what is in this old chest," she said. "I believe it really should be opened. The moths may have got into it through that crack in the lid."

"Why don't you open it, mother?" said Mrs. DeLisle. "I am sure that key of Robert's would fit the lock."

"No," said grandmother in the tone that nobody, not even Aunt Winnifred, ever dreamed of disputing. "I will not open that chest without Eliza's permission. She confided it to my care when she went away, and I promised that it should never be opened until she came for it."

"Poor Eliza," said Mrs. DeLisle, thoughtfully. "I wonder what she is like now. Very much changed like all the rest of us, I suppose. It is almost thirty years since she was here. How pretty she was!"

"I never approved of her," said grandmother, brusquely. "She was a sentimental, fanciful creature. She might have married well but she preferred to waste her life pining over the memory of a man who was not worthy to untie the shoe-lace of a Laurance."

Mrs. DeLisle sighed softly and made no reply. People said that she had had her own romance in her youth and that her mother had sternly repressed it. I had heard that her marriage with Mr. DeLisle was loveless on her part and proved very unhappy. But he had been dead many years and Aunt Winnifred never spoke of him.

"I have made up my mind what to do," said grandmother, decidedly. "I will write to Eliza and ask her if I may open the chest to see if the moths have got into it. If she refuses, well and good. I have no doubt that she *will* refuse. She will cling to her old sentimental ideas as long as the breath is in her body."

I rather avoided the old chest after this. It took on a new significance in my eyes and seemed to me like the tomb of something—possibly some dead and buried romance of the past.

Later on a letter came to grandmother; she passed it over the table to Mrs. DeLisle.

"That is from Eliza," she said. "I would know her writing anywhere—none of your modern sprawly, untidy hands, but a fine lady-like script, as regular as copper-plate. Read the letter, Winnifred; I haven't my glasses and I daresay Eliza's rhapsodies would tire me very much. You need not read them aloud—I can imagine them all. Let me know what she says about the chest."

Aunt Winnifred opened and read the letter and laid it down with a brief sigh.

"This is all she says about the chest. 'If it were not for one thing that is in it I would ask you to open the chest and burn all its contents. But I cannot bear that anyone but myself should see or touch that one thing. So please leave the chest as it is, dear aunt. It is no matter if the moths do get in.' That is all," continued Mrs. DeLisle, "and I must confess that I am disappointed. I have always had an almost childish curiosity about that old chest, but I seem fated not to have it gratified. That 'one thing' must be her wedding dress. I have always thought that she locked it away there."

"Her answer is just what I expected of her," said grandmother impatiently. "Evidently the years have not made her more sensible. Well, I wash my hands of her belongings, moths or no moths."

It was not until ten years afterwards that I heard anything more of the old chest. Grandmother Laurance had died; but Aunt Winnifred still lived at the Grange. She was very lonely, and the winter after grandmother's death she sent me an invitation to make her a long visit.

When I revisited the garret and saw the old blue chest in the same dusty corner my childish curiosity revived and I begged Aunt Winnifred to tell me its history.

"I am glad you have reminded me of it," said Mrs. DeLisle, "I have intended to open the chest ever since mother's death but I kept putting it off. You know, Amy, poor Eliza Laurance died five years ago but even then mother would not have the chest opened. There is no reason why it should not be examined now. If you like we will go and open it at once and afterwards I will tell you the story."

We went eagerly up the garret stairs. Aunt knelt down before the old chest and selected a key from the bunch at her belt.

"Would it not be too provoking, Amy, if this key should not fit after all? Well, I do not believe you would be any more disappointed than I."

She turned the key and lifted the heavy lid. I bent forward

eagerly. A layer of tissue paper revealed itself with a fine tracing of sifted dust in its crinkles.

"Lift it up, child," said my aunt gently. "There are no ghosts for you, at least, in this old chest."

I lifted the paper up and saw that the chest was divided into two compartments. Lying on the top of one was a small, square, inlaid box. This Mrs. DeLisle took up and carried to the window. Lifting up the cover she laid it in my lap.

"There, Amy, look through it and let us see what old treasures have lain hidden there these forty years."

The first thing I took out was a small square case covered with dark purple velvet. The tiny clasp was almost rusted away and yielded easily. I gave a little cry of admiration. Aunt Winnifred bent over my shoulder.

"That is Eliza's portrait at the age of twenty and that is Willis Starr's. Was she not lovely, Amy?"

Lovely indeed was the face looking out at me from its border of tarnished gilt. It was the face of a young girl, in shape a perfect oval, with delicate features and large dark blue eyes. Her hair caught high on the crown and falling on her neck in the long curls of a bygone fashion was a warm auburn and the curves of her bare neck and shoulders were exquisite.

"The other picture is that of the man to whom she was betrothed. Tell me, Amy, do you think him handsome?"

I looked at the other portrait critically. It was that of a young man of about twenty-five; he was undeniably handsome but there was something I did not like in his face and I said so.

Aunt Winnifred made no reply—she was taking out the remaining contents of the box. There was a white silk fan with delicately carved ivory sticks, a packet of old letters and a folded paper containing some dried and crumpled flowers. Aunt laid the box aside and unpacked the chest in silence. First came a ball-dress of pale yellow satin brocade, made with the trained skirt, "baby" waist and full puffed sleeves of a former generation. Beneath it was a case, containing a necklace of small but perfect pearls, and a pair of tiny satin slippers. The rest of the compartment was filled with household linen, fine and costly but yellowed with age—damask table linen and webs of the uncut fabric.

In the second compartment lay a dress. Aunt Winnifred lifted it out reverently. It was a gown of rich silk that had once been white, but now like the linen it was yellow with age. It was simply made and trimmed with cobwebby old lace. Wrapped around it was a long white bridal veil, redolent with some strange, old-time perfume that had kept its sweetness all through the years.

"Well, Amy, this is all," said Aunt Winnifred with a quiver in her voice. "And now for the story! Where shall I begin?"

"At the very beginning, aunty. You see I know nothing at all except her name. Tell me who she was and why she put her wedding dress away here."

"Poor Eliza!" said aunt, dreamily. "It is a sorrowful story, Amy—and it seems so long ago now. I must be an old woman. Forty years ago—and I was only twenty then. Eliza Laurance was my cousin, the only daughter of Uncle Henry Laurance. My father—your grandfather, Amy, you don't remember him—had two brothers each of which had an only daughter. Both these girls were called Eliza after your great-grandmother. I never saw Uncle George's Eliza but once. He was a rich man and his daughter was much sought after but she was no beauty, I promise you that, and proud and vain to the last degree. Her home was in a distant city and she never came to Wyther Grange.

"The other Eliza Laurance was a poor man's daughter. She and I were of the same age and did not look unlike each other, although I was not so pretty by half. You can see by the portrait how beautiful she was, and it does her scant justice, for half her charm lay in her arch expression and her vivacious ways. She had her little faults of course and was rather over much given to romance and sentiment. This did not seem much of a defect to me then, Amy, for I was young and romantic too. Mother never cared much for Eliza, I think, but everyone else liked her. One winter Eliza came to Wyther Grange for a long visit. The Grange was a very lively place then, Amy. Eliza kept the old house ringing with merriment. We went out a great deal and she was always the belle of any festivity we attended. Yet she wore her honors easily; all the flattery and homage she received did not turn her head.

"That winter we first met Willis Starr. He was a new-comer

and nobody knew much about him, but one or two of the best families took him up and his own fascinations did the rest. He became what you would call the rage. He was considered very handsome, his manners were polished and easy, and people said he was rich.

"I don't think, Amy, that I ever trusted Willis Starr. But like all the rest I was blinded by his charm. Mother was almost the only one who did not worship at his shrine, and very often she dropped hints about penniless adventurers that made Eliza very indignant.

"From the first he had paid Eliza marked attention and seemed utterly bewitched by her. Well, his was an easy winning. Eliza loved him with her whole impulsive, girlish heart and made no attempt to hide it.

"I shall never forget the night they were first engaged. It was Eliza's birthday and we were invited to a ball that evening. This yellow gown is the very one she wore. I suppose that is why she put it away here—the gown she wore on the happiest night of her life. I had never seen her look more beautiful; her neck and arms were bare and she wore this string of pearls and carried a bouquet of her favorite white roses.

"When we reached home after the dance Eliza had her happy secret to tell us. She was engaged to Willis Starr and they were to be married in early spring.

"Willis Starr certainly seemed to be an ideal lover, and Eliza was so perfectly happy that she seemed to grow more beautiful and radiant every day.

"Well, Amy, the wedding day was set. Eliza was to be married from the Grange, as her own mother was dead, and I was to be bridesmaid. We made her wedding-dress together, she and I. Girls were not above making their own gowns then, and not a stitch was set in Eliza's save those put there by loving fingers and blessed by loving wishes. It was I who draped the veil over her sunny curls; see how yellow and creased it is now, but it was as white as snow that day.

"A week before the wedding Willis Starr was spending the evening at the Grange. We were all chattering gaily about the coming event, and in speaking of the invited guests Eliza said something about the other Eliza Laurance, the great heiress, looking archly at Willis over her shoulder as she spoke. It was some merry badinage about the cousin whose namesake she was but whom she so little resembled.

"We all laughed, but I shall never forget the look that came over Willis Starr's face. It passed quickly, but the chill fear that it gave me remained. A few minutes later I left the room on some trifling errand, and as I returned through the dim hall I was met by Willis Starr. He laid his hand on my arm and bent his evil face—for it *was* evil then, Amy—close to mine.

"'Tell me,' he said in a low but rude tone, 'is there another Eliza Laurance who is an heiress?'

"'Certainly there is,' I said sharply. 'She is our cousin and the daughter of our Uncle George. Our Eliza is not an heiress. You surely did not suppose she was!'

"Willis stepped aside with a mocking smile.

"'I did—what wonder? I had heard much about the great heiress, Eliza Laurance, and the great beauty, Eliza Laurance. I supposed they were one and the same. You have all been careful not to undeceive me.'

"'You forget yourself, Mr. Starr, when you speak so to me,' I retorted coldly. 'You have deceived yourself. We have never dreamed of allowing any one to think that Eliza was an heiress. She is sweet and lovely enough to be loved for her own sake.'

"I went back to the parlor full of dismay. Willis Starr remained gloomy and taciturn all the rest of the evening, but nobody seemed to notice it but myself.

"The next day we were all so busy that I almost forgot the incident of the previous evening. We girls were up in the sewing room putting the last touches to the wedding gown. Eliza tried it and her veil on and was standing so, in all her silken splendor, when a letter was brought in. I guessed by her blush who was the writer. I laughed and ran down stairs, leaving her to read it.

"When I returned she was still standing just where I had left her in the middle of the room, holding the letter in her hand. Her face was as white as her veil, and her wide-open eyes had a dazed, agonized look as of some one who had been stricken a mortal blow. All the soft happiness and sweetness had gone out of them. They were the eyes of an old woman, Amy.

"'Eliza, what is the matter?' I said. 'Has anything happened to Willis?'

"She made no answer, but walked to the fireplace, dropped the letter in a bed of writhing blue flame and watched it burn to white ashes. Then she turned to me.

"'Help me take off this gown, Winnie,' she said dully. 'I shall never wear it again. There will be no wedding. Willis is gone.'

"'Gone!' I echoed stupidly.

"'Yes. I am not the heiress, Winnie. It was the fortune, not the girl, he loved. He says he is too poor for us to dream of marrying when I have nothing. Oh, such a cruel, heartless letter! Why did he not kill me? It would have been so much more merciful! I loved him so—I trusted him so! Oh, Winnie, Winnie, what am I to do!'

"There was something terrible in the contrast between her passionate words and her calm face and lifeless voice. I wanted to call mother but she would not let me. She went away to her own room, trailing along the dark hall in her dress and veil, and locked herself in.

"Well, I told it all to the others in some fashion. You can imagine their anger and dismay. Your father, Amy—he was a hot-blooded, impetuous young fellow then—went at once to seek Willis Starr. But he was gone, no one knew where, and the whole country rang with the gossip and scandal of the affair. Eliza knew nothing of this, for she was ill and unconscious for many a day. In a novel or story she would have died, I suppose, and that would have been the end of it. But this was in real life and Eliza did not die, although many times we thought she would.

"When she did recover how frightfully changed she was! It almost broke my heart to see her. Her very nature seemed to have changed too—all her joyousness and light heartedness were dead. From that time she was a faded, dispirited creature, no more like the Eliza we had known than the merest stranger. And then after awhile came other news—Willis Starr was married to the other Eliza Laurance, the true heiress. He had made no second mistake. We tried to keep it from Eliza but she found it out at last. That was the day she came up here alone and packed this old chest. Nobody ever knew just what she put into it. But you and I see now, Amy—her ball-dress, her wedding-gown, her love letters, and, more than all else, her youth and happiness; this old chest was the tomb of it all. Eliza Laurance was really buried here.

"She went home soon after. Before she went she exacted a promise from mother that the old chest should be left at the Grange unopened, until she came for it herself. But she never came back and I do not think she ever intended to, and I never saw her again.

"That is the story of the old chest. It was all over so long ago—the heartbreak and the misery—but it all seems to come back to me now. Poor Eliza!"

My own eyes were full of tears as Aunt Winnifred went down the stairs, leaving me sitting dreamily there in the sunset light, with the old yellowed bridal veil across my lap and the portrait of Eliza Laurance in my hand. Around me were the relics of her pitiful story—the old, oft-repeated story of a faithless lover and a woman's broken heart—the gown she had worn, the slippers in which she had danced light-heartedly at her betrothal ball, her fan, her pearls, her gloves—and it somehow seemed to me as if I were living in those old years myself, as if the love and happiness, the betrayal and pain were part of my own life. Presently Aunt Winnifred came back through the twilight shadows.

"Let us put all these things back in their grave, Amy," she said. "They are of no use to any one now. The linen might be bleached and used, I dare say—but it would seem like a sacrilege. It was mother's wedding present to Eliza. And the pearls—would you care to have them, Amy?"

"Oh, no, no," I said with a little shiver. "I would never wear them, Aunt Winnifred. I should feel like a ghost if I did. Put everything back just as we found it—only her portrait. I would like to keep that."

Reverently we put gowns and letters and trinkets back into the old blue chest. Aunt Winnifred closed the lid and turned the key softly. She bowed her head over it for a minute and then we went together in silence down the shadowy garret stairs of Wyther Grange.

(1903)

Aunt Ethelinda's Monument

In chapter 11 of *Anne of the Island* (1915), Diana and Anne drop in on the former's aunt Atossa, who, according to Diana's father, "has a face like a hatchet—it cuts the air. But her tongue is sharper still." Aunt Atossa proves to be singularly insulting and disagreeable, but Anne and Diana soon forget all about her as they carry on with their day. Aunt Atossa is based on Aunt Ethelinda, the title character in this next story, published in *The Christian Advocate* of New York late in 1904. Montgomery would lift much of Ethelinda's dialogue for Aunt Atossa, but while circumstances prompt Aunt Ethelinda to learn self-awareness about the effects of her sharp tongue on those around her, such self-awareness is not granted to Aunt Atossa. When that character dies later in *Anne of the Island*, Anne reflects that it is "a most dreadful thing to go out of the world and not leave one person behind you who is sorry you are gone."

"I SUPPOSE," SAID AUNT ETHELINDA, IN HER MOST BIT-ing tones, "that you never do anything like this, Elizabeth. You would be afraid of spoiling your hands."

Elsbeth—her name was Elsbeth, not Elizabeth, but Aunt Ethelinda was prejudiced against "foreign" names—laughed. There was nothing better to do, and she was so used to Aunt Ethelinda's sarcasm that it did not hurt her much—now. There had been a time when the sharp things that Aunt Ethelinda said would cut her sensitive little soul to the quick. But Elsbeth had learned to make allowances for Aunt Ethelinda, who wasn't her aunt at all, or anybody else's, although everybody in Brookvale called her so.

"O, yes, I always help when it is to be done," Elsbeth said, pleasantly. "We were cutting sets at home three days last week. But I do my hands up in lemon juice and kid gloves for the night after it," she added, by way of teasing Aunt Ethelinda a trifle.

Aunt Ethelinda sniffed.

"I suppose you got that notion out of some of those silly magazines you read so much of. I wonder your mother allows you. Girls weren't brought up so in my time. But your mother has always spoiled her children. We all thought when George Sheldon married her that she wouldn't be a suitable wife for him."

Aunt Ethelinda sighed heavily, as if all her forebodings upon the occasion of George's marriage had been amply and darkly fulfilled. Elsbeth made no answer this time. A little red spot came out on each of her soft round cheeks, and she primmed up her rosy mouth as if shutting in some hasty words. Elsbeth did not care what Aunt Ethelinda said to her, but she had not yet learned to take slurs at her mother amiably. Sue Barrie, who had come in with Elsbeth and was sitting very demurely back in the corner, looked indignant. But she had a wholesome fear of Aunt Ethelinda, and so she too held her tongue.

Aunt Ethelinda was cutting potato sets with great energy. She wore a faded old wrapper, and her crisp gray hair was decidedly untidy. In short, Aunt Ethelinda was in a mess, and she did not like being caught "in a kilter" by anybody. Moreover, she detested cutting potato sets, and so she went out of her way to be disagreeable. To be sure, that was nothing new for Aunt Ethelinda.

Finding that her last taunt did not visibly ruffle Elsbeth's composure, she returned to personal weapons.

"You'd rather be strumming on the piano than doing anything else, I suppose. That wouldn't stain your soft hands—and it's a good deal easier than work."

"Of course," said Elsbeth, good-naturedly, "I'm very fond of music, Aunt Ethelinda."

"The Martins all were," said Aunt Ethelinda. Elsbeth's mother had been a Martin, and from the indescribable emphasis which Aunt Ethelinda put into her sentence you would have understood that the Martins' fondness for music was the distinct hallmark of their degeneracy and utter unfitness to live. "They never were good at much else. It's a pity you take after them. Jingling tunes won't do much for you. I heard that you wanted to go to Riverside and take music lessons. Are you going?"

"No, indeed," said Elsbeth, with a little sigh. "Father can't afford it."

"I should think not, Elizabeth. Your father is worked and harried to death as it is. It's pretty hard for a man to support an extravagant family. You take my advice and give up your notions of music and just settle down to some good honest work that'll earn your keep. Look at Mary Ann Dilson—teaching school at the Corner. Mary Ann's a smart girl."

"Yes," agreed Elsbeth, ungrudgingly. She was never envious of other people. "But you know I couldn't teach school, Aunt Ethelinda. I'm the worst dunce at arithmetic that ever lived. I thought if I could take music for a few months in Riverside that I'd be able to teach music to beginners in Brookvale. I could get a good class. But there is no use in thinking about it just now. Mother sent me down to bring you this little pot of jelly. We made it yesterday, and she thought you might fancy some."

"My appetite has been dreadful poor lately," admitted Aunt Ethelinda. "It needs coaxing—but your mother's jelly is always too sweet for my taste. However, you can leave it, and I daresay I can worry some down. If it isn't too much trouble will you be condescending enough to put it in the pantry? I'm in a dreadful hurry today—I want to get these spuds done by night. I'm cutting them for Mrs. Dunn, and the money I'll get goes into my monument fund."

"Are you getting on with it pretty well?" asked Elsbeth, with a smile. Brookvale people generally smiled when Aunt Ethelinda's monument fund was spoken of.

"I've got eighty dollars saved up," replied Aunt Ethelinda, with chastened triumph. "But I want twenty more. One hundred is the price of the monument I picked out at Carter & Seaman's the last time I was in town. It's a real handsome one, I tell you. I've always been bound and determined to have a good handsome white marble monument. All the Clydes have them, but I'm the last of the family, and there won't be anyone to put up one for me; so I'll get it myself beforehand. It's bigger than Mrs. Roderick Clyde's. I'll be buried next to her, alongside of mother, and I wouldn't rest in my grave if her monument was better than mine. You're not going so soon, are you? Well, I suppose you can't find much amusement in talking to an old woman like me."

"O, it isn't that, Aunt Ethelinda," protested Elsbeth. "But I must go—mother wants me home to help her this evening."

"Anything does for an excuse, of course," said Aunt Ethelinda, amiably. "Just whip in and whip out before you have time to say how-do decently. Well, it's the style nowadays. Tell your mother I'm obliged for the jelly. You ought to wear a bigger hat when you go out, Elizabeth. You're freckling something scandalous—Martin-like. Give your mother my respects, Miss Barrie. It's over a year since she's been to see me, but I suppose I can't complain. There's nothing very attractive for stylish folks here, no doubt."

"O, isn't she dreadful?" gasped Sue, when they were safely out of earshot down the lane. "How could you put up with her insults, Elsbeth? I'd have lost my temper and 'sassed back,' as Teddy says; I know I would."

"She isn't always quite so biting as she was today," said Elsbeth. "Sometimes when I go she'll be just as nice and kind as can be—and, you know, she is always really pleased to have people go and see her, for all she talks to them so sarcastically. Mother has always impressed on us that we must be kind to Aunt Ethelinda and not resent her sharp speeches. She has had a very hard, lonely life, and it has soured her. Perhaps it has been largely her own fault, but that must make it all the harder to bear, don't you think?"

"Yes, I suppose so. It must be pretty dismal when the only interest you have left in life is buying your own tombstone," admitted Sue. "Will she pick out her own epitaph, I wonder? I'm sure I can't think of many good qualities to inscribe on it."

"I'm really sorry for Aunt Ethelinda," said Elsbeth, "but I must admit it never cheers me up much to go there. She has made me feel that I ought never to mention music in father's hearing again."

"It is too bad you can't have a chance, Elsbeth. You have such a beautiful voice, and you play better now than lots of girls who have been taking lessons for years. Perhaps you will be able to go to Riverside, after all."

"Perhaps," said Elsbeth, quietly, and changed the subject. It hurt her to think about it. After Sue had turned into her own lane she walked slowly homeward, thinking over her own disappointed little hopes and plans and Aunt Ethelinda's remarks.

"Anyway," she concluded, with a little sigh, "I won't let father see that it hurts me. He has a good deal to worry him—Aunt Ethelinda was right there, although it's not exactly the fault of his family, as she insinuates."

Six weeks later Aunt Ethelinda fell down her cellar stairs, broke her leg and arm and wrenched the muscles of her back. Elsbeth went to see her three days after the accident and found her lying in bed, scowling darkly at Cyrilla Potter, who had come in to wait on her and attend to her small household affairs. At least nothing had happened to Aunt Ethelinda's tongue.

"So you did manage to remember me at last, Elizabeth," she said. "I suppose I ought to feel quite flattered that you took the time to do it from more important duties."

"Mother hasn't been very well," said Elsbeth, gently, "and I couldn't come before. I'm very sorry about your accident, Aunt Ethelinda."

"So am I," said Aunt Ethelinda, crisply. "Sorrow won't mend broken bones. I've got to lie here for six weeks at the least, the doctor says. To think that Cyrilla Potter will be in charge here all that time! I never could abide Cyrilla. Well, it might have been worse, I suppose. I might have broken my neck instead of my leg, and then my monument fund would never have been completed. As it is, the doctor's bill will make a nice hole in it. I don't know as I'd grumble so much if I'd any way of passing the time. It's terrible tedious to lie here day in and day out. If my eyes would let me read I might worry through, but they won't; and as for getting Cyrilla to read to me, I'd rather listen to a buzz saw—as I told her flat when she offered. There's swarms of people coming here to see me, of course, but I get desperate tired of their chattering. I never was much interested in gossip. And how am I going to put in six weeks of this and maybe more?"

That afternoon Elsbeth went around to all the girls she knew and asked them to take turns going to read to Aunt Ethelinda. One and all declined. They could not do it, they declared. They could never endure Aunt Ethelinda's tongue. Besides, she wouldn't want them; she was so critical that nobody could please her.

Elsbeth sighed a little. Summer in Brookvale was a very pleasant time, and just now what might be called "the season" was in full swing. There were picnics and drives and sails and rambles galore. It was not a very charming alternative to think of spending long hours reading to Aunt Ethelinda. But Elsbeth went to her and offered to do it.

Aunt Ethelinda did not appear to be particularly grateful.

"Well, I don't know," she said. "I don't suppose you are an extra good reader—though I'd be glad of most anybody, short of Cyrilla. But if it's to be come one day and stay away another I'd as lief not. If I could depend on you to come every day I might accept."

"I'll come every afternoon," promised Elsbeth.

"Well, see that you do. And ask the minister's wife to send me up some good solid books. I don't propose to listen to anything frivolous."

Thereafter Elsbeth went faithfully every afternoon and read for long hours to Aunt Ethelinda. It was not an easy or pleasant employment. Aunt Ethelinda's choice of literature was not precisely interesting when taken in such large doses, and she had an especial penchant for volumes of gloomy, old-fashioned sermons and treatises. Moreover, she was very hard to please and criticized Elsbeth's elocution and pronunciation until even the girl's sunny temper almost failed her—almost, but not quite. Elsbeth always managed to choke down any angry retort that rose to her lips.

"The idea of your making such a martyr of yourself!" protested Sue. "Why, you are missing all the fun cooped up there reading to that cross old woman."

"She suffers a great deal," said Elsbeth, gently. "And I think my reading helps to pass the time for her. If I were in her place I'd want people to make allowances for me."

The six weeks spun out to eight before Aunt Ethelinda could use her broken arm again and dismiss Cyrilla Potter to her own place. One day when Elsbeth came she found her knitting.

"Thank goodness, I'm my own woman again," Aunt Ethelinda announced. "I'm all right, now that I can knit. I feel as if I didn't want ever to see a book opened again, such a dose of reading as I've had. Not but what I admit I'd never have survived without it. I'd have died of sheer lonesomeness and other folks' gossip. And you've been real good to come so constant, and that when you might have had more agreeable occupation, no doubt."

"I'm glad if I have been of any service to you, Aunt Ethelinda," said Elsbeth.

"Yes, I actually believe you are. Once I'd have thought you were just putting on if you talked like that, but actions speak louder than words. What are you going to do with yourself this fall? Is your father going to send you to Riverside?"

Elsbeth shook her head.

"O, no. He cannot afford it. I—I think I will go into Ronald Gresham's store at the Corner for the winter. He wants a clerk—"

"Now, don't tell me that any Sheldon could come down to clerking for a Gresham," interrupted Aunt Ethelinda, acridly. "I draw the line at that. Go into my bedroom and bring me out that inlaid box on the bureau."

Aunt Ethelinda took the box, selected a key from the huge bunch dangling at her belt, and opened it. From it she took a little roll of money.

"Here, Elizabeth, is sixty dollars—what was left of my monument fund after the doctor's bill was paid. It's for you. It'll pay your board and get you a quarter's lessons in Riverside at least."

"Aunt Ethelinda," protested Elsbeth, "I could never dream of taking it—never! But thank you, just the—"

"Fiddlesticks! Of course you're going to take it. I've given up the idea of a monument. When I was lying there on my back thinking, thinking, thinking half the day and most of the night, I can tell you, Elizabeth Sheldon, I took count of the things that were worth while, and monuments weren't among them. 'What's the use of my trying to have a handsomer monument than Mrs. Roderick's?' I thought. 'If I toiled and moiled for a hundred years I could never get such a monument as Mrs. Roderick has, the memory in folks' hearts of all her kind deeds and words and smiles. If I had tons of marble over me it would only serve to remind folks what a cantankerous old crank I was.' So I just said to myself, 'Ethelinda Clyde, you will take what money you've got and do some good with it before you die. And you'll hurry, for you're an old woman and will likely go off sudden, like all the Clydes.' Now, Elizabeth, you've been as good as an angel to me this summer in spite of all the biting things I've said right along. It used to be a real satisfaction to say them at the time, but after you had gone they hurt me worse than they ever hurt you. If you won't take this money it'll be about the cuttingest revenge you can get on me."

Elsbeth flushed crimson.

"Aunt Ethelinda," she said, gently, "I will take it—as a loan. You must let me pay you back in time. I'll be able to do it after I get a start."

"Well, well, if nothing else will do you we can arrange it so. But you're not to feel hurried about paying it back, mind that. I'm never going to use it for a monument, anyhow. And—thank you, Elizabeth, for all your goodness to me this summer."

Elsbeth ran over and threw her arms about Aunt Ethelinda's neck.

"Thank you, a hundred times over, dear Aunt Ethelinda," she said, kissing her. "You've given me my heart's desire."

"Well, well, don't say anything more about it," said Aunt Ethelinda, beginning to knit furiously. "Thanks are embarrassing things. I declare they are, whether they're given or taken. Now, you go to Riverside and do your best. But I must say I hope when you come home you won't be like Amelia Fisher—able to play nothing but them shivery, up-high-there-and-way-down-here 'classical' things. For pity's sake, get your professor to learn you something with a tune to it."

(1904)

Aunt Susanna's Birthday Celebration

This next story, published in *New Idea Woman's Magazine* of New York in February 1905, a few months before Montgomery apparently started writing *Anne of Green Gables*, concerns the rocky relationship of another couple named Anne and Gilbert. While the parallels between these characters and the more famous couple of her book series are slight, this story does show Montgomery's first attempt to write about a bumpy courtship involving characters with these names.

"GOOD-AFTERNOON, NORA MAY. I'M REAL GLAD TO see you. I've been watching you coming down the hill and hoping you'd turn in at our gate. Going to visit with me this afternoon? That's good. I'm feeling so happy and delighted an' I've been hankering for some one to tell it all to.

"Tell you about it? Well, I guess I might as well. It ain't any breach of confidence.

"You didn't know Anne Douglas? She taught school here three years ago, afore your folks moved over from Talcott. She belonged up Montrose way and she was only eighteen when she came here to teach. She boarded with us and her and me were the greatest chums. She was just a sweet girl.

"She was the prettiest teacher we ever had, and that's saying a good deal, for Springdale has always been noted for getting good-looking schoolmarms, just as Miller's Road is noted for its humly ones.

"Anne had *yards* of brown, wavy hair and big, dark-blue eyes. Her face was kind o' pale, but when she smiled you would have to smile, too, if you'd been chief mourner at your own funeral. She was a wellspring of joy in the house, and we all loved her.

"Gilbert Martin began to drive her the very first week she was here. Gilbert is my sister Julia's son, and a fine young fellow he is. It ain't good manners to brag of your own relations, but I'm always forgetting and doing it. Gil was a great pet of mine. He was so bright and nice-mannered everybody liked him. Him and Anne were a fine-looking couple, Nora May. Not but what they had their shortcomings. Anne's nose was a mite too long and Gil had a crooked mouth. Besides, they was both pretty proud and sperrited and high-strung.

"But they thought an awful lot of each other. It made me feel young again to see 'em. Anne wasn't a mossel vain, but nights she expected Gil she'd prink for hours afore her glass, fixing her hair this way and that, and trying on all her good clothes to see which become her most. I used to love her for it. And I used to love to see the way Gil's face would light up when she came into a room or place where he was. Amanda Perkins, she says to me once, 'Anne Douglas and Gil Martin are most terrible struck on each other.' And she said it in a tone that indicated that it was a dreadful disgraceful and unbecoming state of affairs. Amanda had a disappointment once and it soured her. I immediately responded, 'Yes, they are most terrible struck on each other,' and I said it in a tone that indicated I thought it a most beautiful and lovely thing that they should be so.

"And so it was. You're rather too young to be thinking of such things, Nora May, but you'll remember my words when the time comes.

"Another nephew of mine, James Ebenezer Lawson—he calls himself James E. back there in town, and I don't blame him, for I never could stand Ebenezer for a name myself; but that's neither here nor there. Well, he said their love was idyllic. I ain't very sure what that means. I looked it up in the dictionary after James Ebenezer left—I wouldn't display my ignorance afore him—but I can't say that I was much the wiser for it. Anyway, it meant something real nice; I was sure of that by the way James Ebenezer spoke and the wistful look in his eyes. James Ebenezer isn't married; he was to have been, and she died a month afore the wedding-day. He was never the same man again.

"Well, to get back to Gilbert and Anne. When Anne's school

year ended in June she resigned and went home to get ready to be married. The wedding was to be in September, and I promised Anne faithful I'd go over to Montrose in August for two weeks and help her to get her quilts ready. Anne thought that nobody could quilt like me. I was as tickled as a girl at the thought of visiting with Anne for two weeks; but I never went; things happened before August.

"I don't know rightly how the trouble began. Other folks—jealous folks—made mischief. Anne was thirty miles away and Gilbert couldn't see her every day to keep matters clear and fair. Besides, as I've said, they were both proud and high-sperrited. The upshot of it was they had a terrible quarrel and the engagement was broken.

"When two people don't care overly much for each other, Nora May, a quarrel never amounts to much between them, and it's soon made up. But when they love each other better than life it cuts so deep and hurts so much that nine times out of ten they won't ever forgive each other. The more you love anybody, Nora May, the more he can hurt you. To be sure, you're too young to be thinking of such things.

"It all came like a thunderclap on Gil's friends here at Greendale, because we hadn't ever suspected things were going wrong. The first thing we knew was that Anne had gone up West to teach school again at St. Mary's, eighty miles away, and Gilbert, he went out to Manitoba on a harvest excursion and stayed there. It just about broke his parents' hearts. He was their only child and they just worshiped him.

"Gil and Anne both wrote to me off and on, but never a word, not so much as a name, did they say of each other. I'd 'a' writ and asked 'em the rights of the fuss if I could, in hopes of patching it up; but I can't write now—my hand is too shaky—and mebbe it was just as well, for meddling is terribly risky work in a love trouble, Nora May. Ninety-nine times out of a hundred the last state of a meddler and them she meddles with is worse than the first.

"So I just set tight and said nothing, while everybody else in the clan was talking Anne and Gil sixty words to the minute.

"Well, last birthday morning I was feeling terrible disperrited. I had made up my mind that my birthday was always to be a good thing for other people, and there didn't seem one blessed thing

I could do to make anybody glad. Emma Matilda and George and the children were all well and happy and wanted for nothing that I could give them. I begun to be afraid I'd lived long enough, Nora May. When a woman gets to the point where she can't give a gift of joy to anyone, there ain't much use in her living. I felt real old and worn out and useless.

"I was sitting here under these very trees—they was just budding out in leaf then, as young and cheerful as if they wasn't a hundred years old. And I sighed right out loud and said, 'Oh, Grandpa Holland, it's time I was put away up on the hill there with you.' And with that the gate banged and there was Nancy Jane Whitmore's boy, Sam, with two letters for me.

"One was from Anne up at St. Mary's and the other was from Gil out in Manitoba.

"I read Anne's first. She just struck right into things in the first paragraph. She said her year at St. Mary's was nearly up, and when it was she meant to quit teaching and go away to New York and learn to be a trained nurse. She said she was just broken-hearted about Gilbert, and would always love him to the day of her death. But she knew he didn't care anything more about her after the way he had acted, and there was nothing left for her in life but to do something for other people, and so on and so on, for twelve mortal pages. Anne is a fine writer, and I just cried like a babe over that letter, it was so touching; although I was enjoying myself hugely all the time, I was so delighted to find out that Anne loved Gilbert still. I was getting skeered she didn't, her letters all winter had been so kind of jokey and frivolous, all about the good times she was having, and the parties she went to, and the new dresses she got. New dresses! When I read that letter of Anne's, I knew that all the purple and fine linen in the world was just like so much sackcloth and ashes to her as long as Gilbert was sulking out on a prairie farm.

"Well, I wiped my eyes and polished up my specs, but I might have spared myself the trouble, for, in five minutes, Nora May, there was I sobbing again over Gilbert's letter. By the most curious coincidence he had opened his heart to me, too. Being a man, he wasn't so discursive as Anne; he said his say in four pages, but I could read the heartache between the lines. He wrote that he was going to Klondike and would start in a month's time. He was sick of living now that he'd lost Anne. He said he loved her better than his life and always would, and could never forget her, but he knew she didn't care anything about him now after the way she'd acted, and he wanted to get as far away from her and the torturing thought of her as he could. So he was going to Klondike—going to Klondike, Nora May, when his mother was writing to him to come home every week and Anne was breaking her heart for him at St. Mary's.

"Well, I folded up them letters and, says I, 'Grandpa Holland, I guess my birthday celebration is here ready to hand.' I thought real hard. I couldn't write myself to explain to those two people that they each thought the world of each other still—my hands are too stiff; and I couldn't get anyone else to write because I couldn't let out what they'd told me in confidence. So I did a mean, dishonorable thing, Nora May. I sent Anne's letter to Gilbert and Gilbert's to Anne. I asked Emma Matilda to address them, and Emma Matilda did it and asked no questions. I brought her up that way.

"Then I settled down to wait. In less than a month Gilbert's mother had a letter from him saying that he was coming home to settle down and marry Anne. He arrived home yesterday and last night Anne came to Springdale on her way home from St. Mary's. They came to see me this morning and said things to me I ain't going to repeat because they would sound fearful vain. They were so happy that they made me feel as if it was a good thing to have lived eighty years in a world where folks could be so happy. They said their new joy was my birthday gift to them. The wedding is to be in September and I'm going to Montrose in August to help Anne with her quilts. I don't think anything will happen to prevent this time—no quarreling, any-how. Those two young creatures have learned their lesson. You'd better take it to heart, too, Nora May. It's less trouble to learn it at second hand. Don't you ever quarrel with your real beau—it don't matter about the sham ones, of course. Don't take offense at trifles or listen to what other people tell you about him—out-siders, that is, that want to make mischief. What you think about him is of more importance than what they do. To be sure, you're too young yet to be thinking of such things at all. But just mind what old Aunt Susanna told you when your time comes."

(1905)

57

The Hurrying of Ludovic

When Montgomery agreed to rewrite some of her best short stories and compile them as a book eventually entitled *Chronicles of Avonlea* (1912), she mostly disregarded her publisher's request that the stories be revised to include Anne Shirley prominently. Instead, the one story to feature Anne ended up being the lead story in the volume, in which Anne, visiting her friends the Irvings at Echo Lodge, ends up meddling in the courtship of Theodora Dix and the ironically named Ludovic Speed. In this early version of the story, published in *The Canadian Magazine* of Toronto in May 1905, Anne's role is played by Juliet Sherman and the setting occurs in the more generic Deland River instead of Middle Grafton (in close proximity to Avonlea).

JULIET SHERMAN WAS CURLED UP BY THE WINDOW OF Theodora Dix's sitting-room on Saturday evening when she saw Ludovic Speed coming down the lane. He was yet far from the house, for the Dix lane was a long one, but Ludovic could be recognised as far as he could be seen. No one else in Deland River had such a tall, gently-stooping, placidly-moving figure. In every kink and turn of it there was an individuality that was all Ludovic's own.

Juliet thought it would be only tactful to go home. Ludovic was courting Theodora. Everybody in Deland River knew that, or, if anyone were in ignorance of the fact, it was not because he had not had time to find out. Ludovic had been coming down that lane to see Theodora, in the same ruminating, unhastening fashion, for fifteen years!

When Juliet, who was slim and girlish and romantic, rose to go, Theodora, who was plump and middle-aged and practical, said with a twinkle in her eye:

"There isn't any hurry, child. Sit down. You've seen Ludovic coming down the lane, and I suppose you think you'll be what Aunt Martha up the river calls, with a good English pronunciation, 'de trop.' But you won't. Ludovic rather likes a third person around and so do I. It spurs up the conversation as it were. When a man has been coming to see you straight along, twice a week for fifteen years, you get rather talked out by spells."

Theodora never pretended to bashfulness where Ludovic was concerned. She was not at all shy of referring to him and his dilatory courtship. Indeed, it seemed to amuse her.

Juliet sat down again and together they watched Ludovic coming down the lane, gazing calmly about him at the shorn harvest fields and the blue loops of the river as it wound in and out of the autumnal valley below.

Juliet looked at Theodora's placid, finely-moulded face and tried to imagine what she herself would feel like if she were sitting there, waiting for an elderly lover who had, seemingly, taken so long to make up his mind. But her imagination failed her.

"Anyway," she thought, impatiently, "if I wanted him I think I'd find some way of hurrying him up. Ludovic *Speed*. Was there ever such a glaring misnomer?"

Presently Ludovic got to the house and stood so long on the doorstep in a brown study, gazing into the tangled russet boscage of the orchard, that Theodora finally went and opened the door before he knocked. As she brought him into the sitting-room she made a comical grimace at Juliet over his shoulder.

Ludovic smiled pleasantly at Juliet. He liked her; she was the only young girl he knew, for he generally avoided young girls— they made him feel awkward and out-of-place. But Juliet did not affect him in this fashion; she had a way of getting on with all kinds of people and, although she had not lived in Deland River very long, both Theodora and Ludovic looked upon her as an old friend.

Ludovic was tall and somewhat ungainly, but his unhesitating placidity gave him the appearance of a dignity that did not otherwise pertain to him. He had a drooping, silky, brown moustache, and a little curly tuft of imperial—a fashion which was regarded as eccentric in Deland River, where men had clean-shaven chins or went full-bearded. His eyes were dreamy and pleasant, with a touch of melancholy in their blue depths.

He sat down in the big, bulgy, old armchair that had belonged to Theodora's father. Ludovic always sat there and Juliet declared that the chair had come to look like him.

The conversation soon grew animated enough. Ludovic was a good talker when he had somebody to draw him out. He was well read, and frequently surprised Juliet by his shrewd comments on men and matters out in the great world, of which only the faint echoes reached Deland River. He had also a liking for religious arguments with Theodora, who did not care much for politics or the making of history, but was avid of doctrines, and read everything pertaining thereto. When the conversation drifted into an eddy of friendly wrangling over Christian Science between Ludovic and Theodora, Juliet understood that her usefulness was ended for the time being, and that she would not be missed. She went away quietly and had to stop to laugh when she was well out of sight of the house, in the thick grove of birches that grew between the Dix establishment and the "old Seawell place" now belonging to the Shermans.

Juliet leaned against a birch tree and laughed heartily, as she was apt to do at thought of Theodora and Ludovic. To her eager youth this courtship of theirs seemed an amusing thing. She liked Ludovic, but she allowed herself to be provoked at him.

"The big, dear, irritating goose!" she said aloud. "There never was such a lovable idiot before."

The next time Juliet went over to the Dix place she and Theodora drifted into conversation about Ludovic. Theodora, who was the most industrious soul alive, and had a mania for fancy work into the bargain, was busying her smooth, plump fingers with a very elaborate Battenburg lace centrepiece. Juliet, who never did anything when she could avoid it and hated a needle, was lying back in a little rocker, with her slim hands folded in her lap, watching Theodora. She discovered again that day that Theodora was very handsome in a stately, Juno-like fashion of firm, white flesh; large, clearly-chiselled outlines, and great, cowey, brown eyes. When Theodora was not smiling she looked very imposing. Juliet thought it was likely that Ludovic held her in awe.

"Did you and Ludovic talk about Christian Science *all* Saturday evening?" she asked.

Theodora overflowed into a smile.

"Yes, and we even quarrelled over it. At least, I did. Ludovic wouldn't quarrel with anyone. You have to fight air when you spar with him. I hate to square up to a person who won't hit back."

"Theodora," said Juliet coaxingly, "I am going to be curious and impertinent. You can snub me if you like. Why don't you and Ludovic get married?"

Theodora laughed comfortably.

"That's a question Deland River folks have been asking for quite a while, I reckon, Juliet. Well, I'd have no objection to marrying Ludovic. That's frank enough for you, isn't it? But even in this century a woman can hardly marry a man until he asks her. And Ludovic has never asked me!"

"Is he too shy?" persisted Juliet. Since Theodora was in the mood she meant to sift this puzzling affair to the bottom.

Theodora dropped her work and looked meditatively out over the dull slopes of the sere world.

"No, I don't think it is that. Ludovic isn't shy. It's just his way—the Speed way. The Speeds are all dreadfully deliberate. They spend years thinking over a thing before they make up their minds to do it. Sometimes they get so much in the habit of thinking about it that they never get over it—like old Alder Speed, who was always talking of going to England to see his brother, but never went. They're not lazy, you know, but they love to take their time. Ludovic is an aggravated case of Speedism, so to speak. He never hurried in his life. Why, he has been thinking of getting his house painted for the last six years. He talks it over with me every little while, and picks out the colour and there the matter stays. He's fond of me and he means to ask me to have him some time. The only question is—will the time ever come?"

"Why don't you hurry him up?" asked Juliet impatiently.

Theodora went back to her stitches with another laugh.

"If Ludovic could be hurried up I'm not the one to do it. I'm too shy. It sounds ridiculous to hear a woman of my age and inches say that, but it is true. Of course, I know it is the only way any Speed ever did make out to get married. For instance, there's a cousin of mine married to Ludovic's brother. I don't say she proposed to him out and out, but she certainly helped the lame dog cannily over the stile. I couldn't do that. I *did* try once. When I realised that I was getting sere and mellow and all the girls of my generation were going off on either hand, I tried to give Ludovic a hint. But it stuck in my throat. And now I don't mind. If I don't change Dix to Speed until I take the initiative it will be Dix to the end of life. Ludovic doesn't realise that we are growing old, you know. He thinks we are giddy young folks yet, with plenty of time before us. That's the Speed failing. They never find out they're alive until they're dead."

"You're fond of Ludovic, aren't you?" asked Juliet, detecting a note of real bitterness among Theodora's paradoxes.

"Laws, yes," said Theodora candidly. She did not think it worth while to blush over so settled a fact. "I think the world and all of Ludovic. And he certainly does need somebody to look after him. He's neglected—he looks frayed—you can see that for yourself. That old aunt of his looks after his house in some fashion, but she doesn't look after *him*. And he is coming now to the age when a man needs to be looked after and coddled a bit. I'm lonesome here, and Ludovic is lonesome up there, and it does seem ridiculous, doesn't it? I don't wonder that we're the standing joke of Deland River. Goodness knows, I laugh at it enough myself. I've sometimes thought that if Ludovic could be made jealous it might spur him along. But I never could flirt and there's nobody to flirt with if I could. Everybody hereabouts looks upon me as Ludovic's property, and nobody would dream of interfering with him."

"Theodora," cried Juliet, "I have a plan!"

"Now, what are you going to do?" exclaimed Theodora.

Juliet told her. At first Theodora laughed and protested. In the end she yielded somewhat doubtfully, overborne by Juliet's enthusiasm.

"Well, try it, then," she said, resignedly. "If Ludovic gets mad and leaves me I'll be worse off than ever; but nothing venture, nothing win. And there is a fighting chance, I suppose. Besides, I must admit I'm tired of his dilly-dallying."

Juliet went home under the birches tingling with delight in her plot. She hunted up the uncle whose housekeeper she was, and told him what was required of him. Arnold Sherman listened and laughed. He was an elderly widower, playing at farming after a more strenuous life elsewhere, but more interested in books and out-of-the-way hobbies than in crops and stock. He was handsome in a mature style, and he had a dash of mischief in him still, so that he entered readily enough into Juliet's plan. It amused him to think of hurrying Ludovic Speed, and he knew that Theodora could be depended on to do her part. The comedy would not be dull, whatever its outcome.

The curtain rose on the first act after prayer meeting on the next Thursday night. It was bright moonlight when the people came out of the church, and everybody saw it plainly. Arnold Sherman stood upon the steps close to the door and Ludovic Speed leaned up against a corner of the graveyard fence, as he had done for years. The boys said he had worn the paint off that particular place. Ludovic knew of no reason why he should paste himself up against the church door. Theodora would come out as usual and he would join her as she went past the corner.

This was what happened: Theodora came down the steps, her stately figure outlined in its darkness against the gush of lamplight from the porch. Arnold Sherman asked her if he might see her home. Theodora took his arm calmly, and together they swept past the stupefied Ludovic, who stood helplessly gazing after them as if unable to believe his eyes.

For a few minutes he stood there limply; then he started down the road after his fickle lady and her new admirer. The boys and irresponsible young men crowded after, expecting some excitement; but they were disappointed. Ludovic strode on until he overtook Theodora and Arnold, and then fell meekly in behind them.

Theodora hardly enjoyed her walk home, although Arnold Sherman laid himself out to be especially entertaining. Her heart yearned after Ludovic, whose shuffling footsteps she heard behind her. She feared she had been very cruel but she was in for it now. She steeled herself by the reflection that it was for his own good, and she talked to Arnold Sherman as if he were the one man in the world. Poor, deserted Ludovic, following humbly behind, heard her, and if Theodora had known how bitter the cup she was holding to his lips really was, she would never have been resolute enough to present it, no matter for what ultimate good.

When she and Arnold turned in at her gate Ludovic had to stop. Theodora looked over her shoulder and saw him standing stock still on the road. His forlorn figure haunted her thoughts all night. If Juliet had not run over the next day and bolstered up her convictions, she might have spoiled everything by prematurely relenting.

Ludovic stood still on the road, quite oblivious to the hoots and comments of the vastly amused small boy contingent, until Theodora and his rival disappeared from his view under the firs in the hollow of her lane. Then he turned about and went home, not with his usual leisurely amble, but with a perturbed stride which proclaimed his inward disquiet.

He felt bewildered. If the world had suddenly come to an end or if the lazy, meandering Deland River had turned about and flowed uphill, Ludovic could not have been more astonished. For fifteen years he had walked home from meeting with Theodora, and now this elderly stranger, with the glamour of the outside world still hanging around him, had coolly walked off with her under Ludovic's very nose. Worse—most unkindest cut of all—Theodora had gone with him willingly; nay, she had evidently enjoyed his company. Ludovic felt the stirring of a righteous anger in his easy-going soul.

When he reached the end of his long lane—all the lanes were long in Deland River, whose early settlers had a passion for solitude—he paused at his gate and looked at his old house, set back from the lane in a crescent of leafless white birches. Even in the moonlight its weather-worn aspect was plainly visible. He thought of the trimness of the old Seawell place since the advent of the Shermans, and stroked his chin nervously with his sunburnt fingers. Then he doubled up his fist and struck it smartly on the gate-post.

"Theodora needn't think she is going to jilt me in this fashion after our keeping company for fifteen years," he said. "*I'll* have something to say to it, Arnold Sherman or no Arnold Sherman. The impudence of the puppy!"

The next morning Ludovic drove to Delandville and engaged Ewen Matheson to come and paint his house. And that evening, although he was not due until Saturday night, he went down to see Theodora.

Arnold Sherman was there before him and was actually sitting in Ludovic's own prescriptive chair. Ludovic had to deposit himself in Theodora's new wicker rocker, where he looked and felt lamentably out of place.

If Theodora felt the situation to be awkward she carried it off superbly. She had never looked handsomer, and Ludovic perceived that she wore her second best silk dress. He wondered miserably if she had donned it in expectation of his rival's call. She had never put on silk dresses for him. Ludovic had always been the meekest and mildest of mortals, but he felt quite murderous as he sat mutely there and listened to Arnold Sherman's polished conversation.

"You should just have been here to see him glowering," Theodora told the delighted Juliet the next day. "It may be wicked of me, but I felt real glad. I was afraid he might stay away and sulk. So long as he comes here and sulks I don't worry. But he is feeling badly enough, poor soul, and I'm really eaten up by remorse. He tried to outstay your uncle last night, but he didn't manage it. You never saw a more depressed looking creature than he as he hurried down the lane in the moonshine. Yes, he actually hurried."

The following Sunday evening Arnold Sherman walked to church with Theodora and sat with her. When they came in Ludovic Speed suddenly stood up in his pew under the gallery. He sat down again at once, but everybody in view had seen him, and that night folks in all the length and breadth of Deland River discussed the dramatic occurrence with keen enjoyment.

"Yes, he jumped right up as if he was pulled to his feet when the minister was reading the chapter," said his cousin, Lorella Speed, who had been in church, to her brother, Chalmers Speed, who had not. "His face was as white as a sheet, and his eyes were just glaring out of his head. I never felt so thrilled. I declare, I almost expected him to fly at them then and there. But he just gave a sort of gasp and sat down again. I don't know whether Theodora Dix saw him or not. She looked as cool and unconcerned as you please."

Theodora had not seen Ludovic, but if she looked cool and unconcerned, her appearance belied her, for she felt miserably flustered. She could not prevent Arnold Sherman coming to church with her, but it seemed to her like going too far. People did not go to church together in Deland River unless they were next thing to being engaged. What if this filled Ludovic with the narcotic of despair instead of wakening him up? She sat through the service in misery and heard not one word of the sermon.

But Ludovic's spectacular performances were not yet over for the night. The Speeds might be hard to get started, but once they were started their momentum was irresistible. When Theodora and Arnold came out Ludovic was waiting on the steps. He stood up straight and stern, with his head thrown back and his shoulders squared. There was open defiance in the look he cast on his rival, and masterfulness in the mere touch of the hand he laid on Theodora's arm.

"May I see you home, Miss Dix?" was what he said, but what he meant was, "I am going to see you home whether or no."

Theodora, with a deprecating look at Arnold Sherman, took his arm and Ludovic marched her across the green amid a silence which the very horses tied to the storm fence seemed to share.

Juliet ran over to the Dix place early in the morning. Theodora smiled consciously.

"Yes, it is really settled at last, Juliet. Coming home last night Ludovic asked me plump and plain to marry him—Sunday night and all as it was. It's to be right away, so I'll have to do some hurrying. And you must be my bridesmaid."

"So Ludovic Speed has been hurried up to some purpose at last," said Arnold Sherman, when Juliet went home brimful with her news. "And you are all delighted, of course, and my poor pride must be the scapegoat. I shall always be regarded in Deland River as the man who wanted Theodora Dix and couldn't get her."

"But that won't be true, you know," said Juliet comfortingly.

Arnold Sherman thought of Theodora's ripe beauty and the mellow companionableness she had revealed in their brief intercourse.

"I'm not so sure of that," he said with a sigh.

(1905)

The Little Fellow's Photograph

In *Anne of Windy Poplars* (1936), a twenty-something Anne Shirley, now principal of Summerside High School, decides to raise funds for her school's dramatic club by canvassing the community for subscriptions, alongside her student Lewis Allen, a budding photographer who is working his way through high school without family support. This episode originates in the following short story, published thirty years earlier in *The Classmate* of Cincinnati, regarding two adolescent boys who are spending part of their vacation from boarding school on an extended bicycle jaunt in the countryside.

IT WAS LATE IN THE SUMMER AFTERNOON WHEN NEWTON Carter and I dismounted from our bicycles, and sat down to rest on an old-fashioned stone dyke under some huge willows. The day was hot and we had wheeled a long distance since the morning. Just where we were to spend the night we had only a very hazy idea; we were making a vacation bicycle tour and took pot luck wherever we found it. We had been out for a week, and had thoroughly enjoyed our jaunt. There was to be only one more day of it; then we would return to Newton's home, at Hallerton, where I was spending my vacation.

"This is great," sighed Newton, stretching himself out luxuriously among the ferns that grew thickly over the dyke. "I vote we stay here until that blazing sun cools down a bit."

"I wonder if we could get something to eat up there," I said, peering over the dyke at a house about two hundred yards away.

"We had such an early dinner that my inner boy is uncomfortable already. Let's amble up and see."

The house in question was a very quaint, old-fashioned one, low in the eaves, with square, small-paned windows. Big willows stretched their patriarchal arms over it, and an apparent wilderness of perennial flowers and shrubs crowded all about it. It was weather-gray and shabby, but the big barns beyond it were finely finished and prosperous looking, up-to-date in every respect.

"I've always heard that when a man's barns are bigger than his house it's a sign that his income exceeds his expenditure," said Newton.

"I should say it was a sign he thought more of his horses than his family," I observed laughing. "Anyway I'm going to see if I can forage out any edibles. Coming?"

Newton stowed our cameras away behind the gate-post and we sauntered up the deep-rutted, grassy lane.

"This lane doesn't look as if it were much traveled," said Newton, with a shrug. "Evidently the folks who live here aren't strongly sociable."

The house seemed deserted, but we knocked at the little red kitchen door. We expected a welcome; throughout our whole trip we had found the country people exceedingly kind and hospitable, glad to furnish us with meals and sleeping accommodations, and very seldom accepting any payment therefor, although we always offered it.

Consequently, we were decidedly taken aback when the door was jerked open and on the threshold appeared, not the sonsy farmer's wife or daughter we had expected to see, but a tall, broad-shouldered man of about fifty, who demanded unceremoniously:

"What do you want?"

"We are making a bicycle tour of the country, and called to see if we could get our suppers here," explained Newton.

"No, you can't," was the uncompromising answer, and the door was promptly shut in our faces.

We walked away rather amused than not, since our case was not very desperate.

"Nice amiable gentleman, that," said Newton with a grin. "I'm sorry for his wife, if he has one. On second thoughts, I don't think he can have, or she would civilize him a trifle. Well, anyhow, I'm going to sit on his stone dyke until I'm rested unless he comes out and orders us off."

We had just got comfortably sprawled out again, when we heard something pushing softly through the willow undergrowth to our right. Then a small boy of about eight years of age came into view and stood surveying us bashfully, with a big apple turnover clasped tightly in his chubby hands. He was a pretty child, with long, carefully-combed brown curls, big, trustful brown eyes, and delicately-modeled features. There was an air of refinement about him, very different from the rugged, sunburnt types of country children we had met. He was barelegged and bareheaded, with a little blue cotton shirt and a pair of faded velvet knickerbockers between head and legs. But he looked like a small prince in disguise.

Just behind him was a big, black Newfoundland dog, whose head was almost on a level with the lad's shoulder.

"Hello, sonny," said Newton amiably. "Who belongs to you?"

The boy came forward with a smile, holding out his turnover.

"This is for you to eat," he said shyly. "Dad made it for me, but I'd rather give it to you. I've lots to eat."

I daresay I should have been clumsy enough to refuse to take the little chap's snack, but Newton had more tact. He accepted it gravely, broke it in two, handed me one half of it and proceeded to devour the other. I had my doubts as to "dad's" ability in the cooking line, but my first mouthful dissipated them. "Dad" might not be strong on hospitality, but he could certainly make turnovers. As I was really very hungry I enjoyed my half immensely.

"What's your name, sonny-boy?" asked Newton between mouthfuls.

"Tommy Armstrong," said our small benefactor. "But dad always calls me 'Little Fellow.' I'm all he has, you know. Dad is awful fond of me, and I'm awful fond of dad. I'm afraid you think my dad is impolite 'cause he shut the door so quick, but he doesn't mean to be. I heard you asking for something to eat—I was in the garden behind the hollyhocks. So I just thought I'd bring you my turnover 'cause I'm always so sorry for poor people who haven't plenty to eat. I have, always. My dad is a splendid cook. You ought to see the puddings he can make."

"Haven't you a mother anywhere about?" I said.

The Little Fellow shook his head gravely. He had settled down among the grasses by the side of his big, shaggy playmate, his arms clasped about his sunburned knees.

"No, my mother is dead. Mrs. Merrill told me once that she'd gone to heaven, but my dad says there's no such place and I guess he knows. My dad is an awful wise man. He's read thousands of books. I mean to be just exactly like him when I grow up—only I'll always give people things to eat when they want them. My dad isn't very fond of people, you know, but my, he's awful good to me."

"Do you go to school?" asked Newton.

"No. My dad teaches me at home. I think I'd like to go to school and have some little boys to play with, but I guess dad knows what's best. I've got Carlo, and dad himself is splendid to play with when he has time. My dad is pretty busy, you know. He has to run the farm and keep the house clean, too. That's why he can't be bothered having people around, you see. When I get bigger I'll be able to help him lots, and then he'll have more time to be polite to folks."

"That turnover was just about right, Little Fellow," said Newton, swallowing the last crumb.

The Little Fellow's eyes beamed.

"I'm so glad you liked it," he said.

"Would you like to have your picture taken?" I said, feeling that it would hardly do to offer this generous small soul money. "If you would I'll take it."

"O, wouldn't I!" said the Little Fellow eagerly. "Carlo, too?"

"Certainly."

I posed the two prettily before a background of hanging willows, the little chap standing with his arm about his big, curly playmate's neck, both dog and boy seeming equally well-pleased, and took the picture with my last remaining plate.

"If it comes out good I'll send you one by mail," I promised. "How shall I address it?"

"'Tommy Armstrong, care of Mr. James Armstrong, Glencove,'" said the Little Fellow. "O, won't it be fine to have something coming to me mineself through the post-office! I tell you I'll feel awful proud. I won't say a word to dad about it so that it'll be a splendid surprise for him."

"Well, look out for your parcel in a fortnight, or three weeks," I said as we bade him good-by. We looked back at the curve of the road and saw him standing on the dyke waving his hand to us.

A mile down the road we had supper at a farmhouse, where we made inquiries about the Armstrongs.

"James Armstrong has never got over his wife's death five years ago," said our host. "He was a decent, kindly man before that—always a bit of a hermit, but still hospitable and agreeable enough. He was just wrapped up in his wife; she was a mere girl, twenty years younger than he was. Her death was an awful shock to him. It just seemed to change his nature completely. He got soured and cranky. Wouldn't even get a housekeeper— looked after his house and child himself. He'd kept bachelor's hall for years before he was married, so he ain't a bad hand at it, neither. He don't want to see people, and he never goes to church or to a neighbor's house. But he's certainly awful fond of that leetle boy—just about worships him."

The next day found us back at Newton's home. Newton and I had attended the Hallerton Academy together the previous winter. In the fall Newton was going to college, while I intended to start for the West. My father, who had been a quiet, bookish man, in delicate health, had died the year before and I was abso- lutely alone in the world, my mother having died at my birth. Father's small annuity ceased with his death, and I faced the future with just enough money to give me a year at the Academy and pay my fare west. There I intended to take up land and go into wheat-raising, as I always had a taste for farming. My pros- pects were somewhat uncertain, but I was young and strong, not afraid of work, and confident that I could get along once I secured a start. Nevertheless, I felt my isolation and loneliness very keenly.

It was almost three weeks before we found time to develop our pictures. The Little Fellow's came out splendidly—one of the best, both as regards likeness and artistic merit that I had ever taken. The Little Fellow smiled frankly at me from the proof as natural as life. When I showed the picture to Mrs. Carter she exclaimed,

"Why, Allan, he's very much like you!"

"So he is," broke in Newton. "I thought when I saw him his face reminded me of somebody I knew, but I couldn't think who it was. The likeness is ten times stronger in the photograph, though. Why, his eyes, his forehead—his whole expression resemble yours. Did you suppose you were ever such a good-looking little chap as that once, Al?"

"I have a picture of you taken when you were about eight years old," said Mrs. Carter. "Your father sent it to me. It is remarkably like this one."

Mrs. Carter got out her picture—I had always laughed over that photograph of a solemn-eyed little chap with long curls and lace collar—and I had to admit that the resemblance was surprising.

"It is very curious," I said, "but it must be only a coincidence. The Little Fellow can't be any relation of mine. However, I think I'll take this picture down to Glencove myself instead of sending it by mail, and investigate a little. He may be a distant cousin or something. I really know nothing about my mother's people if she had any living. I've always been under the impression that she hadn't. Father hadn't, I know."

"I don't think I'd want to discover a relationship with that amiable Mr. Armstrong," laughed Newton.

I finished the picture nicely, mounting it as artistically as possible; and a few days later I wheeled over the forty miles to Glencove, arriving late in the day at the house where Newton and I had had our supper. The folks readily agreed to take me in for the night, and after supper I told them why I had come.

Mr. Bowen, my host, who was sitting beside me on the veranda, removed his corn-cob pipe from his mouth, leaned forward, and stared at me.

"D'ye mean to say that you've got a photo of little Tommy Armstrong?"

"That I have and a good one," I replied. "Don't believe a professional could have taken better."

Mr. Bowen slapped his knee resoundingly.

"Well, if that don't beat all! Why, little Tommy Armstrong is dead, and his father is just about wild, and all the worse that he hasn't got any kind of a picture of him at all. And now you tell me you've got a good one! Well, well."

"The Little Fellow dead! Impossible!" I exclaimed.

"No, sad to say it's only too true. He was killed two days after you were here. Was driving a load of grain into the barn for his dad when he slipped off and the truck wheel went right over him. He only lived six hours. Suffered awful, but was just as patient and brave as anyone could be, they say. I dunno what'll become of James Armstrong now. They say he's like a crazy man, just moping and muttering to himself all the time, and sort of moaning now and again, 'If I only had a picture of my Little Fellow.' I tell you I'm sorry for that man."

I was shocked and grieved to hear of the Little Fellow's tragic death. Somehow, he had won my affection, even in our brief intercourse. I made some inquiries of Mr. Bowen about James Armstrong's family connections but he could give me no information. Armstrong had come to Glencove twenty years ago. He had lived alone for ten years, then married a Glencove girl. Nothing was known of his family; it was generally believed that he had no relatives.

I was tired after my long ride, but I determined to take the Little Fellow's picture to his father at once. It was sunset when I walked up the lane under the big willows. Carlo was lying on the stone before the red door. He got up, came to me, and licked my hand, lifting his big, brown eyes wistfully as if asking for news of his little playmate. The door was open, and in the dim room beyond I saw a man with his head bowed on the table.

At my knock he started up and came to the door. I expected a repulse at first, but he seemed to recognize me for he said listlessly:

"So you're back? The Little Fellow said you talked to him and was good to him. He liked you. I was sorry I had been so churlish to you. What is it you want?"

"I want to show you something," I said.

James Armstrong went to a shelf in the corner of the room and lighted a lamp. As the light flared up I was shocked at the change in him. He was hollow-cheeked, haggard, and unshaven, and his eyes flashed with a fitful fire.

Without a word I took the Little Fellow's photograph from its wrappings and held it out to him. He snatched it up, gave it one amazed, hungry look, then dropped into his chair and burst into sobs and tears. I had never seen a man weep so before, and I stood aside in mute sympathy until he partially recovered self-control.

"O, you don't know what this means to me," he said brokenly at last. "I hadn't any picture of him. And I'm not like other folks—I can't recall a face—any face, no matter whose, in my memory. I can't see faces as most folks can in their mind. It's been awful since the Little Fellow died—I couldn't even remember what he looked like. And now you've brought me this—after I was so churlish to you, too. Sit down, young sir. I wish I could express my thanks in some way. I guess you've saved my reason—maybe my life. O, sir, isn't it like him? My dear Little Fellow! How am I going to live without him! First his mother—now him."

"He was a dear little chap," I said warmly.

"That he was. Such a cruel death for him, too. He was so bright and full of life—and to be crushed out like that! And he was so patient and never complained. Once he smiled up in my face and said, 'Dad, I think you've been mistaken in one thing—just one. I guess there is a heaven, isn't there? Isn't there, dad?' I said to him, yes, there was—God forgive me for ever trying to teach him anything else. He smiled again, contented-like, and said, 'Well, dad, I'm going there, and mother and God are there, so I'll be pretty well off. But I'm worried about you, dad. You'll be so awful lonesome without me. But just do the best you can, and be a good, kind man always, and be polite to folks; and come to us by-and-by.' He made me promise I'd try, but when he was gone I couldn't stand the blankness of it. I'd have gone mad if you hadn't brought me this. It won't be so hard now."

He talked on about the Little Fellow for some time as if he found relief and pleasure in it. His reserve and gruffness seemed to have fallen from him like a garment.

At last I produced the small photograph of myself and showed it to him.

"Ever see anybody who looked like this?" I asked him.

He peered at it in perplexity.

"It's awful like the Little Fellow," he said at last. "Whose might it be?"

"Mine, when I was eight years old. It was because of the curious resemblance that I came to Glencove. I thought that you and I or the Little Fellow and I might be some distant relation. My name is Allan Tracy, and my father was George Tracy."

James Armstrong shook his head. Then he said, "What was your mother's name?"

"Mary Gardiner."

"She was my half-sister," he said quietly. "I hardly knew her—never saw her but once. I was brought up with an uncle's family after my mother's death. My father moved away and married again. He brought his wife and little daughter to see me once. He died soon after, and I never saw them again. I soon lost all trace of them. You are my nephew and the Little Fellow's cousin."

This was surprising news indeed, to a lad who had fancied himself alone in the world. I spent the whole evening with my newly-found uncle, and found him to be a well-read and intelligent man. We had much to talk of and I told him freely of my plans and situation. Somehow, I took a liking to him. His former inhospitable reception was forgotten, and I saw only the real worth of the character and temperament below the unpromising shell that had hitherto concealed him. He urged me to stay all night with him, but I knew Mr. Bowen would be expecting me back, so I had to decline but promised to spend the next day with him. I did so; and before it was over he said to me gravely:

"Lad, never mind the west. Come here and live with me. You are my nephew, and all I have will be yours some day. I can do well by you—what I would have done for my own son if he'd lived. You're alone in the world, and so am I. I need you. I'll grow hard and bitter again if I'm left here alone. I want you to help me keep my promise to the Little Fellow. His place is empty. Come you and fill it."

"Thank you, uncle, I will," I said frankly, holding out my hand.

(1906)

The Old South Orchard

In a letter to Ephraim Weber dated April 1906, Montgomery reported that a piece she had written more than a year earlier—"It wasn't a story but just a sort of essay relating fictional incidents about an old homestead garden"—had been accepted by *The Outing Magazine* (published out of Deposit, New York), whose editor had reportedly admired the "fine simplicity" of the piece. It was published nearly two years later, in the January 1908 issue. Although Montgomery made no comment to Weber about the editor's apparent suggestion that she expand this essay into a book, it would later form the basis of her fourth novel, *The Story Girl*.

IT IS NOW MORE THAN SEVENTY YEARS SINCE IT HAD ITS beginning, when grandfather brought his bride home. Before the wedding he had fenced off the big south meadow that sloped to the sun; it was the finest, most fertile field on the farm and the neighbors told young Abraham King that he would raise many a crop of wheat in that meadow. Abraham King smiled, and, being a man of few words, said nothing, but in his mind he had a vision of the years to be, and in that vision he saw, not rippling acres of harvest gold, but great leafy avenues of wide-spreading trees, laden with fruit to gladden the eyes of children and grandchildren yet unborn. It was a vision to develop slowly into fulfillment. Grandfather King was in no hurry. He did not set his whole orchard out at once, for he wished it to grow with his life and history and be bound up with all of good and joy that came to the household he had founded. So on the morning after he had brought his young wife home they went together to the south meadow and planted their bridal trees. Those two trees were yet living when we of the third generation were born, and every spring bedecked themselves in blossom as delicately tinted as Elizabeth King's face when she walked through the old south meadow in the morn of her life and love.

That was the beginning of the famous King orchard. When a son was born to Abraham and Elizabeth a tree was planted in the orchard for him. They had ten children in all and each child had its birthtree. Every family festival was commemorated in like fashion, and every beloved visitor who spent a night under their roof was expected to plant a tree in the orchard. So it came to pass that every tree in it was a fair green monument to some love or delight of the past years.

We, the grandchildren of Abraham and Elizabeth, were born into this heritage. The orchard was old when we came to know it and, for us, was one of the things that must have existed forever, like the sky and the river and the stars. We could not think of a world without the old south orchard. Each grandchild—and there were many of us, both on the homestead where father lived and scattered abroad in far lands—had its tree there, set out by grandfather when the news of its birth was announced to him.

In our day there was a high stone wall around it instead of grandfather's split rail fence. Our uncles and father had built the wall in their boyhood, so that it was old enough to be beautiful with moss, and green things growing out of its crevices, violets purpling at its base in early spring days, and goldenrod and asters making a September glory in its corners.

Grandmother, as long as she was able, liked to go through the orchard with us, down to the farther gate, where she never omitted to kiss us all good-bye, even if we were to be gone for no more than an hour. She would wait at the gate, her sweet old face all aglow, until we were out of sight; then she would visit Uncle Stephen's avenue before going back to the house.

"Uncle Stephen's avenue," as we always called it, was a double row of apple trees running down the western side of the orchard—a great green bowery arcade it was. To walk through it in blossom time was something not to be forgotten. It realized for us our most extravagant dreams of fairyland wherein we wandered under the gorgeous arches of kings' palaces over pavements of pearl and emerald. Heaven, we thought, must surely be an endless succession of Uncle Stephen's avenues in blossom that never faded.

Uncle Stephen was that first-born whose birth-tree stood nearest to the two gnarled old patriarchs in the center of the orchard. Father, who was one of the youngest members of the family, had but one remembrance of him—as a handsome youth of eighteen home from a long sea voyage, with all the glamor of faraway lands and southern seas about him. In Uncle Stephen the blood of a seafaring race claimed its own. He had none of grandfather's abiding love of woods and meadows and the kindly ways of the warm red earth; to sea he must go, despite the fears and pleadings of the reluctant mother, and it was from the sea he came to set out his avenue in the south orchard with trees brought from his voyage.

Then he sailed away again, and the ship was never heard of more. The gray first came in grandmother's brown hair in those months of waiting. Then, for the first time in its life, the old orchard heard the sound of weeping and was consecrated by a sorrow.

To us children Uncle Stephen was only a name, but a name to conjure with. We never wearied of speculating on his fate and harrowing our small souls with fearful imaginations concerning his last moments. He played an important part in many of our games and make-believes; he was always the good fairy who appeared mysteriously in the nick of time and rescued us from all difficulties. He was all the more delightful in that he never grew old like our other uncles. For us he was always the curly-headed youngster, with the laughing blue eyes, of the framed daguerreotype hanging up in grandmother's room. If he had ever come back in reality we would have expected him to look just like that. We all, I think, cherished a secret belief that he was yet living—probably on a desert island—and would some day return home, glittering with the gold and jewels of the pirate hoard discovered on the said island. To this day we middle-aged men and women who were the children of that old south orchard do not say "when my ship comes in" but "when Uncle Stephen comes home."

There was another spot in the orchard which had a great attraction for us, albeit mingled with something of awe and fear. This was "Aunt Una's seat," a bench of mossy stone slabs arched over by a couple of gnarled pear trees and grown thickly about with grasses and violets. We never cared to play there—it would have seemed like desecration, but in our quiet moods we sought the old stone bench to dream. Aunt Una mingled in those dreams, but not after the fashion of Uncle Stephen, for there was no doubt concerning her fate. She had died thirty years before, on her twentieth birthday.

We children heard much of Aunt Una, for she was one of those people who are not soon forgotten, whose personality seems to haunt the scenes of their lives long after they have gone thence. She had been very beautiful, with a strange moonlight beauty of white skin and night-black eyes and hair, foreign to the fair, rosy King style of loveliness; a dreamy, spiritual girl, one of those souls who have no real abiding place in this world and only tarry for a brief while. She had been gifted with the power of expression, and a sort of journal she had written was one of grandmother's treasures. She sometimes read portions of it to us, and so we seemed to make a very real acquaintance with Aunt Una. The book contained verses that appeared quite wonderful to us—indeed, I think even yet that they were wonderful—and bits descriptive of the orchard, blent with a girl's dreams and longings. Her phrases lingered in our memories and the whole orchard seemed full of her. Besides, there was a bit of her romance connected with it.

Aunt Una had had a lover. This man was still living; he was little more than fifty, but we thought him very old because of his snow-white hair. He had never married, and lived some distance away. Every June, on Aunt Una's birthday, he made a pilgrimage to the old orchard to see her tree, all ablow with never-failing blossoms, and sit on her bench. At such times we children were not allowed to go into the orchard, but we sometimes peeped over the wall and saw him sitting there, a melancholy, lonely figure. It gave us, I think, a deep and lasting sense of the beauty and strength of love which could thus outlive time and death. We were too young then to understand its full beauty. The romance of it appealed more strongly to us; we girls had our favorite dream of dying young and having our lovers come to visit our trees thirty years after.

But the orchard had happier memories. There had been a wedding in it for one thing—long before we were born. It was that of Aunt Iris, who had been a celebrated beauty. She was married in the orchard under the apple blossoms of June. We never tired of hearing grandmother tell of it. We had heard the story so often that we could picture it almost as plainly as grandmother herself—the lanes of white, fragrant trees, the gay dresses of the guests, the beautiful bride in her white silk dress and old lace veil. It was a favorite game with us to enact it all over, and so coveted was the honor of playing the bride's part that it had to be settled by lot. Aunt Iris' pear tree, planted by the bride herself after the ceremony, was in our time a huge old tree just within the entrance gate. The most delicious pears that I have ever eaten grew on it. There are no such pears nowadays. I suppose they had a catalogue name, but the old south orchard had a nomenclature all its own, and we knew them as "Aunt Iris' pears."

There were many plum trees in the orchard, as well as cherries—great luscious ox-hearts and a sweet white kind—pears and quinces, but of course more of apple trees than of any other kind. Uncle Bob's tree was our favorite, because it bore a delicious, juicy, yellow apple with a streak of red on one side. There were two big trees—the twins' trees—which were given over to us entirely, because nobody except children could eat their big, green, dead-sweet apples. And there was a seedling tree which had come up unbidden in a sunny corner, the fruit of which we used when our games called for a "trial by ordeal." The apples of it were the sourest that ever grew; hard, bitter, unpalatable. The "ordeal" consisted in eating one of them in large bites without making a single grimace! Few of us ever passed it, but there was one who never failed—our little French cousin, Laure. She could munch those dreadful apples without so much as a change of expression on her little dark, elfin face. But then, Laure could do anything she attempted. We could never "stump" her, as our juvenile slang expressed it.

Every season brought new beauties to the old orchard. It would have been hard to say when we loved it best. In spring it was a rare spot; the grass was green there when everywhere else was only sere brown sod; the trees were in leaf and bud a full week earlier there than in other orchards. Summer brought ripe luxuriance of growth. Long ago grandmother had sown a little plot with caraway just inside the gate and it had spread half over the orchard. In July, when it came into blossom, the long arcades were white with its billowy waves that swayed and foamed in the moonshine of summer eves like seas of silver. One day a three-year-old baby wandered into the caraway thicket that met over her head, lay down in it, and went to sleep. When she was missed, great was the consternation in the house of King. Everybody turned out to search, distracted by direful possibilities of well and river. Search as they might they could not find her. It was sunset, with a mother in hysterics, before an answering gurgle came from the caraway in response to frantic calls. Father plunged over the stone wall and into the caraway where he came upon a rosy sleep-warm baby curled up in a nest of her own fashioning and very loath to leave it.

Autumn was, I think, the time we loved best, for then came the apple-picking. What fun it was! The boys would climb the trees and shake the apples down until we girls cried for mercy. The days were crisp and mellow, with warm sunshine and a tang of frost in the air, mingled with the woodsy odors of the withering leaves. The hens and turkeys prowled about picking at windfalls, and our pet kittens made mad rushes at each other among the leaves.

Then came winter, when the orchard was heaped with drifts. It was a wonderful place on moonlit nights, when the snowy arcades shone like magic avenues of ivory and pearl and the bare trees cast fairy-like traceries over them. Uncle Stephen's avenue was a fine place for coasting, and when a thaw came, followed by a frost, we held high carnival there.

Any history of the old south orchard would be incomplete if it failed to mention the "King Bubble." This was a spring of peculiarly sweet, pure water which gurgled up in the southwest corner at the foot of a gentle slope. Grandfather had rimmed it round with a circle of hewn stones, and in this basin the water brimmed up like a great amber bubble until it found its way through ferns and mosses to the brook below. In our games the King Bubble played the part of every famous fount in song and story of which we had ever read—especially the well of Urda and Ponce de Leon's fountain of youth. On summer days, tired and warm, we would fling ourselves down on its fern-fringed brink and drink deep draughts from an old blue china cup which always sat on a little stone shelf below the brim and never chanced to be broken despite the dozens of careless little hands that seized it. To-day weary men and women all over the world think often of that spring and long for a cup of its matchless water.

Near the spring was a huge granite bowlder as high as a man's head, straight and smooth in front, but hollowed out into natural steps behind. It also played an important part in all our games, being fortified castle, Indian ambush, throne, pulpit, or concert platform as occasion required. A certain gray-haired minister, famous in two continents for eloquence and scholarly attainments, preached his first sermon at the age of ten from that old gray bowlder, and a woman whose voice has delighted thousands sang her earliest madrigals there.

"If you're a King, you sing," was a countryside proverb in those days, and certainly it was true of all the descendants of grandfather and grandmother. We all sang more or less, although none could equal Laure, and among the dearest memories of the old south orchard are those of the long, mellow twilights of summer Sundays, when old and young assembled in the orchard and sang hymns, grandfather beating time. How clearly the whole scene comes out on the wall of memory's picture gallery—grandfather and grandmother, father and mother, sitting on Aunt Una's bench, while we children, with all Uncle George's brood from the next farm, sat on the grass around them. Two voices sound out for me above all the others—Laure's glorious and silvery, grandmother's sweet, quavering, tremulous. Dear old Grandmother King! How much she enjoyed those summer evenings of song!

Grandfather and grandmother used to walk much in the orchard on fine evenings, hand in hand, lovers still, lingering in Uncle Stephen's arcade or at Aunt Una's seat. Their devotion to each other was beautiful to see. We children never thought it a sad or unlovely thing to grow old with so fair an example before us. One summer grandmother grew very frail and could not walk in the orchard. Yet grandfather was the first to go; they found him sitting in his armchair on one afternoon, a smile on his fine old face and the sunshine making a glory of his white hair. Grandmother called him by name, but for the first time he failed to answer her.

They carried Grandfather King through the old orchard on his last journey. It had been his wish. Children and grandchildren walked behind him under boughs laden with the mellow fruit of trees his hands had planted. The next June Grandmother King was carried to him over the same way—the bride going once more to her bridegroom under the glory of their bridal trees.

I visited the orchard not long ago on a mellow afternoon. It did not seem much changed. Most of the old trees were standing; grandfather's and grandmother's were gone, but their places were filled with two flourishing young trees planted when the homestead boy had brought his bride home. Aunt Una's seat was there and Uncle Stephen's avenue; the King Bubble was as clear and sparkling as of yore—truly, it was a fountain of youth, for it never grew old. And at the big granite bowlder children were playing "Ivanhoe" and besieging it valiantly with arrows and popguns. My best wish for them was that in the years to come the old orchard might hold for them as many sweet and enduring memories as it held for me.

(1908)

The Life-Book of Uncle Jesse

This next story, published in the August 1909 issue of *The Housekeeper* (a women's magazine in Minneapolis), was subsequently "recycled" and "replanted" in *Anne's House of Dreams* (1917), to use Claire E. Campbell's recent terminology. It contains the first of two prototypes of Captain Jim, a retired sea captain whose talents as an oral storyteller do not translate into print and who fears that his life stories will be forgotten once he is no longer alive to tell them. Elizabeth Rollins Epperly suggests that Captain Jim acts as "a kind of living emblem of chivalry and kindness and truth," hints of which are already apparent in Uncle Jesse.

UNCLE JESSE! THE NAME CALLS UP THE VISION OF HIM as I saw him so often in those two enchanted summers at Golden Gate; as I saw him the first time, when he stood in the open doorway of the little, low-eaved cottage on the harbor shore, welcoming us to our new domicile with the gentle, unconscious courtesy that became him so well. A tall, ungainly figure, somewhat stooped, yet suggestive of great strength and endurance; a clean-shaven old face deeply lined and bronzed; a thick mane of iron gray hair falling quite to his shoulders; and a pair of remarkably blue, deep-set eyes, which sometimes twinkled and sometimes dreamed, but oftener looked out seaward with a wistful quest in them, as of one seeking something precious and lost. I was to learn one day what it was for which Uncle Jesse looked.

It cannot be denied that Uncle Jesse was a homely man. His spare jaws, rugged mouth, and square brow were not fashioned on the lines of beauty; but though at first sight you thought him plain you never thought anything more about it—the spirit shining through that rugged tenement beautified it so wholly.

Uncle Jesse was quite keenly aware of his lack of outward comeliness and lamented it, for he was a passionate worshipper of beauty in everything. He told mother once that he'd rather like to be made over again and made handsome.

"Folks say I'm good," he remarked whimsically, "but I sometimes wish the Lord had made me only half as good and put the rest of it into looks. But I reckon He knew what He was about, as a good Captain should. Some of us have to be homely or the purty ones—like Miss Mary there—wouldn't show up so well."

I was not in the least pretty but Uncle Jesse was always telling me I was—and I loved him for it. He told the fib so prettily and sincerely that he almost made me believe it for the time being; and I really think he believed it himself. All women were lovely and of good report in his eyes, because of one he had loved. The only time I ever saw Uncle Jesse really angered was when someone in his hearing cast an aspersion on the character of a shore girl. The wretched man who did it fairly cringed when Uncle Jesse turned on him with lightning of eye and thunder cloud of brow. At that moment I no longer found it hard to reconcile Uncle Jesse's simple, kindly personality with the wild, adventurous life he had lived.

We went to Golden Gate in the spring. Mother's health had not been good and her doctor recommended sea air and quiet. Uncle James, when he heard it, proposed that we take possession of a small cottage at Golden Gate, to which he had recently fallen heir by the death of an old aunt who had lived in it.

"I haven't been up to see it," he said, "but it is just as Aunt Elizabeth left it and she was the pink of neatness. The key is in the possession of an old sailor living near by—Jesse Boyd is the name, I think. I imagine you can be very comfortable in it. It is built right on the harbor shore, inside the bar, and it is within five minutes' walk of the outside shore."

Uncle James' offer fitted in very opportunely with our limp family purse, and we straightway betook ourselves to Golden

Gate. We telegraphed to Jesse Boyd to have the house opened for us and one crisp spring day, when a rollicking wind was scudding over the harbor and the dunes, whipping the water into white caps, and washing the sandshore with long lines of silvery breakers, we alighted at the little station and walked the half mile to our new home, leaving our goods and chattels to be carted over in the evening by an obliging station agent's boy.

Our first glimpse of Aunt Elizabeth's cottage was a delight to soul and sense; it looked so like a big gray seashell stranded on the shore. Between it and the harbor was only a narrow strip of shingle and behind it was a gnarled and battered fir wood where the winds were in the habit of harping all sorts of weird and haunting music. Inside, it was to prove even yet more quaint and delightful, with its low, dark-beamed ceilings and square, deep-set windows by which, whether open or shut, sea breezes entered at their own sweet will. The view from our door was magnificent, taking in the big harbor and sweeps of purple hills beyond. The entrance of the harbor gave it its name—a deep, narrow channel between the bar of sand-dunes on the one side and a steep, high, frowning red sandstone cliff on the other. We appreciated its significance the first time we saw a splendid golden sunrise flooding it, coming out of the wonderful sea and sky beyond and billowing through that narrow passage in waves of light. Truly, it was a golden gate through which one might sail to "faerie lands forlorn."

As we went along the path to our little house we were agreeably surprised to see a blue spiral of smoke curling up from its big, square chimney; and the next moment Uncle Jesse (we were calling him Uncle Jesse half an hour after we met him, so it seems scarcely worth while to begin with anything else) came to the door.

"Welcome, ladies," he said, holding out a big, hard, but scrupulously clean hand. "I thought you'd be feeling a bit tired and hungry, maybe, so when I came over to open up I put on a fire and brewed you up a cup of tea. I just delight in being neighborly and 'tain't often I have the chance."

We found that Uncle Jesse's "cup of tea" meant a veritable spread. He had aired the little dining room, set out the table daintily with Aunt Elizabeth's china and linen—"knowed jest where to put my hands on 'em—often and often helped old Miss Kennedy wash 'em. We were cronies, her and me. I miss her terrible."—and adorned it with mayflowers which, as we afterwards discovered, he had tramped several miles to gather. There was good bread and butter, "store" biscuits, a dish of tea fit for the gods on high Olympus, and a platter of the most delicious sea trout done to a turn.

"Thought they'd be tasty after traveling," said Uncle Jesse. "They're fresh as trout can be, ma'am. Two hours ago they was swimming in Johnson's pond yander. I caught 'em—yes, ma'am. It's about all I'm good for now, catching trout and cod occasional. But 'tweren't always so—not by no manner of means. I used to do other things, as you'd admit if you saw my life-book."

I was so hungry and tired that I did not then "rise to the bait" of Uncle Jesse's "life-book." I simply wanted to begin on those trout. Mother insisted that Uncle Jesse sit down and help us eat the repast he had prepared, and he assented without undue coaxing.

"Thank ye kindly. 'Twill be a real treat. I mostly has to eat my meals alone, with the reflection of my ugly old phiz in a looking glass opposite for company. 'Tisn't often I have the chance to sit down with two such sweet purty ladies."

Uncle Jesse's compliments look bald enough on paper; but he paid them with such gracious, gentle deference of tone and look that the woman who received them felt that she was being offered a queen's gift in kingly fashion.

He broke bread with us and from that moment we were all friends together and forever. After we had eaten all we could, we sat at our table for an hour and listened to Uncle Jesse telling us stories of his life.

"If I talk too much you must jest check me," he said seriously, but with a twinkle in his eyes. "When I do get a chance to talk to anyone I'm apt to run on terrible."

He had been a sailor from the time he was ten years old and some of his adventures had such a marvelous edge that I secretly wondered if Uncle Jesse were not drawing a rather long bow at our credulous expense. But in this, as I found later, I did him injustice. His tales were all literally true and Uncle Jesse had the gift of the born story teller, whereby "unhappy, far-off things" can be brought vividly before the hearer and made to live again in all their pristine poignancy. Mother and I laughed and shivered over Uncle Jesse's tales, and once we found ourselves crying. Uncle Jesse surveyed our tears with pleasure shining out through his face like an illuminating lamp.

"I like to make folks cry that way," he remarked. "It's a compliment. But I can't do justice to the things I've seen and helped do. I've got 'em all jotted down in my life-book but I haven't got the knack of writing them out properly. If I had I could make a great book, if I had the knack of hitting on just the right words and stringing everything together proper on paper. But I can't. It's in this poor human critter." Uncle Jesse patted his breast sorrowfully; "but he can't get it out."

When Uncle Jesse went home that evening mother asked him to come often to see us.

"I wonder if you'd give that invitation if you knew how likely I'd be to accept it," he remarked whimsically.

"Which is another way of saying you wonder if I meant it," smiled mother. "I do, most heartily and sincerely."

"Then I'll come. You'll likely be pestered with me at any hour. And I'd be proud to have you drop over to visit me now and then too. I live on that point yander. Neither me nor my house is worth coming to see. It's only got one room and a loft and a stovepipe sticking out of the roof for a chimney. But I've got a few little things lying around that I picked up in the queer corners I used to be poking my nose into. Mebbe they'd interest you."

Uncle Jesse's "few little things" turned out to be the most interesting collection of curios I had ever seen. His one neat little living room was full of them—beautiful, hideous, or quaint, as the case might be, and almost all having some weird or exciting story attached.

Mother and I had a beautiful summer at Golden Gate. We lived the life of two children with Uncle Jesse as a playmate. Our housekeeping was of the simplest description and we spent our hours rambling along the shores, reading on the rocks, or sailing over the harbor in Uncle Jesse's trim little boat. Every day we loved the simple-souled, true, manly, old sailor more and more. He was as refreshing as a sea-breeze, as interesting as some ancient chronicle. We never tired of listening to his stories; and his quaint remarks and comments were a continual delight to us. Uncle Jesse was one of those interesting and rare people who in the picturesque phraseology of the shore folks, "never speak but they say something." The milk of human kindness and the wisdom of the serpent were mingled in Uncle Jesse's composition in delightful proportions.

One day he was absent all day and returned at nightfall.

"Took a tramp back yander." "Back yander" with Uncle Jesse might mean the station hamlet or the city a hundred miles away, or any place between—"to carry Mr. Kimball a mess of trout. He likes one occasional and it's all I can do for a kindness he did me once. I stayed all day to talk to him. He likes to talk to me, though he's an eddicated man, because he's one of the folks that's *got* to talk or they're miserable, and he finds listeners scarce round here. The folks fight shy of him because they think he's an infidel. He ain't *that* far gone exactly—few men is, I reckon—but he's what you might call a heretic. Heretics are wicked but they're mighty interesting. It's just that they've got sorter lost looking for God, being under the impression that He's hard to find—which He ain't, never. Most of 'em blunder to Him after awhile I guess. I don't think listening to Mr. Kimball's arguments is likely to do *me* much harm. Mind you, I believe what I was brought up to believe. It saves a vast of trouble—and back of it all, God is good. The trouble with Mr. Kimball is, he's a leetle *too* clever. He thinks he's bound to live up to his cleverness and that it's smarter to thrash out some new way of getting to heaven than to go by the old track the common, ignorant folks is traveling. But he'll get there sometime all right and then he'll laugh at himself."

Nothing ever seemed to put Uncle Jesse out or depress him in any way.

"I've kind of contracted a habit of enjoying things," he remarked once, when mother had commented on his invariable cheerfulness. "It's got so chronic that I believe I even enjoy the disagreeable things. It's great fun thinking they can't last. 'Ole rheumatiz,' I says, when it grips me hard, 'you've *got* to stop aching sometime. The worse you are the sooner you'll stop, perhaps. I'm bound to get the better of you in the long run, whether in the body or out of the body.'"

Uncle Jesse seldom came to our house without bringing us something, even if it were only a bunch of sweet grass.

"I favor the smell of sweet grass," he said. "It always makes me think of my mother."

"She was fond of it?"

"Not that I knows on. Dunno's she ever saw any sweet grass. No, it's because it has a kind of motherly perfume—not too young, you understand—something kind of seasoned and wholesome and dependable—just like a mother."

Uncle Jesse was a very early riser. He seldom missed a sunrise.

"I've seen all kinds of sunrises come in through that there Gate," he said dreamily, one morning when I myself had made a heroic effort at early rising and joined him on the rocks half way between his house and ours. "I've been all over the world and, take it all in all, I've never seen a finer sight than a summer sunrise out there beyant the Gate. A man can't pick his time for dying, Mary—jest got to go when the Captain gives his sailing orders. But if I could I'd go out when the morning comes in there at the Gate. I've watched it a many times and thought what a thing it would be to pass out through that great white glory to whatever was waiting beyant, on a sea that ain't mapped out on any airthly chart. I think, Mary, I'd find lost Margaret there."

He had already told me the story of "lost Margaret" as he always called her. He rarely spoke of her but when he did his love for her trembled in every tone—a love that had never grown faint or forgetful. Uncle Jesse was seventy; it was fifty years since lost Margaret had fallen asleep one day in her father's dory, and drifted—as was supposed, for nothing was ever known certainly of her fate—across the harbor and out of the Gate, to perish in the black thunder squall that had come up suddenly that long ago afternoon. But to Uncle Jesse those fifty years were but as yesterday when it is past.

"I walked the shore for months after that," he said sadly, "looking to find her dear, sweet, little body; but the sea never gave her back to me. But I'll find her sometime. I wisht I could tell you just how she looked but I can't. I've seen a fine silvery mist hanging over the Gate at sunrise that seemed like her—and then again I've seen a white birch in the woods back yander that made me think of her. She had pale brown hair and a little white face, and long slender fingers like yours, Mary, only browner, for she was a shore girl. Sometimes I wake up in the night and hear the sea calling to me in the old way and it seems as if lost

Margaret called in it. And when there's a storm and the waves
are sobbing and moaning I hear her lamenting among them. And
when they laugh on a gay day it's *her* laugh—lost Margaret's
sweet little laugh. The sea took her from me but some day I'll
find her, Mary. It can't keep us apart forever."

I had not been long at Golden Gate before I saw Uncle
Jesse's "life-book," as he quaintly called it. He needed no coaxing to show it and he proudly gave it to me to read. It was an
old leather bound book filled with the record of his voyages
and adventures. I thought what a veritable treasure trove it
would be to a writer. Every sentence was a nugget. In itself the
book had no literary merit; Uncle Jesse's charm of story telling failed him when he came to pen and ink; he could only jot
roughly down the outlines of his famous tales and both spelling
and grammar were sadly askew. But I felt that if anyone pos-
sessing the gift could take that simple record of a brave, adventurous life, reading between the bald lines the tale of dangers
stanchly faced and duties manfully done, a wonderful story
might be made from it. Pure comedy and thrilling tragedy were
both lying hidden in Uncle Jesse's "life-book," waiting for the
touch of the magician's hand to waken the laughter and grief and
horror of thousands. I thought of my cousin, Robert Kennedy,
who juggled with words in a masterly fashion, but complained
that he found it hard to create incidents or characters. Here were
both ready to his hand; but Robert was in Japan in the interests
of his paper.

In the fall, when the harbor lay black and sullen under
November skies, mother and I went back to town, parting with
Uncle Jesse regretfully. We wanted him to visit us in town during
the winter but he shook his head.

"It's too far away, Mary. If lost Margaret called me I mightn't
hear her there. I must be here when my time comes. It can't be
very far off now."

I wrote often to Uncle Jesse through the winter and sent him
books and magazines. He enjoyed them but he thought—and
truly enough—that none of them came up to his life-book for
real interest.

"If my life-book could be took and writ by someone that
knowed how it would beat them holler," he wrote in one of his
few letters to me.

In the spring we returned joyfully to Golden Gate. It was as golden as ever and the harbor as blue; the winds still rollicked as gaily and sweetly and the breakers boomed outside the bar as of yore. All was unchanged save Uncle Jesse. He had aged greatly and seemed frail and bent. After he had gone home from his first call on us mother cried.

"Uncle Jesse will soon be going to seek lost Margaret," she said.

In June Robert came. I took him promptly over to see Uncle Jesse, who was very much excited when he found that Robert was a "real writing man."

"Robert wants to hear some of your stories, Uncle Jesse," I said. "Tell him the one about the captain who went crazy and imagined he was the Flying Dutchman."

This was Uncle Jesse's best story. It was a compound of humor and horror, and though I had heard it several times I laughed as heartily and shivered as fearsomely over it as Robert did. Other tales followed; Uncle Jesse told how his vessel had been run down by a steamer, how he had been boarded by Malay pirates, how his ship had caught fire, how he had helped a political prisoner escape from a South American republic. He never said a boastful word but it was impossible to help seeing what a hero the man had been—brave, true, resourceful, unselfish, skillful. He sat there in his poor little room and made those things live again for us. By a lift of the eyebrow, a twist of the lip, a gesture, a word, he painted some whole scene or character so that we saw it as it was.

Finally, he lent Robert his "life-book." Robert sat up all night reading it and came to the breakfast table in great excitement.

"Mary, this is a wonderful book. If I could take it and garb it properly—work it up into a systematic whole and string it on the thread of Uncle Jesse's romance of lost Margaret it would be the novel of the year. Do you suppose he would let me do it?"

"Let you! I think he would be delighted," I answered.

And he was. He was as excited as a schoolboy over it. At last his cherished dream was to be realized and his "life-book" given to the world.

"We'll collaborate," said Robert. "You will give the soul and I the body. Oh, we'll write a famous book between us, Uncle Jesse. And we'll get right to work."

Uncle Jesse was a happy man that summer. He looked upon the little back room we gave up to Robert for a study as a sacred shrine. Robert talked everything over with Uncle Jesse but would not let him see the manuscript. "You must wait till it is published," he said. "Then you'll get it all at once in its best shape."

Robert delved into the treasures of the life-book and used them freely. He dreamed and brooded over lost Margaret until she became a vivid reality to him and lived in his pages. As the book progressed it took possession of him and he worked at it with feverish eagerness. He let me read the manuscript and criticize it; and the concluding chapter of the book, which the critics, later on, were pleased to call idyllic, was modeled after my suggestions, so that I felt as if I had a share in it too.

It was autumn when the book was finished. Robert went back to town but mother and I decided to stay at Golden Gate all winter. We loved the spot; and, besides, I wished to remain for Uncle Jesse's sake. He was failing all the time; and after Robert went and the excitement of the book-making was past he failed still more rapidly. His tramping expeditions were over and he seldom went out in his boat. Neither did he talk a great deal. He liked to come over and sit silently for hours at our seaward window, looking out wistfully toward the Gate with his swiftly-whitening head leaning on his hand. The only keen interest he still had was in Robert's book. He waited and watched impatiently for its publication.

"I want to live till I see it," he said, "just that long—then I'll be ready to go. He said it would be out in the spring—I must hang on till it comes, Mary."

There were times when I doubted sadly if he would "hang on." As the winter wore away he grew frailer and frailer. But ever he looked forward to the coming of spring and "the book," *his* book, transformed and glorified.

One day in young April the book came at last. Uncle Jesse had gone to the postoffice faithfully every day for a month, expecting it; but this day he was too feeble to go and I went for him. The book was there. It was called simply, "The Life-Book of Jesse Boyd," and on the title page the names of Robert Kennedy and Jesse Boyd were printed as collaborators.

I shall never forget Uncle Jesse's face as I handed it to him. I came away and left him reading it, oblivious to all else. All night the light burned in his window and I looked out across the sands to it and pictured the delight of the old man poring over the printed pages whereon his own life was portrayed. I wondered how he would like the ending—the ending I had suggested. I was never to know.

After breakfast I went over to Uncle Jesse's house, taking some little delicacy mother had cooked for him. It was an exquisite morning, full of delicate spring tints and sounds. The harbor was sparkling and dimpling like a girl; the winds were playing hide and seek roguishly among the stunted firs, and the silver-flashing gulls were soaring over the bar. Beyond the Gate was a shining, wonderful sea.

When I reached the little house on the point I saw the lamp still burning wanly in the window. A quick alarm struck at my heart. Without waiting to knock I lifted the latch and entered.

Uncle Jesse was lying on the old sofa by the window, with the book clasped to his heart. His eyes were closed and on his face was a look of the most perfect peace and happiness—the look of one who has long sought and found at last.

We could not know at what hour he had died; but somehow I think he had his wish and went out when the morning came in through the Golden Gate. Out on that shining tide his spirit drifted, over the sunrise sea of pearl and silver, to the haven where lost Margaret waited beyond the storms and calms.

(1909)

A Garden of Old Delights

Like "The Old South Orchard" earlier in this volume, this story, first published in *The Canadian Magazine* of Toronto in June 1910, contains an embryonic version of the setting of *The Story Girl*—the phrase "our orchard of old delights" appears in chapter 4 of its sequel, *The Golden Road*—as well as an early incarnation of the titular character (referred to here sometimes as "the Story Girl" and sometimes as "the Story-Girl"). It consists of descriptions of an old garden told by an adult narrator through the lens of memory and contains several family legends that would be retold by Sara Stanley—as well as one that Montgomery saved for *Emily of New Moon* (1923). Furthermore, the Story Girl's "garden book," which closes this short story, anticipates the garden book that Emily Starr writes as an adolescent when she is forbidden to write fiction in *Emily Climbs* (1925).

WHAT WONDER THAT WISE OLD EDEN STORY PLACED the beginning of life in a garden? A garden fitly belongs to the youth of the world and the youth of the race, for it never grows old. The years, which steal so much from everything else, bring added loveliness and sweetness to it, enriching it with memories beautiful and tender, but never blighting its immortal freshness. It is foolishness to speak as we do of "old" gardens: gardens are perennially young, the haunt of flowers and children. And Grandmother's garden was always full of both.

Some of her many grandchildren always came to the old homestead for their summer holidays. One summer there were a half-dozen there as guests; and, counting the other ten who lived near her and spent more time at grandmother's than at their own homes, we were the merriest little crew in the world. The garden was our favourite haunt, and we passed most of our waking moments there. It was to us an enchanted pleasure-ground, and there is nothing in all our store of remembrance so sweet and witching as our recollections of it. Places visited in later years have grown dim and indistinct, but every nook and corner of grandmother's garden is as vivid in memory as on the day I saw it last. That was many years ago; but I could go straight with shut eyes at this very moment to the bed beside the snowball tree where the first violets grew.

The door of the big living-room opened directly into the garden. You went down four wide shallow steps, formed of natural slabs of red sandstone which great-grandfather had brought up from the shore. The lower one was quite sunk into the earth, and mint grew thickly about its edges. Often crushed by so many little feet, it gave out its essence freely and the spicy odour always hung around that door like an invisible benediction.

The garden was long and narrow and sloped slightly to the west. On two sides it was surrounded by a high stone wall; at least, we thought it high; but I have a mature suspicion that I might not think so now. Things have such an unwholesome habit of dwindling as we grow older; but then we could barely see over it by standing on tiptoe, and we had to climb to its top by the little ladder fastened against the western end if we wanted to get a good view of the wide, sloping green fields beyond, and the sea calling so softly on its silvery, glistening sand shore.

The third side was shut in by the house itself, a long, quaint, white-washed building, lavishly festooned with Virginia creeper and climbing roses. Something about the five square windows in the second storey gave it an appearance of winking at us in a friendly fashion through its vines; at least, so the story-girl said; and, indeed, we could always see it for ourselves after she had once pointed it out to us.

At one corner of the house a little gate opened into the kitchen garden, where the vegetables grew; but we never felt much interest in that—perhaps because grandmother's old servant Jean looked upon it as her special domain and discouraged intruders.

"Get awa' wi' ye into the floor garden—that's the proper place for bairns," she would say, with an instinctive perception of the fitness of things.

The fourth side was rimmed in by a grove of fir trees, a dim, cool place where the winds were fond of purring, and where there was always a resinous, woodsy odour. On the farther side of the firs was a thick plantation of slender silver birches and whispering poplars; and just beyond it what we called the "wild garden"—a sunny triangle shut in by the meadow fences and as full of wild flowers as it could hold: blue and white violets, dandelions, Junebells, wild-roses, daisies, buttercups, asters, and goldenrod, all lavish in their season.

The garden was intersected by right-angled paths, bordered by the big white clam-shells which were always found in abundance by the bay, and laid with gravel from the shore—coloured pebbles and little white shells well ground into the soil. In the beds between the paths and around the wall grew all the flowers in the world, or so, at least, we used to think. The same things were always found in the same place; we always looked for the clove pinks, sown in grandmother's bridal days, behind the big waxberry bush, and the shadowy corner behind the sumacs was always sweet in spring with white narcissus.

There were many roses, of course, roses that grew without any trouble and flung a year's hoarded sweetness into luxuriant bloom every summer. One never heard of mildew or slugs or aphis there, and nothing was ever done to the rose-bushes beyond a bit of occasional pruning. There was a row of big double pink ones at one side of the front door, and the red and white ones grew in the middle plot. There was one yellow rose-tree to the left of the steps; but the ones we loved best were the dear little "Scotch roses"—oh, how fragrant and dainty and thorny were those wee semi-double roses with their waxen outer petals and the faint shell-pink of their hearts! Jean had brought the rose-bush with her all the way from an old Scottish garden when she was a "slip of a lassie," so that in our eyes there was a touch of romance about them that the other roses lacked.

Grandmother's bed of lavender and caraway and sweet clover was very dear to her heart. The caraway and sweet clover had a tendency to spread wildly, and it was one of our duties to keep them in proper bounds, rooting up every stray bit that straggled from the allotted space. We picked and dried the lavender for grandmother's linen closet; and she made us delicious caraway cookies such as I have never eaten anywhere else. I am afraid such cookies are not made nowadays.

All the beds were edged with ribbon grass. The big red peonies grew along the edge of the fir grove, splendid against its darkness, and the hollyhocks stood up in stiff ranks by the kitchen garden gate. The bed next to them was a sight to see when the yellow daffodils and tulips came out. There was a clump of tiger-lilies before the door and a row of madonna-lilies farther down. One big pine tree grew in the garden, and underneath it was a stone bench, made, like the steps, of flat shore stones worn smooth by the long polish of wind and wave. Just behind this bench grew pale, sweet flowers which had no name that we could ever find out. Nobody seemed to know anything about them. They had been there when grandfather's father bought the place. I have never seen them elsewhere or found them described in any catalogue. We called them the White Ladies—the Story Girl gave them the name. She said they looked like the souls of good women. They were very ærial and wonderfully dainty, with a strange, haunting perfume that was only to be detected at a little distance and vanished if you bent over them. They faded whenever they were plucked, and although strangers, greatly admiring them, often carried away roots and seeds they could never be coaxed to grow elsewhere.

There was one very old-fashioned bed full of bleeding hearts, Sweet William, bride's bouquet, butter-and-eggs, Adam-and-Eve, columbines, pink and white daisies, and Bouncing Bets. We liked this bed best, because we might always pluck the flowers in it whenever we pleased. For the others, we had to ask permission, which, however, was seldom refused.

Poppies were the only things in the garden with a license to ramble. They sprang up everywhere; but the bed of them was in the northwest corner, and there they shook out their fringed silken skirts against a low coppice of young firs. Asparagus, permitted because of the feathery grace of its later development, grew behind the well-house, near the lilies-of-the-valley; the middle path was spanned at regular intervals by three arches, and these were garlanded with honeysuckle.

The well-house was a quaint, lichened old structure built over the well at the bottom of the garden. Four posts supported an odd peaked little roof like the roof of a Chinese pagoda, and it was almost covered with vines that hung from it in long swinging festoons nearly to the ground. The well was very deep and dark, and the water, drawn up by a windlass and chain in a mossy old bucket shaped like a little barrel and bound with icy hoops, was icy cold. As far down as we could see, the walls of the well were grown over with the most beautiful ferns.

The garden was full of birds; some of them we regarded as old friends, for they nested in the same place every year and never seemed afraid of us. A pair of bluebirds had an odd liking for a nook in the stonework of the well; two yellowhammers had preëmpted an old hollow poplar in the south-western corner. Wild canaries set up housekeeping in the big lilac bush before the parlour windows. One exciting summer a pair of hummingbirds built a nest in the central honeysuckle arch. A wild August gale and rainstorm tore it from its frail hold and dashed it to the ground, where we found it the next morning. We girls cried over it; and then we cast lots to decide who should have the wonderful thing, fashioned of down and lichen, and no bigger than a walnut. The hummingbirds never came back, though we looked wistfully for them every summer. Robins were numerous, especially in early spring, great, sleek, saucy fellows, strutting along the paths. In the summer evenings after sunset they would whistle among the firs, making sweet, half melancholy music.

A garden with so many years behind it would naturally have some legends of its own. There was one fascinating story about "the poet who was kissed." One long-ago day, so long ago that grandfather was only a little boy, a young man had come into this garden—one whose name had already begun to bud out with the garland of fame that later encrowned it. He went into the garden to write a poem, and fell asleep with his head pillowed on the old stone bench. Into the garden came great-aunt Alice, who was nobody's aunt then, but a laughing-eyed girl of eighteen, red of lip and dark of hair, wilful and sweet, and a wee bit daring. She had been away and had just come home, and she knew nothing at all of her brother's famous guest; but in the garden, fast asleep under the pine tree, with his curly head on the hard stones and his half-finished poem beside him was the handsomest youth she had ever seen.

Mischievous Alice took him for an unexpected cousin from Scotland, and, bending over until her long dark curls swept his shoulder, she dropped a kiss, light and dainty as a falling rose-petal, on his sunburned cheek. Then he opened his big blue eyes and looked into Alice's blushing face—blushing hotly, for she realised all at once that this could not be the Scotch cousin. She knew, for she had been told, that *he* had eyes as velvet brown as her own. Fair Alice sprang to her feet and fled through the garden in dire confusion—a confusion which was not mended any when she found out who the sleeping prince really was. But it all ended happily, as one would expect, in wedding-bells for Alice and her poet.

The story which had the greatest fascination for us was that of "The Lost Diamond." Soon after grandfather and grandmother were married a certain great lady had come to visit them, a lady on whose white, high-bred hand sparkled a diamond ring. She had gone to walk in the garden; the diamond was in the ring when she went down the sandstone steps, for grandmother noted its sparkle as the great lady lifted her silken gown; but when she came in again the setting was empty and the diamond gone. Nor was it ever found, then or afterwards, search as they might. And never was anything better searched for. This story had a perennial charm for us children; we always had a secret hope that we might find the stone, and it made our labours seem light indeed. Nobody objected to pulling up weeds when every pull stood the chance of being rewarded by the starry glitter of the lost gem.

And then our garden had its ghost. We children were not sup-posed to know anything about this—grandmother thought it would frighten us and had forbidden any allusion to it in our presence. Her precaution was useless, for we knew all about it— the Story Girl had told us. How the Story Girl knew it I cannot say; but the legend did not frighten us at all. Instead, we were intensely interested and very proud of it. Not every garden had a ghost. So it seemed to confer a certain distinction on ours. We never saw our ghost, but that was not for lack of looking for it.

The legend, as related to us one misty twilight by the Story Girl, and told in whispers with furtive glances backward that rendered it very impressive—oh, she knew how to tell a story, that Girl—was as follows:

Long ago, even before grandfather was born, an orphaned cousin of his lived with his parents. Her name was Edith and she was small and sweet and wistful eyed, with very long sleek brown curls and a tiny birthmark like a pink butterfly right on one oval cheek. She had a lover, the young son of a neighbour, and one day he had told her shyly that he was coming on the morrow to ask her a very important question and he wanted to find her in the garden when he came. Edith promised to meet him at the old stone bench; and on the morrow she dressed herself in her pale blue muslin and sleeked her curls and waited smiling at the trysting spot. To her there came a heedless cousin bursting out boyishly that her lover had been killed that morning by the accidental discharge of his gun. Edith was never quite herself after that; and she was never contented unless she was dressed in her blue gown and sitting on the old bench waiting for him—because he would be sure to come sometime, she said. She grew paler every day, but the little pink butterfly grew redder until it looked like a stain of blood against the whiteness of her face. When the winter came she died, but the next summer it began to be whispered about that Edith was sometimes seen sitting on the bench, waiting. More than one person had seen her.

"Grandfather saw her when he was a little boy," said the Story Girl, nodding mysteriously. "And my mother saw her once, too, only once."

"Did *you* ever see her?" the skeptical boy wanted to know.

The Story-Girl shook her head.

"No, but I shall some day, if I keep on believing," she said confidently.

"*I* wouldn't like to see her—I should be afraid," said the timid girl, with a little shiver.

"There wouldn't be anything to be afraid of," said the Story Girl reassuringly. "It's not as if it were a stranger ghost. It's our own family ghost, so, of course, it wouldn't hurt us."

We often "acted out" the story of Alice and her poet; we discovered the lost diamond in a thousand different ways and places; but we never acted the story of Edith. Ghosts are not chancy folk to meddle with—even when they are your own family ghosts.

We had our own games and sports, mostly original, for the Story-Girl could invent them more easily than most children could talk. Our playhouse was in the fir grove. We had shelves on the trees covered with a dazzling array of broken dishes and pieces of coloured glass; and we had "cupboards" scooped out among the big roots and lined with moss. We wove wreaths and crowns of pink daisies and every girl was queen for a day, turn about. We had picnics and little festivals galore. But when all was said and done we liked best to hear the Story-Girl tell stories.

We would climb to the top of the western wall, or sit on the grass under the swinging fir boughs, and listen for hours. The Story-Girl was an orphan grandchild who had always lived at grandmother's. She was a slim, light-footed thing, with an oval brown face and large, dark-blue, dreamy eyes. She had a marvellous memory and a knack of dramatic word-painting. Half her stories she "made out of her own head," and we thought them wonderful. Even now I still think they *were* wonderful, and if she had lived I believe the world would have heard of her. She died in her early teens in a foreign land, far away from her beloved garden. It was she kept the "garden book." I found it in a box in the attic the last time I was at the old homestead, and brought it away with me. Many of its entries made the past seem the present again:

April twentieth.

It is spring, and I am so glad. The beauty of winter is that it makes you appreciate spring. Little green things are poking up everywhere in the garden. I always run out first thing every morning to see how much they have grown since yesterday. I helped grandmother plant the sweet peas to-day and I planted a little bed of my own. I am not going to dig them up this year to see if they have sprouted. It is bad for them. I am going to try to cultivate patience.

I read a new fairy book in the fir grove to-day. A fir grove is the right kind of a place to read fairy stories. Sally says she can't see that it makes any difference where you read them, but, oh, it does.

May tenth.

Warm, with south wind. Grandmother and Jean finished

planting the vegetable garden to-day. I never like the vegetable garden except when I am hungry. Then I do like to go and look at the nice little rows of onions and beets.

May twenty-eighth.

I was busy weeding all day. Sally and Jack came over and helped me. I don't mind weeding but I always feel so sorry for the poor weeds. It must be hard to be rooted up; but then you should not grow in the wrong place. I suppose if weeds ever get to heaven they will be flowers. I hope heaven will be all flowers. I think I could be always good if I lived in a garden all the time. But then Adam and Eve lived in a garden and they were not always good—far from it.

June eighth.

It rained this morning. The garden is always so sweet after a rain. Everything is so fresh and clean and the perfumes are lovelier than ever. I wish one could see perfumes as well as smell them. I am sure they would be beautiful. Billy says it is just like a girl to wish something silly. Billy is very practical—he would never think of being sorry for the weeds. Grandfather says he is very level-headed. It is best to be level-headed, of course, but you miss lots of fun.

Our Canterbury-Bells are out. I think "Canterbury-Bells" is a lovely name. It makes you think of cathedrals. Sweet William is a dreadful name for a flower. William is a man's name, and men are never sweet. They are a great many admirable things, but they are not sweet and shouldn't be. That is for women.

June seventeenth.

The garden does not look the same by moonlight at all. It is very beautiful but it is different. When I was a little wee girl I used to believe that fairies danced in the garden by moonlight. I would like to believe it still, but it is so hard to believe things you know are not true. Uncle James told me there were no such things as fairies. He is a minister, so, of course, I knew he spoke the truth. It was his duty to tell me and I do not blame him, but I have never felt quite the same to Uncle James since.

We acted Alice and the poet to-day. I like it mostly, but not to-day, for Billy was the poet and he didn't look a bit poetical—his face was so round and freckled. I just wanted to laugh and that spoiled it all for me. I always like it better when Jack is the poet; he looks the part and he never screws his eyes up as tight as Billy does. But you can seldom coax Jack to be the poet, and Billy is so obliging that way.

July twentieth.

We all helped grandmother make her rose jar to-day. We picked quarts of rose leaves. The most fragrant ones grow on grandmother's wedding bush. When grandmother was married she had a bouquet of white roses and she stuck one of the green shoots from it down in the garden, never thinking it would really grow, but it did, and it is the biggest bush in the garden now. It does seem so funny to think that there ever was a time when grandfather and grandmother were not married. You would think to look at them that they always had been. What a dreadful thing it would have been if they had not got married to each other! I don't suppose there would have been a single one of us children here at all; or if we were we would be part somebody else, and that would be almost as bad. When I think how awful it would have been to have been born part somebody else, or not born at all, I cannot feel sufficiently thankful that grandfather and grandmother happened to marry each other, when there were so many other people in the world they might have married.

I am trying to love the zinnias best, because nobody seems to like them at all, and I am sure they must feel it; but all the time deep down in my heart I know I love the roses best. You just can't help loving the roses.

August nineteenth.

Grandmother let us have our tea in the garden this afternoon, and it was lovely. We spread the tablecloth on the grass by the well-house, and it was just like a picnic. Everything tasted twice as good, and we did not mind the ants at all.

I am going to call the southernwood "apple-ringie" after this. Jean says that is what they call it in Scotland, and I think it sounds ever so much more poetical than southernwood. Jack says the right name is "boy's love," but I think that is silly.

September fifth.

Billy says that a rich man in town has a floral clock in his garden. It looks just like the face of a clock, and there are flowers in it that open every hour, and you can always tell the time. Billy wishes we had one here but I don't. What would be the good of it? Nobody ever wants to know the time in a garden.

It was my turn to be queen, and I wore the daisy crown all day. I like to be queen, but there is really not as much fun in it as in being a common person, after all. Besides, the rest all call you "Your Majesty," and curtsy whenever they come into your presence, if they don't forget, and it makes you feel a little lonely.

September twenty-seventh.

Shadows are such pretty things and the garden is always full of them. Sometimes they are so still you would think them asleep. Then again they are laughing and skipping. Outside, down on the shore fields, they are always chasing each other. They are wild shadows; the shadows in the garden are tame shadows.

October twentieth.

Everything seems to be rather tired of growing. The pine tree and the firs and the 'mums. The sunshine is thick and yellow and lazy, and the crickets sing all the time. The birds have nearly all gone.

The other day I thought I saw the ghost at last. I was coming though the fir grove and I saw somebody in blue sitting on the bench. How my heart beat! But it was only a visitor, after all. I don't know whether I was glad or disappointed. I don't think it would be a pleasant experience to see the ghost; but after you had seen it, think what a heroine you would be.

November tenth.

There was a little snow last night but it all melted as soon as the sun came out. Everything in the garden has gone to sleep and it is lonely and sad there now. I don't think I shall write any more in my garden book till spring.

Early morning was an exquisite time in the garden. Delicate dews glistened everywhere, and the shadows were black and long and clear-cut. Pale, peach-tinted mists hung over the bay, and little winds crisped across the fields and rustled in the poplar leaves in the wild corner. But the evening was more beautiful still, when the sunset sky was all aglow with delicate shadings and a young moon swung above the sea in the west. The robins whistled in the firs, and over the fields sometimes came lingering music from the boats in the bay. We used to sit on the old stone wall and watch the light fading out on the water and the stars coming out over the sea. And at last grandmother would come down the honeysuckle path and tell us it was time that birds and buds and babies should be in bed. Then we would troop off to our nests in the house, and the fragrant gloom of a summer night would settle down over the Garden of Old Delights.

(1910)

A Pioneer Wooing

In chapter 7 of *The Story Girl*, Sara Stanley and her cousins pay a visit to local curmudgeon Mr. Campbell in the hopes of persuading him to make a donation to their school library fund. When he asks Sara to tell him a story and offers to pay her "in proportion to the entertainment you afford me," Sara meets his challenge by proposing to "tell [him] the story of the Sherman girls, and how Betty Sherman won a husband"—even though, as the narrator adds, "Betty Sherman was Mr. Campbell's own great-grandmother [and] her method of winning a husband was not exactly in accordance with maidenly traditions." This story, based on a family legend involving Montgomery's great-grandparents Donald Montgomery and Betsy Penman, first appeared in fictional form in *The Farm and Fireside*, a weekly periodical published out of Springfield, Ohio, in 1903 (mere days before the publication of "The Old Chest of Wyther Grange") and was reprinted with minor changes in *The Canadian Courier* of Toronto in May 1911, coinciding with the publication of *The Story Girl*.

D ONALD FRASER, SITTING BY THE LOW, FOUR-PANED window of his new house, was playing old Scotch airs on his fiddle to beguile dull time away on a cold winter afternoon more than a hundred years ago. The place was a remote settlement in a nascent Canadian province, where the settlers were engaged in the arduous task of carving out homes for themselves in the wilderness.

Donald's new house had only four rooms, but it was considered quite a pretentious edifice in those primitive days. Before it, the cleared fields of his farm sloped down to the ice-bound bay; behind it, great woods stretched inland, intersected here and there by trails and wood roads. In winter the ice was the great highway of traffic, and people from far and wide passed Donald's door, often calling to warm themselves before his fire and exchange news of the various scattered settlements.

The day was bitter cold and a storm threatened. Few travellers were abroad and Donald had no callers. He felt lonely and got his fiddle down for company. It was too early yet to go across the bay to Shermans'. Donald smiled to himself as he played *Annie Laurie*, and thought of Nancy Sherman, more beautiful than the heroine of the old ballad.

"'Her face it is the fairest that e'er the sun shone on,'" hummed the young Scotch Canadian softly.

The Frasers were one of the best families in the little colony, which was as yet so thinly populated that everybody in it knew everybody else. Alexander Fraser, Donald's father, had been one of the earliest immigrants from Scotland. He was a man liked and respected by all, and had taken a prominent part in shaping the affairs of the colony. From him, Donald, his first born, inherited his broad shoulders, sandy hair, deep-set gray eyes, and resolute jaw. But it was from his Irish mother that Donald got the qualities which made him a favourite with all who knew him. The merry curve of his mobile mouth, the twinkle in his gray eyes, the gay smile, the flashing wit, the irrepressible good comradeship that distinguished him from the more reserved, pure-bred Scotch folk, even the faint suggestion of "brogue" in his ringing tones, all contributed to form a personality which was destined to stamp its influence on those rude early days. Many a blue-eyed Scotch and English lassie would have been glad and willing to listen had Donald Fraser come a-wooing, and many a girlish heart a hundred years ago beat quicker at his step and voice. But Donald cared only for one whom many others wooed likewise. He was not openly favoured above his rivals. He did not know whether Nancy Sherman cared for him or not, but he knew that if she would not come to be the mistress of his new house none other ever should. So he dreamed of her as he drew his bow over the strings and filled the low room with the sweetness of old Lowland ballads, the fine frenzy of Highland reels and strathspeys, and the rollicking abandon of Irish jigs.

When he played the last the Irish fun in his nature overwhelmed him, drowning out the Scottish romance, and he wished that somebody would drop in and crack a joke with him.

When he left the north window, which he liked best because it looked over the bay to Shermans', and went to the south one, looking out over a dreary expanse of stumps and half-cleared land, he saw a sleigh emerge from the woods. He knew the driver at a glance and, rushing to the door, threw it open with hearty hospitality. Anyone would have been welcome, but this visitor was Neil Campbell, who was Donald's especial crony. Friends they had always been, and friends they were yet . . . and they were also rivals. People had expected to see their friendship blotted out by their rivalry, but it had stood the test. Each loved Nancy Sherman and each knew that the other knew it; each was determined to win her, and neither would have hesitated over any ruse that would give him the advantage. But no ill-feeling found place between them, and when Neil came from Berwick he always called to see Donald before he crossed the bay; and sometimes, so free from bitterness was their rivalry, he even took Donald over.

He got out of the door and shook Donald's proffered hand heartily. Then he tied his restive young mare to a post, threw the buffalo robe over her, and followed Donald into the kitchen. Neither in appearance nor temperament was there the slightest resemblance between the two men. In point of looks Neil Campbell could not compare for an instant with Donald Fraser. He was smaller and slighter, with a dark, melancholy face and intensely blue eyes . . . the vivid blue of the St. Lawrence water on a windy autumn day when the sun breaks out after a storm. In parentage he was pure Highland, with all the Highlander's mystic, poetic temperament. He was not so widely popular as the gay and dashing Donald, and he was not a favourite with women; but his few friends loved him rarely, and it was said by some that if a woman once loved him she would do and dare all things to win him.

Neil threw himself down before the roaring fire with a sigh of satisfaction. It was ten miles from Berwick to the bay shore, and though a lover thought little of that when his lass waited for him at the end, a blazing back log and a "taste" of good Scotch whisky were not to be despised at the halfway station.

"It's cold the day," he said briefly.

"You'll be going over the bay, I'm thinking," said Donald, good humouredly.

A slight tinge of color showed itself on Campbell's dark face. While he bore Donald no grudge for their rivalry, he could not refer to it in the unreserved way of his friend. To him, Donald's offhand way of looking at the situation savored of greater confidence than he himself possessed, and this stung him. He only nodded in reply to Donald's remark.

The latter had meanwhile been rummaging in his untidy bachelor cupboard, and now he emerged with a bottle of whisky and a couple of tumblers. This was a matter of course a hundred years ago. A woman might offer her women friends a cup of hot tea, but a man treated his callers to a "taste" of the best whisky obtainable. If he failed to do so he was looked upon as seriously lacking in what were then considered the most rudimentary rites of hospitality.

"You look cold," said Donald. "Sit nearer to the fire, man, and let this put a bit of warmth in your veins. You'll need it before you get over the bay. It's bitter cold on the ice to-day. Now for the Berwick news! Has Jean McLean made up with her man yet? And is it true that Sandy Macdonald is to marry Kate Ferguson? 'Twill be a match, now. Sure, and with her red hair Sandy will not be like to lose his bride past finding."

Berwick was Donald's boyhood home, and Neil had plenty of news for him concerning friends and kin. At first he talked little and cautiously, as was his wont, while Donald bantered and joked, but presently the whisky, which neither spared, began to tell upon the different temperaments. Donald's volatile spirits evaporated, and the Scotch element of his nature came uppermost. He grew cautious and watchful, talked less, but made shrewder remarks. The Highlander, on the contrary, lost his reserve, and became more and more confidential. At last, after being shrewdly manipulated by Donald, Neil Campbell confessed that he meant to put his fate to the test that very night. He was going over the bay to ask Nancy Sherman to marry him. If she consented, then Donald and the rest should see such a wedding as the colony had never yet seen!

Donald rose abruptly and went to the window, leaving Neil to sip his grog and gaze into the fire with the air of a man very well satisfied with himself. As for Donald, he was for the moment non-plussed. This was worse than he had expected. He had never dreamed that Neil would dare to bring matters to a crisis yet. But there was no time to be lost if he meant to get ahead of his rival. In his heart Donald believed that Nancy cared for him. What else could those modestly bestowed favors and shy looks, such as she gave to no other, mean? Yet he might be mistaken. She might like Neil the better after all; and, whether or no, the first man there stood the better chance. Donald knew all too well that Nancy's father favoured Neil Campbell, as being by far the richer man in worldly goods. If Neil asked Nancy to marry him when he, Donald, had not yet spoken, Elias Sherman would have the most to say in the matter, and Nancy would never dream of disputing her father's command. Donald looked far out over the bay, and realized that his chance of winning Nancy depended on his crossing that white expanse before Neil did. How could it be managed? A twinkle came into Donald's eye. All was fair in love and war. He went back to the table.

"Have some more, man, have some more," he said, persuasively. "'Twill keep the life in you in the teeth of that wind. Help yourself. There's plenty more where that came from."

"Is it going over the bay the night that yourself will be doing?" asked Neil as he obeyed.

Donald shook his head.

"I had thought of it," he owned, "but it looks a wee like a storm and my sleigh is at the blacksmith's to be shod. If I went it must be on Black Dan's back, and he'd like a canter over the ice in a snowstorm as little as I. His own fireside is the safest place for a man to-night, Campbell."

Neil nodded drowsily. His potations, after his long cold drive, were beginning to have their effect. Donald, with laughter in his deep-set eyes, watched his friend and persuaded him again and again to have yet another "tasting." When Neil's head at last fell heavily on his arm Donald arose with the smile of a man who has won in a doubtful game. Neil Campbell was sound asleep and would remain so for some hours. The question was, how long. It might be for hours, and it might be for only a few minutes; but half an hour's start would be enough. For the rest, it would depend on Nancy. But there was no time to lose.

Donald flung on his stout homespun overcoat, pulled his fur cap warmly over his ears, and wrapped a knitted muffler of handspun yarn round his neck. Then he caught his mitts and riding whip from the nail over the fireplace, and strode to the door with a parting glance at the reclining figure of his unconscious friend.

"May your sleep be long and sweet, man," he laughed softly. "As for the waking 'twill be betwixt you and me."

With an amused smile he untied Neil's horse, climbed into Neil's sleigh, and tucked Neil's buffalo robe comfortably around him.

"When he wakes Black Dan will carry him as well as he would have carried me," thought the schemer, "but if the snow comes after sunset it's little we'll see of either over the bay to-night. Now, Bess, old girl, do your bonniest. There's more than you know hangs on your speed. If the Campbell wakes too soon Black Dan could show you a pair of clean heels for all your good start. On, my girl."

Brown Bess, one of the best mares in the county, sprang forward over the ice like a deer. The sun was nearing its setting. The gleaming white expanse of the bay, gemmed here and there with wooded, purple islets, and rimmed in by dark, violet coats, glittered like the breast of a fair woman decked with jewels. Above, the curdled gray rolls of cloud flushed faintly pink, but the north and east were gray with the presage of night and storm.

Donald thought of none of these things, nor of the rare spiritual beauty of the wastes about him. As he urged Brown Bess forward, with now and then a glance behind to see if Black Dan were yet following, he thought only of what he should say to Nancy Sherman, and of what her answer would be.

The Shermans were a family of United Empire Loyalists who had come to Canada at the close of the American War of Independence. They never spoke of their former fortunes, but it was the general opinion that they had once been wealthy. However that might be, they were poor enough now, and life was even a harder struggle for them than it was for the Scotch immigrants who had already obtained a footing on the Canadian soil.

Elias Sherman was a genial, friendly soul, and his wife was a pale, proud woman who had been beautiful once, and was dignified and gracious yet. When they came to the little maritime colony they brought two children with them. These two children, Nancy and Betty, grew up amid many hardships and privations; but as they blossomed out into young womanhood they were widely famed for their beauty, and lovers from the best and wealthiest of the colonial families came a-wooing to the little cottage on the bay shore, and thought themselves richly repaid if they won a smile or a kind glance from "the beautiful Sherman girls." Beautiful and stately they were, indeed, with a grace and charm of manner which triumphed over mean attire and surroundings. A hundred years ago, Nancy and Betty Sherman, now sleeping forgotten in mossy, grass-grown graves on a hill that slopes down to the moaning St. Lawrence gulf, had the pick of five counties to their hands. Not one of the blue-eyed, fresh-faced Scotch and English lassies, the Jeans and Kates and Margarets, could for a moment compare with them. They were envied bitterly enough, no doubt, and caused many a long forgotten heartache. Yet the fault was not theirs—they made no effort to win or retain the homage offered them. The boldest lover could not boast of favors received. A kind word or gracious smile was all they ever won, and was esteemed enough. Even Donald Fraser could but own to himself that Nancy was as likely to say "No" as "Yes." She had said it calmly and sweetly to better men. Well, he would face the question bravely, and if he were refused—"Neil will have the laugh on me, then. Sure, and he's sleeping well. And the snow is coming soon. There'll be a bonny swirl on the bay ere long. I hope no harm will come to the lad if he starts to cross. When he wakes he'll be in such a fine Highland temper that he'll never stop to think of danger. Well, Bess, my girl, here we are at last. Now, Donald Fraser, pluck up heart and play the man. Remember you're a Scotchman, with a dash of old Ireland to boot, and never flinch because a slip of a lass looks scornful at you out of the bonniest dark blue eyes on earth."

In spite of his bold words, however, Donald's heart was thumping furiously when he drove into the farmyard. Nancy was there, milking a cow by the stable door, but she stood up when she saw him coming, grasping her pail with one hand, and holding the other out to him in the gracious, untroubled way for which she was noted. Haloed by the sunset light that was flinging its rosy splendors over all the wide white wastes around them, the girl was so beautiful that Donald's courage failed him almost completely. Was it not the wildest presumption to hope that this exquisite creature could fare for him or would come to be the mistress of his little house—she, who was fit for a king's halls. In all the humility of a true lover he stood before her, and Nancy, looking into his bonny face, understood with woman's instinct, why he had come. A color and light that was not of the sunset crept into her face and eyes. She did not withdraw her hand from his grasp, but she turned her face aside and bent her head.

Donald knew that he must make the most of this unexpected chance. He might not see Nancy alone again before Neil came. Clasping both of his hands over the slender one he held he said, breathlessly, "Nan, less, I love you. You may think 'tis a hasty wooing, but that's a story I can tell you later, maybe. I know well I'm not worthy of you, but if true love could make a man worthy there'd be none before me. Will you have me, Nan?"

Nancy's head in its crimson shawl drooped lower still. For a moment Donald endured an agony of suspense. Then he heard her answer—oh, such a low, sweet answer!—and he knew that she was won.

The snow was beginning to fall as they walked together to the house. Donald looked over the bay, misty white in the gathering gloom, and laughed light heartedly.

"I must tell you that story, lass," he said, catching Nancy's look of wonder, "and you'll see what a trick I played on my best friend to win you."

And tell it he did, with such inimitable drollery and such emphasized brogue that Nancy could not but laugh as heartily as he did. She was not proof against the humour of the situation even amid the sweeter romance of it.

"Black Dan goes well, but he'll not be quick enough," he said, as he helped Nancy in. Half an hour later Neil Campbell, with a blackly bent brow and a fire in his blue eyes that was woe to see, dismounted from his smoking horse at the Shermans' door, and strode into the kitchen. Had Donald Fraser been there the comedy might shortly have been turned into tragedy, for there was blood fury in Campbell's heart and eyes. But the wily rival was far away, and the kitchen was empty. Neil stood and chafed at the door until Mrs. Sherman came down the rude stairs from the loft above. At sight of Campbell she started in surprise, for though many a wooer came to her house they did not usually come so early in the day; but she went forward to meet him in a gracious manner.

"Good morning, Mr. Campbell. 'Tis a fair day after the storm, but a cold. Come nearer the fire."

Neil felt his blind fury ebbing away before this woman of the queenlike presence and pale, sorrowful face, so little in keeping with the rude, low room. Mrs. Sherman always imposed a sense of deference upon the person to whom she spoke. Neil could not bring himself to demand of her where Donald Fraser or Nancy was. Yet he must say something.

"Where is Betty this morning?" he said, trying to speak calmly, though his voice shook.

On being told that she had gone to the well for a pail of water he went out, vowing that he would discover from her the whereabouts of his false friend.

Betty Sherman saw him coming across the snow, and stood up erectly beside the well with a smile on her face. Her lips parted and her breath fluttered over them quickly. She put up her slender brown hands and nervously caught the crimson fringes of her knitted shawl together under her chin, while into her eyes leaped a strange light of fear and passion, and some undefined emotion that strove to conquer the other two.

As far as feature and bearing went Nancy and Betty Sherman looked marvellously alike. Yet so different were they in coloring and more than all in expression that they were scarcely held to resemble each other. The hair that lay in skeins of silken fairness on Nancy's white forehead rippled off from Betty's in locks as richly brown as October nuts. The misty purple of Nan's eyes was so dark and deep in Betty's as to be almost black; and while Nancy was oftener pale than not a dusky red always glowed in Betty's cheeks and deepened to scarlet in the curves of a very sweet, very scornful mouth. As for their expression, Nancy's was always gracious and charming, while Betty's was mocking and maddening.

Though Betty had many lovers they were afraid of her. Her tongue was a sharp and unsparing one, and she satirized them to their faces. Woe betide the rash youth with a squint or a stutter who came courting Betty Sherman! And even those who had no defect of person or manner fared little better. Yet come they did, for there was that about the girl that held a man, though she treated him as the dust under her feet.

When Neil Campbell had first come to the cottage on the bay shore it had been Betty whom he came to see. In those days he had thought Nan by far the less bonny. But Betty, always cruel to her suitors, was doubly so to Neil. She mimicked his Highland accent, mocked at his Highland ways, and laughed at his shyness as "Highland pride." Neil, believing his suit hopeless, left the scornful maid to her own devices, and was gradually drawn into the train of Nancy's lovers, soon to become the most devoted of them. Thenceforth Betty had treated him with unvarying indifference, although generally she made as much fun of Nancy's lovers as of her own. Neil now felt that his humiliation would be doubly bitter from Betty's probable railing, but in his passionate anger—an anger that quite overmastered the sting of baffled love—he did not care what she might say.

"Good morning, Mr. Campbell," said Betty's silver clear voice as he came up to her. "It is early abroad you are. And on Black Dan, no less! Was I mistaken in thinking that Donald Fraser said that his favourite horse should never be backed by any man but him? But doubtless a fair exchange is no robbery, and Brown Bess goes well and fleetly."

"Where is Donald Fraser?" said Neil thickly. "It is him I am seeking, and it is him I will be finding. Where is he, Betty Sherman?"

"Donald Fraser is far enough away by this," said Betty lightly. "He is a prudent fellow, that Donald, and has some quickness of wit under that sandy thatch of his. He came here last night at sunset, with a horse and sleigh not his own, or lately gotten, and he asked Nan in the stable yard to marry him. Did a man ask me to marry him while I was at the cow's side, with my milking pail in my hands, 'tis a cold answer he'd get for his pains. But Nan was ever o'erfond of Donald, and 'tis kindly she must have answered him, for they sat late together last night, and 'twas a bonny story that Nan wakened me to hear when she came to bed—the story of a braw lover, who let his secret out when the whiskey was abune the wit, and then fell asleep while his rival was away to woo and win his lass. Did you ever hear a like story, Mr. Campbell?"

Neil clenched his fists.

"Oh, yes," he said, fiercely, "it is laughing at me over the country side that Donald Fraser will be doing, and telling that story! But when I meet him it is not laughing he will be doing! Oh, no! There will be another story to tell!"

"What will you do to him?" cried Betty in alarm. "Don't meddle with the man. Now, what a state to be in because a slip of a good looking lass prefers sandy hair and gray eyes to Highland black and blue. You have not the spirit of a wren, Neil Campbell! Were I you I would show Donald Fraser that I could woo and win a maid as speedily as any Lowlander of them all, that would I! There's many a girl would say 'yes' gladly for your asking. I know one myself, as bonny as Nan, if folks say true, who would think herself a proud and happy woman if you looked kindly on her, and would love you as well as Nan loves her Donald—aye, and ten times better."

Betty's face went crimson, and her eyes faltered down to the pail at her feet.

"And who may it be, Betty?" asked Neil after a brief silence.

Betty did not answer in words. She came a step nearer, and put one hand on Neil's shoulder, with her head still drooping, but her eyes looking up at him, and an expression, half defiant, half yielding, wholly captivating, that answered as plainly as words.

Neil took the cold hands in his.

"If this be so, lass," he said gently, "why did you mock at me so when I came first?"

"What simpletons men are!" pouted Betty. "Why, 'twas because I liked you best, to be sure!"

Then she suddenly sprang away from him with flushing cheeks and clouded eyes.

"Oh, what must you think of me?" she cried. "Bold—unmaidenly—that is what you will call me, and truly. But when I saw you coming—and I had loved you so long! 'What,' thought I 'to lose all for want of one little bold word!' 'Twas hard to speak, but I have spoken it; and now you will despise me."

She clasped her hands and stood meekly before him, with her face hanging on her breast. Neil came nearer and drew her into his arms.

"Thank you for that word," he said simply. "Betty, it was you I liked best at first, and if you will marry me it is a good husband I will try to make you, and a proud and happy man I'll be."

Betty looked up at him with eyes in which tenderness and mischief were mingled.

"Then maybe Donald Fraser will not do as much laughing after all," she said. "Look you, Neil. Leave me to manage this. When Nan comes back I'll say to her, 'Nan, is Donald so very sure that Neil Campbell said your name when he told his errand? 'Tis a mistake your Lowlander has made, sister.' And then I'll tell her how you came this morning and asked me to marry you. Though 'twas I that did the asking, was it not? But I'll not tell her that."

(1903/1911)

A Chip of the Old Block

In chapter 16 of *Rainbow Valley* (1919), minister's daughter Faith Meredith decides to ask neighbourhood tyrant Norman Douglas to return to church, mainly to offset a loss in her father's salary. Already in a bad mood because of a recent argument with his housekeeper, Norman initially drives Faith to tears with his questions, prompting her to leave. But when her distress turns to anger, she marches back and tells him off, with the unexpected result that he promises to resume contributing to the minister's salary if she forgives him. Faith's often unintentionally humorous speech ("Your wife never had a new hat for ten years—no wonder she died") originates in this next story, focalized through the perspective of a surprisingly self-aware bully who terrorizes his wife and children. This story, whose title is now more commonly expressed as "a chip off the old block" (referring to a person who resembles a parent), appeared initially in the *Springfield Republican* of Massachusetts in January 1907. The version included here is the one that appeared in *The Canadian Courier* of Toronto in early 1913 and that anchors the narrative in the world of Avonlea, presumably the same revised version that Montgomery had prepared for possible inclusion in her collection of linked stories *Chronicles of Avonlea*.

W HEN DAVID CARTER CAME HOME FROM PLOUGHING in the shore field one still, spring evening, he understood that something had happened to disturb his women folks. His meek, timid wife had been crying, although she tried to hide it; his meek, timid daughter, Mary, the youngest of his family and the only one left at home, looked even more cowed and lifeless than usual. Her meekness and paleness and general negativeness of personality angered her father, as always happened. Why couldn't she be like other men's daughters—like his own sisters had been—girls of spirit and fire and laughter? But no, like all his children, she must take after her mother in character and appearance. They had all been meek and apologetic and afraid of him; and he had bullied them as unmercifully as he had bullied his wife.

"What's the matter with you two?" he demanded, in his great, resounding voice, after the silent supper had been eaten. "You look as if you wanted to say something and was scared to say it. You haven't got as much spirit as a flea, neither of you. Mary, what's up?"

But Mary only cast an appealing look at her mother—a look that angered her father still more. He knew that she was afraid of him with good reason, but he despised her for it.

"Reckon you'll have to speak up, ma, since the cat's got Mary's tongue," he said, sneeringly. "I wouldn't have supposed that all my children would be cowards, boys and girls alike. It's your bad breed coming out in them, that's what it is. Your folks were always sneaking and white-livered. What's troubling you, woman, I say? Confound it, speak up, can't you?"

"Oh!" Mrs. Carter's pinched and faded face grew white. She was afraid of her husband, and always had been afraid of him in all the forty years since she had married him because her father ordered her to. "Oh, Pa, Robert Glover is dead—he died this afternoon."

The poor little woman paused in sheer terror. Robert Glover was a forbidden name in that household. She had not ventured to utter it in her husband's hearing for fifteen years.

"Is he? Well, it's a good thing!" David Carter lifted his cup and drained it at a gulp. A shocked look passed over his wife's face, but she dared make no protest. "A good thing!" repeated David, striking the table with his huge, brown fist. "There's one less fool and cumberer of the ground on earth. And what business have you to be whining because he's dead—what business, I say? Don't you let me see any more of it in either of you. If he's dead it's a good riddance. Now, remember, no more sniffling."

David Carter got up from the table and strode from the room.

Jim Boulter, the hired boy, who had heard all that had passed, also went out and hied him away to the blacksmith's shop to spread the story of David Carter's speech and behaviour when told of his son-in-law's death. It shocked people but did not surprise them; they were too well used to David Carter for that. By next day Agnes Glover, in her widowed home, heard the tale. She wept over it, but showed no anger. She was very like her mother, even more like her than the pale Mary.

When David Carter had married, people said he had been lucky enough to get the only woman on earth who could live with him. She bore with his bullying temper in a placidly-unresisting, colourless fashion that always goaded him into fresh displays of it. Their four children—two sons and two daughters—were all meek, quiet little creatures, who submitted without remonstrance to their father's tyranny. Tyrannize over them he did, railing at them unceasingly, twitting them with their very submission, thwarting and denying every wish of their childish lives.

When Agnes was eighteen Robert Glover began to come to see her. Robert was a rather shiftless fellow, and as soon as David Carter had got his eyes opened to the amazing fact that this spiritless girl, whom he had always despised, was grown-up and actually had a lover, he stormily forbade the young man the house. Agnes he overwhelmed with invectives. She listened to him meekly and wordlessly; but the next week she slipped away from home one night and married Robert.

Her father disowned her, promptly and wholly. He sent all her belongings contemptuously after her, erased her name from the family Bible, and commanded his wife and older children never to mention Robert or Agnes Glover's name in his hearing again. This command was obeyed. For fifteen years Agnes had been as dead to her father as if she had been buried under six feet of turf.

They had been hard years for her. She had a large family, and Robert was a careless and improvident husband. For the last two years he had been ill with consumption and if it had not been for kindly neighbours his family would have been in utter want.

On the day of the funeral Mrs. Carter took her poor courage in both hands and asked her husband if she could go—or at least if Mary might go, for appearance's sake. David Carter furiously demanded what appearances needed to be consulted in the case of a stranger's funeral. He ordered her and Mary to dress in their best and go with him to a political picnic in Carmody. They obeyed, and great was the scandal of that same shrinking, shame-faced obedience in Avonlea.

But Robert Glover was buried and then the neighbours took up the case of his wife and family. A delicate woman—seven young children—nothing for them to live on! What was to be done? The answer was prompt. Her father must help her; he was well able to do it. But who was to beard the lion in his den and tell him so? One and all, the Avonlea people refused. Finally, they took a mean advantage of their new minister, who had not been long enough among them to have learned fully what manner of man David Carter was. They told him that it was his duty and privilege to reconcile father and daughter, so he went obligingly.

Poor Mr. Bentley! To his dying day he never forgot that interview. He met David Carter in the yard. Carter was surlier than usual that day; he did not even ask the minister in. His wife and Mary crouched behind the curtains of the open parlour window to listen; they knew why the minister had come; Jim Boulter also knew and he took care to hoe the onion beds within earshot.

"Good afternoon, Mr. Carter," said Mr. Bentley affably.

"Good afternoon. What have you come for?" said David Carter bluntly.

Mr. Bentley was not accustomed to being asked his reason for calling so unceremoniously. It rattled him.

"Oh—I—ahem—I have called—been asked to call—to—to tell you—about your daughter, Mr. Carter. I"—

"Why, what has Mary been doing?" asked David Carter stolidly.

"Mary? Oh, your younger daughter? I did not refer to her, but to your other daughter, Mrs. Glover."

"I have no other daughter." David Carter planted the pitchfork he was carrying in the ground before him, put his hands on top of it, bowed his chin on them, and looked squarely at the minister with a black scowl. "I have only one daughter, Mary, who lives here with me. If you have anything to say of her, say it and have done."

The minister had got his second wind, and, being a plucky little man, did not quail.

"You have another daughter, Mr. Carter," he said firmly. "You cannot do away with the relationship by any arbitrary decree.

Mrs. Glover is your daughter and she is at present in very poor circumstances. It is your duty to help her, Mr. Carter, since you are amply able to do so. Have you no pity? I sincerely hope—"

"Stop!" David Carter fairly shouted the word. He was purple with rage. "Hold your tongue," he went on furiously. "I won't hear another word from you. Mind your own business. You come here and talk to me about religion and I'll listen to you. But leave my family affairs alone. That woman and her young ones are nothing to me—nothing. They needn't come whining to me for help, for I'll never give it. And you go! If you wasn't a minister I'd teach you to interfere with what doesn't concern you. As it is, get out."

The minister got out. He realized that this was one of the times when discretion is the better part of valour. He went away, pale and horror-stricken, and told the people who had sent him that he could not influence Mr. Carter. He did not give them the particulars of the interview, but Jim Boulter did. By the next day Agnes Glover heard them. Mrs. Peter Sloane, her next door neighbour, dropped in and told her that her father had abused the minister scandalous and hoped she'd starve—the latter assertion being a bit of embroidery on somebody's part. Agnes wept, and said, oh, wasn't it hard? Her own father, to be so bitter! She didn't see how he could!

Her children were all around her, wistful, pale-faced, frightened—all except Christina, the second girl. Christina sat back in a corner, with her hands gripping the chair rungs on either side. She neither talked nor cried, although she could do both when she had a mind to. She did not look like the other children, who were all meek and drab-coloured. Christina had black hair, hanging in a heavy, straight braid, deepset black eyes, and crimson cheeks. Her mouth was close-shut and determined, her chin gave the world assurance of a chin. As she listened to Mrs. Sloane's story, at which her mother whimpered, her eyes grew blacker, her cheeks redder, her lips tighter. Finally she got up and left the room.

Nobody noticed her departure. She put on her little black hat and left the house. It was a mile and a half to David Carter's place, and thither Christina proceeded, silently and determinedly. She had never been there in her life, but she walked unhesitatingly across the yard and into the house, without knocking. There was nobody in the kitchen so Christina marched across it and pushed open the sitting room door.

Mrs. Carter and Mary were working in the garden. David Carter was sitting by the window, reading his newspaper. Christina's eyes flashed dangerously when she saw him. She walked inflexibly across the room, caught the paper from his hand, threw it on the floor, and stamped on it.

David Carter stared at her in blank amazement. He had not the least idea who she was, but he felt that she was an enemy. Antagonism radiated from every curve of her body, every feature of her face; it exhaled from her like a breath.

"Who the devil are you?" he demanded, more in bewilderment than in anger.

Christina drew a long breath. Unquailingly she glared back into the eyes against which so few people could hold their own.

"I am Christina Glover," she said, clenching her brown fists, "and I have come here to tell you to your face just what I think of you. You are a bad-tempered, cruel, unjust old man! I hate you! I despise you! I wouldn't have you for a grandfather! I am not afraid of you. And I am glad you disowned my mother! She is far too good to have such a man as you for her father. You said you were glad my father was dead. My father was a good man, and people loved him but nobody ever loved you. You said you hoped we'd starve. Well, we won't starve! But I'd rather starve than take any help from you! You are a tyrant! You make grandma's life miserable, and you make Aunt Mary's life miserable, and you made Uncle Henry's and Uncle Reuben's lives miserable before they went away. They were all frightened of you, but I am not. I don't care what you say or do. If you strike me I'll strike you back. I'll scratch you. I came here just to tell you my opinion of you and it's this—you are not fit to live!"

David Carter had listened to this tirade in the silence of absolute amazement. When Christina stopped for lack of breath, with a final stamp of her foot, he suddenly burst into loud laughter. With a mighty slap of hand on knee he exclaimed:

"I vow you've got spunk! You're a chip of the old block! There's nothing white-livered about you. You're a Carter. I didn't know Agnes had such a daughter. You're worth doing something for. I like spunk. Sit down—sit down."

"I will not." Christina's eyes flashed more than ever. She thought that she was being made fun of—treated contemptuously. It cut deep. She would have enjoyed an explosion of anger. But this was maddening. "I will not sit down in your house! I am going home. But I am glad I came up here and told you just what I think of you."

"So am I—so am I," chuckled David Carter. "There's a drop of the old Carter blood left yet—it was bound to come out somewhere. I'm glad to see it. Come now, my dear, sit down. No, she won't. I swear she's off. There she goes through the yard with her head up and her eyes snapping. There's gait and vim for you. There's spunk. No whining and snivelling about her! Ho, ho! So she hates me—she despises me—the little baggage! I like her—I like her—she's fine—she's great! I'll have to make up with Agnes, that's plain, or that spitfire of a girl of hers will never own me for a grandfather. Told me I wasn't fit to live! Ho, ho! She's a rare one! Wasn't she mad, though! The real Carter temper's there. I thought it had mighty near died out. Reckon I won't have to get mad so often in future by way of keeping up its reputation. That saucebox will help me. Ho, ho!"

He laughed again, uproariously, just as his wife's pale, alarmed face appeared in the doorway.

"Get tea, ma—and then put on your bonnet and we'll drive down to Agnes'. She's got a young hussy in her brood that I want to get better acquainted with. If they'd sent her in the first place instead of sending the minister they'd have been wiser. She ain't afraid to speak her mind—and she's got a mind to speak, too. You can ask the whole gang here to dinner Sunday if she'll come with 'em. I'll give Agnes all the money she needs—she'll take it fast enough, no fear of her. Christina would fling it back in my face, the young Tartar. But I'll bring her to terms yet. We've got to be good friends. Come, ma, hurry the tea. Since I've got to make it up with Agnes I'm anxious to have it over. You women will be bound to do a lot of crying and snivelling. Chris won't cry, I'll bet my last dollar. She'll flash them black eyes of hers at me and tell me she hates me. Laws, but it'll be fun bringing her round. I haven't felt so good-humoured for years, ma."

(1907/1913)

The Indecision of Margaret

Soon after her arrival at Redmond College in *Anne of the Island*, Anne makes a new friend in Philippa Gordon, an intelligent but frivolous young woman of a wealthy Nova Scotia family, who is, in her own words, "always afflicted with indecision," especially where her matrimonial prospects are concerned. Motivated to study for an undergraduate degree partly to delay having to choose between suitors named Alec and Alonzo, Philippa ends up falling in love with a man who meets none of her criteria for a husband. The character of Philippa and her matrimonial dilemma originated in this short story, first published in the September 1906 issue of New York's *Gunter's Magazine* but appearing again with fairly extensive revisions in the January 1915 issue of Toronto's *Maclean's Magazine*, six months before *Anne of the Island* was published.

"MARGARET," SAID MY AUNT ROBERTA, NOT WASTING words, "you must marry!"

Experience should have told me that it was hopeless to argue with Aunt Roberta. Experience *did* tell me so. But one cannot see the last glimmer of freedom snuffed out without at least a feeble protest.

"Why must I marry, Aunt Roberta? I'm sure I'm very happy as I am."

"You can't be," said Aunt Roberta positively. "No woman of your age can be happy unless she's married. Now, Margaret, I have been very patient with you—very patient. But there is a limit to my patience. If you had no chance to marry I should not say anything to you. I should only pity you in discreet silence. But with three unexceptional young men wanting to marry you, your shilly-shallying is disgraceful. You have flirted with those men shamefully. You know you have."

"It was the only amusement Providence sent me," I interjected feebly.

But Aunt Roberta went on with a rush. "There must be an end to this. One of these men you must marry, Margaret—I don't care which—but one of them it must be. When I meet your poor, dear, dead father in the other world I am not going to have him casting it up to me that I let his daughter become an old maid."

"But I am an old maid now, Aunty," I said flippantly. "I'm twenty-eight, and you know twenty-five is the first corner. And it doesn't hurt. Really it doesn't."

"Margaret, you know I dislike frivolity. I am serious, distinctly serious. You must marry, or else—"

Aunt Roberta paused darkly.

"Or else—what?" I asked, wishing to know the worst.

"Or else I'll wash my hands of you and send you home to your stepmother and her family of seven," concluded Aunt Roberta, triumphantly.

I wilted on the spot, wilted visibly. Aunt Roberta saw it and beamed.

"I thought that would bring you to your senses. Now, just make up your mind which of those three men you want to marry and we'll have the wedding in September."

"But that is just the trouble, Aunty," I said dolefully. "I don't want to marry any of them, so I can't decide between them. I suppose I shall simply have to draw lots."

"I don't like the light way in which you treat such a solemn subject, Margaret," observed Aunt Roberta severely. "The selection of a life partner is a very important matter. I leave your choice unrestricted. They are all well off, so that I shall feel I have done my duty by you and your poor, dear, dead father when I see you established as the wife of any one of them. It's not as if I could do anything for you at my death. You know that I have only a life interest in everything. What will become of you if you don't marry?"

"There is a special Providence for the unprotected," I answered. "I think I will go for a walk in the beech lane."

I felt that the beech lane would do me good. I always carried my troubles and perplexities to the beech lane. It was so green and still that it was an excellent place for thinking things out. And I foresaw that I should have a lot of thinking out to do. Oh, for somebody to help me in it—somebody to advise me! I do so hate to have to make up my mind on any point myself. I am always afflicted with indecision. Just as soon as I decide on one course I feel in my bones that some other would have been the correct one. I was born a see-saw and all Aunt Roberta's steady pressure could never prevent me from teetering. Just now I felt that it would be the greatest relief in the world to have somebody assist me in selecting a husband from the availables. Aunt Roberta wouldn't do it. Aunt Roberta is a living embodiment of the reconciliation between predestination and free-will. She decrees what you must do; but she leaves it to your own choice how you will do it.

Before I went to the lane I stepped up to my room and looked at myself in the glass. I always go and look at myself in the glass after I have looked at Aunt Roberta for a while. I want to reassure myself that I don't resemble her. I really don't, but I am always afraid that my nose will develop Byrne tendencies as I grow older, and I examine it anxiously every day to see that it hasn't. Aunt Roberta has the Byrne nose in the Byrnest degree. I am so thankful I escaped it.

My nose looked passable so far and so did everything else about me. My hair was smooth as brown satin and my eyes were grey; they are green sometimes when my dress doesn't suit them, or when I am in a vixenish mood. But it took me half an hour to decide what hat to wear for, even though I was comfortably sure I should not meet anyone in the beech lane, I wanted to feel for my own personal satisfaction that the hat was harmonious. At first I inclined to the pale nile-green one with the daisy wreath; but I had no sooner put it on than I thought the pink one with the floppy brim would be much more becoming. When I got *it* pinned in place I liked the nile-green one better. At last I put them close together on the bed, shut my eyes, and jabbed with a hat pin. The pin speared the pink one, so I put it on.

The beech lane was lovely, all sunshine and green shadow and purring wind. I would have enjoyed it all so much if I hadn't had to decide which of those three detestable men I must marry. They *were* detestable. I had liked them all very well before, but now I hated them. I couldn't decide. No sooner did I think favorably of one of them than the others seemed less detestable. It was just as it had been about the hats, only worse, because there were three of them. How I wished I could settle it the same way by standing them up together and jabbing with a hat pin!

But the worst of it all was I knew perfectly well that, whichever I married, I should regret all my life that I hadn't married one of the others.

At last I stopped midway in the lane and leaned my elbows on the fence with a despairing groan.

"Oh, I can't decide," I exclaimed miserably. "I do wish I had somebody to help me!"

"How will I do?" said a voice.

I didn't jump. Aunt Roberta says I never do anything that might be expected of me. I looked calmly around and I saw a man, a young man—an ugly young man—sitting on the fence between two big grey beeches and smiling at me as if he had known me from my cradle.

I really thought that he was the ugliest young man I had ever seen. He had a big, loose-jointed figure with absurdly long legs. His hair was brick red and all tously under a tweed cap. His eyes were green and his mouth was crooked. As for his ears—but I never think about his ears if I can help it.

He was so ugly that I felt he could be trusted to the last degree. Providence would never have made anybody like that without giving him a most beautiful soul and disposition to atone for it. Perhaps Providence had sent him to my assistance. I was so glad I had on my pink hat because the nile-green one always does make me look a little pale.

"I think you would do very well if I knew who you are," I said.

"Oh, it's all in the family. I'm Peter Campbell."

"Cousin Peter," I cried.

"Only a third cousin," he protested.

"And you're a minister, too!" I exclaimed incredulously.

"All the better to help you. That's what ministers are for. Now, what is the trouble?"

"I'm in dreadful perplexity and I can't make up my mind," I sighed. "I was born that way, so there is no use blaming me for it as Aunt Roberta does."

"I'm the very person you're looking for," averred Peter. "I'm the best hand at making up minds I ever met. What is your difficulty?"

"Well," I began, "there are three men."

"Only *three?*" he remarked in a skeptical tone.

"It is three too many," I said decidedly. "I wish there was none at all. These three men want to marry me."

"Naturally."

"And Aunt Roberta says I have to marry one of them."

"Which one?"

"That's the difficulty," I cried. "Aunt Roberta won't say which and I can't. *You* must aid me to decide. You must tell me which of those men I am to marry."

"Let me see," he said meditatively, putting the tips of his big, long, knotty fingers together. "I must understand this matter thoroughly. You say your Aunt Roberta says you must marry one of them. Now, *why* must you?"

"Because Aunt Roberta thinks it is an indelible disgrace to be an old maid. She is determined that I shan't be any old-maider than I am already. And she says she'll send me home if I won't marry. I *can't* be sent home. There's a stepmother and seven children. And I couldn't get along without Aunt Roberta's flesh pots now that she has accustomed me to them. I've lived with her for five years, ever since father died. I'm the most useless person in the world. So I have to obey her. Oh, that's all settled. The question is—which?"

"You must tell me something about The Three," commanded Cousin Peter. "I must know what I'm doing."

"Well, there's Alec Walker," I said. "He's very nice and very handsome. He's a doctor, and he's good-tempered, and he has the loveliest curly black hair. I do so admire curly black hair."

The young minister took off his cap, ran his fingers through his rampant red hair, and crushed the cap down on it again.

"Is there any particular objection to Alec?" he asked.

"No. But that's just the trouble. He's so perfect. Fancy how horrible it would be to have a perfect husband—somebody you could never find fault with!"

"Well, that's one. Go on with the others."

"Dave Boyd is a hustling business man. He's fairly good-looking, dresses well, and has a classic nose. I adore classic noses.

"I mean," I added hastily, "that it would be a comfort to have a nose in the family that could be depended on. I can't depend on mine. It may turn Byrney any day."

"What is Dave's capital fault?" asked Peter.

"I'm afraid he's a little mean. I *know* he has picked up bargains in chocolates at bankrupt sales. But he's as good as gold and a member of the church."

"Remains but one. What about him?"

"His name is Alonzo Grant. He is rich enough to live without working so he would have plenty of time to help me make up my mind about everything. And he has the most adorable dark blue eyes."

Peter actually winked one of his green ones at me.

"Why not marry Alonzo?"

"Think of marrying a man named Alonzo," I said dolefully. "Besides, I have an instinct that warns me that he is one of those men who would open their wives' letters. Now, you know all about them. Which one shall I marry?"

Peter shook his head.

"I don't know enough about them. Look here. Ask your aunt for three weeks in which to reflect. Meanwhile I shall cultivate their acquaintance, size up their dispositions, and get a good working idea which one will suit you best. I'm up here on my vacation and I'm staying over at Bob Reid's."

"That will be the very thing," I exclaimed. Then I sighed. "You must think me horribly frivolous," I said.

Somehow I didn't want him to think me frivolous. That was ridiculous, of course. Why should I care what a redheaded person, whom I had never seen before, was likely to think of me? But then he was my third cousin. One likes one's relations to think decently of one.

"I shall tell you in three weeks' time what I think of you," he said.

He got down off the fence and we walked home together. I took him in to see Aunt Roberta. Aunt Roberta was decidedly cool to him. He is my cousin on my mother's side and Aunt

Roberta never liked the Campbells. But Peter didn't seem to mind her chilliness.

"A very plain young man," observed Aunt Roberta, when he had gone. "Really, Margaret, it is fortunate you didn't take after your mother's people."

"But I did—in the matter of noses," I returned wickedly, patting mine. "And I don't think Peter is so very ugly at all."

I did. But I wasn't going to admit it.

"It is not very good taste to call a young man by his given name on the first occasion of meeting him," said Aunt Roberta majestically.

"But he's my cousin," I protested. "You wouldn't have me call my cousin Mr. Campbell? Besides, he told me to call him Peter."

Aunt Roberta sniffed.

"Third cousin is a very diluted relationship. And are you going to do everything this Peter tells you?"

That reminded me.

"Aunty," I said hastily, "you remember what we were discussing before I went out? Well, I find that I can't make up my mind right off. You must really give me a little time. Let me have three weeks to think it over in. It's such a solemn subject—you said it was yourself. I'll promise that I'll tell you which man I'm going to marry at the end of three weeks."

"Very well," assented Aunt Roberta.

Alec and Dave and Alonzo all came up that evening; and Peter came over, too. He didn't say a great deal, just sat back in a corner and watched and listened; but he outstayed them all. Not that it did him much good. Aunt Roberta sat in the room and read a magazine stonily. I went to the door with him when he went away and walked across the lawn with him. He didn't look so homely in the moonlight, and oh, he was so nice! Niceness fairly exhaled from him.

"What do you think of them, Peter?" I asked.

"Nice fellows—but don't ask me anything more about them till the three weeks are up," said Peter. "There are better things to talk of on a moonlight night than matrimonial candidates. Look at those white lilies over there by the old beech. They look like you, Margaret. Will you pick one for me?"

I picked him a whole bunch.

THE INDECISION OF MARGARET

When I went back to the house Aunt Roberta met me in the hall.

"I hope, Margaret, that you are not going to flirt with this Peter Campbell," she said majestically.

"Indeed, I am not, Aunt," I assured her solemnly.

And I meant it. I had no intention of flirting with Peter. I didn't feel much like flirting, knowing that I had to marry one of "The Three" in September. But it was such a relief to know I wouldn't have to do the choosing. I slept like a child that night.

During the rest of the week Peter haunted our house. He came over when "The Three," or any fraction of them, were up because he said he wanted to study them to see which would suit me; and he came over when none of them was about because he said he wanted to study me and see which one I would suit. "The Three" liked Peter because he never butted into anything and spoiled it; and he was so ugly and cousinly that they never dreamed of being jealous of him as they were of one another. Aunt Roberta apparently didn't like him and went on consistently not liking him. This puzzled me. I couldn't see how anybody could help liking Peter.

Came Sunday, and Peter preached in the village church. I went, of course; but I couldn't realize that Peter could be going to preach. The fact that he was a minister persisted in seeming a huge joke to me. I put on my prettiest dress and spent an agonized ten minutes deciding on my hat, for our pew was right in front of the pulpit and I wanted to look nice under Peter's eye.

Well, Peter preached. And by the time he had preached ten minutes I felt so small and insignificant that I thought I must be all but invisible to the naked eye.

Peter never said a word about women; and he never even looked at me. But I realized then and there what a pitiful, frivolous, soulless, little butterfly I was, and how horribly different I must be from Peter's ideal woman. *She* would be grand and strong and noble—I felt it—I knew it. He was so earnest and tender and true; he was everything a minister ought to be. I wondered how I could ever have thought him ugly, with that intellectual brow, which the roughly falling hair hid on week-days, those inspired eyes, and that thrilling voice.

People said it was a splendid sermon. I am no judge of sermons, but I know I could have listened to him forever and that I felt utterly wretched. I just wanted to slip down on my knees and bury my face in my hands and pray God to make me a better girl and more worthy of such a third cousin as Peter.

He caught up with me on the road home and grinned as cheerfully as usual. But his grin could never deceive me again. I had seen the *real* Peter behind the outer mask.

"Peter," I said, "you were born to be a minister. You *couldn't* be anything else."

"No, I couldn't," he replied soberly. "I tried to be something else for a long while. I didn't want to be a minister. But I came to see at last that it was the work given me to do; and, God helping me, I shall try to do it."

His voice was low and reverent, almost as if he were speaking to himself. I thought that he would do his work and do it well and nobly; and happy the woman fitted by nature and training to help him do it. *She* would be no feather blown about by every fickle wind of fancy. *She* would always know what hat to put on. Probably she would have only the one. Ministers never have much money. But who would mind having only one hat or none at all, when she had a Peter?

Aunt Roberta frowned at me when I went in. I suppose she thought Peter and I had stayed too long talking at the garden gate.

"I thought you assured me that you were not going to flirt with that young man," she observed.

"I'm not flirting with him," I said piteously. "Why, Aunty, he is a minister."

"Ministers are oddly like other men," commented Aunt Roberta.

"Peter isn't," I responded decisively. "He isn't like any other man in the world."

Then did Aunt Roberta push up her spectacles and look at me.

Next day when Peter came over she asked him right before me if his congregation was a desirable one and what his salary was.

Peter told her his salary. It wasn't much more than I had known Aunt Roberta to spend on my dresses in one year.

"As for my congregation, it isn't a very fashionable one," he remarked gravely. "It is a little mission church in the slums down on Patterson street. I have to live there; the surroundings are not pleasant nor the people exteriorly attractive. But it's *mine*—my chosen life work."

Peter didn't say and Aunt Roberta didn't know—that he had received a call to more than one wealthy and cultured congregation but he had refused them all because he believed that he had his Master's call to labor among the poor and downtrodden of the earth. And Bob told me that the people of that little mission church just worshipped Peter, and that he was a burning and shining light in the darkness of the neighborhood where he worked.

"I suppose," observed Aunt Roberta distinctly, "that you have no intention of marrying? You would hardly care to ask a gently-bred woman to share such prospects?"

Aunt Roberta is so horridly outspoken. It is a Byrne habit and goes with the nose. I felt myself blushing to the roots of my hair, but Peter's expression never changed. He looked gravely and staunchly at the coyote skin at his feet.

"You are right in supposing so," he said. "I don't see how I could ask any woman to share such an existence of toil and poverty."

That seemed to settle it. I felt a queer, heavy dull feeling in my heart as if some new-born hope had fallen dead. And it didn't seem worth while to wonder if two people could really live on Peter's salary. But I wondered it now and then for all, and I concluded they could, if the woman was a very good manager and very economical and everything I wasn't. I wished that I had learned to make over dresses and do marketing.

Aunt Roberta's mind seemed easier after that and she didn't nag me about Peter. Meanwhile, "The Three" kept coming, and I drove with one and walked with another and sat and talked nonsense with the third. And I was, oh, so glad when the driving or the walking or the talking was over and I was free to fly to Peter who was always somewhere handy to be flown to. He was so good and jolly, that dear Peter, and he would talk lightly or seriously, just as I was in the mood.

He told me all about his work—I asked him for details—and it did seem hard and dull from his way of putting it. But it certainly agreed with Peter. Then why shouldn't it agree with other people?

"When you get married, Peter, I suppose your wife will be a great help to you," I suggested once.

"I don't expect to ever marry," said Peter gravely.

"Why not?" I asked.

"You heard what your Aunt Roberta said the other day. How could I ask a woman to go and live with me in the slums?"

"But she might want to go. She—she might be dying to be asked," I faltered. "She wouldn't mind the slums if you were there—if she loved you."

"What do you know about love?" demanded Peter, looking at me, I thought, accusingly.

I understood that he meant to imply that I didn't know anything about it, I who was going to marry some man in September because I didn't want to be sent home to a stepmother.

"I daresay I know as much about it as you do," I said. "At any rate, I'm sure that if I loved anybody I'd be willing to go anywhere with him—to the slums, or to Greenland's icy mountains. Besides, you would choose such a superior woman—wouldn't you Peter?—that she would positively exalt in the slums. You would choose—wouldn't you—a very good, noble, sensible, learned woman who could always make up her mind about everything, and lead the prayer meeting and never care whether her hat was nile-green or floppy pink or just plain slummy brown? Wouldn't you, Peter?"

Peter shook his head. He was leaning his folded arms on the beech lane fence and looking down into a curly bed of young, spicy ferns.

"No, that is just the trouble. If I fell in love with such a woman I might ask *her* to go down to Patterson street with me. But I never would fall in love with such a woman, you see. I'd be fatally sure to hanker after a little, non-sensible girl with brown-satin hair and big greenish-grey eyes. She would have to be beautiful because I am so ugly, to even matters up. I wouldn't want her to make up her mind with any especial readiness—*I* make up my mind very quickly and firmly, and it would be uncomfortable to have too much mind in the same house, especially a Patterson street house, as they are rather small. I should like her to like frills. And, of course, I could never dream of asking a girl like that to marry me—*never*, Margaret."

There was such an unpleasant ring of determination in his voice that it made me miserable; although his description of his ideal had caused my heart to flutter pleasantly.

I thought I knew somebody a little like it, but what good would that do if he didn't ask me—her, I mean—to marry him? And Aunt Roberta had ordained I *must* marry somebody.

When I counted up that night in my room I found that there were only five more days before I would have to decide—or, rather, Peter—which of "The Three" was to be groom at my wedding. Only five days! My heart stood still and my head spun round. Just for a minute, though—then everything cleared up—and I knew. I made up my own mind for my own self then and there and it wasn't a bit hard, not a bit.

The five days simply flew. Peter and "The Three" came and went, Aunt Roberta looked fifty different things and my mind simply stayed made up without a shadow of turning. It almost awed me; it had never been so before. You can't imagine what a delightful sensation it was to feel so sure and know it was your own sureness and not somebody else's. I envied more than ever those fortunate people who can make up their own minds about everything. I knew I should never be able to do it again. But that didn't matter so much since I had made it up on the only really important point in the whole universe.

"Well," remarked Peter, "I suppose I have to pick out a husband for you to-night?"

We were in the beech lane, just at the spot where I had first met Peter three weeks ago by the almanac; three years by some other computation of time. Peter was going away the next day and beyond that there wasn't *anything*—time, space, or thought.

"No, you haven't," I replied. "I've made up my own mind about 'The Three.'"

"Oh?" my companion certainly turned a little pale. "Then which of the gentlemen is to be my third cousin-in-law?"

"*None of them*," I said decidedly. "I wouldn't marry one of those men for anything, not even to escape from fifteen step-mothers with fifteen children apiece."

Peter turned away, folded his arms on the fence and looked across the clover field.

"What will your Aunt Roberta say?"

"All sorts of things. But it won't matter in the least," I cried recklessly.

"Then," responded Peter, "I suppose my responsibility is at an end. I am glad. I didn't realize what I was doing when I rashly took upon myself to decide which of four men you should marry."

"*Four* men?" I echoed. "Why, there are only three."

"*Four*," returned Peter, with the tone of one not to be contradicted.

"I have been brought up to believe everything a minister says," I remarked. "If you say there are four, four there must be. But my powers of resistance have all been exhausted in disposing of three. If the fourth man asks me to marry him I shall have to do it."

"And what if he doesn't?" muttered Peter moodily.

"But he will, don't you think?" I asked piteously. "Why shouldn't he? I suppose I'm not good enough for a min— for a fourth man's wife. Is that the trouble? Not good enough, or smart enough, or economical enough?"

"You are everything he would want his wife to be," rejoined Peter savagely. "But how could he ask you to leave your luxurious home and share his life of self-denial and poverty? You would have to give up so much."

"But I'd have *him*," I argued, "I wouldn't miss the other things."

"Oh, you don't know—you don't realize," groaned Peter. "I *can't* ask you to marry me—I love you better than my life. I love you too well to drag you down to Patterson street. I'm poor and I always will be poor. Remember what your Aunt Roberta said to me. It's been burning into my brain ever since. But I knew it anyway. No, I'm going away. I'll never forget you—but I'll never be coward enough to ask you to be my wife under the circumstances."

"Then I'll have to ask you," I faltered. "Won't you marry me, Peter?"

Peter whirled around, clenching his hands.

"Margaret! Don't!"

"Now, Peter, surely you aren't going to reject me. I never thought to see the day when I'd be asking a man to marry me and he wouldn't. It isn't polite, Peter. And while I wouldn't be a model minister's wife to start with I'd improve. I know I would, Peter.

I'm not half so fond of frills as you imagine and I could learn to cook before September if I went right at it; and I once taught a Sunday School class all summer. *Please*, Peter! If you won't—oh, Peter—if you won't—"

There I just broke down and cried. It was so mortifying.

"Oh, Margaret, darling." And there I was, with Peter's arms about me and his lips on mine.

"Well," said Aunt Roberta that night, "have you decided which of those men you are going to marry?"

"Yes. I'm going to marry Peter," I said.

Aunt Roberta looked things, unwholesome things.

"Margaret Byrne, didn't you promise me you wouldn't flirt with that man?"

"You can hardly call it flirting with a man to promise to marry him," I protested.

"And he told me he would never ask any woman to share such a life," sniffed Aunt Roberta.

"He didn't say just that, Aunty. He said he didn't *see how* he could. I suppose he has had some new light since. But, anyhow, he *didn't* ask me. *I* asked *him*."

"So you think you'll like living on Patterson street?"

"Why, of course. Won't Peter be there too?"

Aunt Roberta looked at me over her glasses.

"Humph! Do you think you really love this Peter?"

"*Think*? I don't think! I *know* it," I cried.

Aunt Roberta took off her glasses.

"Well, that is all that is really necessary," said that astonishing relative. "Come and kiss me, my dear."

(1906/1915)

Aunt Philippa and the Men

In *Anne's House of Dreams*, Montgomery introduces a dynamic new character: forty-something man hater Miss Cornelia Bryant, who, according to Elizabeth Rollins Epperly, "is merciless in her faulting of men for all the ills in and out of Four Winds." Miss Cornelia's startling speeches were so well-received that three of them were included in Donald Graham French's 1921 anthology *Standard Canadian Reciter: A Book of the Best Readings and Recitations from Canadian Literature*. A prototype of Miss Cornelia appeared in the form of Aunt Philippa in the following short story, published in the January 1915 issue of *The Red Book Magazine* (Chicago), which referred to this story as one "In Which a Man-Hater Joins Hands with Cupid." Aunt Philippa and Miss Cornelia are almost identical to each other in their dress and in their anecdotes about men behaving badly, except for slightly different catchphrases (*"That's* the men for you" in the case of the former, "Isn't that like a man?" in the case of the latter), even if the characters differ in terms of their motivation for telling these anecdotes.

I KNEW QUITE WELL WHY FATHER SENT ME TO PRINCE Edward Island to visit Aunt Philippa that summer. He told me he was sending me there "to learn some sense;" and my stepmother, of whom I was very fond, told me she was sure the sea air would do me a world of good. I did not want to learn sense or be done a world of good; I wanted to stay in Montreal and go on being foolish—and make up my quarrel with Mark Fenwick. Father and Mother did not know anything about this quarrel;

they thought I was still on good terms with him—and that was why they sent me to Prince Edward Island.

I was very miserable. I did not want to go to Aunt Philippa's. It was not because I feared it would be dull—for without Mark, Montreal was just as much of a howling wilderness as any other place. But it was so horribly far away. When the time came for Mark to want to make up,—as come I knew it would,—how could he do it if I were seven hundred miles away?

Nevertheless, I went to Prince Edward Island. In all my eighteen years I had never once disobeyed Father. He is a very hard man to disobey. I knew I should have to make a beginning some time if I wanted to marry Mark, so I saved all my little courage up for that and didn't waste any of it opposing the visit to Aunt Philippa.

I couldn't understand Father's point of view. Of course, he hated old John Fenwick, who had once sued him for libel and won the case. Father had written an indiscreet editorial in the excitement of a red-hot political contest—and was made to understand that there are some things you can't say of another man even at election time. But then, he need not have hated Mark because of that; Mark was not even born when it happened.

Old John Fenwick was not much better pleased about Mark and me than Father was, though he didn't go to the length of forbidding it; he just acted grumpily and disagreeably. Things were unpleasant enough all round without a quarrel between Mark and me; yet quarrel we did—and over next to nothing, too, you understand. And now I had to set out for Prince Edward Island without even seeing him, for he was away in Toronto on business.

When my train reached Copely the next afternoon, Aunt Philippa was waiting for me. There was nobody else in sight, but I would have known her had there been a thousand. Nobody but Aunt Philippa could have that determined mouth, those piercing gray eyes, and that pronounced, unmistakable Goodwin nose. And certainly nobody but Aunt Philippa would have come to meet me arrayed in a wrapper of chocolate print with huge yellow roses scattered over it, and a striped blue-and-white apron!

She welcomed me kindly but absentmindedly, her thoughts evidently being concentrated on the problem of getting my trunk home. I had only the one, and in Montreal it had seemed to be of moderate size; but on the platform of Copely station, sized up by Aunt Philippa's merciless eye, it certainly looked huge. "I thought we could a-took it along tied on the back of the buggy," she said disapprovingly, "but I guess we'll have to leave it, and I'll send the hired boy over for it to-night. You can get along without it till then, I s'pose?"

There was a fine irony in her tone. I hastened to assure her meekly that I could, and that it did not matter if my trunk could not be taken up till next day.

"Oh, Jerry can come for it to-night as well as not," said Aunt Philippa, as we climbed into her buggy. "I'd a good notion to send him to meet you, for he isn't doing much to-day, and I wanted to go to Mrs. Roderick MacAllister's funeral. But my head was aching me so bad I thought I wouldn't enjoy the funeral if I did go. My head is better now, so I kind of wish I had gone. She was a hundred and four years old and I'd always promised myself that I'd go to her funeral."

Aunt Philippa's tone was melancholy. She did not recover her good spirits until we were out on the pretty, grassy, elm-shaded country road, garlanded with its ribbon of butter-cups. Then she suddenly turned around and looked me over scrutinizingly.

"You're not as good looking as I expected from your picture, but them photographs always flatter. That's the reason I never had any took. You're rather thin and brown. But you've good eyes and you look clever. Your father writ me you hadn't much sense, though. He wants me to teach you some, but it's a thankless business. People would rather be fools."

Aunt Philippa struck her steed smartly with the whip and controlled his resultant friskiness with admirable skill.

"Well, you know it's pleasanter," I said, wickedly. "Just think what a doleful world it would be if everybody were sensible."

Aunt Philippa looked at me out of the corner of her eye and disdained any skirmish of flippant epigram.

"So you want to get married?" she said. "You'd better wait till you're grown up."

"How old must a person be before she is grown up?" I asked gravely.

"Humph! That depends. Some are grown up when they're born, and others ain't grown up when they're eighty. That same

Mrs. Roderick I was speaking of never grew up. She was as foolish when she was a hundred as when she was ten."

"Perhaps that's why she lived so long," I suggested. All thought of seeking sympathy in Aunt Philippa had vanished. I resolved I would not even mention Mark's name.

"Mebbe 'twas," admitted Aunt Philippa with a grim smile. "*I'd* rather live fifty sensible years than a hundred foolish ones."

Much to my relief, she made no further reference to my affairs. As we rounded a curve in the road where two great overarching elms met, a buggy wheeled by us, occupied by a young man in clerical costume. He had a pleasant, boyish face, and he touched his hat courteously. Aunt Philippa nodded very frostily and gave her horse a quite undeserved cut.

"There's a man you don't want to have much to do with," she said portentously. "He's a Methodist minister."

"Why, Aunty, the Methodists are a very nice denomination," I protested. "My step-mother is a Methodist, you know."

"No, I didn't know, but I'd believe anything of a step-mother. I've no use for Methodists or their ministers. This fellow just came last spring, and it's *my* opinion he smokes. And he thinks every girl who looks at him falls in love with him—as if a Methodist minister was any prize! Don't you take much notice of him, Ursula."

"I'll not be likely to have the chance," I said with an amused smile.

"Oh, you'll see enough of him. He boards at Mrs. John Callman's, just across the road from us, and he's always out sunning himself on her veranda. Never studies, of course. Last Sunday they say he preached on the iron that floated. If he'd confine himself to the Bible and leave sensational subjects alone it would be better for him and his poor congregation, and so I told Mrs. John Callman to her face. I should think *she* would have had enough of his sex by this time. She married John Callman against her father's will, and he had delirious trembles for years. That's the men for you."

"They're not *all* like that, Aunt Philippa," I protested.

"Most of 'em are. See that house over there? Mrs. Jane Harrison lives there. Her husband took tantrums every few days or so and wouldn't get out of bed. She had to do all the barn work till he'd got over his spell. That's men for you. When he died, people writ her letters of condolence but *I* just sot down and writ her one of congratulation. There's the Presbyterian manse in the hollow. Mr. Bentwell's our minister. He's a good man and he'd be a rather nice one if he didn't think it was his duty to be a little miserable all the time. He won't let his wife wear a fashionable hat, and his daughter can't fix her hair the way she wants to. Even being a minister can't prevent a man from being a crank. Here's Ebenezer Milgrave coming. You take a good look at him. He used to be insane for years. He believed he was dead and used to rage at his wife because she wouldn't bury him. *I'd* a-done it."

Aunt Philippa looked so determinedly grim that I could almost see her with a spade in her hand. I laughed aloud at the picture summoned up.

"Yes, it's funny, but I guess his poor wife didn't find it very humorsome. He's been pretty sane for some years now, but you never can tell when he'll break out again. He's got a brother, Albert Milgrave, who's been married twice. They say he was courting his second wife while his first was dying. Let that be as it may, he used his first wife's wedding ring to marry the second. That's the men for you."

"Don't you know *any* good husbands, Aunt Philippa?" I asked desperately.

"Oh, yes, lots of 'em—over there," said Aunt Philippa sardonically, waving her whip in the direction of a little country graveyard on a distant hill.

"Yes, but *living*—walking about in the flesh?"

"Precious few. Now and again you'll come across a man whose wife won't put up with any nonsense and he *has* to be respectable. But the most of 'em are poor bargains—poor bargains."

"And are all the wives saints?" I persisted.

"Laws, no, but they're too good for the men," retorted Aunt Philippa, as she turned in at her own gate. Her house was close to the road and was painted such a vivid green that the landscape looked faded by contrast. Across the gable end of it was the legend, "Philippa's Farm," emblazoned in huge, black letters two feet long. All its surroundings were very neat. On the kitchen doorstep a patchwork cat was making a grave toilet. The groundwork of the cat was white, and its spots were black, yellow, gray and brown.

"There's Joseph," said Aunt Philippa. "I call him that because his coat is of many colors. But I ain't no lover of cats. They're too much like the men to suit me."

"Cats have always been supposed to be peculiarly feminine," I said, descending.

"'Twas a man that supposed it, then," retorted Aunt Philippa, beckoning to her hired boy. "Here, Jerry, put Prince away. Jerry's a good sort of boy," she confided to me as we went into the house. "I had Jim Spencer last summer and the only good thing about *him* was his appetite. I put up with him till harvest was in, and then one day my patience give out. He upsot a churnful of cream in the back yard—and was just as cool as a cowcumber over it—laughed and said it was good for the land. I told him I wasn't in the habit of fertilizing my back yard with cream. But that's the men for you. Come in. I'll have tea ready in no time. I sot the table before I left. There's lemon pie. Mrs. John Cantwell sent it over. I never make lemon pie myself. Ten years ago I took the prize for lemon pies at the county fair, and I've never made any since for fear I'd lose my reputation for them."

The first month of my stay passed not unpleasantly. The summer weather was delightful, and the sea air was certainly splendid. Aunt Philippa's little farm ran right down to the shore, and I spent much of my time there. There were also several families of cousins to be visited in the farm-houses that dotted the pretty, seaward-sloping valley, and they came back to see me at "Philippa's Farm." I picked spruce gum and berries and ferns, and Aunt Philippa taught me to make butter. It was all very idyllic—or would have been if Mark had written. But Mark did not write. I supposed he must be very angry because I had run off to Prince Edward Island without so much as a note of good-by. But I had been so sure he would understand!

Aunt Philippa never made any further reference to the reason Father had sent me to her; but she allowed no day to pass without holding up to me some horrible example of matrimonial infelicity. The number of unhappy wives who walked or drove past "Philippa's Farm" every afternoon, as we sat on the veranda, was truly pitiable.

We always sat on the veranda in the afternoon, when we were not visiting or being visited. I made a pretense of fancy work, and

Aunt Philippa spun diligently on a little old-fashioned spinning-wheel that had been her grandmother's. She always sat before the wooden stand which held her flowers, and the gorgeous blots of geranium blossom and big green leaves furnished a pretty background. She always wore her shapeless but clean print wrappers, and her iron-gray hair was always combed neatly down over her ears. Joseph sat between us, sleeping or purring. She spun so expertly that she could keep a close watch on the road as well, and I got the biography of every individual who went by. As for the poor young Methodist minister, who liked to read or walk on the veranda of our neighbor's house, Aunt Philippa never had a good word for him. I had met him once or twice socially and had liked him. I wanted to ask him to call but dared not—Aunt Philippa had vowed he should never enter her house.

"If I was dead and he came to my funeral I'd rise up and order him out," she said.

"I thought he made a very nice prayer at Mrs. Seaman's funeral the other day," I said.

"Oh, I've no doubt he can pray. I never heard anyone make more beautiful prayers than old Simon Kennedy down at the Harbor, who was always drunk or hoping to be—and the drunker he was the better he prayed. It ain't no matter how well a man prays if his preaching isn't right. That Methodist man preaches a lot of things that ain't true, and what's worse they ain't sound doctrine. At least, that's what I've heard. I never was in a Methodist church, thank goodness."

"Don't you think Methodists go to heaven as well as Presbyterians, Aunt Philippa?" I asked gravely.

"That ain't for us to decide," said Aunt Philippa solemnly. "It's in higher hands than ours. But I ain't going to associate with them on *earth*, whatever I may have to do in heaven. The folks round here mostly don't make much difference and go to the Methodist church quite often. But *I* say if you are a Presbyterian, *be* a Presbyterian. Of course, if you ain't, it don't matter much what you do. As for that minister man, he has a grand-uncle who was sent to the penitentiary for embezzlement. I found out *that* much."

And evidently Aunt Philippa had taken an unholy joy in finding it out.

"I dare say some of our own ancestors deserved to go to the

penitentiary, even if they never did," I remarked. "Who is that woman driving past, Aunt Philippa? She must have been very pretty once."

"She was—and that was all the good it did her. 'Favor is deceitful and beauty is vain,' Ursula. She was Sarah Pyatt and she married Fred Proctor. He was one of your wicked, fascinating men. After she married him he give up being fascinating but he kept on being wicked. *That's* the men for you. Her sister Flora weren't much luckier. *Her* man was that domineering she couldn't call her soul her own. Finally he couldn't get his own way over something and he just suicided by jumping into the well. A good riddance—but of course the well was spoiled. Flora could never abide the thought of using it again, poor thing. *That's* men for you.

"And there's that old Enoch Allan on his way to the station. He's ninety if he's a day. You can't kill some folks with a meat ax. His wife died twenty years ago. He'd been married when he was twenty so they'd lived together for fifty years. She was a faithful, hard-working creature and kept him out of the poor-house, for he was a shiftless soul, not lazy, exactly, but just too fond of sitting. But he weren't grateful. She had a kind of bitter tongue and they did use to fight scandalous. O' course it was all his fault. Well, she died, and old Enoch and my father drove together to the graveyard. Old Enoch was awful quiet all the way there and back; but just afore they got home, he says solemnly to Father: 'You mayn't believe it, Henry, but this is the happiest day of my life.' *That's* men for you. His brother, Scotty Allan, was the meanest man ever lived in these parts. When his wife died she was buried with a little gold brooch in her collar unbeknownst to him. When he found it out he went one night to the graveyard and opened up the grave and the casket to get that brooch."

"Oh, Aunt Philippa, that is a horrible story," I cried, recoiling with a shiver over the gruesomeness of it.

"'Course it is, but what would you expect of a man?" retorted Aunt Philippa.

Somehow, her stories began to affect me in spite of myself. There were times when I felt very dreary. Perhaps Aunt Philippa was right. Perhaps men possessed neither truth nor constancy. Certainly Mark had forgotten me. I was ashamed of myself because this hurt me so much, but I could not help it. I grew pale and listless. Aunt Philippa sometimes peered at me sharply, but she held her peace. I was grateful for this.

But one day a letter did come from Mark. I dared not read it until I was safely in my own room. Then I opened it with trembling fingers.

The letter was a little stiff. Evidently Mark was feeling sore enough over things. He made no reference to our quarrel or to my sojourn in Prince Edward Island. He wrote that his firm was sending him to South Africa to take charge of their interests there. He would leave in three weeks time and could not return for five years. If I still cared anything for him, would I meet him in Halifax, marry him, and go to South Africa with him? If I would not, he would understand that I had ceased to love him and that all was over between us.

That, boiled down, was the gist of Mark's letter. When I had read it I cast myself on the bed and wept out all the tears I had refused to let myself shed during my weeks of exile.

For I could not do what Mark asked—I *could not*. I couldn't run away to be married in that desolate, unbefriended fashion. It would be a disgrace. I would feel ashamed of it all my life and be unhappy over it. I thought that Mark was rather unreasonable. He knew what my feelings about runaway marriages were. And was it absolutely necessary for him to go to South Africa? Of course his father was behind it somewhere, but surely he could have got out of it if he had really tried.

Well, if he went to South Africa he must go alone. But my heart would break.

I cried the whole afternoon, cowering among my pillows. I never wanted to go out of that room again. I never wanted to see anybody again. I hated the thought of facing Aunt Philippa with her cold eyes and her miserable stories that seemed to strip life of all beauty and love of all reality. I could hear her scornful "That's the men for you," if she heard what was in Mark's letter.

"What is the matter, Ursula?"

Aunt Philippa was standing by my bed. I was too abject to resent her coming in without knocking.

"Nothing," I said spiritlessly.

"If you've been crying for three mortal hours over nothing you want a good spanking and you'll get it," observed Aunt Philippa, placidly, sitting down on my trunk. "Get right up off that bed this minute and tell me what the trouble is. I'm bound to know, for I'm in your father's place at present."

"There, then!" I flung her Mark's letter. There wasn't anything in it that it was sacrilege to let another person see. That was one reason why I had been crying.

Aunt Philippa read it over twice. Then she folded it up deliberately and put it back in the envelope.

"What are you going to do?" she asked in a matter-of-fact tone.

"I'm not going to run away to be married," I answered sullenly.

"Well, no, I wouldn't advise you to," said Aunt Philippa reflectively. "It's a kind of low-down thing to do, though there's been a terrible lot of romantic nonsense talked and writ about eloping. It may be a painful necessity sometimes, but it ain't in this case. You write to your young man and tell him to come here and be married respectable under my roof, same as a Goodwin ought to."

I sat up and stared at Aunt Philippa. I was so amazed that it is useless to try to express my amazement.

"Aunt—Philippa," I gasped. "I thought—I thought—"

"You thought I was a hard old customer, and so I am," said Aunt Philippa. "But I don't take my opinions from your father nor anybody else. It didn't prejudice me any against your young man that your father didn't like him. I knew your father of old. I have some other friends in Montreal and I writ to them and asked them what he was like. From what they said I judged he was decent enough as men go. You're too young to be married, but if you let him go off to South Africa he'll slip through your fingers for sure, and I s'pose you're like some of the rest of us—nobody'll do you but the one. So tell him to come here and be married."

"I don't see how I can," I gasped. "I can't get ready to be married in three weeks. I can't—"

"I should think you have enough clothes in that trunk to do you for a spell," said Aunt Philippa sarcastically. "You've more than my mother ever had in all her life. We'll get you a wedding dress of some kind. You can get it made in Charlottetown, if country dress-makers aren't good enough for you; and I'll bake you a wedding cake that'll taste as good as anything you could get in Montreal, even if it won't look so stylish."

"What will Father say?" I questioned.

"Lots o' things," conceded Aunt Philippa grimly. "But I don't see as it matters when neither you nor me'll be there to have our feelings hurt. I'll write a few things to your father. He hasn't got much sense. He ought to be thankful to get a decent young man for his son-in-law in a world where 'most every man is a wolf in sheep's clothing. But that's the men for you."

And that was Aunt Philippa for you. For the next three weeks she was a blissfully excited, busy woman. I was allowed to choose the material and fashion of my wedding suit and hat myself, but almost everything else was settled by Aunt Philippa. I didn't mind; it was a relief to be rid of all responsibility; I did protest when she declared her intention of having a big wedding and asking all the cousins and semi-cousins on the island, but Aunt Philippa swept my objections lightly aside.

"I'm bound to have one good wedding in this house," she said. "Not likely I'll ever have another chance."

She found time amid all the baking and concocting to warn me frequently not to take it too much to heart if Mark failed to come after all.

"I know a man who jilted a girl on her wedding day. That's the men for you. It's best to be prepared."

But Mark did come, getting there the evening before our wedding day. And then a severe blow fell on Aunt Philippa. Word came from the manse that Mr. Bentwell had been suddenly summoned to Nova Scotia to his mother's death bed; he had started that night.

"That's the men for you," said Aunt Philippa bitterly. "Never can depend on one of them, not even on a minister. What's to be done now?"

"Get another minister," said Mark easily.

"Where'll you get him?" demanded Aunt Philippa. "The minister at Cliftonville is away on his vacation, and Mercer is vacant; and that leaves none nearer than town. It won't do to depend on a town minister being able to come. No, there's no help for it. You'll have to have that Methodist man."

Aunt Philippa's tone was tragic. Plainly she thought the ceremony would scarcely be legal if that Methodist man married us. But neither Mark nor I cared. We were too happy to be disturbed by any such trifles.

The young Methodist minister married us the next day in the presence of many beaming guests. Aunt Philippa, splendid in black silk and point-lace collar, neither of which lost a whit of dignity or luster by being made ten years before, was composure itself while the ceremony was going on. But no sooner had the minister pronounced us man and wife than she spoke up.

"Now that's over I want some one to go right out and put out the fire on the kitchen roof. It's been on fire for the last ten minutes."

Minister and bridegroom headed the emergency brigade, and Aunt Philippa pumped the water for them. In a short time the fire was out, all was safe, and we were receiving our deferred congratulations.

"Now, young man," said Aunt Philippa solemnly as she shook hands with Mark, "don't you ever try to get out of this, even if a Methodist minister did marry you."

She insisted on driving us to the train and said good-by to us as we stood on the car steps. She had caught more of the shower of rice than I had, and as the day was hot and sunny she had tied over her head, atop of that festal silk dress, a huge, home-made, untrimmed straw hat. But she did not look ridiculous. There was a certain dignity about Aunt Philippa in any costume and under any circumstance.

"Aunt Philippa," I said, "tell me this: Why have you helped me to be married?"

The train began to move.

"I refused once to run away myself, and I've repented it ever since." Then, as the train gathered speed and the distance between us widened, she shouted after us, "But I s'pose if I had run away I'd have repented of that too."

(1915)

By the Grace of Sarah May

In June 1905, around the time Montgomery apparently began writing *Anne of Green Gables*, she published in *Modern Women* of Boston a short story entitled "By the Grace of Sarah Maud." Irene Gammel uses the terms "prototype," "silhouette," and "kernel" to describe the ways that the story's eight-year-old protagonist, Sarah Maud Molloy, anticipates the young Anne Shirley, including "an intuitive and poetic understanding of nature's beauty," her propensity for asking adults difficult questions, and her temper. Gammel also notes that Montgomery "must have felt that this sparkling little redhead was a kindred spirit" due to her choice to share with the character her middle name (Maud) and initials similar to hers. Yet when Montgomery republished this short story in *Maclean's Magazine* of Toronto in August 1916, eight years after the publication of *Anne of Green Gables*, the only major alteration she made was to rename the character "Sarah May."

NESBITT PANTED INTO THE STATION—TOO LATE. THE train, with its load of picnickers, was gone; and there was no other train going west until late in the afternoon.

"Confound it," he said blackly. "And confound Murchison," he added, thinking of the acquaintance who had delayed him on the street to discuss a slight matter of business.

He was left—there was no blinking that fact. The selected picnic ground was fifty miles away, so that the wild notion that had crossed his brain of getting a team and driving thereto had to be dismissed. No, there was no picnic for him; and, as things were, much depended on that picnic.

Nesbitt left the station in a mood of sickening depression. All the hope and exhilaration of the morning had vanished. Betty would think he did not care—and Clark was on the train. For a whole day Clark could wander with Betty through romantic haunts, while he, Nesbitt, sulked in town. Only a fool could fail to make use of such a golden opportunity; and Clark was no fool.

"That is *my* role," thought Nesbitt bitterly.

He was in love with Betty Stewart. But Betty was independent. They had had some tiffs, with a resulting coolness. Nesbitt had not been sure enough of his welcome to call for a fortnight. Then with her usual caprice, Betty unbent. She had sent him a note the previous day inviting him to join a private picnic party to Maiden Lake.

> "We will leave on the 10.15 train," she wrote, "so be a good boy, stop sulking, and come with us. If you come I shall know how to be very nice to you, but if you don't I shall know you are still sulking and I shall be nice to—other people."

Nesbitt had not been sulking—take his word for it; he was merely on his dignity. That, of course, went to the winds at Betty's beck. And this was the result—he was wandering homeward alone through the People's Square; and Betty and Clark were on their way to Maiden Lake.

Nesbitt sat down on a bench in the Square and was about to give himself over to sulking in right good earnest when he heard somebody crying. Some twisting of neck discovered a small girl of about eight or nine curled up on a bench across the walk behind him, with her face buried in her arms and the ragged sailor hat on her head shaking in the emphasis of her woe. She was sniffling in an unrestrained luxury of grief, evidently thinking herself alone.

"Hello," said Nesbitt, who hated to see children or animals suffering, "it seems there is somebody besides myself in the world who is miserable after all. This must be seen to."

He went over and sat down on the other bench.

"What is the matter, sissy?" he asked gently.

Sissy squirmed around with a start, revealing a freckled, tear-spotted face, and a very red little nose. She was not shy and she did not at all resent his intrusion into her private troubles.

"I—can't—get—to—the—picker—nic," she said, between sobs.

"Did you miss your train, too?" asked Nesbitt with a smile. He could still smile, even in the wreck of all things, and his smile was very winning. It won Sarah May Molloy's young heart on the spot.

"Train nothing. We wasn't going on a train. We was going to ride out to Deerville in livery rigs—all Miss Beecham's Mission School kids. We was going to have a bully time. Ice cream, too. Oh, gee! And I can't go."

Sarah May's pale blue eyes brimmed up with tears again.

"Tell me why," said Nesbitt. "If it isn't a secret I'd really like to know."

"'Tain't any secret. I hain't got any dress but this"—touching the faded print she wore—"and Ma, she said at first I could go. And when the Jones kids got new white dresses for to wear, and Ma, she says she won't lemme go 'cause she can't git me a new dress and she ain't going to have the Jones kids dressed bettern hern at a pickernic. And I jest howled and Ma, she said she'd skelp me if I didn't dry up, so I kem out here and I feel awful bad. I'd gone to the pickernic 'thout any dress *at all* ruther'n miss it. I never was in the country afore and I wanted to see it."

"I'm very sorry for you," said Nesbitt gravely. "I can sympathize with you for I also have missed my picnic to-day."

"*Your* clothes look pretty good," said Sarah May, eyeing them critically.

"It's not a matter of clothes in my case—but the principle is the same. Now, look here—but first, what is your name?"

"Sarah May Molloy."

"Very well, Sarah May, listen to me. We have both been disappointed—let us pool our disappointments and have a strictly exclusive picnic of our own. There's a train leaving for the east in half an hour. Come with me and we'll go out to the Junction and turn ourselves loose in the woods there. I don't know if I can manage any ice cream, but we'll have heaps of other good things."

Sarah May put her finger in her mouth.

"Say, are you bluffin'?"

"No, indeed! I'm in downright earnest. Go and ask your mother if she'll lend you to me for the day."

"Can't do that 'cause she's gone up to the north end to scrub for a woman and she won't be back till night. But she won't care. If you ain't puttin' up a job I'll go, mister."

"It's a bargain. You wait here while I rush up town and invest in some ready-to-wear eatables. We've been unjustly cheated out of our picnic, Sarah May, but we'll get even with Fate yet."

Nesbitt, smiling at his own whim, hurried to the nearest fruit and confectionery store and soon came back, loaded with parcels. Sarah May was waiting for him. She had pushed her carroty hair back under her hat, scrubbed her face dry with her apron, and was ready to adventure forth on any quest with this astonishing new friend of hers.

"Gee, but you've got whacks of things," she exclaimed. "What's them? Or'nges? Or'nges are the clear stuff. Gimme one to suck on the train. Ain't I glad you come along, though!"

"I'm not sorry myself," said Nesbitt. "You are what I really needed, Sarah May—a diversion."

"Ain't!" said Sarah May indignantly. "I'm Irish."

"Oh, it's all the same thing, dearie. Come, let us away to Arcady now. Begone, dull care and haunting remorse; we'll daff the world and sneering rivals and over-dressed Joneses aside for one day at least, Sarah May."

"You talk just like a crazy uncle of me father's," said Sarah May tolerantly.

They got on a lazy little freight train that took half an hour to crawl out to the Junction, a small village where the east and west roads branched off. When Nesbitt left the train his eye caught a sign over a small restaurant near the station and he took Sarah May in and treated her to unlimited ice cream. Sarah May ate three saucersful and chattered blithely between rapturous gulps. Evidently Sarah May had no sorrow that ice cream could not cure.

Then they went away into the big beech woods beyond the village, following a winding forest path until they came to the banks of a brook where they sat down and had another feast, Sarah

May rummaging cheerfully in Nesbitt's parcels and squealing with delight over her discoveries.

"Say, ain't it great here?" she said, when they had finished their lunch, pillowing her elbows in the moss and looking up into the great green arches above her. "These woods make me feel I don't know how—like I do at Mass sometimes—all kind of solemn and happy-like. The country is all right, mister."

"Would you like to live out here?" asked Nesbitt.

Sarah May shook her head decidedly.

"Nope. It'd be too lonesome for a steady thing. I'd ruther people than trees. But for a day it's fine. Say, Mister, let's mosey on a bit. I want to see all that's to be seen."

Accordingly they moseyed on. Sarah May seemed tireless and they rambled through woods and fields and country lanes the whole afternoon. They gathered flowers and hunted for birds' nests, and Nesbitt answered Sarah May's questions, of which she asked a few thousand, more or less. The inquisition was wholesome for Nesbitt; he could not brood much over what might be doing at Maiden Lake when he had to satisfy Sarah May's rapacious appetite for information about everything she saw.

It was sunset when Sarah May's legs gave out. Nesbitt set her up on the gate of a wood lane on the hill above the Junction and they watched the sunset together while they waited for their train.

"It's been boss," said Sarah May, with a deep sigh of satisfaction. "I'll bet I wouldn't have had half as good a time if I'd gone with the other kids. Them Joneses would have put on too much side. I wisht I could go to a pickernick with you every week."

"Much obliged," said Nesbitt absently.

"You'd ruther gone to the other, though," said Sarah May shrewdly. "You've been thinking about it all the time. Why? Did your girl go on it?"

"Yes," said Nesbitt, moved by a whimsical impulse to confidence in this red-headed mite of the slums. "And you see, Sarah May, the other fellow went too."

"I savvy," Sarah May nodded comprehendingly. Then, desiring to comfort him, and drawing on her own feminine possibilities, she added: "That needn't worry you, 'cause she'll be so mad at you not coming that she'll likely give him the cold shoulder and the marble heart for spite. See?"

"You are a comforting young woman, Sarah May. But—I'm afraid—you see, I think she is *my* girl, but I'm not sure *she* thinks so."

"Does she want the earth with a gilt fence round it?" demanded Sarah May scornfully. "I'll bet the other fellow ain't half as good looking as you. I wisht *I* was grown up."

"Thank you. I wish she had your excellent taste."

"I s'pose she's a good looker?" queried Sarah May curiously.

"She is the most beautiful woman in the world, dearie. Look—do you see that little cloud away down in the north-west sky—that bright gold one? That is just the color of her hair. And do you see that sky in the south-west with that one clear star in it? Her eyes are as blue as that sky and as brilliant as that star, Sarah May. And those wild roses you picked by the brook to-day have never seen her face or they would not think it worth their while to be roses."

"Say, but you've got it bad," commented Sarah May drowsily. Her red head nodded against Nesbitt's arm. He lifted her off the gate and carried her down to the station where a train presently rolled in. Nesbitt got on the rear car with Sarah May in his arms. Her head was cuddled on his shoulder, and in one of her scrawny little hands she still clutched her big bouquet of wild roses and limp daisies.

Nesbitt had supposed the train was the freight they had come out on. He now discovered that it was the western train and that the car was full of the returning Maiden Lake picnickers.

Nesbitt's appearance was hailed with laughter and jests. He felt foolish, but he looked nobly serene as he stalked down the aisle and dropped into the only vacant place in the car—beside Betty Stewart!

He wondered why it was vacant. Where in the world was Clark? Then he saw Clark down at the other end, scowling gloomily out of a window.

Betty said "Good evening" very icily, and completely ignored the fact of Sarah May. Nesbitt made the little red head more comfortable on his shoulder before he spoke. Then he said:

"Did you take the trouble to wonder why I did not show up this morning?"

"I supposed you were not sufficiently interested in the picnic—or picnickers—to come," said Betty in an indifferent tone which had the effect of adding: "And then I dismissed the matter from my mind."

"I missed the train," said Nesbitt. "My watch was slow to begin with and then I met Murchison and he delayed me. You were gone ten minutes when I reached the station. I can't tell you how I felt about it. On my way back I found this baby crying in the People's Square because she couldn't get to a mission picnic. So I took her out to the Junction for an outing, and I think she had a good time at least."

He paused in suspense. He expected Betty to give a cruel little laugh and make some satirical speech about his newly-fledged philanthropy. But Betty could always be depended on for the unexpected.

Her eyes softened. She gave him a look that gladdened him and said in a low tone, as she bent forward and gently pushed back the moist, sandy locks from Sarah May's flushed face:

"I think it was lovely of you."

Her touch, or the jerk of the train as it came to a stand-still at the water-tank, wakened Sarah May. She lifted her head, rather dazed by the lights and strangers around her, and found herself looking into the face of the very prettiest young lady she had ever seen.

Sarah May sat up on Nesbitt's knee, pointed a brown finger at Betty, and said, sleepily, but in a voice whose awful distinctness was heard to the farthest end of the car:

"Are you his girl?"

Nesbitt gasped and looked for the end of all things. At that awful moment he wished he had never seen Sarah May.

But Betty smiled again and said in a voice, low but equally distinct:

"Yes, dear, I am."

(1905/1916)

Abel and His Great Adventure

Published in the February 1917 issue of *The Canadian Magazine* of Toronto, six months before the publication of *Anne's House of Dreams*, this next short story contains the second of two prototypes of Captain Jim. As Elizabeth Rollins Epperly notes in a comparison of the short story and the novel that would follow, "Why Montgomery would publish this short story—in Canada—when her novel was in the works is a mystery." Indeed, as Genevieve Wiggins notes, "The story of 'Abel' appeared while the author was reading the proofs for *Anne's House of Dreams*, certainly an unusual publishing decision."

"COME OUT OF DOORS, MASTER—COME OUT OF doors. I can't talk or think right with walls around me—never could. Let's go out to the garden." These were almost the first words I ever heard Abel Armstrong say. He was a member of the board of school trustees in Stillwater, and I had not met him before this late May evening, when I had gone down to confer with him upon some small matter of business. For I was "the new schoolmaster" in Stillwater, having taken the school for the summer term.

It was a rather lonely country district—a fact of which I was glad, for life had been going somewhat awry with me and my heart was sore and rebellious over many things that have nothing to do with this narration. Stillwater offered time and opportunity for healing and counsel. Yet, looking back, I doubt if I should have found either had it not been for Abel and his beloved garden.

Abel Armstrong (he was always called "Old Abel," though he was barely sixty) lived in a quaint, gray house close by the harbour shore. I heard a good deal about him before I saw him. He was called "queer," but Stillwater folks seemed to be very fond of him. He and his sister, Tamzine, lived together; she, so my garrulous landlady informed me, had not been sound of mind at times for many years; but she was all right now, only odd and quiet. Abel had gone to college for a year when he was young, but had given it up when Tamzine "went crazy." There was no one else to look after her. Abel had settled down to it with apparent content: at least he had never complained.

"Always took things easy, Abel did," said Mrs. Campbell. "Never seemed to worry over disappointments and trials as most folks do. Seems to me that as long as Abel Armstrong can stride up and down in that garden of his, reciting poetry and speeches, or talking to that yaller cat of his as if it was a human, he doesn't care much how the world wags on. He never had much git-up-and-git. His father was a hustler, but the family didn't take after him. They all favoured the mother's people—sorter shiftless and dreamy. 'Tain't the way to git on in this world."

No, good and worthy Mrs. Campbell. It was not the way to get on in your world; but there are other worlds where getting on is estimated by different standards, and Abel Armstrong lived in one of these—a world far beyond the ken of the thrifty Stillwater farmers and fishers. Something of this I had sensed, even before I saw him; and that night in his garden, under a sky of smoky red, blossoming into stars above the harbour, I found a friend whose personality and philosophy were to calm and harmonize and enrich my whole existence. This sketch is my grateful tribute to one of the rarest and finest souls God ever clothed with clay.

He was a tall man, somewhat ungainly of figure and homely of face. But his large, deep eyes of velvety nut-brown were very beautiful and marvellously bright and clear for a man of his age. He wore a little pointed, well-cared-for beard, innocent of gray; but his hair was grizzled, and altogether he had the appearance of a man who had passed through many sorrows which had marked his body as well as his soul. Looking at him, I doubted Mrs. Campbell's conclusion that he had not "minded" giving up college. This man had given up much and felt it deeply; but he had outlived the pain and the blessing of sacrifice had come to him. His voice was very melodious and beautiful, and the brown hand he held out to me was peculiarly long and shapely and flexible.

We went out to the garden in the scented moist air of a maritime spring evening. Behind the garden was a cloudy pine wood; the house closed it in on the left, while in front and on the right a row of tall Lombardy poplars stood out in stately purple silhouette against the sunset sky.

"Always liked Lombardies," said Abel, waving a long arm at them. "They are the trees of princesses. When I was a boy they were fashionable. Anyone who had any pretensions to gentility had a row of Lombardies at the foot of his lawn or up his lane, or at any rate one on either side of his front door. They're out of fashion now. Folks complain they die at the top and get ragged-looking. So they do—so they do, if you don't risk your neck every spring climbing up a light ladder to trim them out as I do. My neck isn't worth much to anyone, which, I suppose, is why I've never broken it; and *my* Lombardies never look out-at-elbows. My mother was especially fond of them. She liked their dignity and their stand-offishness. *They* don't hobnob with every Tom, Dick and Harry. If it's pines for company, master, it's Lombardies for society."

We stepped from the front doorstone into the garden. There was another entrance—a sagging gate flanked by two branching white lilacs. From it a little dappled path led to a huge apple-tree in the centre, a great swelling cone of rosy blossom with a mossy circular seat around its trunk. But Abel's favourite seat, so he told me, was lower down the slope, under a little trellis overhung with the delicate emerald of young hop-vines. He led me to it and pointed proudly to the fine view of the harbour visible from it. The early sunset glow of rose and flame had faded out of the sky; the water was silvery and mirror-like; dim sails drifted along by the darkening shore. A bell was ringing in a small Catholic chapel across the harbour. Mellowly and dreamily sweet the chime floated through the dusk, blent with the moan of the sea. The great revolving light at the channel trembled and flashed against the opal sky, and far out, beyond the golden sand-dunes of the bar, was the crinkled gray ribbon of a passing steamer's smoke.

"There, isn't that view worth looking at?" said old Abel, with a loving, proprietary pride. "You don't have to pay anything for it either. All that sea and sky free—'without money and without price.' Let's sit down here in the hop-vine arbour, master. There'll be a moonrise presently. I'm never tired of finding out what a moonrise sheen can be like over that sea. There's a surprise in it every time. Now, master, you're getting your mouth in the proper shape to talk business—but don't you do it. Nobody should talk business when he's expecting a moonrise. Not that I like talking business at any time."

"Unfortunately it has to be talked of sometimes, Mr. Armstrong," I said.

"Yes, it seems to be a necessary evil, master," he acknowledged. "But I know what business you've come upon, and we can settle it in five minutes after the moon's well up. I'll just agree to everything you and the other two trustees want. Lord knows why they ever put *me* on the school board. Maybe it's because I'm so ornamental. They wanted one good-looking man, I reckon."

His low chuckle, so full of mirth and so free from malice, was infectious. I laughed also, as I sat down in the hop-vine arbour.

"Now, you needn't talk if you don't want to," he said. "And I won't. We'll just sit here, sociable-like, and if we think of anything worth while to say we'll say it. Otherwise, not. If you can sit in silence with a person for half an hour and feel comfortable, you and that person can be friends. If you can't, friends you'll never be, and you needn't waste time in trying."

Abel and I passed successfully the test of silence that evening in the hop-vine arbour. I was strangely content to sit and think— something I had not cared to do lately. A peace, long unknown to my stormy soul, seemed hovering near it. The garden was steeped in it; old Abel's personality radiated it. I looked about me and wondered whence came the charm of that tangled, unworldly spot.

"Nice and far from the marketplace, isn't it?" asked Abel suddenly, as if he had heard my unasked question. "No buying and selling and getting gain here. Nothing was ever sold out of *this* garden. Tamzine has her vegetable plot over yonder, but what we don't eat we give away. Geordie Marr down the harbour has a big garden like this and he sells heaps of flowers and fruit and vegetables to the hotel folks. He thinks I'm an awful fool because

I won't do the same. Well, he gets money out of his garden and I get happiness out of mine. That's the difference. S'posing I could make more money—what then? I'd only be taking it from people that needed it more. There's enough for Tamzine and me. As for Geordie Marr, there isn't a more unhappy creature on God's earth—he's always stewing in a broth of trouble, poor man. O' course, he brews up most of it for himself, but I reckon that doesn't make it any easier to bear. Ever sit in a hop-vine arbour before, master?"

I was to grow used to Abel's abrupt change of subject. I answered that I never had.

"Great place for dreaming," said Abel complacently. "Being young, no doubt, you dream a-plenty."

I answered hotly and bitterly that I had done with dreams.

"No, you haven't," said Abel meditatively. "You may *think* you have. What then? First thing you know you'll be dreaming again—thank the Lord for it. I ain't going to ask you what's soured you on dreaming just now. After awhile you'll begin again, especially if you come to this garden as much as I hope you will. It's chockful of dreams—*any* kind of dreams. You take your choice. Now, *I* favour dreams of adventures, if you'll believe it. I'm sixty-one and I never do anything rasher than go out cod-fishing on a fine day, but I still lust after adventures. Then I dream I'm an awful fellow—blood-thirsty."

I burst out laughing. Perhaps laughter was somewhat rare in that old garden. Tamzine, who was weeding at the far end, lifted her head in a startled fashion and walked past us into the house. She did not look at us or speak to us. She was reputed to be abnormally shy. She was very stout and wore a dress of bright red-and-white striped material. Her face was round and blank, but her reddish hair was abundant and beautiful. A huge, orange-coloured cat was at her heels; as she passed us he bounded over to the arbour and sprang up on Abel's knee. He was a gorgeous brute, with vivid green eyes, and immense white double paws.

"Captain Kidd, Mr. Woodley." He introduced us as seriously as if the cat had been a human being. Neither Captain Kidd nor I responded very enthusiastically.

"You don't like cats, I reckon, master," said Abel, stroking the Captain's velvet back. "I don't blame you. I was never fond of them myself until I found the Captain. I saved his life and when you've saved a creature's life you're bound to love it. It's next thing to giving it life. There are some terrible thoughtless people in the world, master. Some of those city folks who have summer homes down the harbour are so thoughtless that they're cruel. It's the worst kind of cruelty, I think—the thoughtless kind. You can't cope with it. They keep cats there in the summer and feed them and pet them and doll them up with ribbons and collars; and then in the fall they go off and leave them to starve or freeze. It makes my blood boil, master.

"One day last winter I found a poor old mother cat dead on the shore, lying against the skin and bone bodies of her three little kittens. She had died trying to shelter them. She had her poor stiff claws around them. Master, I cried. Then I swore. Then I carried those poor little kittens home and fed 'em up and found good homes for them. I know the woman who left the cat. When she comes back this summer I'm going to go down and tell her my opinion of her. It'll be rank meddling, but, lord, how I love meddling in a good cause."

"Was Captain Kidd one of the forsaken?" I asked.

"Yes. I found him one bitter cold day in winter caught in the branches of a tree by his darn-fool ribbon collar. He was almost starving. Lord, if you could have seen his eyes! He was nothing but a kitten, and he'd got his living somehow since he'd been left till he got hung up. When I loosed him he gave my hand a pitiful swipe with his little red tongue. He wasn't the prosperous freebooter you behold now. He was meek as Moses. That was nine years ago. His life has been long in the land for a cat. He's a good old pal, the Captain is."

"I should have expected you to have a dog," I said.

Abel shook his head.

"I had a dog once. I cared so much for him that when he died I couldn't bear the thought of ever getting another in his place. He was a *friend*—you understand? The Captain's only a pal. I'm fond of the Captain—all the fonder because of the spice of deviltry there is in all cats. But I *loved* my dog. There isn't any devil in a good dog. That's why they're more lovable than cats—but I'm darned if they're as interesting."

I laughed as I rose regretfully.

"Must you go, master? And we haven't talked any business after all. I reckon it's that stove matter you've come about. It's like those two fool trustees to start up a stove sputter in spring. It's a wonder they didn't leave it till dog-days and begin then."

"They merely wished me to ask you if you approved of putting in a new stove."

"Tell them to put in a new stove—any kind of a new stove—and be hanged to them," rejoined Abel. "As for you, master, you're welcome to this garden any time. If you're tired or lonely, or too ambitious or angry, come here and sit awhile, master. Do you think any man could keep mad if he sat and looked into the heart of a pansy for ten minutes? When you feel like talking, I'll talk, and when you feel like thinking, I'll let you. I'm a great hand to leave folks alone."

"I think I'll come often," I said, "perhaps too often."

"Not likely, master—not likely—not after we've watched a moon-rise contentedly together. It's as good a test of compatibility as any I know. You're young and I'm old, but our souls are about the same age, I reckon, and we'll find lots to say to each other. Are you going straight home from here?"

"Yes."

"Then I'm going to bother you to stop for a moment at Mary Bascom's and give her a bouquet of my white lilacs. She loves 'em and I'm not going to wait till she's dead to send her flowers."

"She's very ill just now, isn't she?"

"She's got the Bascom consumption. That means she may die in a month, like her brother, or linger on for twenty years, like her father. But long or short, white lilac in spring is sweet, and I'm sending her a fresh bunch every day while it lasts. It's a rare night, master. I envy you your walk home in the moonlight along that shore."

"Better come part of the way with me," I suggested.

"No." Abel glanced at the house. "Tamzine never likes to be alone o' nights. So I take my moonlight walks in the garden. The moon's a great friend of mine, master. I've loved her ever since I can remember. When I was a little lad of eight I fell asleep in the garden one evening and wasn't missed. I woke up alone in the night and I was most scared to death, master. Lord, what shadows and queer noises there were! I darsn't move. I just sat there quaking, poor small mite. Then all at once I saw the moon looking down at me through the pine boughs, just like an old friend. I was comforted right off. Got up and walked to the house as brave as a lion, looking at her. Good-night, master. Tell Mary the lilacs 'll last another week yet."

From that night Abel and I were cronies. We walked and talked and kept silence and fished cod together. Stillwater people thought it very strange that I should prefer his society to that of the young fellows of my own age. Mrs. Campbell was quite worried over it, and opined that there had always been something queer about me. "Birds of a feather," she quoted darkly to her husband.

I loved that old garden by the harbour shore. Even Abel himself, I think, could hardly have felt a deeper affection for it. When its gate closed behind me it shut out the world and my corroding memories and discontents. In its peace my soul emptied itself of the bitterness which had been filling and spoiling it, and grew normal and healthy again, aided thereto by Abel's wise words. He never preached, but he radiated courage and endurance and a frank acceptance of the hard things of life, as well as a cordial welcome of its pleasant things. He was the *sanest* soul I ever met. He neither minimized ill nor exaggerated good, but he held that we should never be controlled by either. Pain should not depress us unduly, nor pleasure lure us into forgetfulness and sloth. All unknowingly he made me realize that I had been a bit of a coward and a shirker. I began to understand that my personal woes were not the most important things in the universe, even to myself. In short, Abel taught me to laugh again; and when a man can laugh wholesomely things are not going too badly with him.

That old garden was always such a cheery place. Even when the east wind sang in minor and the waves on the gray shore were sad, hints of sunshine seemed to be lurking all about it. Perhaps this was because there were so many yellow flowers in it. Tamzine liked yellow flowers. Captain Kidd, too, always paraded it in panoply of gold. He was so large and effulgent that one hardly missed the sun. Considering his presence I wondered that the garden was always so full of singing birds. But the Captain never meddled with them. Probably he understood that his master would not have tolerated it for a moment.

So there was always a song or a chirp somewhere. Overhead flew the gulls and the cranes. The wind in the pines always made a glad salutation. Abel and I paced the walks, followed by Captain Kidd, and held high converse on matters beyond the ken of cat or king.

"I like to ponder on all problems, though I can never solve them," Abel used to say. "My father held that we should never talk of things we couldn't understand. But, lord, master, if we didn't the subjects for conversation would be mighty few. I reckon the gods laugh many a time to hear us, but what matter? So long as we remember that we're only men, and don't take to fancying ourselves gods, really knowing good and evil, I reckon our discussions won't do us or anyone much harm. So we'll have another whack at the origin of evil this evening, master."

Tamzine forgot to be shy with me at last, and gave me a broad smile of welcome every time I came. But she rarely spoke to me. She spent all her spare time weeding the garden, which she loved as well as Abel did. She was addicted to bright colours and always wore wrappers of very gorgeous print. She worshipped Abel and his word was a law unto her.

"I am very thankful Tamzine is so well," said Abel one evening as we watched the sunset. The day had begun sombrely in gray cloud and mist, but it ended in a pomp of scarlet and gold. "There was a time when she wasn't, master—you've heard? But for years now she has been quite able to look after herself. And so, if I fare forth on the last great adventure some of these days Tamzine will not be left helpless."

"She is ten years older than you. It is likely she will go before you," I said.

Abel shook his head and stroked his smart beard. I always suspected that beard of being Abel's last surviving vanity. It was always so carefully groomed, while I had no evidence that he ever combed his grizzled mop of hair.

"No, Tamzine will outlive me. She's got the Armstrong heart. I have the Marwood heart—my mother was a Marwood. We don't live to be old, and we go quick and easy. I'm glad of it. I don't think I'm a coward, master, but the thought of a lingering death gives me a queer sick feeling of horror. There, I'm not going to say any more about it. I just mentioned it so that some day when you hear that old Abel Armstrong has been found dead, you won't feel sorry. You'll remember I wanted it that way. Not that I'm tired of life either. It's very pleasant, what with my garden and Captain Kidd and the harbour out there. But it's a trifle monotonous at times and death will be something of a change, master. I'm real curious about it."

"I hate the thought of death," I said gloomily.

"Oh, you're young. The young always do. Death grows friendlier as we grow older. Not that one of us really wants to die, though, master. Tennyson spoke truth when he said that. There's old Mrs. Warner at the Channel Head. She's had heaps of trouble all her life, poor soul, and she's lost almost everyone she cared about. She's always saying that she'll be glad when her time comes, and she doesn't want to live any longer in this vale of tears. But when she takes a sick spell, lord, what a fuss she makes, master! Doctors from town and a trained nurse and enough medicine to kill a dog! Life may be a vale of tears, all right, master, but there are some folks who enjoy weeping, I reckon."

Summer passed through the garden with her procession of roses and lilies and hollyhocks and golden glow. The golden glow was particularly fine that year. There was a great bank of it at the lower end of the garden, like a huge billow of sunshine. Tamzine revelled in it, but Abel liked more subtly-tinted flowers. There was a certain dark wine-hued hollyhock which was a favourite with him. He would sit for hours looking steadfastly into one of its shallow satin cups. I found him so one afternoon in the hop-vine arbour.

"This colour always has a soothing effect on me," he explained. "Yellow excites me too much—makes me restless—makes me want to sail 'beyond the bourne of sunset.' I looked at that surge of golden glow down there to-day till I got all worked up and thought my life had been an awful failure. I found a dead butterfly and had a little funeral—buried it in the fern corner. And I thought I hadn't been any more use in the world than that poor little butterfly. Oh, I was woeful, master. Then I got me this hollyhock and sat down here to look at it alone. When a man's alone, master, he's most with God—or with the devil. The devil rampaged around me all the time I was looking at that golden glow; but God spoke to me through the hollyhock. And it seemed to me that a man who's as happy as I am and has got such a garden has made a real success of living."

"I hope I'll be able to make as much of a success," I said sincerely.

"I want you to make a different kind of success, though, master," said Abel, shaking his head. "I want you to *do* things—the things I'd have tried to do if I'd had the chance. It's in you to do them—if you set your teeth and go ahead."

"I believe I *can* set my teeth and go ahead now, thanks to you, Mr. Armstrong," I said. "I was heading straight for failure when I came here last spring; but you've changed my course."

"Given you a sort of compass to steer by, haven't I?" queried Abel with a smile. "I ain't too modest to take some credit for it. I saw I could do *you* some good. But my garden has done more than I did, if you'll believe it. It's wonderful what a garden can do for a man when he lets it have its way. Come, sit down here and bask, master. The sunshine may be gone to-morrow. Let's just sit and think."

We sat and thought for a long while. Presently Abel said abruptly:

"You don't see the folks I see in this garden, master. You don't see anybody but me and old Tamzine and Captain Kidd. I see all who used to be here long ago. It was a lively place then. There were plenty of us and we were as gay a set of youngsters as you'd find anywhere. We tossed laughter backwards and forwards here like a ball. And now old Tamzine and older Abel are all that are left."

He was silent a moment, looking at the phantoms of memory that paced invisibly to me on the dappled walks and peeped merrily through the swinging boughs. Then he went on:

"Of all the folks I see here there are two that are more vivid and real than all the rest, master. One is my sister Alice. She died thirty years ago. She was very beautiful. You'd hardly believe that to look at Tamzine and me, would you? But it is true. We always called her Queen Alice—she was so stately and handsome. She had brown eyes and red gold hair, just the colour of that nasturtium there. She was father's favourite. The night she was born they didn't think my mother would live. Father walked this garden all night. And just under that old apple-tree he knelt at sunrise and thanked God when they came to tell him that all was well.

"Alice was always a creature of joy. This old garden rang with her laughter in those years. She seldom walked—she ran or danced. She only lived twenty years, but nineteen of them were so happy I've never pitied her over much. She had everything that makes life worth living—laughter and love, and at the last sorrow. James Milburn was her lover. It's thirty-one years since his ship sailed out of that harbour and Alice waved him good-bye from this garden. He never came back. His ship was never heard of again.

"When Alice gave up hope that it would be, she died of a broken heart. They say there's no such thing; but nothing else ailed Alice. She stood at yonder gate day after day and watched the harbour; and when at last she gave up hope life went with it. I remember the day: she had watched until sunset. Then she turned away from the gate. All the unrest and despair had gone out of her eyes. There was a terrible peace in them—the peace of the dead. 'He will never come back now, Abel,' she said to me.

"In less than a week she was dead. The others mourned her, but I didn't, master. She had sounded the deeps of living and there was nothing else to linger through the years for. *My* grief had spent itself earlier, when I walked this garden in agony because I could not help her. But often, on these long warm summer afternoons, I seem to hear Alice's laughter all over this garden; though she's been dead so long."

He lapsed into a reverie which I did not disturb, and it was not until another day that I learned of the other memory that he cherished. He reverted to it suddenly as we sat again in the hop-vine arbour, looking at the glimmering radiance of the September sea.

"Master, how many of us are sitting here?"

"Two in the flesh. How many in the spirit I know not," I answered, humouring his mood.

"There is one—the other of the two I spoke of the day I told you about Alice. It's harder for me to speak of this one."

"Don't speak of it if it hurts you," I said.

"But I want to. It's a whim of mine. Do you know why I told you of Alice and why I'm going to tell you of Mercedes? It's because I want someone to remember them and think of them sometimes after I'm gone. I can't bear that their names should be utterly forgotten by all living souls.

"My older brother, Alec, was a sailor, and on his last voyage to the West Indies he married and brought home a Spanish girl. My father and mother didn't like the match. Mercedes was a foreigner and a Catholic, and differed from us in every way. But I never blamed Alec after I saw her. It wasn't that she was so very pretty. She was slight and dark and ivory-coloured. But she was very graceful, and there was a charm about her, master—a mighty and potent charm. The women couldn't understand it. They wondered at Alec's infatuation for her. I never did. I—I loved her, too, master, before I had known her a day. Nobody ever knew it. Mercedes never dreamed of it. But it's lasted me all my life. I never wanted to think of any other woman. She spoiled a man for any other kind of woman—that little pale, dark-eyed Spanish girl. To love her was like drinking some rare sparkling wine. You'd never again have any taste for a commoner draught.

"I think she was very happy the year she spent here. Our thrifty women-folk in Stillwater jeered at her because she wasn't what they called capable. They said she couldn't do anything. But she could do one thing well—she could love. She worshipped Alec. I used to hate him for it. Oh, my heart has been very full of black thoughts in its time, master. But neither Alec nor Mercedes ever knew. And I'm thankful now that they were so happy. Alec made this arbour for Mercedes—at least he made the trellis, and she planted the vines.

"She used to sit here most of the time in summer. I suppose that's why I like to sit here. Her eyes would be dreamy and far-away until Alec would flash his welcome. How that used to torture me! But now I like to remember it. And her pretty soft foreign voice and little white hands. She died after she had lived here a year. They buried her and her baby in the graveyard of that little chapel over the harbour where the bell rings every evening. She used to like sitting here and listening to it. Alec lived a long while after, but he never married again. He's gone now, and nobody remembers Mercedes but me."

Abel lapsed into a reverie—a tryst with the past which I would not disturb. I thought he did not notice my departure, but as I opened the gate he stood up and waved his hand.

Three days later I went again to the old garden by the harbour shore. There was a red light on a distant sail. In the far west a sunset city was built around a great deep harbour of twilight. Palaces were there and bannered towers of crimson and gold. The air was full of music; there was one music of the wind and another of the waves, and still another of the distant bell from the chapel near which Mercedes slept. The garden was full of ripe odours and warm colours. The Lombardies around it were tall and sombre like the priestly forms of some mystic band. Abel was sitting in the hop-vine arbour; beside him Captain Kidd slept. I thought Abel was asleep, too; his head leaned against the trellis and his eyes were shut.

But when I reached the arbour I saw that he was not asleep. There was a strange, wise little smile on his lips as if he had attained to the ultimate wisdom and were laughing in no unkindly fashion at our old blind suppositions and perplexities.

Abel had gone on his Great Adventure.

(1917)

The Schoolmaster's Bride

In chapter 7 of *Anne's House of Dreams*, entitled "The Schoolmaster's Bride," Captain Jim Boyd tells newlyweds Anne and Gilbert and their guests the story of Persis Leigh, who had travelled to Prince Edward Island from Scotland six decades earlier as the bride of Captain Jim's dear friend John Selwyn. Pausing occasionally to keep "a passing tryst with visitants Anne and Gilbert could not see" and to "gaz[e] into the glowing fire in a quest of the bygones," Captain Jim puts his talents as an oral storyteller to good use, engaging his listeners with questions and asides as he goes. Montgomery's process of writing this story proved to be more complicated than Captain Jim's oral delivery of it, however. According to her journals, she had outlined the plot of the story shortly before the death of her maternal grandmother in March 1911 but had only been able to resume work on it in late 1915. She ended up publishing this version of the story in *Everywoman's World*, a Toronto periodical, in July 1917, just a month before the release of *Anne's House of Dreams*; the issue in question also contained an instalment of her celebrity memoir, "The Alpine Path: The Story of My Career."

I HAVE BEEN THINKING TO-NIGHT OF THE SCHOOLMAS- ter's bride. A man must die to forget her, or the schoolmaster either, for that matter. They were the two people who made the deepest impression on my life. Now, in my late evening, I think of them a great deal, recalling for my own delight their words and looks and loveliness. They died some twenty years ago, nei- ther of them living to be very old, which I think part of their good fortune. But to me they and their love story are of yesterday; and, in my fireside musings, while my grandchildren romp around me, little recking what is going on in grandfather's old white head, I like to relive that summer in Lindsay when the schoolmaster waited for his bride, and built a home for her.

John Selwyn came to teach school in Lindsay when I was a boy of sixteen. He was an Englishman, but very different from the usual run of derelicts who came from the Old Country to teach school in Prince Edward Island in those days. They had brains, and knew their trade when sober—else it had been, God help the poor scholars! But they were not like John Selwyn. He was young and stalwart and handsome. I remember him as he was when he spent that first fortnight in my father's house; for, as was the custom then, he "boarded around" and my father, Alexander Kennedy, was Secretary of the Board of Trustees. He was very tall, with gray eyes that turned black in excitement, or with deep feeling; women thought his mouth very beautiful, but I liked it for its strength and tenderness and humour. He was full of courage and pity and noble enthusiasms. He was my senior by eight years, but from the first I loved him as David loved Jonathan. My soul was knit to his. I owe more to John Selwyn than to any other human creature. I was too old to be spared to school, save for a few weeks in winter; but I was his pupil, none more earnest and eager. We read and walked and talked together. He quoted poetry for me which I had never heard, Byron and Scott and Wordsworth, Shelley and Keats, those giants of old time; even kindly and tender Mrs. Hemans, for in those days a man was not ashamed to quote Mrs. Hemans. He told me tales of history and romance and chivalry. Never shall I forget the delight with which I listened to those old legends on moonlit evenings by the silver sea. He filled my mind and soul with his own aspirations and ideals, as a full vessel might pour off its fullness into an empty one. He made me; he was more my father than the dour, black-browed, sternly-upright but cold man to whom I owed mere existence. Wherefore I loved him with a varied love, son and comrade and pupil, all in one. But this is not my story; and I only tell of what he did for me and was to me that you, who read of him, may understand what manner of man he was.

One spring evening I met him by the pond, near the little log school-house. It was a clear, apple-green night. There was a milk-white mist on the edge of the sea with a young moon kissing it. The ceaseless voice of many waters came up from the tawny shore. The chill and freakish wind of sunset was shrilling in the old year's dry grasses on the dunes between the pond and the Gulf; there was an emerald mist on the willows of the creek.

And there was a light on John Selwyn's face and a flash in his eyes that I had not seen before.

"I've been up on the hill, looking at the sunset through the beeches, Andrew," he said. "Come into the schoolhouse and sit with me awhile. I have something to tell you."

We went in. The schoolmaster lighted a candle and stirred up the logs in the fireplace. They were still glowing, for the day had been cold and he had stayed, after school let out to study. He gazed so long into the fire, smiling, that I thought he had forgotten what he meant to tell me. But at length he looked into my eyes.

"I've a sweetheart back home, lad," he said.

I had thought he must have, for he had never taken any notice of even our prettiest Lindsay lasses, and they would have been so willing that he should, poor girls!

"Her name is Persis Gray," he went on, "and she is coming out to me. Think of that, Andrew."

I was glad for his sake and said so. For my own, I was not so glad. I was afraid she might come between us.

"Thank you, Andrew. I wanted you to be the first to know. When you see her you will realize what a fortunate man I am."

"She is very beautiful, I suppose?" I said.

"Beautiful?" He laughed. "Don't start me on that subject, Andrew, or you'll think I'm daft. If a diamond and a ruby could be fused into one the result might symbolize her. She would have come out with me if it had not been for her old uncle. He was an invalid and had cared for her when her parents died, and she felt she could not leave him. I thought she was right, though I loved him as little as he loved me. It was a hard parting, and it has been a hard waiting. But her uncle is dead and she is free. Her friends do not want her to come, but she is coming in spite of them. Think of the courage of her—and the trust! God make me worthy of it, Andrew. Some day I hope you'll love a woman as I love Persis. It's the greatest blessing a man can have. Before I met her my life was very hungry. Now it is nourished to the full by her love. And she is coming to me!"

His happiness was so great that I warmed to it and rejoiced with him.

"When do you expect her?" I asked.

"She sails on the *Royal William* late in June, so she should be here by mid-July. God grant her a fair passage. I must set Carpenter Johnson to building me a home for her. Her letter came to-day. I knew before I opened it that it held good news. I saw her a few nights ago."

"You saw her?" I asked stupidly.

He looked at me queerly.

"Ay, lad. I saw her. You don't understand, I've never told you. But I have a gift, lad, a gift—or a curse. Who knows? My poor great-great-grandmother, Mercy Selwyn, must have found it a curse. She had it, and they burned her for a witch because of it, Andrew—burned her on the hill behind the town back home."

"What is the gift?" I asked wonderingly.

"Certain weird seizures come upon me at long intervals," he answered slowly. "The scientists call them trances, I believe, but they understand them as little as the rabble that burned my ancestress. As a child I had them and my poor mother worried greatly over it. As I grew older I ceased to talk of them for I saw that people looked queerly at me, though they could not haul me to the stake because of them. I see things in them, lad—things that are happening—things that will happen. Sometimes they have been a comfort to me—sometimes a horror. I have not had one since I came to Lindsay until four nights ago. I was sitting here, so, gazing at the dying fire. It faded from before my eyes, and in its stead I saw an old room I know well in England. Persis was there, gazing at me with tears in her eyes; but behind the tears I saw a radiance and a joy. The vision passed quickly, but I knew it foretokened good news of my love."

"You dreamed it," I said uncomfortably. Somehow, I did not like to believe in his gift. It seemed to set him apart from common humanity in a rather uncanny fashion. Had I lived two hundred years sooner I daresay I would have been as bitter a persecutor of poor Mercy Selwyn as any.

He smiled.

"No, I did not dream it. But we shall not talk of this again. You will not be so much my friend if you think much of it. No, don't protest, lad. I understand, and I do not blame you. There are times when I scarce feel friendly to myself because of it. Such a power has a bit of divinity in it, whether of a good or an evil divinity, who shall say? And we mortals all shrink from a too close contact with god or devil."

I did not quite understand him, but I willingly let the subject drop.

Soon all the Lindsay people knew that the schoolmaster's bride was coming, and all were glad because they loved him. Every one sympathised with him in the building of the new home which went on apace. He chose a site for it not far from the school-house, within sound of the rhythmic thunder of the sea. The old house, for it is an old house now, is still there, looking seaward through its small windows. But no one has lived in it for many years. The winds blow around it mournfully and the gray rain beats upon it, and the white mists come in from the Gulf to enfold it. And the moonlight falls over it and lights up the old paths where John Selwyn walked and planned, that happy, busy summer.

The sand dunes were not far away, the sea tempests blew over them and the sea spray smote upon them. But a thick spruce grove protected the garden which the schoolmaster made for his bride. The gate of it was between two large fir trees, the hinge on one, the catch on the other.

"This gate will shut out all the world but my friends," he said to me one evening. "How she will love this garden! There shall be a white sisterhood of lilies here by the gate and over yonder we shall have a gayety of poppies, the silken ladies of the garden. My schoolgirls have set out yonder rose-bushes for her, pink for her cheek and white for her brow and red for her lips. I wonder if to-day has been kind to her."

At last the new house was finished, waiting only to be sanctified by love and joy to be a home. One dim, star-lighted twilight he took me over it. It was furnished very plainly. The men and women who loved him had sent many simple, wholesome gifts to the new house for his bride. Even blind and crippled old Aunt

Margaret Kennedy had woven for her a basket of the sweet-scented grass that grows on our sand dunes. There were logs in the big fireplace ready for the lighting.

"We shall sit here," he said, "just she and I, alone with the twilight and the sweetness. But sometimes we shall let a friend come in and share it. You will be our most welcome guest, Andrew."

"Perhaps Mistress Selwyn may not want me," I said, rather churlishly, not knowing then what an added wealth of friendship Persis Gray was to bring into my life.

John Selwyn only laughed. Knowing her as I did not, he needed to waste no words refuting so silly a speech.

It was the first of July when the house was finished. The schoolmaster began to count the days like silver beads on a rosary. We saw him walking alone by the shore and in the beech wood, and said to each other kindly, "She will soon be with him now."

She was to come with mid-July, but she came not. This was not alarming. Vessels were often delayed many days and even weeks beyond their expected time. The time lagged away. The *Royal William* was a week—two weeks—three weeks, overdue. As slowly and subtly and remorselessly as a sea-fog stealing landward fear crept into our hearts, fear that grew deeper and deadlier as the weeks lengthened out. The time came when I could not bear to look into John Selwyn's eyes. They were so terribly like what Mercy Selwyn's must have been at the stake. He said little, even to me. He had taken me into his joy, but he could not take me into his sorrow. My soul was at that time washed empty of every wish and hope and desire save that I might see the *Royal William* sailing up the harbour. He taught school as a man in a dream and then hurried to the shore. One dark, streaming night, when the white waves were ravening on the black strand, they said he walked on the shore until morning. We did not torture him with expressions of sympathy; but everything else tortured him. When he saw a farfoam wreath tossing he thought of a woman's white arm flung for an appealing moment from the wave. The seaweed ribbons seemed like a woman's floating hair. Every heart in Lindsay ached for him. He never went near the house he had made ready for his bride and the weeds grew wild and thick in the garden, where the petals of the last red rose were scattered by a September wind. Summer was over and the schoolmaster's bride had not come— never would come now.

"There is an hour in which a man might be happy all his life could he but find it. But I cannot find it, lad," he said wildly, when I met him one evening in the beech grove overlooking the sea, where he had been wont to walk and dream of her. His looks frightened me. I knew people said he was losing his mind.

"The *Royal William* may come yet," I said stupidly. "Ten years ago the *Georgina* was a month overdue, but she came at last. The *Royal William* is only seven weeks overdue."

"Oh, I shall see Persis again," he said, with a strange calm I liked less than his wildness. "I have only to wait very, very patiently and I shall see her coming to me from yonder shore and the garland gold of her hair mirrored in that still pond."

Suddenly he gripped my arm so savagely that I flinched.

"Boy, boy, I cannot bear it!" he whispered hoarsely. "I picture a hundred deaths for her. *The ship may have caught fire.* I shall go mad soon. Pray that the agony I feel may never be your portion."

He rushed away from me shoreward and I did not follow him. I went home and wept, though I counted myself a man.

A great tempest ravaged the Gulf for the next three days; on the evening after it abated I went to the shore. It was clean-washed after the storm and not a wind stirred, but the surf was dashing on the sand in a splendid silver turmoil. The schoolmaster was there, gazing eastward across the tossing water; he and it were the only restless things in all that great stillness and peace. But presently he gave over his moody striding and leaned with folded arms against a great upstanding red rock worn smooth by long buffeting of wind and wave.

The sunken sun had sucked all the rosy light out of the great blue bowl of the sky and twilight came down over the white foam before us. Behind us people were singing in a harvest field.

I spoke to the schoolmaster, but he did not answer. I looked fearfully into his gaunt face. It was very white and set, and his great hollow eyes were gazing past me unseeingly. I knew not what they looked at, but an icy feeling crept over me and I drew a little away from my friend.

"John! John Selwyn!" I cried imploringly. Then, like a frightened child, "Waken! Waken!"

Slowly the fixed stare faded out of his eyes. Slowly he turned his head and looked at me. I have never seen anything so transfigured and glorified as John Selwyn's face at that moment.

"All is well, lad," he said. "Rejoice with me. I have seen the *Royal William* coming around East Point. She will be here by dawn. To-morrow night I shall sit with my bride by my own hearth fire."

Did he see it? God knows. I doubted. I was only a boy and knew not what marvels great love and great pain may compass. But I know that in the first faint gray dawn of the next day I wakened to find my father standing by my bed; and on the cheeks of that stern man were tears.

"Rise, Andrew," he said. "Malcolm MacNaughton has brought word that the *Royal William* is outside the harbour."

We lived some distance from the harbour and, although I lost no time, almost every soul in Lindsay was there before me, for the tidings had spread rapidly. The schoolmaster was there, standing apart from us all, his hat drawn low over his face. He had, as I learned later, watched there all night, in a glad confidence. No one spoke to him; he had known his own bitterness and we might not intermeddle in his joy. Many women were weeping and the eyes of many men were wet. There was little talking. It seemed as though the sea had given up its dead.

It was a lovely dawn. The sky in the east was all rosy-silver and the sea beneath it dancing ripples. The grass was green and dew-wet on the cliffs. Birds do not often sing in September but one sang that morning in the wind-beaten firs near the old wharf. Over the harbour bar hung a milky mist; then the rising sun rent it apart and made a rainbow of it. And as it did so the *Royal William* came through it, sailing swiftly before a fair wind over a glistening pathway through the transparent air. We went mad for a little while, at the sight, and cheered wildly. Then again we kept silence as the gray, battered ship came onward up the channel and at last furled her sails in the long desired haven.

Two women came ashore, the captain's sonsy wife and one other, a tall girl wrapped in a dark cloak. We had but a brief glimpse of her ere she was folded in John Selwyn's arms and led away. I remember that we were all a little disappointed. We had looked for, I know not what, radiant beauty; but this girl, with her hair all closely hidden in her dark hood, was pale and worn. Only her eyes were very wonderful as for one instant they swept over the waiting crowd. They were sea-blue and star-like—the eyes of a woman a man might die for. They haunted my fancy as I went home, leaving the others to crowd around the crew of the *Royal William*, and listen to their tale of the fearful storms and accidents which had all but brought her voyage to a disastrous end.

That night, in James MacNaughton's house, John Selwyn and Persis Gray were married at early candle-lighting, and every man, woman, and child in Lindsay was there to see it. Some had been saying, through the day, that the schoolmaster's bride was not very bonny after all; but they never said it again. Flushed with her happiness, she was a sight to make an old man young. She wore a wonderful dress of rose brocade such as we had never seen in Lindsay, nor ever saw again, for Mistress Selwyn did not wear it after her marriage, going quietly clad in home-spuns like our own matrons. But that night she looked the queen, with a foam of laces on her full bosom and her heavy coils of shining, pale-gold hair pinned closely over her head. All the pain and joy of past generations had bequeathed to her a legacy of love and loyalty, and it shone in those wonderful eyes of hers and lighted her face like a rosy lamp shining through alabaster. The hardships and dangers of her long, lonely voyage were forgotten; only perfect trust and exquisite happiness breathed from her as she clasped her bridegroom's hand and took her vows upon her.

They walked to their home in the September moonlight, and Persis Selwyn's hand kindled the fire on their hearth-stone. We left them sitting before it, hand in hand, even as the schoolmaster had foreseen.

(1917)

Our Neighbors at the Tansy Patch

This next story appeared in the August 1918 issue of *Canadian Home Journal* (Toronto), following an announcement in the preceding issue:

From the time that little "Anne of Green Gables" came skipping into the hearts of Canadian readers, L.M. Montgomery's stories have been eagerly sought. Something new from her pen is a treat, indeed, and her story, "Our Neighbors at the Tansy Patch," . . . will be no exception. After you have read this exceedingly delightful sketch of rural country life you will feel you know the Conways—Timothy Benjamin, better known as T.B., Joe, Aunt Lily, but most of all Granny—"everyone [sic] of them," as Salome expressed it, "crazier than the others." Crazy they may have been, but very human and interesting when pictured by L.M. Montgomery.

While Montgomery's best-known books could arguably also be called "delightful sketch[es] of rural country life," in this story there's a fascinating reversal, in that the dysfunctional country folks are viewed with equal parts distance and disdain by the city-dwelling narrator. And while most of the story exists in this form only, attentive readers will recognize anecdotes and speeches from several of Montgomery's subsequent books, including *Rainbow Valley*, *Rilla of Ingleside*, *Emily of New Moon* (in which the Tansy Patch figures as the home of Teddy Kent), *Emily Climbs*, and *The Blue Castle*, as well as some episodes reworked for chapter 12 of *Magic for Marigold*.

Montgomery's accompanying author byline includes a reference to a story entitled "The Cats of the Tansy Patch," suggesting that she had recently published an earlier story about this place or these characters (possibly set during the Bruce family's first summer in this location), but that story has not yet been located.

PART I.

WHEN, DURING OUR SECOND SUMMER AT THE TANSY Patch, the whiskers of one of our cats were cut off mysteriously we always blamed a small boy pertaining to a family living near us, behind a thick spruce grove. Whether we were right or wrong in this conclusion I cannot say. None of us, not even our redoubtable Salome, cared to accuse any member of this family openly. We had too well-founded dread of "Granny's" tongue. So nothing was ever said about "Doc's" whiskers, and our amiable relations with our neighbors remained undisturbed.

They were certainly a curious assortment. Salome always referred to them as "Them lunatics behind the bush," and asserted vehemently that "everyone of them is crazier than the others, ma'am." She thought it quite dreadful that Dick and I should allow the children to consort with them so freely; but the children liked them, and we ourselves found an endless source of amusement in their peculiarities. They were even better fun than our cats, we thought.

The head of the house was a handsome, middle-aged man whom we seldom saw and with whom, save on one memorable occasion, we never had any conversation. His legal name appeared to be William Conway. His offspring called him "Paw," Aunt Lily always referred to him pathetically as "My poor brother," and Granny called him "My worthless skinamulinx of a son-in-law." What his wife had called him I wot not. She had died, it appears, eight years previously, when Millicent Mary Selina Munn Cook Conway had been born. If she resembled her mother it is not probable that her bereaved spouse sorrowed as one without hope.

When Timothy Benjamin, the oldest son—better known, it may be said as T.B.—paid us a long, friendly, first call, Salome had asked him bluntly, "What does your father do for a living?"

"Nawthing, mostly," was T.B.'s frank and laconic response.

"Then how do you get along?" demanded Salome.

"My old beast of a granny has a little money. We live on that," said T.B. easily. "Folks round here call paw lazy, but he says no, he's just contented."

"Does he never work?"

"Nope. He fiddles and fishes. And he hunts for buried treasure."

"Buried treasure?"

"Yip—down on them sand-hills 'cross from the hotel. He says Captain Kidd buried millions there. He keeps a-digging for it, paw does. Says when he finds it we'll all be rich."

"Your father'd better be digging in his garden," said Salome, severely. "I *never* saw such a scandal of weeds."

"That's what Granny says," retorted T.B.

Salome was squelched for the time being. The thought that she and Granny could be of the same opinion about anything enraged her into silence.

Of Mr. Conway's prowess as fisherman and treasure-seeker I know nothing, but I can testify to his ability as a violinist. When he fiddled, on his tumble-down "back stoop," on the summer evenings, the music that drifted over to the Tansy Patch, through the arches of the spruce wood, was enchanting. Even Salome, who prided herself on her ear for music, admitted that.

"It's angelic, ma'am, that's what it is," she said with solemn reluctance. "And to think that lazy good-for-nothing could make it! What could Providence have been thinking of, ma'am? My good, hard-working brother John tried all his life to learn to play well on the fiddle and he never could. And this Bill Conway can do it without trying. Why, he can almost make me dance, ma'am."

That would have been a miracle, indeed! But Dick and I often did dance, on our own stoop, in time to the witching lilts of the invisible musician beyond the spruces.

In appearance Mr. Conway looked like a poet run to seed. He had a shock of wavy, dark auburn hair, a drooping moustache and a goatee, and brilliant brown eyes. He was shy or unsociable, we did not know which. At all events, he never came near us. "Jest too lazy to talk, that's all," T.B. assured us. "Paw hasn't nothin' again' yous."

The first member of the family to call on us—and the only one who ever paid us a formal call—was Aunt Lily—Miss Lilian Alethea Conway, according to the limp, broken-cornered card she left behind. The formality of her call consisted in her leaving this card. For the rest, she stayed the afternoon, took supper with us, and then remained for the evening.

"I am not, my dear Mrs. Bruce, a soulless society woman," was her somewhat unnecessary introductory remark. She swam up the steps—she really had a very graceful walk—and subsided limply into a rocker. She wore a rumpled dress of pale blue muslin with a complicated adornment of black velvet ribbon, and her long, thin arms were encased in cream lace gloves—remarkably nice gloves, of their kind, at that. Some of Granny's money must have gone into those gloves. She had a pale, freckled face and reddish hair. Yet she was not absolutely lacking in beauty. Later on I saw her once in the moonlight and was surprised by her good looks. Her features were quite classical and if she had known how to do anything with her hair she would have been a pretty woman.

I asked her to come into the house, but she assured me she preferred to remain outside.

"I love to sit and watch the golden bees plundering the sweets of the clover," she said dreamily, clasping her lace-covered hands. Neither bees nor clover were noticeable about the Tansy Patch, but that did not worry Aunt Lily. She rolled her large, blue eyes upon me and added,

"I adore the country, Mrs. Bruce. The city is so artificial. Don't you truly think the city is so artificial? There can be no real interchange of soul in the city. Here, in the beautiful country, under God's blue sky, human beings can be their real and highest selves. I am sure you agree with me, Mrs. Bruce."

I did, or pretended to; Salome and I knitted the afternoon away while Aunt Lily swayed idly and unceasingly in her rocker, and talked quite as idly and unceasingly. She told us all there was to be told about her family and herself. She kept a diary, it appeared.

"I must have some place to pour out my soul in, Mrs. Bruce," she said pathetically. "Some day, if you wish, I will show you my journal. It is a self-revelation. And yet I cannot write out what burns in my bosom. I envy my niece Dorinda her powers of expression. Dorinda is a poetess, Mrs. Bruce. She experiences the divine afflatus. My poor brother can express the deepest emotions of his soul in music, but I can only wield my halting pen.

Yet my journal is not devoid of interest, Mrs. Bruce, and I should not object to sharing it with a sympathetic friend."

"I should like to see it," I assured her—sincerely enough, for I suspected that journal would be rather good fun.

"I will bring it to you some day then," said Aunt Lily, "and when you read it, remember, oh pray, remember, that it was written by a being with a tired heart. I suffer greatly, Mrs. Bruce, from a tired heart."

I did not know whether this was a physical or an emotional ailment. Salome understood it to be the former and asked quite sympathetically,

"Did you ever try a mustard plaster at the pit of your stomach, Miss?"

"I fear that would not benefit a weary heart, Miss Silversides," sighed Aunt Lily. "Possibly you have never suffered, as I have, from a weary, wounded heart."

"No, thank the Lord, my heart's all right," said Salome, briskly. "My only trouble is rheumatism in the knee j'int. Ever have rheumatism in your knee j'int, Miss?"

No, Aunt Lily's knee joints were all right. In fact, Aunt Lily proved to be a remarkably healthy woman. Her wearied heart evidently found no difficulty in pumping sufficient blood through her body and her appetite, as supper-time showed, was anything but feeble.

"When I can forget what might have been, I am happy," she sighed. "I have had my romance, Mrs. Bruce. Alas, that it should be in the past tense! I once thought I had found my true soul mate, Mrs. Bruce, and I dreamed of happy, real marriage."

"What happened that you didn't get married?" queried Salome, pricking up her ears. Salome is always rather interested in blighted romances, despite her grim exterior.

"A misunderstanding, Miss Silversides—a misunderstanding that severed two fond hearts. He wedded another. Never since that sad day have I met a man who could stir the dead ashes of my heart to tingling life again. But let us not talk of my sorrows, dear friends. Will you tell me how to can peas?"

When Aunt Lily went away I asked her to come again and she assured me that she would.

"I think you will understand me—I have always been misunderstood," she said. Then she trailed her blue draperies down the

hill to the wood, looking, when kindly distance had lent enchant-
ment, quite a graceful, romantic and attractive figure.

"Did you ever hear such a lunatic, ma'am?" demanded Salome.
"Her and her soul mates and her tired hearts! Her hair looks as
if she'd swept it up with a broom and her nails weren't cleaned
and her stockings were scandalous dirty. And yet, for all, there's
something about the creature I like, ma'am."

That was the eventual verdict of our household upon
Aunt Lily. In spite of everything there was a queer charm
about her to which we succumbed. The same thing could
be said of that absurd diary of hers, which she brought over
to us during our second summer. It was as ridiculous, and
sentimental, and lackadaisical as Aunt Lily herself. And yet
there was an odd fragrance about it that lingered in our memories. We could not, somehow, laugh quite as much over it as we
wanted to.

T.B. was also an early and frequent caller. He was thirteen
years old, in our first summer at the Patch. He had thick, fair,
thatch-like hair and keen blue eyes—the only intelligent eyes
in the family. He was, it developed, much addicted to creeping
and crawling things; he always had bugs, toads, frogs or snakes
secreted about his anatomy. The only time he ever had a meal
with us a small green snake slipped from the pocket of his ragged
shirt and glided over the table.

"Do you think he is *human*, ma'am?" Salome asked, with
bated breath, after he was gone.

"He is a born naturalist," said Dick. "He is making a special
study of ants this summer, it appears. Snakes are only a side
issue at present. If he could be educated he would amount to
something."

There did not seem to be much likelihood of this. T.B. himself
had no illusions on the subject.

"There ain't any chance for me—never was and never will be,"
he once told me gloomily.

"Perhaps your grandmother would help you," I suggested.

T.B. grinned.

"Perhaps—when stones bleed," he said scornfully. "I don't
s'pose the old beast has enough money. None of us knows how
much she *has* got—she just doles it out. But she wouldn't give
me any if she had pecks. She hates me. If there's any money left

when she dies—s'posen she *ever* does die—Joe's to get it. He's her baby."

If Joseph—T.B. was the only one who ever called him Joe— was Granny's favorite he was not the favorite of anybody else. However we of the Tansy Patch might differ concerning the other members of the Conway family we all united in cordially detesting Joseph. He was such a sly, smug little wretch—"a born hypocrite, that child is, ma'am," declared Salome solemnly. We had no proof that it was really he who had cut off Doc's whiskers, but there was no doubt that it was Joseph who painted poor Una's legs with stripes of red and green paint one day. Una came home in tears, quickly followed by T.B. and Aunt Lily, the latter in tears also.

"I would rather have lost my right hand than have this happen, dear Mrs. Bruce," she wailed. "Oh, do not cherish it against us. Your friendship has been such a sweet boon to me. And turpentine will take it off—it can't be very dry yet."

"Jest wait till Granny goes to sleep and I'll lambaste Joe within an inch of his life," said T.B.

He did, too; when Granny wakened from her nap she heard the sobbing Joe's tale and shrieked objurgations at T.B. for an hour. T.B. sat on the fence and laughed at her; we could hear him and hear Granny also. Granny's vocal powers had not failed with advancing years, and every word came over distinctly to the Tansy Patch through the clear evening air.

"May you be eaten by pigs," vociferated Granny—and we knew she was brandishing her stick at the graceless T.B. "I'll bite your face off—I'll tear your eyes out—I'll rip your heart out! You blatant beast! You putrid pup!"

"Oh, listen to that awesome woman, ma'am," said Salome, shuddering. "Ain't it a wonder she isn't struck dead?"

But Granny was every inch alive—except that she could not walk, having what Aunt Lily called "paralattics in the hips." She was confined to a chair, generally placed on the back verandah, whence she could command a view of the main road. From this point of vantage she could scream maledictions and shake her long, black stick at any person or objects which incurred her dislike or displeasure.

Granny was of striking appearance. She had snow-white hair and dead-white face, and flashing black eyes. She still possessed all her teeth, but they were discolored and fang-like; and when she drew her lips back and snarled she was certainly a rather wolf-like old dame. She always wore a frilled widow's cap tied tightly under her chin, and was addicted to bare feet.

It was war to the hilt between Granny and Salome from the start. Granny attacked first, without the slightest provocation. Salome had gone through the spruce wood to call the children home to dinner. Perhaps Granny found Salome's expression rather trying. Salome always did look very well satisfied with herself. At least, something about her seemed to grate on Granny's nerves.

"Yah!" she shrieked vindictively, "your grandfather hanged himself in his horsestable. Go home, jail-bird, go home."

Outraged Salome was too much overcome to attempt a reply. She came home almost in tears.

"Ma'am, my grandfathers both died most *respectable* deaths."

"You mustn't mind what Granny says, Salome," I said soothingly.

"Indeed, ma'am, nobody should mind what a lunatic says. But it is hard for a decent woman to have her grandfathers insulted. I do not mind the name she called me, ma'am, but she might respect the dead."

Granny respected nothing on earth. T.B. who, although he hated her, had a certain pride in her, told tales of her repartee. On one occasion a new minister had stopped on the road and accosted Granny over the fence. He was young and callow, and perhaps Granny's eyes disconcerted him, for he certainly worded his question rather inanely.

"Can you tell me, madam, where I am going?" he asked politely.

"How should I know where you are going, gosling?" retorted Granny. Then she had burst into a series of chuckles which had completed his discomfiture. The poor young man drove hastily away, crimson of face—"looking like thirty cents," declared T.B. with a relish.

On another occasion Granny routed an automobile. One, filled with gay hotel guests, had stopped at the gate. Its driver had intended to ask for some water, but Granny did not allow him to utter a word.

"Get out of this with your demon machine," she yelled. She caught up the nearest missile, which happened to be her dinner plate, and hurled it at him. It missed his face by a hair's breadth and landed squarely, grease and all, in a fashionable lady's silken lap. Granny followed this up by a series of fearsome yells and maledictions, of which the mildest were "May ye never have a night without a bad dream," and "May ye always be looking for something and never finding it," and—finally—"May ye all die to-night. I'll pray for it, that I will."

The dismayed driver got his car away as quickly as possible and Granny laughed loud and long.

"My old Granny's the limit," declared T.B.

If Joseph was Granny's favorite, poor Charity was her pet detestation. Charity was the oldest of the family; she was eighteen and a good-hearted, hard-working creature. Almost all the work that was done in that house was done by Charity. Consequently, she had little time for visiting, and her calls on us were few. She was a dark, rather stocky girl, but had her share of the family's good looks. She had dusky red cheeks and a very pretty red mouth. Granny vowed that Charity was "a born fool"; Charity was very far from being that, but she certainly did not possess very much "gumption," as Salome said. She had no taste in dress and went about one summer wearing an old rose gown with a bright scarlet hat.

"Oh, if only something would happen to one of them, ma'am, before they dislocate my eyes," groaned Salome.

One day something did happen. A glad Salome told us of it.

"Charity Conway won't wear that dress again, ma'am. Yesterday when she was going to church she found a nest of five eggs in the field. So she put them in the pocket of her petticoat and when she got to church she forgot all about them and sat down on them and the dress is ruined, ma'am. It is a good thing, but I am sorry for poor Charity, too, for Granny is mad at her and says she won't buy her another dress this summer."

PART II.

If Charity came to see us but seldom, Dorinda made up for it. Dorinda was a constant guest. Dorinda was sixteen and Dorinda wrote poetry—"bushels of it," so said T.B.

The first time Dorinda came she wanted to borrow some mutton tallow.

"I have chapped hands and I find it difficult to write poetry with chapped hands."

"I should think you would, miss," said Salome; but she got out the mutton tallow.

Dorinda bored us to death with her poetry. It really was the most awful trash. One line, however, in a poem which Dorinda addressed to the returned soldiers of the Boer War, always shone like a star in our family memory.

"Canada, like a maiden, welcomes back her sons."

But Salome thought it wasn't quite decent!

"If there was only a wood-pool near here!" sighed Dorinda. "I can write my best only by a wood-pool."

"Why not try the pond?" suggested Salome.

"My Muse," said Dorinda, with dignity, "only inspires me by a wood pool."

I cannot remember the names of all Dorinda's poems. Some of them were, "Lines on a Birch Tree," "Lines to My Northern Birds," "A Romantic Tail," and "Lines Written on a Friend's Tansy Patch."

Dorinda was stout but very good-looking. She had magnificent hair—great masses of silky brown curls. She always dressed it beautifully, too. But, like all mortals, Dorinda was not satisfied.

"I wish I was sylph-like, Mrs. Bruce," she sighed. "A poetess should be sylph-like."

The relations between Dorinda and Aunt Lily were not as cordial as their common addiction to literary pursuits might presuppose. There was some antagonism between them, the cause of which we never knew. But it resulted in T.B. hating Dorinda with an unbrotherly hatred and deriding her poems unmercifully.

One little white blossom of pure affection bloomed in the arid desert of T.B.'s emotional life. He loved his Aunt. She sympathized with his pursuits and, in spite of her lackadaisical ways, was not afraid of his snakes. T.B. would not allow Granny to abuse Aunt Lily.

"How did you stop it?" queried Salome, anxiously.

TWICE UPON A TIME

"The first time she turned her tongue loose on Aunt Lily I went up to her and bit her," said T.B., coolly.

"You ought to bite her oftener," said Salome, vindictively.

"There ain't none of the rest of us worth standing up for," said T.B. "Granny's tough biting."

T.B. figured conspicuously in Aunt Lily's diary. She seemed to centre her maternal affection in him.

"I wish I could educate T.B.," she wrote, "but alas, I am poor. How bitter a thing is grinding poverty! My poor brother is a genius, but he makes no money. And I fear he will never find the treasure he seeketh. Like myself, he is misunderstood and unappreciated. My beloved T.B. lacks many things which should pertain to youth. I patched his best trousers to-day."

Many of T.B.'s speeches and exploits figured in the diary.

"For, perhaps, in spite of all, he may be famous some day," wrote Aunt Lily, "and then this neglected diary, written by a woman whose hopes in life have been blighted, will be of inestimable value to a biographer in search of material. I have noticed that the boyish pranks of great men are of surpassing interest. I could wish that T.B. used less slang. But English undefiled is seldom heard to-day. Alas, for it! I feel that T.B.'s association with the refined family who are now sojourning at the Tansy Patch may be of great help to him."

I don't know that we "helped" T.B. very much, but Salome tried to do him good in a spiritual way. She was much horrified to find that T.B. was a skeptic and prided himself on it. Accordingly, Salome took to lending him books and tracts and bribing him to read them, with doughnuts. One of them was the "Memoir of Susanna B. Morton"—an account of the life and early death of a child of extraordinary piety. Salome used to read it and weep over it Sunday afternoons. T.B. enjoyed the book, but scarcely, I fear, in the way Salome desired.

"Ain't Susanna a holy terror?" he would say to me with a grin. T.B. had a sense of humor and that book tickled it.

Una, too, told him sweetly that she meant to pray for him; but this roused T.B.'s dander instantly.

"You ain't! Don't you dast! I won't be prayed for," he shouted.

"Oh, T.B., aren't you afraid of going to the bad place?" whispered poor Una, quite aghast.

192

"Nix on that"—contemptuously. "I don't believe there's any hell or heaven either. When you die that's the end of you."

"Wouldn't you like to go on living?" asked Dick, who enjoyed drawing T.B. out.

"Nope. There's no fun in it," said the youthful misanthrope. "Heaven's a dull place from all the accounts I've heard of it. I'd like a heaven full of snakes and ants and things, though. There'd be some sense in that kind."

"How are your ants coming on?" I queried.

T.B. was transformed in a moment. He sat up, eager, alert, bright-eyed.

"They're durned int'resting," he exclaimed. "I sat all day yesterday and watched their doings in that nest below the garden. Say, but they're quarrelsome little cusses—some of 'em like to start a fight 'thout any reason, far's I can see. And some of 'em are cowards. They gits so scared they just double theirselves up into a ball and let the other fellow bang 'em round. They won't put up no fight. Some of 'em are lazy and won't work. I've watched 'em shirking. And there was one ant died o' grief 'cause another ant got killed—wouldn't eat—wouldn't work—just died. Tell *you*, I wish humans was as interesting as ants. Well, so long. I must be gitting home to dinner."

Always in the winter, which we spent in our town home, the children kept up a correspondence with T.B. He wrote very interesting letters, too, allowing for eccentricities of grammar and spelling. Aunt Lily wrote me wondrous underlined epistles, full of sentiment, and Dorinda sent us a poem every week—on "Memories of Other Days" or some kindred subject. We often wondered what life must be in the house beyond the spruces in winter, when Granny must perforce be cooped up indoors. Salome shuddered over the thought of it.

It was not until our fourth and last summer at the Tansy Patch that we were ever asked to partake of a meal in the Conway establishment. One day, not long before our final departure, T.B. came over and gravely handed us a formal invitation, in Aunt Lily's handwriting, on a soiled, gilt-edged correspondence card. We were asked to supper the next evening at seven o'clock. Salome got one, too.

"Surely, ma'am, you'll never try to eat a meal in that house!" she exclaimed. "Why, I *have* heard that they've been known to mix up cakes *in the wash-pan*, ma'am. And remember the dog and the soup, ma'am."

"But they threw the soup out," said Una.

"I think Mr. Bruce and I must go," I said. "I do not want to hurt Aunt Lily's feelings. But you can please yourself about going, Salome."

Salome drew a deep breath.

"I'd rather go to supper with the king of the Cannibal islands, ma'am," she said. "But if you are determined to go, I'll go too, and we'll all be poisoned together."

I really believe Salome was curious. She wanted to see what sort of meal "them lunatics" would put up.

We all got a surprise. The Conway supper table was as pretty a one as I have ever sat down to. The linen was spotless. The china and silver old and good—evidently relics of Granny's palmy days. The decorations of ferns and wild flowers were charming, and the awful lamp, with its hideous red globe, which stood on a corner table, cast a very becoming rose-light over everything.

"You see, we can put on style when we want to," said T.B., slyly.

All the family were dressed up for the occasion. "Paw" in a dark suit and white shirt, was handsome and presentable. Aunt Lily for once had her hair done nicely and she and the girls, in their pretty muslins, looked quite charming. Even Granny had on a new black silk and a fresh cap; and, if she could only have held her tongue, might have passed for a decidedly handsome and aristocratic old dame. But that Granny could not do.

"I hope you've got more in your head than you carry on your face," she said when Dick was introduced.

Having said that, however, she behaved herself quite well during supper. The bill of fare presented to us was surprisingly good and—what was still more surprising—quite fashionable. Charity must have studied household magazines to some effect. Everything was so delicious that we could not but enjoy it—despite sundry disconcerting recollections of gossip concerning snakes and wash-pans. We had angel cake that night and, whatever it was mixed up in, it was toothsome. Salome, in particular, was much impressed by the "style" and menu. She never spoke quite so scornfully of them afterwards.

"They may be lunatics, ma'am," she said, as we went home. "But that silver was solid, ma'am, and that cloth was double damask and there was initials on the spoons; and when all's said and done, ma'am, there's *family* behind them whatever they've come to."

"I hope you got your craws full," was Granny's parting salutation.

We all noticed how pretty and chipper Aunt Lily was that night. She was quite bright and animated. The reason therefor was disclosed soon after when Aunt Lily informed us that she was going to be married. She was very well satisfied about it too, in spite of her tired heart and blighted life. We discovered that the bridegroom elect was a common-place farmer living near the hotel.

"He's no beauty," T.B. informed us, "and Granny twits Aunt Lily with it. But Aunt Lily says she'd marry him if he was as ugly as a gorilla because it is his soul she loves. I dunno nawthing about his soul, but he's got the dough and he's going to educate me. Aunt Lily told him she wouldn't have him if he didn't. I'm going to live with 'em, too. Say, won't I be glad to get away from Granny's tongue and Dorinda's poetry? It makes me feel young again."

"How on earth will that woman ever keep a house, ma'am?" said Salome. "I pity that poor man."

"He is very well able to keep a servant," I said, "and I have always had a suspicion that Aunt Lily is not by any means as die-away as her looks, Salome. The woman who arranged that supper table must have something of what you call 'gumption.' Anyhow, everybody is so well satisfied that it seems a pity to carp."

"Oh, I like the creature and I wish her well, ma'am," Salome rejoined, with a toss of her head. "And I'm glad poor T.B. is to have his chance. But say what you will, ma'am, George Black is marrying into a queer lot, and that is my final opinion, ma'am."

Aunt Lily meant to give up keeping a diary, so she informed me.

"I shall not need it," she said. "I can pour out my soul to my husband. I have put the past and all its sadness behind me. Will you help me select my bridal suit, Mrs. Bruce? I *did* want to be wedded in a sky-blue gown—the tint of God's own heaven, Mrs. Bruce. But George says he would like a plain dark suit better and I believe that a wife should reverence and obey her husband. I am no new woman, Mrs. Bruce, and I believe in the sacredness of the conjugal tie. The secret of life is devotion, Mrs. Bruce."

"I'm very glad you are taking T.B. with you," I said.

"I could not dream of leaving him behind, Mrs. Bruce. My heart is knit to his. I trust that in my home his surroundings will be more uplifting than they have hitherto been. In an atmosphere of calm and joy I feel sure that he will develop, Mrs. Bruce."

The next week Aunt Lily and T.B. went to the new atmosphere of calm and joy and we departed regretfully from the Tansy Patch. As we drove away in the still evening we heard "Paw" fiddling gloriously on his stoop; and as we turned the corner of the road and passed the house Granny shook her stick at us with a parting malediction.

"May yer potatoes always be rotten," she shrieked.

But—"Paw's" fiddle followed us further than Granny's howls, and our memories of our Tansy Patch neighbors were not unpleasant ones.

"When all is said and done, ma'am," was Salome's summing up, "them lunatics were interesting."

(1918)

The Matchmaker

In chapter 15 of *Anne of Ingleside* (1939), the last book Montgomery published in her lifetime, Anne decides to play matchmaker for Stella Chase, a young woman she met at choir practice who is "one of the most charming girls she had ever met." The problem? Both Stella and the man who is apparently perfect for her, Alden Churchill, have never met each other, and both Stella's father and Alden's mother are opposed to their adult child marrying at all! But Anne has tremendous experience in matchmaking, reminding Gilbert of all the couples whose marriages she has helped bring about: "Theodora Dix and Ludovic Speed . . . Stephen Clark and Prissie Gardner . . . Janet Sweet and John Douglas . . . Professor Carter and Esme Taylor . . . Nora and Jim . . . Dovie and Jarvis." This multi-chapter sequence originated in the following short story, published two decades earlier, also in *Canadian Home Journal*. In place of a thirty-something Anne is widowed Ellen Churchill, whose motivation for fixing up her niece and her late husband's nephew is that there are no other young people, let alone children, in their settlement.

66 THERE IS NOT A SINGLE BABY IN LANCASTER," SAID Mrs. Churchill. "There is not *one* young married couple in Lancaster. And, what's worse, nobody is getting married or has any notion of getting married. It's a disheartening state of affairs."

Mrs. Churchill was talking to her friend, Mrs. Mildred Burnham, as they sat on her verandah in the clear, spring twilight. They were both middle-aged widows and had been chums since they had shared the same desk at school. Mrs. Burnham was a tall, thin lady, who admitted that she had a sensitive disposition. Mrs. Churchill, who was a large, placid, slow-moving person, never jarred on this sensitiveness; so they were very fond of each other.

"Well," said Mrs. Burnham, "all the people who have been married in Lancaster for the last ten years have gone away. Just now there doesn't seem to be any candidates. What young folks there are hereabouts are *too* young—except Alden Churchill and this new niece of yours—what's her name?"

"Stella Chase."

"Now, if *they* would take a notion to each other?" suggested Mrs. Burnham.

Mrs. Churchill gazed earnestly at the rose in her filet crochet. She had already made up her mind that her nephew Alden should marry her niece Stella, but matchmaking is something requiring subtlety and discretion, and there are things you do not tell, even to your intimate friend.

"I don't suppose there's much chance of that," she said, "and if they did it wouldn't be any use. Mary will never let Alden marry as long as she can keep him from it—the property is hers until he marries and then it goes to him, you know. And as for Richard, he has never let poor Stella have a beau in her life. All the young men who ever tried to come to see her he simply terrified out of their senses with sarcasm. He is the most sarcastic creature you ever heard of. Stella can't manage him—her mother before her couldn't manage him. They didn't know how. He goes by contraries, but neither of them ever seemed to catch on to that."

"I thought Miss Chase seemed very devoted to her father."

"Oh, she is. She adores him. He is a most agreeable man when he gets his own way about everything. He and I get on beautifully. *I* know the secret of coming it over him. I'm real glad they've moved up here from Clancy. They're such company for me. Stella is a very sweet girl. I always loved her, and her mother was my favorite sister. Poor Lisette!"

"She died young?"

"Yes—when Stella was only eight. Richard brought Stella up himself. I don't wonder they're everything to each other. But he should have more sense about Stella's marrying. He must know he can't live forever—though to hear him talk you'd think he meant to; he's an old man—he wasn't young when he married. And what is Stella to do after he's gone? Just shrivel up, I suppose."

"It's a shame," agreed Mrs. Burnham. "I don't hold with old folks spoiling young folks' lives like that."

"And Alden's another whose life is going to be spoiled. Mary is *determined* he shan't marry. Every time he's gone about with a girl she puts a stop to it somehow."

"Do you s'pose it's all her doings?" queried Mrs. Burnham, rather drily. "Some folks think Alden is very changeable. I've heard him called a flirt."

"Alden is handsome and the girls chase him," cried Mrs. Churchill, up in arms against any criticism of her favorite. "I don't blame him for stringing them along a bit and dropping them when he's taught them a lesson. But there's been one or two nice girls he really liked and Mary just blocked it every time. She told me so herself—told me she went to the Bible—she's always 'going to the Bible,' you know—and turned up a verse, and every time it was a warning against Alden getting married. I've no patience with her and her odd ways. Why can't she go to church and be a decent creature like the rest of us in Lancaster? But no, she must set up a religion for herself, consisting of 'going to the Bible.' Last fall, when that valuable horse took sick—worth four hundred if he was a dollar—instead of sending for the Clancy vet. as we all begged her to do she 'went to the Bible'—and turned up a verse, 'The Lord gave and the Lord taketh away. Blessed be the name of the Lord.' So send for the vet. she would not—and the horse died. Fancy applying that verse in such a way! I call it irreverent."

Mrs. Churchill paused, being rather out of breath. Her sister-in-law's vagaries always made her impatient.

"Alden isn't much like his mother," said Mrs. Burnham.

"Alden's like his father—a finer man never stepped. Why he ever married Mary was something we could never fathom. Of course, she had lots of money but *that* wasn't the reason. George was really in love with her. I don't know how Alden stands his mother's whims. *He* rather plumes himself on his liberal views—believes in evolution and that sort of stuff. Going, are you? What's your hurry?"

"Well," sighed Mrs. Burnham, "I find that if I'm out in the dew much my neuralgia troubles me considerable. We're getting old, Ellen."

"To be sure we are," agreed Mrs. Churchill. "*My* rheumatism takes hold this spring, too, if I'm not mighty careful. Good-night—mind the step."

Mrs. Churchill continued rocking on her verandah, crocheting, and plotting. When her brother-in-law, Richard Chase, had moved from Clancy to Lancaster, Mrs. Churchill had been delighted. She was very fond of Stella and, as Clancy was ten miles away, she had never been able to see as much of her as she wished. And she had made up her mind that Stella and Alden Churchill must be married off to each other by hook or by crook. Stella was twenty-four and Alden was thirty and it was high time they were married, so Mrs. Churchill thought.

"I've no doubt I can bring it about," she said to herself. "But I'll have to be careful—it would never do to let one of them suspect a thing. It's going to mean a lot of trouble and bother—and some fibbing, as well, I'm afraid. But it's all in a good cause. Neither Alden nor Stella will ever get married to anybody if I don't lend a hand, that's certain. And they won't take a fancy to each other without some help, that's equally certain. Stella isn't the kind of girl Alden *thinks* he fancies—he imagines he likes the high-colored, laughing ones. But we'll see, Ellen,—we'll see. *I* know how to deal with pig-headed people of all sorts."

Mrs. Churchill laughed comfortably. Then she decided she must get to work at once. Stella had been living in Lancaster for three weeks and the new minister was casting sheep's eyes at her. Mrs. Churchill had caught him at it. She did not like *him*—he was too anaemic and short-sighted—she was not going to help *him* to Stella. Besides, Alden, who hadn't been dangling after any girl all winter, might begin at any moment. There was a new and handsome school-teacher down on the Base Line Road and spring was a dangerous time. If Alden began a new flirtation he would have no eyes for Stella.

As yet, they were not even acquainted. The first thing to do was to have them meet each other. How was this to be managed? It must be brought about in some way absolutely innocent in appearance. Mrs. Churchill racked her kindly brains but could think of only one way. She must give a party and invite them both. She did not like the way. She was intensely proud of her beautiful, beautifully-kept house, with its nice furnishings and the old heirlooms that had come down to her through three generations. She hated the thought of its being torn up by preparations for a party and desecrated by a horde of young romps. The Lancaster boys and girls were such romps. But a good cause demands sacrifices. Mrs. Churchill sent out her invitations, alleging that she was giving the party as a farewell send-off for her cousin Alice's daughter, Janet, who was going away to teach in the city. Janet, who hadn't expected Aunt Ellen to come out like this, was rather pleased. But Mrs. Churchill's other cousin, Elizabeth, two of whose daughters had gone away without any such farewell party, was bitterly jealous and offended, and never forgave Ellen.

Mrs. Churchill cleaned her house from attic to cellar for the event and did all the cooking for the supper herself, help being impossible to get in Lancaster. She was woefully tired the night before the party. Every bone in her body ached, her head ached, her eyes ached. But instead of going to bed she sat out on the verandah, in the chilly spring night, and talked to Alden, who had dropped in, but would not go into the house. Mrs. Churchill was very anxious to have a talk with him, so she braved the damp and the chill.

Alden sat on the verandah steps with his bare head thrown back against the post. He was, as his aunt had said, a very handsome fellow—tall, broad-shouldered, with a marble-white face, that never tanned, and dead-black hair and eyes. He had a laughing, velvety voice which no girl could hear without a heart-beat, and a dangerous way of listening to a woman—*any* woman—as if she were saying something he had thirsted all his life to hear. He had gone to Midland Academy for three years and had thought of going to college. But his mother refused to let him go, alleging Biblical reasons, and Alden had settled down contentedly enough on the farm. He liked farming; it was free, out-of-doors, independent work; he had his mother's knack of making money and his father's attractive personality. It was no wonder he was considered a matrimonial prize.

"Alden, I want to ask a favor of you," said Mrs. Churchill. "Will you do it for me?"

"Sure, Aunt Ellen," he answered heartily. "Just name it. You know I'd do anything for you." Alden was very fond of his Aunt Ellen and would really have done a good deal for her.

"I'm afraid it will bore you," said Mrs. Churchill anxiously. "But it's just this—I want you to see that Stella Chase has a good time at the party to-morrow night. I'm so afraid she won't. She doesn't know the young people here—and they're all so much younger than she is—at least the boys are. Ask her to dance and see that she isn't left alone and out of things. She's so shy with strangers. I do want her to have a good time."

"Oh, I'll do my best," said Alden readily.

"But you mustn't fall in love with her, you know," said Mrs. Churchill, laughing carefully.

"Have a heart, Aunt Ellen. Why not?"

"I'm in earnest. It wouldn't do at all, Alden."

"Why not?" persisted Alden.

"Well"—confidentially—"I think the new minister has taken quite a shine to her."

"That conceited young ass!" exploded Alden, with unexpected warmth.

Mrs. Churchill looked mild rebuke.

"Why, Alden, he's a very nice young man—so clever and well-educated. It's only that kind of man who would have any chance at all with Stella's father, you know."

"That so?" asked Alden, relapsing into his indifference.

"Yes: and I don't even know if *he* would. Richard thinks there's nobody alive good enough for Stella. He simply wouldn't let her *look* at a farmer like you. So I don't want you to make trouble for yourself falling in love with a girl you could never get. I'm just giving you a friendly warning."

"Oh, thanks—thanks! What sort of a girl is she anyhow? Looks good?"

"If you'd gone to church as often as you should, Alden, you'd have seen her before now. She's not a beauty. Stella is my favorite niece but I can see what she lacks. She's pale and delicate—she'd never do for a farmer's wife. That's why I'd like to see her and the minister make a match of it. To be sure, she's too fond of dress—she's positively extravagant. But they say Mr. Paxton has money of his own. To my thinking, it would be an ideal match, and that's why I don't want you to spoil it."

"Why didn't you invite Paxton to your spree and tell him to give Stella a good time?" demanded Alden rather truculently.

"You know I couldn't ask the minister to a dance, Alden. Now, don't be cranky—and do see that Stella has a nice time."

"Oh, I'll see that she has a rip-roaring time. Good-night, Aunt Ellen."

Alden swung off abruptly. Left alone, Mrs. Churchill chuckled.

"Now, if *I* know anything of human nature, that boy will sail right in to show me and Richard that he can get Stella if he wants her, in spite of us. And he rose right to my bait about the minister. I declare, it's easy to manage men if you're half cute. Dear me, this shoulder of mine is starting up. I suppose I'll have a bad night."

She had a rather bad night, but the next evening she was a gallant and smiling hostess. Her party was a success. Everybody seemed to have a good time. Stella certainly had. Alden saw to that—almost too zealously for good form, his aunt thought. It was going a little too strong for a first meeting that after supper Alden should whisk Stella off to a dim corner of the verandah and keep her there for an hour. But, on the whole, Mrs. Churchill was satisfied when she thought things over the next morning. To be sure, the parlor carpet had been practically ruined by two spilled saucerfuls of ice-cream; her grandmother's Bristol glass candlesticks had been broken to smithereens; and one of the girls had upset a pitcherful of rainwater in the spareroom which had soaked downwards and discolored the dining-room ceiling in a tragic fashion; but on the credit side of the ledger was the fact that, unless all signs failed, Alden had fallen in love with Stella. Mrs. Churchill thought the balance was in her favor.

Later on, she discovered another and more serious debit item. In a fortnight it transpired that Mrs. Burnham was deeply offended because she had not been asked to the party. That it was strictly a young people's party, and that no elderly people were invited, did not matter. Mrs. Burnham's sensitive nature was terribly hurt, and she told sundry neighbors that she would never feel the same to Ellen Churchill again. She came no more for friendly evening calls and was frostily polite when they met elsewhere. Mrs. Churchill was very blue about it. She missed Mildred terribly, though she thought she was absurdly unreasonable. But she was repaid on the evening she came upon Alden and Stella, loitering along arm in arm in the leafy by-road east of the village which Lancaster folks called Lover's Lane. Mrs. Churchill perked right up. She had not been able to find out if her party had produced any lasting results. Now it was evident things were going all right. Alden was caught; but what about Stella? Mrs. Churchill knew that her niece was not the sort of girl to fall ripely into any young man's outstretched hand. She had a spice of her father's contrariness, which in her worked out in a charming independence.

Stella came to see her aunt the next evening and they sat on the verandah steps. Beside Stella the big "bridal wreath" shrub banked up on its June-tide whiteness, making a beautiful background for the girl. Stella was a pale, slender thing, shy but intensely sweet. She had large, purplish-grey eyes, with very black lashes and brows, and when she was excited a wild-rose hue spread over her cheeks. She was not considered pretty but nobody ever forgot her face.

"I was very sorry to see you strolling in Lover's Lane with Alden Churchill yesterday evening, Stella," said Mrs. Churchill severely.

Stella turned a startled face towards her aunt.

"Why?"

"He isn't the right kind of beau for you at all, Stella."

"He is your nephew, Aunt Ellen—and I thought you were so fond of him."

"He's my nephew by marriage—and I like him well enough. But he's not good enough for you, Stella. He has no *family* behind him. Why, his mother's grandfather *hanged himself*; and her father made his money hawking a medicine he concocted himself around the country. The Churchills all felt dreadful bad when George Churchill married her—and the Churchills themselves weren't strong on family. I have to admit that, though I did marry one myself. But that's not the worst. Alden's awfully fickle, Stella. No girl can hold him long. Lots have tried and they all failed. I don't want to see you left like that the minute his fancy veers. Now, just take your aunty's advice, darling, and have nothing to do with him. You know how fond and proud of you I am."

"I know you've always been awfully good to me, Aunt Ellen," said Stella slowly, "but I think you're mistaken about Alden."

"No fear. I've known him for thirty years and you've known him for two weeks. Which of us is most likely to understand him? He'll act as if he was mad about you for a few months and then he'll drop you. You can't hold him—you're not his type. He likes the bouncing, jolly girls—like the Base Line teacher for example."

"Oh—well—I must be going home," said Stella vaguely. "Father will be lonesome."

When she had gone, Mrs. Churchill chuckled again.

"Now, if *I* know anything of human nature, Miss Stella has gone off, vowing she'll show meddling old aunts that she *can* hold Alden, and that no Base Line schoolma'am shall ever get her claws on him. That little toss of her head and that flush on her cheeks told me that. *I* can read these young geese like a book."

When it became a matter of common gossip that Alden Churchill was "going with" Stella Chase Mrs. Churchill looked out of her door one night with a sigh.

"The wind is east and I wish I could stay home to-night and nurse my rheumatism but I must go a-matchmaking. It's high time I tried my hand on Mary. She'll be the hardest nut to crack. But *I* know how to tackle her. Everyone has a weak point and I found Mary's out long ago."

The Churchill farm was a mile and a half from Lancaster, and Mrs. Churchill was very tired when she got there. Mrs. Mary Churchill did not welcome her too effusively either—she never did. The two sisters-in-law had never cared much for each other. But Aunt Ellen did not worry over Mary's coolness. She sat down in a rocker and took out her filet, while Mary sat opposite to her in a stiff-backed chair, folded her long thin hands, and gazed steadily at her. Mary Churchill was tall and thin and austere. She had a prominent chin and a long, compressed mouth. She never wasted words and she never gossiped. So Ellen found it somewhat difficult to work up to her subject naturally, but she managed it through the medium of the new minister, whom Mary did not like.

"He is not a spiritual man," said Mary coldly. "He believes the kingdom of heaven can be taken by brains. It cannot."

"He's a very clever young fellow," said Ellen, rocking placidly. "His sermons are remarkable."

"I heard but one and do not wish to hear more. My soul sought food and was given a lecture."

"Oh, well, Mary, you know other people don't think and feel as you do. Mr. Paxton is a fine young man. He has quite a notion of my niece Stella Chase, too. I'm hoping it will be a match."

"Do you mean a marriage?" asked Mary.

Ellen shrugged her plump shoulders.

"Now, Mary, you understand what I mean well enough. And it would be just the thing. Stella is especially fitted to be a minister's wife. By the way, I hear that Alden is going with her a bit. You ought to put a stop to that, Mary."

"Why?" asked Mary, without the flicker of an eyelid.

"Because it isn't a bit of use," responded Ellen energetically. "He could never get her in this world. Her father doesn't think anyone is good enough for her—except a minister or doctor or something like that. He'd show a plain farmer to the door in a moment. You'd better tell Alden to give up all notion of Stella Chase, Mary. He'll find himself thrown over before long and made a laughing stock of, if he doesn't. Look at all the girls that have flirted with him and then dropped him. If that goes on much longer he'll never get a decent wife. No nice girl wants shopworn goods."

"No girl ever dropped my son," said Mary, compressing her thin lips. "It was always the other way about. My son could marry any woman he chose—any woman, Ellen Churchill."

"Oh!" said Ellen's tongue. Her tone said, "of course I am too polite to contradict you but you have not changed my opinion." Mary Churchill understood the tone and her white, shrivelled face warmed a little. Ellen went away soon after, very well satisfied with the interview.

"Of course, one can't count on Mary," she reflected, "but if *I* know anything of human nature I've worried her a little. She doesn't like the idea of folks thinking Alden is the jilted one. I s'pose she's busy turning up Bible verses now to solve the problem. Lord, how my shoulders ache! East winds were invented by the old Nick. But I feel I've done Alden and Stella a good turn to-night. There's only Richard to manipulate now. I wonder if he has the slightest idea that Stella and Alden are going together. Not likely. Stella would never dare take Alden to the house, of course. I'll tackle Richard next week."

Mrs. Churchill tackled him, according to programme. He was sitting in his little library reading, but he put his book aside when his sister-in-law came in. He was always courteous to her and they got on surprisingly well. He was a small, thin man, with an unkempt shock of grey hair and little, twinkling, deep-set eyes.

Ellen sat down but said she could not stay long—she had just run up to borrow Stella's recipe for snow pudding.

"I'll sit a minute to cool off. It's dreadful hot to-night. Likely there'll be a thunderstorm. Mercy, that cat is bigger than ever!"

Richard Chase had a familiar in the shape of a huge black cat. It always sat on the arm of his chair while he read. When he put his book away it climbed over into his lap. He stroked it tenderly.

"Lucifer gives the world assurance of a cat," he said. "Don't you, Lucifer? Look at your Aunt Ellen, Lucifer—observe the baleful glances she is casting upon you, from orbs created to express only kindness and affection."

"Don't you call me that beast's Aunt Ellen," protested Mrs. Churchill sharply. "A joke's a joke, but that is carrying things too far."

"Wouldn't you rather be Lucifer's aunt than Neddy Churchill's aunt?" queried Richard Chase plaintively. "Neddy Churchill is a glutton and a wine-bibber, isn't he? You've often given me a catalogue of his crimes. Wouldn't you rather be aunt to a fine, up-standing cat like Lucifer with a blameless record where whiskey and tabbies are concerned?"

"Poor Ned is a human being," retorted Mrs. Churchill. "I can't abide cats. It's the only fault I have to find with Alden Churchill. He's got the strangest liking for cats, too. Lord knows where he got it—his mother and father loathed them as I do."

"What a sensible young man he must be," said Richard Chase ironically.

"Sensible! Well, he's sensible enough—except in the matter of cats and evolution—another thing he didn't inherit from his mother!"

"Do you know, Ellen," said Richard Chase solemnly, "I have a secret leaning towards evolution myself."

"So you've told me for the last thirty years," retorted Mrs. Churchill. "Well, believe what you like, Richard. Thank God, nobody could ever make *me* believe that I was descended from a monkey."

"You don't look it, I confess, you comely woman," said Richard Chase. "I see no simian resemblances in your rosy, comfortable, eminently respectable physiognomy. Still, your great-grandmother a million times removed swung herself from branch to branch by her tail. Science proves that, Ellen—like it or leave it."

"I'll leave it then. I'm not going to argue with you on that or any point. I've got my own religion and no ape-ancestors figure in *it*. By the way, Richard, Stella doesn't look as well this summer as I'd like to see her."

"She always feels the hot weather a good deal. She'll pick up when it's cooler."

"I hope so. Loretta picked up every summer but the last, Richard, don't forget that. Stella has her mother's constitution. She's far from strong. It's just as well she isn't likely to marry."

"Why isn't she likely to marry? I asked from curiosity, Ellen—rank curiosity. The processes of feminine thought are intensely interesting to me. From what premises or data do you draw the conclusion, in your own delightful, off-hand way, that Stella is not likely to marry?"

"Well, Richard, to put it plainly, she isn't the kind of girl that is popular with the men. She's a dear, sweet, good girl but she doesn't take with them."

"She has had admirers. I have spent much of my substance in the purchase and maintenance of shot guns and bull dogs."

"They admired your money bags, I fancy. They were easily discouraged, too. Just one broadside of sarcasm from you and off they went. If they had really wanted Stella they wouldn't have wilted for that—any more than for your imaginary bull dogs. No, Richard, we might as well admit that Stella isn't the girl to win desirable beaus—especially when she's getting on in years.

Loretta wasn't, you know. She never had a beau till you came along."

"But wasn't I worth waiting for? Surely Loretta was a wise young woman. You would not have me give my daughter to any Tom, Dick or Harry, would you—my Star, who, despite your somewhat disparaging remarks, is fit to shine in the palaces of kings?"

"We have no kings in this country," said Mrs. Churchill, getting up. "I'm not saying Stella isn't a lovely girl. I'm only saying the men are not likely to see it, and considering her constitution, I think it is decidedly a good thing. A good thing for you, too. You could never get on without her, you'd be as helpless as a baby. Well, I'm off. I know you are dying to get back to that book of yours."

"Admirable, clear-sighted woman! What a treasure you are for a sister-in-law! I admit it—I am dying. But no other but yourself would have been perspicacious enough to see it or amiable enough to save my life by acting upon it. Good-evening, pearl-of-in-laws."

"Of course, there's never any knowing what effect anything you've said has had on him," mused Mrs. Churchill, as she went down the street. "But if I know anything of human nature, he didn't like the idea of Stella not being popular with the men any too well, in spite of the fact that their grandfathers were monkeys. I think he'd like to show me! Well, I've done all I can—I've interested Alden and Stella in each other and I've made Mary and Richard rather anxious for the match than otherwise. And now I'll just sit tight and watch how things go."

Two evenings later Stella came up to see her Aunt Ellen. It was a hot, smoky evening, so they sat on the verandah steps again. Stella seemed absent-minded and quiet. Presently she said abruptly, looking the while at a crystal-white star hanging over the Lombardy at the gate.

"Aunt Ellen, I want to tell you something."

"Yes, dear?"

"I am engaged to Alden Churchill," said Stella desperately. "We've been engaged ever since last Christmas. We've kept it secret just because it was so sweet to have such a secret. But we are going to be married next month."

Mrs. Churchill dropped her crochet and looked at Stella, who still continued to stare at the star. So she did not see the expression on her aunt's face. She went on, a little more easily.

"Alden and I met at a party in Clancy last September. We—we loved each other from the very first moment. He said he had always dreamed of me—had always been looking for me. He said to himself, 'There is my wife,' when he saw me come in at the door. And I—just felt the same. Oh, we are so happy, Aunt Ellen. The only cloud on our happiness has been your attitude about the matter."

"Bless me!" said Mrs. Churchill feebly.

"Won't you try to approve, Aunt Ellen? You've been like a mother to me. I'll feel so badly if I have to marry against your wish."

There was a sound of tears in Stella's voice. Mrs. Churchill picked her filet up blindly.

"Why—I don't care, child. I like Alden—he's a splendid fellow—only he has had the reputation of being a flirt——"

"But he isn't. He was just looking for the right one, don't you see, Aunty?—and he couldn't find her."

"How will your father regard it?"

"Oh, father is greatly pleased. He has known it all along. He took to Alden from the start. They used to argue for hours about evolution. Father said he always meant to let me marry as soon as the right one came along. I feel dreadfully about leaving him—but Cousin Delia Chase is coming to keep house for him and father likes her very much."

"And Alden's mother?"

"She is quite willing, too. When Alden told her last Christmas that we were engaged, she went to the Bible and the first verse she turned up was, 'A man shall leave father and mother and cleave unto his wife.' She said it was perfectly clear to her then what she ought to do and she consented at once. So you see everyone is pleased; and won't you give us your good wishes, too, Aunty."

"Oh, of course," said Mrs. Churchill rather vaguely. There was not much heartiness in her voice and Stella went away a little disappointed. After she had gone Mrs. Churchill took stock of the preceding weeks.

She had burdened her conscience with innumerable fibs; she had confirmed her rheumatism; she had ruined her parlor carpet, destroyed two treasured heirlooms and spoiled her dining room ceiling; she had alienated the affections of her dearest friend, perhaps forever; she had given Richard Chase something to tease her about the rest of her life; she had put a weapon into Mary Churchill's merciless hand, which, if she, Mrs. Churchill, knew anything about human nature, Mary would not fail to use upon occasion; she had got in wrong with Alden and Stella and could only get out by a confession too humiliating to make. And all for what? To bring about a marriage between two people who were already engaged.

"I have had enough of matchmaking," said Mrs. Churchill firmly.

(1919)

Tomorrow Comes

This next story, published in the July 1934 issue of *Canadian Home Journal*, focuses on a little girl named Judy Grayson, yet the periodical referred to it as "a story of two very proud, very silly, very unreasonable young people who were not all to blame for what happened and who have learned wisdom through suffering"—the term "young people" referring to two adult characters, not a child. Elizabeth Rollins Epperly, coming across random pages from the story's typescript on the backs of the pages of the manuscript of *Mistress Pat* (then called "The Girls of Silver Bush"), notes that this story "is surely the germ for *Jane of Lantern Hill.*" Yet the full version of this story, discovered after the publication of this facet of Epperly's research, while certainly similar to *Jane* in its general focus on a girl who discovers that her father is alive and her parents are separated, also has much in common with the subplot in *Anne of Windy Poplars* involving Anne's young next-door neighbour, Little Elizabeth.

JUDITH GRAYSON . . . WHOSE MOTHER CALLED HER JUDY and whose grandmother called her Hester . . . was born expecting things to happen. That they seldom did happen, even at Bartibog, under the watchful eyes of Grandmother and The Woman never blighted her expectations in the least . . . especially at Bartibog. Things were just bound to happen at Bartibog. If not today then tomorrow. Of course The Woman had once said dourly, when Judy had promised to do something tomorrow, "Tomorrow never comes, Hester." But Judy knew better. Tomorrow *would* come sometime. Some beautiful morning at Bartibog you would wake up and find it was Tomorrow. Not Today but Tomorrow. And then things would happen . . . wonderful things. You might even have a day when you would be free to do as you liked, unwatched by Grandmother and The Woman . . . though that seemed almost too good ever to happen, even in Tomorrow. Or you might find out what was along that road . . . that wandering, twisted road, like a nice red snake . . . which led to the End of the World. You might even discover that the Island of Happiness was at the End of the World. Judy had always, all through her seven years of life, felt sure the Island of Happiness was somewhere if one could but find it.

But how could you explore for it, or for anything else, when Grandmother and The Woman bossed you all the time and wouldn't let you out of their sight? Bossing was not Judy's word. She had taken it over from Timothy Salt and thought it very expressive. Judy especially resented being bossed by The Woman. She did not like it in Grandmother, of course, but you felt reluctantly that perhaps a grandmother had a right to boss you. What right had The Woman?

The Woman's name was really Martha Monkman, as Judy knew perfectly well: but once, long ago, she had heard someone say that Martha Monkman was old Mrs. Sinclair's "woman" and Judy never thought of her as anything else after that. It suited her so well, especially when spelled, as Judy always saw it, with a capital . . . a great, big, forbidding W, as full of angles and corners as Martha Monkman herself.

"I hate her," Judy had once said passionately to mother.

"Hush, hush." Mother was always hush-hushing. Both Grandmother and The Woman would not have any noise about the house. Everybody had to move softly, speak softly, even, so Judy felt, think softly. Judy often felt perversely that she wanted to yell loud and long. She *would* do it sometime . . . when Tomorrow came . . . and oh, how she would enjoy the look on The Woman's face!

"Do *you* like her, mother?" demanded Judy.

"Martha is very honest and faithful," said Mother wearily. "She has been your grandmother's companion for forty years."

Judy did not think this was an answer at all.

"She hates *me*," said Judy.

"Judith Grayson! Martha doesn't . . ."

"She does . . . and grandmother, too. They both do. You know they do, mother."

Mother looked aghast. She tried feebly to change Judy's mind but she did not seem to be able to think of any good arguments. Judy brushed them all aside.

"Why do they hate me, mother?"

"You are an absurd child. Grandmother and Martha are both old people and old people are easily disturbed and worried. Of course you annoy them sometimes. And . . . and . . . when *they* were young, children were brought up much more strictly than they are now. They cling to the old way." There was no use in trying to extract anything from mother. Judy knew this and gave it up. But she permitted herself one satisfaction . . . although she looked carefully around first to make sure the door was shut.

"Grandmother and The Woman are two tyrants," she said deliberately, "and when Tomorrow comes I'm going to escape from them forever."

She had expected Mother would nearly die of horror . . . I am afraid Judy really said that hoping to make a sensation . . . but Mother only looked at her strangely. And said a strange thing.

"There is no escape for either of us now. Tomorrow will never come. As for you . . . they need not be so afraid to let you out of their sight. There is no fear of anyone kidnapping you."

Mother laughed bitterly. It was unthinkable but Judy almost thought Mother was really sorry that there was no danger of her being kidnapped. And yet Judy knew that her mother loved her fiercely and tenderly and wholly . . . knew it just as indisputably as she knew that Grandmother and The Woman didn't love her at all. Why, they never spoke of her by her name, even her middle name, if they could help it. It was always "the child." How Judy hated to be called "the child," just as they might have spoken of "the dog" or "the cat." Only there was no dog or cat in Grandmother's house.

"When Tomorrow comes," Judy told Grandmother once, "I will have a million dogs and forty-five cats."

Grandmother's face had grown dark and angry. Judy had been punished for impertinence.

But at least she was at Bartibog. They always came to Bartibog in the summer. Judy loved it. She hated Grandmother's gloomy, splendid town house in which everything seemed unacquainted with her, although she had lived there as far back as she could remember. But when they came down to Bartibog everything changed magically. She couldn't step outside the door there without stepping into something romantic. She lived in a world of romance once she came to Bartibog. Instead of a long, grim, stately street there was beauty wherever you looked. Luckily Grandmother and The Woman couldn't prevent you from looking, though Judy had no doubt they would if they could. The lighthouse down on the green point, painted in odd red and white rings . . . the dim blue shore where there were happy golden hollows among the dunes and the bones of old vessels . . . the little silvery curving waves . . . the range-lights that gleamed through the violet dusks . . . all gave her so much delight that it hurt. And the sea sunsets! Judy always went up to the north dormer to watch them and the ships that sailed out of the harbour at the rising of the moon. Ships that came back . . . ships that never came back. Judy longed to go in one of them . . . on a voyage to the Island of Happiness. The ships that never came back stayed there . . . where it was always Tomorrow.

She could see the harbour from the north dormer with its smoky islands and its misty bays. She had never seen it any closer but she knew the mysterious road ran in that direction and her feet itched to follow it. When Tomorrow really came she would fare forth on it and perhaps find an island all her own, where she and Mother could live alone and Grandmother and The Woman could never come. They both hated water and would not put foot on a boat for anything. Judy liked to picture herself, standing on her island and mocking them, as they stood vainly glowering on the mainland shore.

"This is Tomorrow," she would taunt them. "You can't catch me any more. You are only in Today."

What fun it would be!

And there was Timothy Salt. At least, there had been Timothy Salt last summer and Judy fervently hoped he would be this summer, too. Of course Grandmother and The Woman would disapprove of him as they had done last summer; but they could not do away with him altogether because he was the nephew of

Tillytuck Salt . . . which was a name out of Tomorrow if ever there was one . . . the man who took care of Grandmother's house at Bartibog and was so useful in various ways that they dared not offend him. Tillytuck stood on his dignity and let it be known that his nephew was good enough for anybody to play with, take it or leave it. Grandmother took it and, under many restrictions, Judy had been allowed to play with Timothy. The most galling restriction, of course, was that they were never to go out of sight of the house. What wonders of adventure and romance might they not have discovered had it not been for that! At least they would have explored the Road to the End of the World. *Where* did that bewitching road lead to? Sometimes Judy thought she would burst if she didn't find out.

In spite of all restrictions she and Timothy had a good deal of fun together. They made sand pies and swung on the side gate . . . and talked. Judy liked to hear Timothy talk. He always said such nice slangy things. He was always very polite, too . . . Tillytuck had told him he would lick the stuffing out of him if he wasn't polite . . . and had a nice lean, brown face with round blue eyes and a delightful grin. He was about a head taller than Judy . . . which made her wonder what on earth The Woman meant by saying he was beneath her. Judy went to bed that night rather sadly because she had as yet seen nothing of Timothy. Perhaps he had gone away. It was a lonesome night, too . . . the first few nights at Bartibog were always like that till you got used to the moan of the sea and the sigh of the wind. Judy wished she could sleep with Mother. But Grandmother wouldn't allow that. Mother couldn't even put her to bed. Judy couldn't understand why but she knew she was never left alone with Mother any oftener than Grandmother could help.

"I'm always so afraid of things in the night," she had told Grandmother piteously. And Grandmother had said there must be no cowards in her house.

Alone and lonesome though she was, Judy went conscientiously through her little ritual of retiring. She folded her clothes and cleaned her teeth and brushed her long straight brown hair with the glints of red in it that always angered Grandmother . . . Judy couldn't imagine why. Of course it wasn't like Mother's lovely golden hair with the ripples in it and the little love-locks that curled about her ears. She didn't look a bit like Mother anyhow.

Her skin was creamy and colourless where Mother's was pink and white, her eyes were as russet as her hair where Mother's were the most heavenly blue, and her chin was square and cleft where Mother's was pointed and little. Of all the things about her Judy knew it was her chin Grandmother hated most.

"It gets more like His every day," Judy had once heard Grandmother say to The Woman.

Whose?

Before Judy got into bed she opened one of the drawers in the high, black, polished old bureau and took a carefully-hidden picture from under a pile of handkerchiefs. She had cut it out of a piece of newspaper that had come wrapped around a parcel. A man's picture . . . she didn't know whose because the name had been torn away. But she liked the face tremendously. The chin was like her own. She thought if she had had a father she would have liked him to look like that. Her father was dead, so Grandmother told her, looking at her so vindictively that Judy knew her father had been hated by this grim, bitter old woman. Mother never would say anything about him. She had forbidden Judy to mention him.

"Your father did not love you," she said, her eyes dark with some kind of feeling and her little red mouth trembling. "He . . . hated you."

Judy wondered why. She had, so they said, been only three when her father died. Why should anyone hate you when you were so small? Could you be worth hating? But Judy never mentioned her father to anybody again.

"Good-night, dear Man." She kissed the picture and returned it to its hiding place. Then she climbed into bed and cuddled down under the blankets . . . for the June nights were cool enough at Bartibog and the sea breeze searching. There was more than a breeze tonight. It whistled and banged and shook and thumped and raged, and she knew the waves were dashing wildly down on the shore. What fun it would be to steal down close to them under the moon! But it was only in Tomorrow one could do that.

Judy lay awake a great deal at nights when the grown-ups were asleep, thinking out things and asking herself questions that were never answered. Why was Mother always so sad? And why was Grandmother angry with her because she was sad? And tonight she had a new mystery to ponder over. She had overheard Grandmother say to Mother,

"*He* is here."

"How . . . how do you know?" Mother had asked in a queer, choked voice.

"Tillytuck told Martha. He is visiting his uncle down at Flying Cloud. James Markham is very ill . . . he is not expected to recover. And *he* will probably stay there until the end."

"It . . . it doesn't matter to me." Mother had spoken breathlessly and defiantly. It was almost like a cry.

"It shouldn't. But you are always so terribly weak, Elaine."

"Why have you told me he was here at all?" cried Mother.

"To prepare you. You might meet him somewhere unexpectedly. And the child must be kept under strict watch and ward. If he thought he could get a hold on you by kidnapping her he would do it in a minute, hate her as much as he may."

"Why should he kidnap her? The law would give her to him if he cared to invoke it."

"He will not go to law. That clan hates publicity. That is why he has never attempted to get a divorce."

"He won't bother his head about Judy. He cares nothing for her . . . or me. You have told me that often enough, mother."

Mother was crying now. Judy clenched her fists. How dared Grandmother make Mother cry? But Grandmother often did that with some queer little speech Judy couldn't understand. Only she always felt that there was far more in what Grandmother said than her words themselves said.

"Is Grace with him?" asked Mother.

"Probably. She wouldn't trust him near Bartibog alone."

"Then," said Mother bitterly, with a little laugh so sad it nearly broke Judy's heart, "you need not be afraid of my meeting him."

Grandmother had come out into the hall and her face darkened when she saw Judy.

"Eavesdropping!" It was only one word but what venom Grandmother could put into a word!

Judy thought it over until her head whirled. Who was "he"? Where was Flying Cloud? What a name! Out of Tomorrow again. It was maddening to be so near Tomorrow and not be able to get into it. What had "he" to do with Mother or herself? Kidnapping!

Judy quivered, hardly knowing whether she were frightened or thrilled. But it was all nonsense. People weren't kidnapped in Bartibog. That only happened in the papers. But she would ask Timothy Salt about it tomorrow. How the wind blew! The waves sounded nearer . . . nearer . . . one of them was a great dark wave of sleep . . . it rolled right over her . . . Judy drowned in it with a delicious sigh of surrender.

She could not ask Timothy about it next day for there was no Timothy. For three days there was no Timothy. Judy simply couldn't stand it any longer so she waylaid Tillytuck and asked him where Timothy was. It was a tremendous relief to learn that Timothy was only visiting another uncle and would be home by the end of the week.

"I was afraid he might have got into Tomorrow ahead of me," Judy confided to Tillytuck.

"Ye're an odd little skeesicks," said Tillytuck. Then added, as if speaking to himself, "And it's my opinion them two old dames are a sight too hard on you."

Timothy was there the next Monday morning, as brown and polite as ever, and at least an inch taller. It was good to see him. Judy smiled to him over the gate with her shy sweetness and said, "What's the news in your neck of the woods?"

Being safely out of Grandmother's and The Woman's hearing she could indulge in a bit of slang. It sounded daring and adventurous. She felt as if she had slipped from some invisible shackle when she said it. Timothy and she swung on the gate the whole forenoon while he told her the news in his neck of the woods. Occasionally The Woman came to a window and scowled at them. But not as often as usual because Grandmother was in bed and The Woman was waiting on her. It was such an unheard-of thing for Grandmother to be in bed in the day time. Judy couldn't recall such a state of affairs before. Of course, Grandmother wasn't really ill. She just had a pain, The Woman said. So Judy felt that it was not altogether too awful of her to be glad that Grandmother had to stay in bed.

"Let's hope," said Timothy, cheerfully and unashamedly, "that she will have a pain for a week."

Judy felt a bit guilty because she couldn't help thinking it *would* be rather nice. And she felt guiltier still when the doctor had to be sent for after dinner.

From then on she didn't feel anything but amazement and bewilderment over the rush of events. Everything was in a whirl of excitement. Grandmother had appendicitis . . . Grandmother must be taken to the hospital at once. The Woman went with her. She would not let Mother go . . . Mother must stay and look after the child. There was nobody left in the house except Judy and Mother and the cook. But Tillytuck promised Grandmother he would sleep in the garage loft at night.

That night Judy slept with Mother. It was almost as if Tomorrow had really arrived. And how heavenly to wake in the morning and see Mother's face on the pillow next to her, all flushed and sweet like a rose, and the little gold knob at the nape of her white neck. Mother was always so beautiful in the mornings. Only Mother's eyes looked sad and restless as if she had not slept a great deal. When Judy laughed in her face Mother shuddered.

"Do *his* eyes still laugh?" she whispered to herself. Judy's quick ears caught it.

"Whose eyes?"

"Never mind. Somebody I used to know."

"Somebody you liked an awful lot," said Judy shrewdly. But she was more taken up with her own hopes than with anything else just then. It was so wonderful that Grandmother and The Woman were gone and she alone with Mother. The cook and Tillytuck didn't count. But Timothy did. And Timothy made a proposition when he came that fairly took Judy's breath away.

"Say, I've got to go down the harbour way on an errand for Uncle Tillytuck. You come with me."

"Oh . . . I couldn't," gasped Judy.

"Why not? The old ladies are away."

Why not, indeed! Judy took a huge gulp of freedom.

"How long will it take?"

"Not more'n two hours. You'll be back in time for dinner. We'll see where that road goes to."

That settled it. This must certainly be Tomorrow. Judy decided then and there to take a chance on it. Mother had gone to lie down with a headache and Judy wasn't going to disturb her, especially as it was quite possible Mother would forbid such an expedition . . . "put the kibosh on it," as Timothy said. It was probably wicked to go without asking permission but things were all upset anyway and old standards had gone by the board . . . and she couldn't resist the lure of that road which had called her so long.

"Now you can yell," Timothy told her as soon as they were out of sight around the first S bend.

Strange! She no longer wanted to yell, now that there was nothing to prevent her doing so. She just wanted to walk quietly on . . . on . . . on, towards that blueness at the end of the world, drinking in the loveliness all around her. Every turn and kink of the road revealed new beauties . . . and it turned and kinked interminably, following the twists of a tiny river that seemed to have appeared from nowhere.

On every side were fields of buttercups and clover where bees buzzed. Now and then they walked through a milky way of daisies. Away to the right the sea laughed at them in silver-tipped waves. On the left, the harbour, ever drawing nearer, was like watered silk. Judy liked it better that way than if it was pale-blue satin. They drank the wind in. The very sky was glad. A sailor with gold rings in his ears . . . the kind of a person one would meet in Tomorrow . . . smiled as he passed them. Far out on the bar was a splendid low thunder. Judy thought of a verse she had learned in Sunday School. "The little hills rejoice on every side." Did the man who wrote that mean the golden dunes at Bartibog?

"I think this road leads right to God," she said dreamily.

"No, it just goes down to the back shore," said Timothy matter-of-factly. "Look . . . you can see the end from here. Soon as I've done my errand we'll go on down to the end. Here . . . we turn off here . . . we've got to go over to that island."

"That island" was a long slender one, lying out in the harbour about a quarter of a mile from the shore. There were trees on it and a house. Judy had always wished she could have an island of her own with a little bay of silver sand in it just like this. But how to get to it?

"We'll row out in this flat," said Timothy, picking up the oars in a small boat tied to a leaning tree.

Judy shrank back for a moment. Even in Tomorrow . . .

"You're afraid," taunted Timothy.

"I'm not." Judy stepped into the boat. She *was* . . . a little . . . but she was not going to let Timothy see it.

"Good stuff," said Timothy approvingly.

He could row. Was there anything Timothy couldn't do? By the time they reached the island Judy had got over her fright and wished the distance were twice as long. But this island was a fascinating place where anything might happen. Of course it was in Tomorrow. Islands like this didn't happen except in Tomorrow. They had no part or lot in unadventurous, humdrum Today.

Timothy's errand was to a certain Mrs. Thompson who appeared to be the housekeeper. A nurse who met them at the door told Timothy he would find her on the far end of the island picking wild strawberries. Fancy! An island where wild strawberries grew! Timothy went to hunt her up and Judy was asked to wait in the living room.

It was a beautiful room, with flowers everywhere and wild sea breezes blowing in. There was something about the room Judy loved. Especially she loved the mirror over the mantel which reflected the room so beautifully and, through the open window, a glimpse of lowland and dune and sea.

And then Judy got the shock of her life. Propped up against the mirror was a large envelope with a typewritten address.

> *James Markham,*
> *Flying Cloud,*
> *Bartibog.*

This island was Flying Cloud! Here was the mysterious "he" who might kidnap her! And there he was, coming through the door.

Judy stood frozen in her tracks, all dismay and terror . . . and something that was neither. For this was the man whose picture lay in her bureau drawer! And he looked even nicer than in his picture, with his crinkly russet eyes and his sleek, red-brown hair. Judy decided, in one swift flash of intuition, that she didn't care an awful lot if he did kidnap her.

"Who are you?" asked the man, smiling.

"I'm . . . I'm me," faltered Judy, still in a swither of various emotions.

"Oh, to be sure . . . you. Popped out of the sea, I suppose . . . come up from the dunes . . . no name known among mortals."

Judy felt she was being made fun of . . . a little. And she liked it. But she answered a bit primly.

"My name is Judith Hester Grayson."

There was a silence . . . a very queer silence. The man looked at her for quite a time without saying anything. Then he merely asked her politely to sit down.

"I'm waiting for Timothy," she explained. "He's gone to tell Mrs. Thompson something. When he has told it we are going back to Bartibog."

"Now, if you have any notion of kidnapping me, Mr. Man!"

"Of course. But meanwhile you might as well be comfortable. And a spot of light refreshment perhaps? What would you like?"

Judy sat down. She felt oddly happy and at home.

"Can I have just what I like?"

"Yes."

"Then," said Judy triumphantly, "I'd like some ice-cream with strawberry jam on it."

The man rang a bell and gave an order. The ice-cream and jam came. Yes, this must be Tomorrow. No doubt about it. Ice-cream and strawberry jam didn't appear in this magical manner in Today.

"We'll set a share aside for Timothy," said the man.

They were good friends right away. The man didn't talk a great deal but he looked at Judy very often. There was a tenderness in his face . . . a tenderness she had never seen before in anybody's face, not even in Mother's. She felt that he liked her very much.

"I have your picture in my bureau drawer," she told him.

He looked startled.

"My picture! Who gave it to you?"

"Nobody. I cut it out of a paper. It hadn't any name but I liked it. Do you notice . . ." Judy was very grave, ". . . that our chins are something alike?"

"Something," agreed the man. Then he laughed . . . bitterly. Did all grown-up people laugh like that? No, Tillytuck didn't. But this man was looking as bitter as his laugh now. He wasn't happy. Judy wished she could make him happy. People who lived in Tomorrow shouldn't be unhappy.

Timothy came in and ate his share of the treat. Then there was nothing to do but go. Judy knew the man hadn't the slightest notion of kidnapping her and she felt the strangest, most unaccountable sensation of disappointment.

"Good-bye and thank you," she said politely. "It is very nice here in Tomorrow."

"Tomorrow?"

"This is Tomorrow," explained Judy. "I've always wanted to get into Tomorrow and now I have."

"Oh, I see. Well, I'm sorry to say it isn't Tomorrow for me. And *I* wouldn't want to get into Tomorrow. *I* would like to get back into Yesterday."

Judy was very sorry for him. She looked longingly back to Flying Cloud as Timothy rowed away. Why did Grandmother hate this man? There was nothing hateful about him. Her heart yearned back to Flying Cloud. Even on the road she turned again for a last, longing look at it.

"Look out," screamed Timothy.

The room went around oddly. The furniture nodded and jigged. The bed . . . how came she to be in bed? She couldn't remember going to bed. Somebody with a white cap on was just going out of the door. What door? How funny one's head felt! There were voices somewhere . . . low voices. She could not see who was talking but somehow she knew. Mother and the man. What were they saying? Judy heard stray sentences here and there, bobbing out of a confusion of murmuring.

"I . . . I thought you always hated her," said Mother. There was a sound of tears in Mother's voice . . . and a sound of laughter, too. Laughter with no bitterness in it.

"My own baby! I loved her," said the man. "Always. But I never knew how much till Timothy Salt came rowing over to tell me she had been struck . . . and killed . . . by a car."

"I knew you loved her as soon as I got here and saw your face bending over her," said Mother.

More murmurs. The room went around again . . . jigged up and down . . . steadied itself.

"I admit I was jealous of her. I thought you cared nothing for me any more . . . you seemed so wrapped up in her."

If that room would only stay put! Really, things behaved very queerly in Tomorrow. Judy hadn't heard what Mother said. The man was speaking again.

"It was your mother told you that. She never liked me or anything about me. You remember she would never call Judy anything but Hester because Judith was *my* choice of a name . . . my mother's. Elaine, you know it was your mother and Martha Monkman who made all the trouble between us."

"Not all." Mother seemed to be spunking up in a rather half-hearted defence of her family. "Not *all*. You know your sister hated me . . . *she* made half the trouble."

"Grace was always a mischief-maker I admit. But I wouldn't have believed her if I thought you still cared. And Judy seemed afraid of me. I thought you were bringing her up to hate me."

"Oh, no, no, Stephen! She *was* frightened of you . . . I didn't know why. I think . . . now . . . mother and Martha told her things . . . and I thought you couldn't forgive her for not being a boy."

"Woman!"

What a delightful way he said "Woman." Judy could fancy his smile. She wished she could see him but when she tried to turn her head round went that room again.

"We were both young fools," Mother was saying when it steadied once more.

"Is it too late to be wise, Elaine?" said the man.

Judy strained her ears for Mother's answer. Somehow, she felt it would be of tremendous significance to everybody in the world. But she could hear nothing . . . only sobs. Judy gave a long sigh of despairing resignation.

There was a brief silence. Then they came over to her bed . . . Mother and the man. She could see them now. Mother, all pale and tearful, looking as if she had been through some terrible experience, but with some strange inner radiance shining behind it all . . . a radiance that seemed part of the golden sunset light which suddenly flooded the room. The man was smiling triumphantly. Judy felt they both loved her very much.

"Are you feeling better, darling?" said Mother.

"Have I been sick?"

"You were knocked down by a car over on the mainland road," said the man. "Timothy came for help. To use his own expressive language, the liver was scared out of him. We brought you over here to Flying Cloud and sent for the doctor . . ."

"And for me," said Mother happily.

"The doctor said you had a very slight concussion . . . nothing serious. You'll be all right soon. Only you must keep very quiet for a few days."

He had such a delightful voice . . . you loved him for his voice. And he had his arm around Mother.

"This is your father," said Mother, "and . . . and . . . we are not going to be separated any more."

"Father is dead," said Judy. "So I suppose I am dead too."

"Father and you are both very much alive, sweet." Father bent down and kissed her. "When you feel quite up to listening you shall hear the whole story of two very proud, very silly, very unreasonable young people who were not all to blame for what happened and who have learned wisdom through suffering."

The woman with the white cap was coming in again. Somehow Judy knew that whatever she had to say must be said before she quite got in.

"Will we live here?"

"Always . . . when we're not living somewhere else," said Father gaily.

"And will Grandmother and The Woman live with us?"

Father seemed as bad as Timothy for slang.

"Not by a jugful," said Father.

The sunset gold was fading and the nurse was looking her disapproval. But Judy didn't care.

"I've found Tomorrow," she said, as Father and Mother went out.

"*I* have found something I thought I had lost forever," said Father as the nurse shut the door on him.

(1934)

I Know a Secret

In chapters 30 and 31 of *Anne of Ingleside*, Anne's daughter Nan has a run-in with an older girl named Dovie, who charms Nan with the promise of a secret. For that narrative sequence, Montgomery drew liberally on this next story, published in the August 1935 issue of *Good Housekeeping* with the following subhead: "Dovie, Who Was Eleven, Knew So Much More Than Jane, Who Was Only Eight." A girl with a propensity for sharing secrets is also featured in chapter 5 of *Jane of Lantern Hill*, except the secret in question turns out to be the truth about Jane's parents' marriage.

"I KNOW A SECRET . . . I KNOW A SECRET . . . I KNOW A secret . . . and I won't tell *you*," chanted Dovie Johnson as she teetered back and forth on the very edge of the wharf.

Jane shuddered to see her, and yet the teetering had a fascination. She was so sure Dovie would fall off sometime, and then what? But Dovie never did. Her luck always held.

Everything Dovie did, or said she did—which were, perhaps, two very different things, although Jane was too innocent and credulous to know that—had a fascination for Jane. Dovie, who was eleven and had lived in Bartibog all her life, knew so much more than Jane, who was only eight and had lived in Bartibog only a year. Bartibog, Dovie said, was the only place where people knew anything. What could you know, shut up in a town?

And Dovie knew so many secrets. She never would tell them, and Jane pined to know them. Secrets must be such wonderful, mysterious, beautiful things. Jane hadn't a single secret. Everything she knew, other people knew—Mother and Aunt Helen and Uncle George. And a secret wasn't a secret if more than two people knew it, so Dovie said. If Dovie would only tell her one single secret, that would be enough. But plead as Jane might and did, Dovie wouldn't. Dovie would only wrinkle up her fat nose and look important and say that Jane was far too young to have secrets. This maddened Jane.

"You'd tell somebody. You couldn't help it," taunted Dovie.

"I wouldn't—I could so," cried Jane. "Oh, Dovie, please tell me a secret, just one. You know so many. You might tell me just one. Dovie—" Jane had a sudden inspiration—"if you tell me a secret, I'll give you six apples for it."

Dovie's queer little amber eyes gleamed. Apples were apples in Bartibog, where orchards were few. The George Lawrences had a small one, and in it were some August apples that ripened sooner than any others in Bartibog.

"Six yellow apples off that tree in the southwest corner?" bargained Dovie.

Jane nodded. Her breath came quickly. Was it—oh, was it possible that Dovie would really tell her a secret?

"Will your aunt let you?" demanded Dovie.

Every one in Bartibog knew that Mrs. George Lawrence was as mean as second skimmings with her apples, as with everything else. Jane nodded again, but rather uncertainly. She was none too sure about it. Aunt Helen let her have one apple a day—"to keep the doctor away"—but six all at once were a pretty big order. Dovie scented the uncertainty.

"You would have to have those apples right here before I could tell you a secret," she said firmly. "No apples, no secret."

"I—I may not be able to get them all at once," said Jane anxiously. "But I'll have them in a week."

Jane had had another inspiration. She would not eat her apple a day. She would save them up till she had six. Perhaps the doctor might come, but what of it? She liked Dr. Nicholas. He had come to see her when she had been sick in the spring, and he was rosy and jolly and twinkling. He had told her mother and Aunt Helen—especially Aunt Helen—that she must be let live in the sunshine all summer and she would be all right by fall.

"Well, I'll think it over," said Dovie doubtfully. "Don't get your hopes up. I don't expect I'll tell you any secret after all. You're too young. I've told you so often enough."

"I'm older than I was last week," pleaded Jane. "Oh, Dovie, you have so many lovely secrets. You might spare me one. Don't be so mean."

"I guess I've got a right to my own secrets," said Dovie crushingly. "Get a secret of your own, Jane Lawrence, if you want one so much."

"I don't know how," cried Jane in despair. "And it would be so lovely to have a secret."

"Oh, it's wonderful," agreed Dovie. "I tell you, Jane, life isn't worth living without secrets. Six apples isn't much to pay for one. If you'd give me that little gold chain of yours now . . ."

"I couldn't do that," said Jane miserably. "It isn't really mine, you see. It's Mother's, though she lets me wear it sometimes. Father gave it to her just before he died. It's almost the only little bit of jewelry she has."

"Oh, of course I know you and your mother are poor as church mice," agreed Dovie. "Ma says she doesn't know what you'd have done when your mother got sick if your Aunt Helen hadn't taken you in. My, she was mad at having to do it, though. She told Ma her and George had enough to do to make both ends meet as it was. And she said as soon as Hester—that's your ma, you know—"

"Of course I know my own mother's name," said Jane, a trifle on her dignity. Secrets or no secrets, there were limits.

"Well, your Aunt Helen said that she bet as soon as Hester got well again she'd have to go back to her work. What did your ma work at in town, Jane?"

"She taught school," said Jane, "and taught it well. But the secret, Dovie—you'll tell me one, won't you?"

"We'll see when you get those six apples," was all Dovie would say.

But she had never conceded so much before, and Jane's hopes were high.

She continued to sit on the wharf long after Dovie had gone. She liked to sit on the wharf and watch the fishing boats going out and coming in, and sometimes a ship drifting down the harbor, bound to fair lands far away—"far, far away"—Jane repeated the words to herself with a relish. They savored of magic. She wished she could sail away in a ship—down the blue harbor, past the bar of shadowy dunes, past Prospect Point, which at sunset became an outpost of mystery; out, out to the blue mist that was a summer sea; on, on to enchanted islands in golden morning seas. Jane flew on the wings of her imagination all over the world as she squatted there on the old, sagging, half-decayed wharf.

This afternoon she was all keyed up about the secret. Dovie Johnson and she had been playmates of a sort ever since Jane had come to Bartibog. The very first time Jane had ever seen her, Dovie had whispered,

"I know a secret."

That is the most intriguing phrase in the world. From that moment Jane was Dovie's humble and adoring satellite. Dovie liked Jane well enough.

"No harm in her—a bit soft," she told the other Bartibog girls, none of whom bothered much about Jane.

Would Dovie really tell her a secret? And what would it be? Something lovely, of course. Secrets were always lovely. Perhaps Dovie had been through the looking glass like Alice. Or perhaps she had seen a tiny white fairy lying on a lily pad in her father's pond. Or a boat sailing down the Bartibog River, drawn by stately white swans attached to silver chains. Perhaps the secret was something the birds told her. Or it might be that she had been to the moon.

The moon, white and frail, was hanging over the sand dunes now. Soon it would be bright and shining. Jane loved the moon. She loved to dream about it. It was a silver world of fancy where she lived a strange dream life. She never told any one about it, not even Mother, so Jane really had a wonderful secret all her own if she had only had sense enough to know it.

Perhaps Dovie knew a princess. Or, since princesses were scarce in Bartibog, just a common, everyday girl who had been changed into a toad by a witch. But no—Jane shivered—that would not be beautiful, and secrets were always beautiful. Surely Dovie would tell her one. How happy she would be when Dovie had told her a secret! She was happy now in the very thought of it, so happy that even Aunt Helen's frown when she came in late to supper couldn't squelch her.

Anyhow Aunt Helen was always frowning. Jane thought she would be glad for more reasons than one when Mother was well enough to go back to town and teach. Somehow she knew Mother would be very glad, too, though Mother was always sweet and never answered back when Aunt Helen said mean little things. Jane didn't mind—much—when Aunt Helen said mean things to her. But she hated it when she said them to Mother. Mother was so dear and pretty and sad. And not strong. Aunt Helen was always twitting her about that. There must be something wicked about not being strong, though Jane couldn't imagine what it was. She wasn't strong herself.

"But how could she be?" she had heard Aunt Helen saying to Uncle George. "Her mother has no constitution. It was a mistake for Beverley ever to marry her. And the girls he might have had!"

Jane liked to speculate on those girls Father might have had. One of them might have been her mother. But that was horrible. Nobody could be her mother except Mother. The thing was simply unthinkable.

"I *think* Dovie Johnson is going to tell me a secret," Jane confided to Mother that night when she was being put to bed. "Of course I won't be able to tell it to you, Mother, because no more than two people can have a secret. You won't mind, will you, darling?"

"Not at all," said Mother, much amused.

Dovie Johnson always amused her. George said she was "a young devil," and Helen didn't approve of Jane's playing with her—"though the Johnsons are *very* respectable." But there was no one else for Jane to play with, and she was so taken up with Dovie.

For a week Jane denied herself her daily apple. When Aunt Helen gave it to her—grudgingly, as she gave everything—Jane would slip away, ostensibly to eat it, but in reality to store it in a box in the granary. She watched the apples anxiously for spot or blemish. Those apples didn't keep. But when she met Dovie on the wharf the next Saturday morning, she had the six apples, fair and unmarred.

"Here are the apples, Dovie," she said breathlessly. "And now tell me the secret."

Dovie looked at the apples rather disdainfully. "They're small," she said.

Jane's heart sank. "They're *all* small this summer," she faltered. Dovie pursed up her lips. "I'll tell you the secret some other time."

"I don't want to hear it some other time," cried Jane. Jane had a spirit of her own, and nothing roused it more quickly than injustice. "A bargain is a bargain, Dovie Johnson. You *said* six apples for a secret. Here are the apples. And you shan't have a bite unless you tell me the secret."

"Oh, very well," said Dovie in a bored way. "Only don't blame me if you don't like it so well when you hear it. Swear you'll never tell any one, cross your heart and hope to die."

"Of course I won't tell. It wouldn't be a secret then."

"Well, listen," said Dovie.

Jane listened. The water swelling around the piers of the wharf listened. The hills across the harbor listened. Or so it seemed to Jane. The whole world was listening. Jane shivered with delicious ecstasy. She was going to hear a secret at last.

"You know the Jimmy Thomases down at the Harbor Mouth?" said Dovie. "Six-toed Jimmy Thomas?"

Jane nodded. Of course she knew the Jimmy Thomases—at least, knew of them. Uncle George got his fish from them. But what could they possibly have to do with the secret?

"And you know Ellen Thomas?" went on Dovie.

Jane had seen Ellen Thomas once, when Six-toed Jimmy had brought her round with him in his fish wagon. She had not liked her much. Ellen was just about her own age, with jet-black bobbed hair and bold black eyes. She had stuck her tongue out at Jane.

"Well—" Dovie drew a long breath—"this is the secret. *You* are Ellen Thomas, and *she* is Jane Lawrence."

Jane stared at Dovie. She hadn't the faintest glimmer of Dovie's meaning. What she had said made no sense.

"I—I—what do you mean?"

"It's plain enough, I should think." Dovie smiled pityingly. "You and her was born the same night. It was when your ma and your dad were living in that little house at the Harbor Head when he was working for the Biligy people. The nurse took you down to Thomases' and put you in Ellen's cradle and brought Ellen back to your ma. Nobody but her ever knew the difference. She did it because she hated your ma. She wanted your dad for herself, and she took that way of getting even. And that is why you are really Ellen Thomas, and you ought to be living down there at the Harbor Mouth, and poor Jane Lawrence ought to be up at your Uncle George's instead of being banged about by that stepmother of hers."

Jane believed every word of this preposterous yarn. Not for one moment did she doubt the truth of Dovie's tale. She gazed at Dovie with anguished, disillusioned eyes. This—*this*—was the beautiful secret!

"How—how did you find out?" she gasped through dry lips.

"The nurse told me on her deathbed," said Dovie solemnly. "I s'pose her conscience troubled her. I've never told any one. The next time I saw Ellen Thomas—Jane Lawrence, I mean—I took a good look at her. She has just the same kind of ears as your ma. And she's dark complected like your ma. *You*'ve got blue eyes and yellow hair. I don't s'pose anything can be done about it now. But I've often thought it wasn't fair, you having such an easy time, and your ma keeping you like a doll, and poor El— Jane in rags and not getting enough to eat many's the time. And old Six-toed beating her when he comes home drunk. Say, these apples are dandy." Dovie took a huge bite out of one. "If you'll give me six more next week, I'll tell you another secret."

"I don't want to hear any more," cried Jane passionately. She could never forget what she *had* heard. Her pain was greater than she could bear. "I *hate* you for telling me this, Dovie Johnson."

Dovie shrugged. "I told you you mightn't like it, didn't I? Where are you going?"

For Jane, white and dizzy, had risen to her feet. "Home, to tell Mother," she said miserably.

"You musn't—you dasn't. Remember, you swore you wouldn't tell any one," cried Dovie. "The Black Man will get you if you do."

Jane didn't know who the Black Man was and didn't care. But it was true she promised not to tell. And Mother always said you must never break a promise.

"I guess I'll be getting home myself," said Dovie, not altogether liking the look of Jane.

She gathered up her apples and ran off, her bare dusty legs twinkling along the old wharf. Behind her she left a broken-hearted child sitting among the ruins of her small universe. Dovie didn't care. Jane was such a softy, it really wasn't much fun to fool her.

Jane sat on the wharf for what seemed hours—blind, crushed, despairing. She wasn't Mother's child; she was Six-toed Jimmy's child—Six-toed Jimmy, of whom she had always had such a secret dread simply because of his six toes. She had no business to be living with Mother, loved by Mother. Oh! Jane gave a piteous little moan. Mother wouldn't love her any more if she knew. All her love would go to Ellen Thomas. And yet she—*she*, Jane Lawrence—was Ellen Thomas.

Jane put her hand to her head. "It makes me dizzy."

"What's the reason you ain't eating nothing?" asked Aunt Helen sharply at the dinner table.

"Were you out in the sun too long, darling?" said Mother anxiously. "Does your head ache?"

"Ye—es," said Jane. Something *was* aching terribly, but it didn't seem to be her head. Was she telling a lie to Mother? And if so, how many more would she have to tell? For Jane knew she would never be able to eat again—never so long as this horrible secret was hers. And she knew she could never tell Mother. Not so much because of the promise—Jane had heard Aunt Helen say that a bad promise was better broken than kept—but because it would hurt Mother. Somehow Jane knew beyond any doubt that it would hurt Mother horribly. And Mother mustn't, shouldn't, be hurt. Jane recalled the time she had heard Mother crying in the night. She could never forget it. She must never breathe the secret to Mother.

And yet, there was Ellen Thomas. She wouldn't call her Jane Lawrence. It made Jane feel awful beyond any description to think of Ellen Thomas as being Jane Lawrence. She felt as if it blotted her out altogether. If she wasn't Jane Lawrence, she wasn't anybody. She would *not* be Ellen Thomas.

But Ellen Thomas haunted her. For a week Jane was beset by her—a wretched, wretched week during which Mother worried herself almost sick over Jane, who wouldn't eat and wouldn't play with Dovie Johnson any more and, just as Aunt Helen scornfully said, "moped around." Mother would have sent for Dr. Nicholas, but Dr. Nicholas was away for his vacation, and his practice was being looked after by some strange doctor who was boarding at the Harbor Hotel, and Aunt Helen didn't hold with strange doctors.

Jane had often wondered why, when people came to Bartibog for vacation, Dr. Nicholas should go away for his. But now Jane wondered over nothing except the one awful question which had emerged from her confusion of mind and taken possession of her. Shouldn't Ellen Thomas have her rights? Was it fair that she, Jane Lawrence—Jane clung to her own identity frantically—should have all the things that Ellen Thomas was denied and which were hers by rights? No, it wasn't fair. Jane was despairingly sure it wasn't fair. Somewhere in Jane there was a very strong sense of justice and fair play. And it became increasingly borne in upon her that it was only fair that Ellen Thomas should be told. After all, she didn't suppose Mother would care so much. She would be a little upset at first, of course, but as soon as she knew that Ellen Thomas was really her own child, all her love would go to Ellen, and Jane would become of no account to her. Mother would kiss Ellen Thomas and sing to her in the twilight when the fog was coming in from the sea—sing the song Jane loved best:

> "I saw a ship a-sailing, a-sailing on the sea,
>   And, oh, it was all laden with pretty things for me."

Jane and Mother had often talked about the time their ship would come in. But now the pretty things would be Ellen Thomas'.

There came a day when Jane knew she could bear it no longer. She must do what was fair. She would go down to the Harbor Mouth—it was only a mile—and tell the Thomasas the truth. They could tell Mother. Jane felt that she simply could not do that.

Jane felt a little better when she had come to this decision; better, but very, very sad. She tried to eat a little at supper because it would be the last meal she would ever eat with Mother.

"I'll always call her 'Mother,'" thought Jane desperately. "And I won't call Six-toed Jimmy 'Father.' I'll just say, 'Mr. Thomas' very respectfully. Surely he won't mind that."

But something choked her. She couldn't eat. Again Mother said timidly she wished she could see the doctor at the hotel.

"Dr. Nicholas will be back next week," said Aunt Helen. "We don't know a thing about that doctor at the hotel, not even his name. And his bill would likely be terrible. There isn't any great rush. You're always worrying over Jane. She runs around too much. That's all that ails her."

"She hasn't run around much lately," said Mother, standing up to Aunt Helen in a way she seldom dared to.

Her eyes sparkled, and a little flush stained her soft round cheeks that had been pale so long. Jane looked at Mother, suddenly seeing her for the first time. Before this she had just been Mother—somebody who cuddled and kissed you and looked after you and comforted you. All at once she had become a different person. Why, Mother was young and pretty—very pretty. She had beautiful soft dark eyes with long lashes, beautiful black hair in little waves about her face. Black hair! Jane's heart was torn by another pang. Ellen Thomas had black hair. Of course. Wasn't she Mother's daughter? Jane herself was fair—"like Beverley," Aunt Helen had said. Only unluckily she had never said it in Jane's hearing.

Nothing came of Mother's little flare-up. Aunt Helen was unmoved. Jane knew that Mother had to be patient until she was strong enough to go back to work.

Jane went right off after supper. She must go before it was dark, or her courage would fail her. Mother and Aunt Helen thought she was going to the wharf to play with Dovie. But Jane walked right past the wharf and down the harbor road, a gallant, indomitable little figure. Jane had no notion that she was a heroine. On the contrary, she felt very much ashamed of herself because it was so hard to do what was right and fair, so hard to keep from hating Ellen Thomas, so hard to keep from fearing Six-toed Jimmy, so hard to keep from turning round and running back to Mother.

It was a lowering evening. Out to sea were heavy black clouds. Fitful lightning played over the harbor and the dark wooded hills beyond it. The village of fishermen's houses at the Harbor Mouth lay flooded in a red light that escaped from under the low-hung clouds. Dozens of children were playing on the sand. They looked curiously at Jane when she stopped to ask which was Six-toed Jimmy's house.

"That one over there," said a boy, pointing. "What's your business with him?"

"Thank you," said Jane, turning away.

"Have ye got no more manners than that?" yelled a girl. "Too stuck up to answer a civil question."

The boy got in front of her. "See that house back of Thomases'?" he said. "It's full of rats, and I'll lock you up in it if you don't tell me what you want with Six-toed Jimmy."

"Come, now, behave like a lady," said a big girl tauntingly. "You're from Bartibog, and the Bartibogers all think they're the cheese. Answer Bill's question."

"If you don't, look out," said another boy. "I'm going to drown some kittens, and I'm quite likely to pop you in, too."

"If you've got a dime about you, I'll sell you a tooth," said a redheaded girl, grinning. "I had one pulled yesterday."

"I haven't a dime, and your tooth would be no use to me," said Jane, plucking up a little spirit. "You let me alone."

"None of your lip," said Redhead.

Jane started to run. The rat boy stuck out a foot and tripped her up. She fell her length on the tide-rippled sand. The others screamed with laughter. But some one exclaimed,

"There's Blue Jack's boat coming in."

Away they all ran. Jane picked herself up. Her dress was plastered with sand, and her stockings were soiled. But she was free from her tormentors. Would these be her playmates in the future?

She must not cry; she must not. She climbed the rickety board steps that led up to Six-toed Jimmy's door. Like all the harbor houses, Six-toed Jimmy's was raised on blocks of wood to be out of reach of any unusually high tide, and the space underneath it was filled with a medley of broken dishes, empty cans, old lobster traps, and all kinds of rubbish. The door was open, and Jane looked into a kitchen the like of which she had never seen in her life. The bare floor was dirty. The sink was full of dirty dishes. The remains of a meal were on a rickety old wooden table, and horrid big black flies were swarming over it. A woman with an untidy mop of grayish hair was sitting on a rocker nursing a baby—a baby gray with dirt.

"*My sister*," thought Jane.

There was no sign of Ellen or Six-toed Jimmy, for which latter fact Jane felt thankful.

"Who are you, and what do you want?" said the woman rather ungraciously.

She did not ask Jane in, but Jane walked in. It was beginning to rain outside, and a peal of thunder made the house shake. Jane knew she must say what she had come to say before her courage failed her, or she would turn and run from that dreadful house and that dreadful baby and those dreadful flies.

"I want to see Ellen, please," she said. "I have something important to tell her."

"Indeed, now!" said the woman. "It must be important from the size of you. Well, Ellen isn't home. Her dad took her up to West Bartibog for a ride, and with this storm coming up there's no telling when they'll be back. Sit down."

Jane sat down on the broken chair. She had known the harbor folks were poor, but she had not known any of them were like this. She had once been in Mrs. Tom Fitch's house with Uncle George, and it was as neat and tidy as Aunt Helen's. Of course, every one knew that Six-toed Jimmy drank up everything he made. And this was to be her home henceforth!

"Anyhow I'll try to clean it up," thought Jane forlornly, but her heart was like lead; the flame of high self-sacrifice which had lured her on was gone out.

"What are you wanting to see Ellen for?" asked Mrs. Six-toed curiously. "If it's about that Sunday school picnic, she can't go—that's flat. She hasn't a decent rag. How can I get her any, I ask you?"

"No, it's not about the picnic," said Jane drearily. She might as well tell Mrs. Thomas the whole story. She would have to know it anyhow. "I came to tell her—to tell her that—that she is me, and I'm her."

Perhaps Mrs. Six-toed might be forgiven for not thinking this very lucid. "Are you cracked?" she exclaimed. "Whatever on earth do you mean?"

Jane lifted her head. The worst was over now. "I mean that Ellen and I were born the same night, and—and—the nurse changed us because she had a spite at Mother, and—and—Ellen ought to be living with Mother and—and—having advantages."

That last phrase was one of Aunt Helen's, but Jane thought it made a dignified ending to a very lame speech.

Mrs. Six-toed stared at her. "Am I crazy, or are you? What you've been saying doesn't make any sense. Whoever told you such a rigmarole?"

"Dovie Johnson."

Mrs. Six-toed threw back her tousled head and laughed. She might be dirty and draggled, but she had an attractive laugh. "I might have knowed it. That's Dovie all over, the young imp. Well, little Miss What's-your-name, you'd better not be believing all Dovie's yarns, or she'll lead you a merry dance."

"Do you mean it isn't true?" gasped Jane.

"Not very likely. You must be pretty green to fall for anything like that. Ellen's a good six months older than you. Who on earth are you, anyhow?"

"I'm Jane Lawrence." Oh, beautiful thought, she *was* Jane Lawrence!

"Jane Lawrence! Beverley Lawrence's little girl? Why, I remember the night you were born. I was down at the Biology Station helping out in the house. I wasn't married to Six-toed then— more's the pity I ever was—and Ellen's mother was living and healthy. I knew your dad well. A nice young feller he was, even if he didn't live long. You look like him—you've got his eyes and hair. And to think you'd no more sense than to fall for that crazy yarn of Dovie's!"

"I am in the habit of believing people," said Jane, rising with a slight stateliness of manner, but too deliriously happy to want to snub Mrs. Six-toed very sharply.

"Well, it's a habit you'd better get out of when you're round with any of the Johnson tribe," said Mrs. Six-toed. "Sit down, child. You can't go home till this storm's over. It's pouring rain and dark as a stack of black cats. Why, she's gone—the child's gone!"

Jane was already blotted out in the downpour. Nothing but the wild exultation born of Mrs. Six-toed's words could have carried her home through that storm. The wind buffeted her, the rain streamed upon her; only the constant glare of the lightning showed her the road. Again and again she slipped and fell. Once she cut her wrist on a sliver of broken glass. But at last she reeled, dripping, mud-plastered, blood-stained, into the kitchen at Uncle George's, where Mother, as pale as ashes, was pacing frantically up and down. Even Aunt Helen was looking disturbed.

Mother ran and caught Jane in her arms. "Darling, what a fright you have given us! Oh, where have you been?"

"I only hope your Uncle George won't get his death out in this rain searching for you," said Aunt Helen, but there was some shrewish relief in her voice.

Jane had almost had the breath battered out of her. She could only gasp as she felt Mother's dear arms enfolding her:

"Oh, Mother, I'm me, really me. I'm not Ellen Thomas."

"That child is delirious," said Aunt Helen. "Well, it's a very inconvenient time for her to be sick."

Much water had flowed under Bartibog Bridge before the October day when Dovie Johnson held a group of girls spell-bound on the school playground while she told them a secret.

"Of course, everybody will soon know it. Jane's mother is going to be married to Dr. Oswald King. It's all very romantic. When Jane was so sick the morning after that thunderstorm in July, her mother just went haywire and vowed she would have the doctor from the hotel, Mrs. George or no Mrs. George. They didn't even know his name, but when he came—what do you think? He was an old beau of Mrs. Lawrence's, and she had liked him real well, too, only she liked Bev Lawrence better. But Dr. King never liked any one else, and he had never married. And now he's going to marry Mrs. Lawrence in a week's time. I'll bet she'll be glad to get away from Mrs. Second-skimmings!"

"How will Jane like it?" asked a girl. "She's always been so wrapped up in her mother."

"Oh, Dr. King was so good to her all the time she was getting over the pneumonia that she's just crazy about him. They're going to take her on their honeymoon in Europe. And when they come back, Jane's going to a very private and 'sclusive school in Halifax. I'm glad of her luck. I always liked Jane, though she was a bit soft! That kid would believe anything you told her!"

(1935)

Retribution

This next short story survives in typescript form among Montgomery's papers at the University of Guelph archives, in a folder containing six stories that she would rework for her final book, *The Blythes Are Quoted*. The typescript for all but one of these stories begins with the address of the home she called "Journey's End," to which she and her husband had retired in April 1935: "Mrs. L.M. Montgomery / 210A Riverside Drive / Toronto, Ont. Can." While the appearance of her mailing address suggests that she submitted (or intended to submit) these six stories to periodicals, none of them has been found in published form or is listed in her ledger of her published work, suggesting that she was not able to find homes for these stories or (less likely) that she had changed her mind about submitting them. But even if she used *Blythes* as a way to salvage stories she had been unable to place in the periodical market of the 1930s, Montgomery did more than insert references to members of Anne's household and shift the setting to rural Prince Edward Island, as she had done thirty years earlier when creating *Chronicles of Avonlea*. As a comparison of both versions of this story shows, she also expanded the characters' back stories, added complexity to the protagonist's motivation, and slowed down the pacing for dramatic effect. This story also demonstrates Montgomery's attempts to offer the magazine marketplace a more realistic story about an embittered woman who has grounds for seeking justice from a man who has never faced consequences for his actions.

CLARISSA WILCOX WAS ON HER WAY TO LONG SHORE. She had heard that David Anderson was dying and she must see him before he died. There were some things she must say to him. She had been waiting for forty years to say them and her chance had come at last.

She had known it must come. Amid all the injustices of life this one monstrous injustice could not be permitted . . . that David Anderson with whom she had danced in youth . . . should die without hearing what she had to say to him.

He could still hear her . . . so much she knew. Dr. Elmsley had told her so. The sudden unheralded stroke that had laid her hated enemy low had robbed him of speech and movement . . . even of sight, since he could not lift his eyelids . . . but he could still hear and was quite conscious. Helpless . . . at her mercy at last . . . she could tell him what had burned in her heart for years. He would have to listen to her. He could not escape . . . could not walk away with his suave, courtly, inscrutable smile. She would avenge Blanche at last . . . beautiful, beloved Blanche, dead in her dark young loveliness.

Clarissa, as usual, was shrouded in black, bent and smileless. She had worn black ever since Blanche had died. Her long, heart-shaped face, with its intense, unfaded blue eyes, was covered with minute wrinkles. Her black hair, with hardly a thread of gray in it, looked rather unnatural around that wrinkled face under the crocheted fascinator Blanche had made her so long ago. She seldom went anywhere and it had lasted well. Clarissa never cared . . . now . . . what she wore. She had a long, thin mouth and a dreadful smile . . . when she smiled at all. She was smiling now. David Anderson was sick . . . sick unto death . . . and her hour had come.

The magic light of a long blue evening was sifting in from the sea but the wind was rising rapidly. It sighed in the tall old pines along the road and it seemed to Clarissa that ghostly years were calling to her in its voice. It was not an ordinary wind . . . it was a wind of death blowing for David Anderson. What if he died before she got to him! She had been late in hearing of his illness. She hurried faster along the road to Long Shore.

Two ships were sailing out of the harbour . . . *his* ships. Where were they off to? Ceylon . . . Singapore . . . Mandalay? Once the names would have thrilled her . . . once she had longed to see those alluring places. But it was Rose who saw them with him . . . Rose, who was dead, too. But the ships still went out, although David Anderson, who had been a ship-builder and owner all his life, carrying on trade with ports all over the world, had long ceased to go in them. He left that to his son. His son? *Perhaps.*

Long Shore was before her . . . David Anderson's rich, splendid house where Rose had queened it for years. Little white cherry-blossom petals were snowing down on the walks through the salty twilight air. The wide door was open and she went in . . . across the hall . . . up the wide, velvet stairs where her foot-steps made no sound. All about her were empty rooms. Through the portieres of dull gold that hung in the library doorway she saw the portrait of Rose hanging on the opposite wall . . . Rose, painted in her wedding gown of ivory satin. Clarissa saw nobody but whispers seemed to haunt the house. It was full of shadows . . . shadows that grasped at you. They had come to attend David Anderson into eternity. But she would not be daunted by them. She had things to say . . . things to say. . . .

Here was his room at last . . . a long, feline room with a little fire at the end of it like the red tongue of a cat. No one was in it except David . . . what good fortune! There was no light and the crowding trees outside made it dim. The perfume of the lilac hedge below came in heavily. Clarissa had always felt that there was something not quite chaste in the scent of lilac blossoms. They were remembering some secret, too-sweet thing . . . like the love between David Anderson and Blanche.

There was a vase on the table full of some white flowers that glimmered spectrally through the dusk. On the wall above them hung Rose's miniature. Clarissa did not hate the portrait in the library but she hated the miniature. It was so intimate and pos-sessive, as if it slyly flaunted its complete ownership of David Anderson. Clarissa hated everything about it . . . the pale, shining golden curls on either side of the vivid rose-and-white face, the large, round blue eyes, the rosebud mouth, the sloping shoulders. The frame was of gold with a golden bow-knot atop. Rose had given it to David one birthday.

After one glance of hatred Clarissa thought no more of it . . . or of anything but David. He was lying in the old-fashioned, canopy-top bed which had been his father's and mother's and in which he and Rose had slept all their married life. His face on the pillow was a face of yellow wax. His eyes, his smoky gray eyes, were hidden under wrinkled lids. His long-fingered, exquisite, rather cruel hands were lying on the spread. The deep dimple in his chin . . . Rose used to put her finger teasingly into that dimple . . . had not changed. His magnificent white hair swept back from his brow. He was an old man but he did not seem old, even as he lay there dying. And, she thought, he still gave you the feeling that he was doing you a favour in allowing you to look at him.

Clarissa sat down on a chair. Her breath came fast. She was unpleasantly surprised to find she was afraid of him. She had always been afraid of him in life but she had not expected to be afraid of him now when he was as good as dead. She had not expected he would still be able to make her feel crude . . . silly . . . always in the wrong. She found her thin, veined hands trembling and she was furious. She had waited a lifetime for this hour . . . she would not be robbed of it.

She fought down her weakness. Her voice was quite steady when she finally spoke. The old house seemed listening to the cold poison of her words. At times the gusts of wind died away as if it, too, were listening. But she must say all she had to say quickly. Someone must come in at any moment.

"Tonight I shall rest well for the first time in years, David Anderson. I shall have told you what I have always wanted to tell you. How I've hated you . . . always . . . always! How I've looked forward to seeing you on your deathbed! You ruined and killed Blanche. You knew she died . . . but you did not know her child lived. You thought it died with the mother. It lived . . . and a cousin of ours took it. It was a boy . . . perhaps your only son, David Anderson. When he was seventeen he came back to Long Shore and you gave him a job in your shipping office. He was called John Lovel. Do you remember, David Anderson? *It was Blanche's son you sent to jail.* Your partner wanted to overlook his fault and give him another chance but you were relentless. Your son went to jail and when he came out after five years he was a criminal. He is in the penitentiary now . . . for life. Your son, David Anderson! I can prove all this and when you are dead I shall publish it. Every one will know that you, the just, upright, censorious man, were the lover of a girl you ruined and the father of an illegitimate son who is a jail-bird. People will point out your grave and say, 'Old David Anderson lies there. He was a hypocrite.' And I shall laugh to hear them, David Anderson . . . oh, how I shall laugh. I have laughed many a time in these past years, knowing that if I opened my mouth I could blacken the spotless reputation of which you were so proud. You were a proud man always, David Anderson . . . proud of your wife . . . your big business . . . your fine, rich house . . . your beautiful wife . . . your handsome son. *Are you sure he's your son, David Anderson?* Rose had a lover. You didn't know that. Perhaps I am the only one who knows it. I've always meant to tell you before you died. You worshipped Rose . . . you put up a beautiful and costly stained glass window to her memory in your big church. Its light falls at night across her grave and touches Lloyd Norman's. He does not come to her now . . . her baby face does not flush for his footsteps as I've seen it flush. Her cheek is cold . . . the grave is a bitter lover, David Anderson. But you know now . . . you know now."

Her passionate words sank into the silence as into a deep well. She had wreaked her hatred at last.

Suddenly she knew that she was alone in the room. With shaking hands she snatched a match and lighted a candle on the table. She held it up . . . its faint flickering light wavered over the face on the pillow. David Anderson, once so tremendously alive, was dead. He had died while she was talking to him. And, lying dead, he smiled. Clarissa had always hated his smile because one could never tell what it meant. Nor could she tell now. Was he mocking her because nothing mattered . . . any longer?

She seemed to go limp like an old dress. She felt aged . . . worn-out . . . foolish. Quickly she went out of the room, leaving him smiling on the pillow, as arrogant in death as in life. Noiselessly she went down and out and along the dark evening road. The embers of sunset smouldered in the west. There were curling crests of ice-white foam on the sea as if it were gnashing its teeth at her. She was very cold.

"I wish I were dead," she whispered. "I loved him so . . . oh, I loved him so. I hope he didn't hear me . . . I hope he didn't hear me! But I'll never know!"

(ca. 1936–1938)

An Afternoon with Mr. Jenkins

In 1933, Montgomery published in *The Family Herald and Weekly Star*, a Montreal farm paper, a short story entitled "An Afternoon with Mr. Jenkins," about an eight-year-old boy named Timothy who worries when the two aunts he lives with receive a distressing letter. Although Montgomery would expand the story for inclusion in *The Blythes Are Quoted*, she also, in a unique form of gender reversal, published a version of this story in London's *Girl's Own Paper* in 1939, replacing Timothy with Sally Jane and shifting the setting from vaguely North American to vaguely British. In this later version, Sally Jane shares many of the characteristics of Timothy, including a fear of the dark, in spite of the fact that her age has been increased by five years.

SALLY JANE YAWNED. IF THIRTEEN YEARS KNEW ANYTHING about such a word, Sally Jane was bored. Saturday was, she reflected, a rather stupid day at Linden Hall, especially when her aunts were away and she could not go down to the village. She was not allowed to go out of the home grounds when her aunts were away, and lately they had been more fussy than ever about this.

Sally Jane was very fond of her aunts, especially Aunt Edith; but she secretly thought they were entirely too fussy about it. She couldn't understand it. Surely a big girl of thirteen, who had been going to school for two years alone, even if she didn't altogether like going to sleep in the dark yet, didn't need to be cooped up at Linden Hall just because her aunts were going to town. They had gone that morning on the early bus, and Sally

Jane felt sure they were worried. More than usual, that is, for they were always worried over something. Sally Jane didn't know what it was, but she had sensed it in everything they had done or said of late. It hadn't been many years ago, Sally Jane reflected, with the air of Mrs. Methusaleh recalling her youth, she could remember them being laughing and jolly, especially Aunt Edith, who was really very jolly for an old maid, as the boys in school called her.

They had laughed less and less these past two years, and Sally Jane had an odd feeling that this was somehow connected with her, although she couldn't understand how that could be. She wasn't a very bad girl. Not even Aunt Kathleen, who—perhaps because she was a widow—took a rather strict view of things, ever said she was a bad girl. Now and then, of course, but it was hard to be perfect. Why, then, did they worry about her? Maybe women had to worry. Men now—if her father had lived! But in that case she, Sally Jane, might not have been living at Linden Hall. That would be terrible. Sally Jane loved Linden Hall. She felt that she could never live anywhere else. When she said this to Aunt Kathleen one day her aunt had sighed and looked at Aunt Edith. She hadn't said anything, but Aunt Edith had replied passionately:

"I can't believe God could be so unjust. Surely, surely, He couldn't be so heartless!"

"S-sh!" said Aunt Kathleen warningly.

"She'll have to know some time," said Aunt Edith bitterly. "The ten years will soon be up, and probably shortened for good behaviour."

Sally Jane was hopelessly puzzled. What was it she would have to know some time, and in any case why should it all be "s-sh-ed" away? Aunt Kathleen had immediately begun talking about her music lessons and the possibility of securing Professor Harvey as a teacher. Now, Sally Jane hated the very thought of taking music lessons. She knew she hadn't a spark of music in her, yet she knew she would have to. Nothing ever made Aunt Kathleen change her mind.

Sally Jane felt aggrieved. Aunt Edith had promised to take her to the lake that day, and they were to go on the bus. Sally Jane adored riding on the bus. She was to be allowed to ride a horse on the merry-go-round, too, another thing she adored.

Then that morning there had been a letter for Aunt Kathleen. She had turned dreadfully pale when she read it, and had said something to Aunt Edith in a queer choked voice. Aunt Edith had turned pale, too, and they had gone out of the breakfast-room. After a little, Aunt Edith came back and told Sally Jane she was very sorry she couldn't take her to the lake after all. She and Aunt Kathleen must go to town on important business.

"You've been crying, Aunt Edith," Sally Jane had said, troubled. She got up out of her chair and hugged Aunt Edith, and the tears had welled up in Aunt Edith's sweet brown eyes again.

Aunt Kathleen was not crying. She was pale and stern and told Sally Jane shortly and unsympathetically that she must not go outside the grounds until they returned.

"Can't I just go down to the village?" Sally Jane had implored. She wanted to buy something for Aunt Edith's birthday to-morrow. She had saved a little out of her pocket money and she meant to spend it on a gift for Aunt Edith, but Aunt Kathleen had been inexorable.

Sally Jane did not sulk; she never sulked. She had, however, a rather dismal forenoon. She practised her music lesson, and oh, how she hated it! She ran races with Merrylegs. She undressed and redressed her dolls. She even made a mud-pie rather guiltily in the back-yard. She had never been actually forbidden to make mud-pies, but she knew Aunt Kathleen did not approve of them. She ate the lunch old Linda set out for her. She had also tried to talk to Linda, for Sally Jane was a sociable little soul, but it was one of Linda's grumpy days. After lunch she said that she had a headache and was going to bed. Sally Jane didn't see what she was going to do in the afternoon.

Well, she would go down to the gate and watch the buses and the cars go by. That wasn't forbidden, anyhow. She wished she had some raisins to eat. Every Sunday afternoon she was given a handful of big juicy purple raisins as "a Sunday treat," but this was only Saturday and when Linda had a headache there was no use asking for anything.

"What are you thinking of, sister?" asked a voice.

Sally Jane jumped. Where had the man come from? There hadn't been any sound, any footstep. Yet there he was, right by Sally Jane's side, looking down at her with a peculiar expression on a handsome, sulky, deeply lined face. He wasn't a tramp—he was too well dressed for that—and Sally Jane, who was always feeling things she couldn't have explained, had an idea that he wasn't used to being so well dressed. The man's eyes were grey and smouldering and Sally Jane felt, too, that he was very cross about something, very cross; cross enough to do any mean thing that occurred to him. And yet there was something about him that Sally Jane liked.

"I was thinking what a splendid day it would have been for the lake," she explained rather stiffly, for she had always been warned not to talk to strangers.

"Oh! the lake. Yes, I remember it was always a fascinating spot for the small fry. Did you want to go there?"

"Yes. Aunt Edith was going to take me. Then she couldn't. She had to go to town on business."

"Oh. And is your Aunt Kathleen at home?"

Sally Jane thawed. This man knew Aunt Kathleen; therefore he was not a stranger and it was allowable to talk to him.

"No. She went, too."

"When will they be back?"

"Not till the evening. They went to town to see their lawyer. I heard them say so."

"Oh!" The man reflected a moment and then gave a queer inward chuckle. Sally Jane didn't like the sound of it, somehow.

"Are you a friend of Aunt Kathleen's?" she inquired politely.

The man laughed again.

"A friend? Oh yes, a very near and dear friend. I'm sure she'd have been delighted to see me."

"You must call again," said Sally Jane persuasively.

"It's quite likely I shall," said the man.

He sat down on the big grey boulder by the gate, lighted a cigarette with fingers that were strangely rough and calloused, and looked Sally Jane over in a cool, appraising manner.

"Whom do you look like, sister?" he said abruptly. "Your dad?"

Sally Jane shook her head.

"No. I wish I did. But I don't know what he looked like. He's dead, and there isn't any picture."

"There wouldn't be," said the man. He laughed again. Again Sally Jane didn't like it.

"My dad was a very brave man," she said quickly. "He was a soldier and he won a medal."

"Who told you that?"

"Aunt Edith. Aunt Kathleen won't talk of him ever. Aunt Edith won't either much, but she told me that."

"Edith was always a bit of a good scout," muttered the man. "You don't look like your mother, either."

"No, I can see that. I have a picture of mother. She died when I was born. Aunt Edith says I look like Grandmother Norris, *her* mother. I'm called Sarah Jane after her."

"Are your aunts good to you?" asked the man.

"They are," said Sally Jane eloquently. She would have said the same thing if they had not been. Sally Jane had a fine sense of loyalty. "Of course, you know, they're bringing me up. I have to be scolded sometimes and I have to take music lessons."

"You don't like that?" said the man, amused.

"No. I haven't any music in me, but I guess maybe it's good dis . . . discipline."

"You have a dog, I see," said the man, indicating Merrylegs. "Good breed, too. I thought Edith and Kathleen never liked dogs."

"They don't, but they let me have one because I wanted one so much. Aunt Edith said Grandmother Norris liked dogs, so Aunt Kathleen gave in. She even doesn't say anything when he sleeps on my bed at nights. She doesn't approve of it, you know, but she lets him stay. I'm glad. Because I don't like going to sleep in the dark."

"Do they make you do that?"

"Oh, it's all right," said Sally Jane quickly. She wasn't going to have any one imagine she was finding fault with her aunts. "I'm quite old enough to go to sleep in the dark. Only——"

"Yes?"

"It's only that when the light goes out I can't help imagining faces looking in at the window, pressed against the pane— awful faces—hateful faces. I heard Aunt Kathleen say once that she was always expecting to look at the window and see 'his' face. I don't know whom she meant, but after that I began to see faces in the dark."

"Your mother was like that," said the man absently. "She hated the dark. They shouldn't make you sleep in it."

"They should, too!" cried Sally Jane. "I know I'm too big a girl to be scared of the dark, and Aunt Edith and Aunt

Kathleen are bricks. I love them and I wish they weren't so worried."

"Oh, so they're worried?"

"Terribly. I don't know what it's about. I can't think it's me, though the way they look at me sometimes—— Do you see anything about me to worry them?"

"Not a thing. So your aunts are pretty good to you? Give you everything you want?"

"Everything that's good for me," said Sally Jane staunchly. "Only they won't have raisins in the rice pudding on Fridays. I can't imagine why. Aunt Edith would be willing, but Aunt Kathleen says the Norrises have never put raisins into rice pudding. Oh, are you going?"

The man had stood up. He was very tall, but he stooped a little. Sally Jane was sorry he was going, although there was something about him she didn't like, just as there was something she did. It was nice to have somebody to talk to.

"I'm going down to the lake," said the man. "Would you like to come with me?"

Sally Jane stared.

"Do you want me?"

"Very much. We'll ride on the bus, and the merry-go-round, and eat ice creams and drink ginger pop, and anything you like."

It was an irresistible temptation.

"But—but," stammered Sally Jane, "Aunt Kathleen said I wasn't to go off the grounds."

"Not alone," said the man. "She meant not alone. I'm sure she'd think it quite lawful for you to go with me."

"Are you quite sure?"

"Quite," said the man, and laughed again.

"About the money," faltered Sally Jane. "You see, I've only sixpence. Of course, I've got some of my pocket money, but I can't spend it; I must get Aunt Edith a birthday present with it. Still, I can spend the sixpence. I've had it a long time. Linda paid it to me one day for sitting still when my aunts were away. It was such hard work I never felt like spending it lightly."

"Sitting still is hard work sometimes," agreed the man. "But this is my treat."

"I must go and shut Merrylegs up," said Sally Jane, much relieved. "You won't mind waiting a few minutes?"

"Not at all."

Sally Jane flew up the driveway and disposed, rather regretfully, of a reluctant Merrylegs.

"It would be more convenient if I knew your name," she hinted timidly as they waited for the bus.

"You may call me Mr. Jenkins," said the man.

Sally Jane had a wonderful afternoon. A glorious trip on the bus, all the merry-go-rounds she wanted, and something better than ice cream.

"I want a decent meal," said Mr. Jenkins. "I didn't have any lunch. Here's a café—the Jo-Jo Café. Shall we go in and eat?"

"The Jo-Jo is an expensive place," warned Sally Jane gravely. "Can you afford it?"

"I think so." Mr. Jenkins laughed mirthlessly.

The Jo-Jo was expensive and exclusive. Mr. Jenkins told Sally Jane to order what she wanted and never think of expense. Sally Jane was in a seventh heaven of delight. It had been a glorious afternoon; Mr. Jenkins had been a very jolly comrade, and now to have a meal at the famous Jo-Jo and order from the menu just as if she were grown up! Sally Jane sighed with rapture.

"Tired, sister?" asked Mr. Jenkins.

Sally Jane liked the way Mr. Jenkins called her "sister." Mr. Black, the village grocer, who was quite a cinema fan, sometimes called her that, too, but not in just the same way, somehow—not as if they really were related.

"Oh no."

"You've had a good time?"

"Splendid. Only——"

"Yes? What?"

"I didn't feel as if *you* were having a good time," said Sally Jane slowly.

"Well, if it comes to that," said Mr. Jenkins, "I wasn't. I kept thinking of a friend of mine, and it rather spoiled things for me."

"Isn't he well?"

"Quite well—too well. Too likely to live. And, you see, he doesn't care much about living."

"Why not?" asked Sally Jane.

"Well, you see, he took a lot of money that didn't belong to him."

"You mean he stole it?" queried Sally Jane, rather shocked.

"Well, let's say embezzled. That sounds better; but the bank thought it sounded bad any way you pronounced it. He was sent to prison for ten years. They let him out when he had been there eight, because he behaved rather well, and he found himself quite rich. An old uncle had died when he was in prison and left him a lot of money. But what good will it do him? He's branded."

"I'm sorry for your friend," said Sally Jane. "Eight years is a very long time. Haven't people forgotten?"

"Some people never forget; his wife's sisters, for instance. They were very hard on him. How he hated them! He brooded all those eight years on getting square with them when he came out."

"How?"

"There is a way. He could take something from them that they want very much to keep. And he's lonely, he wants companionship; he's very lonely! I've been thinking about his future all the afternoon, but you mustn't think I haven't enjoyed myself. It has been something to remember for a long time. Now, is there anything else you want to do before we catch that five-o'clock bus back? You want to get back before your aunts come home, don't you?"

"Yes. But just so they won't be worried. I'm going to tell them about this, of course."

"Won't they scold you?"

"Likely they will, but hard words break no bones, as Linda says," remarked Sally Jane philosophically.

"I don't think they'll scold you much, not if you get the start of them with a message I'm sending them by you. You got that present for your aunt's birthday, didn't you?"

"Yes, but there is one thing. I've got that sixpence yet, you know. I'd like to buy some flowers with it and go over to the park and put them at the base of the soldiers' monument. Because my father was a brave soldier, you know."

"Was he killed at the front?"

"Oh no. He came back and married mother. He was in a bank, too. Then he died."

"Yes, he died," said Mr. Jenkins. "And," he added, "I fancy he'll stay dead."

Sally Jane was rather shocked. It seemed a queer way to speak of any one—what Aunt Kathleen would call flippant. Still, she couldn't help liking Mr. Jenkins.

"Well, good-bye, sister," said Mr. Jenkins, when they got off the bus at the gate of Linden Hall.

"Won't I see you again?" asked Sally Jane wistfully. She felt that she would like to see Mr. Jenkins again.

"I'm afraid not. I'm going away, far away. That friend of mine—he's going far away, to some new land, and I think I'll go too. He's lonely, you know. I must look after him a bit."

"Will you tell your friend I'm sorry he's lonely? And I hope he won't be always lonely."

"I'll tell him. And will you give your aunts a message from me?"

"Can't you give it to them yourself? You said you were coming back to see them."

"I'm afraid I can't manage it, after all. Now listen carefully, because this is important. Tell them they are not to worry over that letter they got this morning. They needn't go to their law-yer again to see if the person who wrote it has the power to do what he threatened to do. I know him quite well and I know he has changed his mind. Tell them he is going away and will never bother them again. You can remember that, can't you?"

"Oh yes. And they won't be worried any more?"

"No, they needn't worry any more. Only there's this! Tell them they must cut out those music lessons and put raisins in the Friday pudding and let you have a light to go to sleep by. If they don't, that person might worry them again."

"I'll tell them about the music lessons and the pudding, but," said Sally Jane staunchly, "not about the light, if it's all the same to that person. You see, I'm getting to be a big girl now and I mustn't be a coward. My dad wasn't a coward. If you see that person, will you please tell him that?"

"Well, perhaps you're right. I'll tell him, anyway. And this is for you alone, sister. We've had a fine time to-day, and it is all right, as it happens, but take my advice and never go off any-where with a stranger again. Most important."

Sally Jane squeezed Mr. Jenkins's hand.

"But *you* aren't a stranger," she said wistfully.

(1933/1939)

Appendix: Dog Monday's Vigil

LUCY MAUD MONTGOMERY

Included as an appendix is a different kind of textual repetition—a stand-alone story adapted from parts of *Rilla of Ingleside* (1921) and appearing in the third edition of *Our Canadian Literature: Representative Prose and Verse*, an anthology compiled by Albert Durrant Watson and Lorne Albert Pierce and published in 1923 by the Ryerson Press (which would publish the first Canadian editions of Montgomery's early books, including *Anne of Green Gables*, starting in 1942). It reworks the threads of the longer narrative focusing on the Blythe family dog, who, according to the narrator of *Rilla of Ingleside*, had been named after a character in Daniel Defoe's *Robinson Crusoe*, and who, as Idette Noomé has observed, "voices the anguish and pain all the humans strive to repress in the face of human loss and absence." In her journals, Montgomery mentioned reading a version of this story to a group of Toronto schoolchildren shortly after the publication of this novel. For Wendy Roy, the inclusion of this story in Watson and Pierce's anthology is evidence of *Rilla* being "considered canonical Canadian literature," but while the third edition also reprinted Montgomery's poems "An Autumn Evening" and "On the Hills" (both published initially in periodicals and included in *The Watchman and Other Poems*), it is worth noting that the initial two editions of this anthology, the first published in late 1922, had not included any material by Montgomery.

DOG MONDAY WAS THE INGLESIDE DOG. HE REALLY belonged to Jem, but he was very fond of Walter also. Monday was not a collie or a setter or a hound or a

Newfoundland. He was just, as Jem said, "plain dog"—"*very*
plain dog," uncharitable people added. Certainly Monday's
looks were not his long suit. Black spots were scattered at random over his yellow carcass, one of them apparently blotting
out an eye. His ears were in tatters, for Monday was never successful in affairs of honour. But he possessed one talisman. He
knew that not all dogs could be handsome or eloquent or vic-
torious, but that every dog could love. Inside his homely hide
beat the most affectionate, loyal, faithful heart of any dog since
dogs were, and something looked out of his brown eyes that
was nearer akin to a soul than any theologian would allow.
Everybody at Ingleside was fond of him, even Susan, although
his one unlucky propensity of sneaking into the spare room and
going to sleep on the bed tried her affection sorely.

On the morning when Jem Blythe left Glen St. Mary for
Valcartier, Dog Monday went to the station with him. He kept
close to Jem's legs and watched every movement of his beloved
master.

"I can't bear that dog's eyes," said Mrs. Meredith.

"The beast has more sense than most humans," said Mary
Vance.

Then the train was coming—mother was holding Jem's
hand—Dog Monday was licking it—everybody was saying
good-bye—the train was in—the train was pulling out—
everybody was waving—Dog Monday was howling dismally
and being forcibly restrained by the Methodist minister from
tearing after the train—they were gone!

The Ingleside folks were half way home when they missed
Dog Monday. Shirley went back for him. He found Dog Monday
curled up in the shipping shed near the station and tried to coax
him home. Dog Monday would not move. He wagged his tail to
show he had no hard feelings, but no blandishments availed
to move him. "Guess Monday had made up his mind to wait
there until Jem comes back," said Shirley, trying to laugh as he
rejoined the others.

Which was exactly what Dog Monday had done. His dear
master had gone; he, Monday, had been deliberately and of malice aforethought prevented from going with him by a demon
disguised in the garb of a Methodist minister; wherefore he, Dog

Monday, would wait there until the smoking, snorting monster which had carried his hero off, carried him back.

For weeks the Ingleside family tried to coax Dog Monday home—and failed. Once Walter went down and brought him home by main force in the buggy, and shut him up for three days. Monday went on a hunger strike and howled like a banshee night and day. They had to let him out or he would have starved to death. So they decided to let him alone, and Dr. Blythe arranged with the butcher near the station to feed him with bones and scraps. Dog Monday lay curled up in the shipping shed, and every time a train came in he rushed over to the platform, wagging an expectant tail, and tore around to everybody who came off the train. Then, when the train was gone, and he realized that Jem had not come, he trotted dejectedly back to his shed, with the funny little sidelong waggle that always made his hind legs appear to be travelling in a totally different direction from his front legs, and lay patiently down to wait for the next train. When cold weather came, Walter built a little kennel in the corner of the shed for him. Monday became quite famous. A Charlottetown reporter came out and photographed him and wrote up the story of Monday's vigil for his paper. It was copied all over Canada. But earthly fame mattered not to Monday. Jem had gone away—Monday didn't know where or why—but he would wait until he came back. Somehow, this comforted the Ingleside folks; it gave them an irrational feeling that Jem would come back, or Monday wouldn't keep on waiting for him.

"Fancy the faithful little beggar watching for me like that," Jem wrote home. "Honestly, dad, on some of these cold, dark nights in the trenches it heartens and braces me up to no end to think that thousands of miles away, at the old Glen station, there is a small spotted dog sharing my vigil."

Walter went away the next year and Dog Monday sent messages by him to Jem. Still another long year went by and still Dog Monday waited. On the September morning after Courcellette Rilla Blythe wakened at dawn and heard distinctly a dog howling in a melancholy way down in the direction of the station. Was it Dog Monday? Rilla shivered—the sound had in it something ominous and boding. She remembered hearing some one say once, "When a dog howls like that the Angel of Death is pass-ing." Rilla listened with a curdling fear at her heart. It *was* Dog Monday—she felt sure of it. Whose dirge was he howling? To whose hovering spirit was he sending that anguished greeting and farewell? Rilla went down to the station after breakfast, and the station master said: "That dog of yours howled from mid-night to sunrise something weird. I dunno what got into him. He kept the wife awake, and I got up once and went out and hollered at him; but he paid no 'tention to me. He was sitting all alone in the moonlight out there at the end of the platform, and every few minutes the poor little beggar'd lift his nose and howl as if his heart was breaking. He never did it afore—always slept in his kennel quiet and canny from train to train. But he sure had something on his mind last night."

Rilla went home anxiously. For four long days she waited. And when the word came that Walter had been killed in action at Courcellette she knew why Dog Monday had cried.

Three years went by—three years that seemed as long as an ordinary life time. Dog Monday, grown old and rheumatic, still kept faithful vigil. And one spring day, when wind and sunshine frolicked in Rainbow Valley, and the maple grove was golden-green, and the harbor all blue and dimpled and white-capped, the news came about Jem. There had been an insignificant little trench raid on the Canadian front, and Lieut. James Blythe was reported "wounded and missing."

That night, when Rilla was lying on her bed in the moonlight praying desperately for a little strength, Susan stepped in like a gaunt shadow and sat down beside her.

"Rilla, dear, do not worry. Little Jem is not dead."

"Oh, how can you believe that, Susan?"

"Because I *know*. Listen to me. When that word came this morning the first thing I thought of was Dog Monday. And to-night, I went down to the station. There was Dog Monday waiting for the night train, just as patient as usual. Now, Rilla dear, that trench raid was last Monday, and I said to the station agent, 'Can you tell me if that dog howled or made any kind of a fuss last Monday night?' He thought it over a bit and then he said, 'No, he did not.' 'Are you sure?' I said. 'There's more depends on it than you think.' 'Dead sure,' he said. 'I was up all night last Monday night because my mare was sick, and there never was a sound out of him.' Now, Rilla, dear, those were the man's very words. And you know how that poor little dog howled all night after the battle of Courcellette. Yet he did not love Walter as much as he loved Jem. If he mourned for Walter like that, do you suppose he would sleep sound in his kennel the night after Jem had been killed? No, Rilla, dear, little Jem is not dead, and that you may tie to. If he were, Dog Monday would have known, just as he knew before, and he would not still be waiting for the trains."

It was absurd and irrational and impossible. But Rilla believed it for all that; and Mrs. Blythe believed it; and the doctor, though he smiled faintly in pretended derision, felt an odd confidence replace his first despair; and foolish and absurd or not, they all plucked up heart and courage to carry on just because a faithful little dog at the Glen station was still watching for his master to come home. Common sense might scorn; incredulity might mutter "mere superstition"; but in their hearts the folks of Ingleside stood by their belief that Dog Monday knew—a belief that was justified six months later when word came that Jem Blythe had escaped from his German prison.

One spring day, when Rainbow Valley was sweet with white and purple violets, the little lazy afternoon accommodation train pulled into the Glen station. It was very seldom that passengers came by that train; so nobody was there to meet it except the new station agent and a small black and yellow dog, who for four and a half long years had met every train that had steamed into Glen St. Mary. Thousands of trains had Dog Monday met, and never had the boy he waited and watched for returned. Yet still Dog Monday watched on with eyes that never quite lost hope. Perhaps his dog heart failed him at times; he was growing old and rheumatic; when he walked back to his kennel after each train he never trotted, but went slowly, with a drooping head, and a depressed tail that had quite lost its old saucy uplift.

One passenger stepped off the train—a tall fellow in a faded lieutenant's uniform, who walked with a barely perceptible limp. He had a bronzed face and there were some grey hairs in the ruddy curls that clustered round his forehead. The new station agent looked at him curiously. He was used to seeing the khaki-clad figures come off the train, some met by a tumultuous crowd; others, who had sent no word of their coming, stepping off quietly like this one. But there was a certain distinction of bearing and feature in this soldier that caught his attention and made him wonder a little more interestedly who he was.

A black and yellow streak shot past the station agent. Dog Monday stiff? Dog Monday rheumatic? Dog Monday old? Never believe it! Dog Monday was a young pup gone clean mad with rejuvenating joy.

He flung himself against the tall soldier, with a bark that choked in his throat from sheer rapture. He flung himself on the ground and writhed in a frenzy of welcome. He tried to climb the soldier's khaki legs and slipped down and grovelled in an ecstasy that seemed as if it must tear his little body to pieces. He licked his boots, and when the Lieutenant had, with laughter on his lips and tears in his eyes, succeeded in gathering the little creature up in his arms, Dog Monday laid his head on the khaki shoulder and licked the sunburned neck, making queer sounds between barks and sobs.

The station agent had heard the story of Dog Monday. He knew now who the returned soldier was. Jem Blythe had come home.

(1923)

Afterword

W HEN L.M. MONTGOMERY'S FIRST BOOK, *ANNE OF Green Gables* (1908), was accepted by L.C. Page and Company (later known as the Page Company) in spring 1907, one of the clauses in her contract committed her to submitting all future book-length manuscripts to Page for the next five years. In her journal, she expressed her misgivings about this requirement given that Page's royalty rate was far below industry standards,[1] but an unanticipated complication was that she ended up being unable to write books fast enough for her publisher, especially after *Anne of Green Gables* proved to be a national bestseller in both the United States and Canada and *Anne of Avonlea* was published as a much-anticipated sequel in 1909.[2] When her intended third novel, *The Story Girl*, progressed more slowly than anticipated, Page suggested that she expand a nine-chapter serial entitled "Una of the Garden" into what would become *Kilmeny of the Orchard* (1910). Then, when she continued to resist writing a third novel about Anne after *The Story Girl* was published in 1911, Page proposed that she revise some of her best short stories for the world of Anne and compile them into a volume that he published as *Chronicles of Avonlea* in 1912.[3]

In her surviving life writing, Montgomery mentioned several times how little she cared for the process of revising previously published periodical material for book publication—she referred to it as "a business I dislike very much"—and how she saw these projects as irritating compromises between literary artistry and the economics of trade publishing. Referring in a letter to her correspondent G.B. MacMillan to the process of transforming

"Una" into *Kilmeny*, for instance, she expressed the opinion that "the 'padding' necessary to increase the length weakened the story very much and it was against my better judgment that I consented to have it appear in book form at all." Three years later, she had little more enthusiasm for *Chronicles*, confiding in her journal on receipt of her author's copies that "to me, from much re-writing they are very stale but to those to whom they come newly they may give pleasure." The fine line between literary fiction and commercial fiction even caused her some worry when a review of *Chronicles* in the *Toronto World* commented on her frantic publication schedule of five books in five years, prompting her to write to the periodical to correct "the mistaken impression that I've been writing a book every year. . . . I take a year to write a book and a year to rest in."[4] In both cases, Montgomery grew concerned that Page's insistence on releasing a book of hers every year would strain her literary reputation even as it helped maximize sales, especially since increased revenue would fill his coffers more than it should have filled hers.

Montgomery's comments about these two books imply a disconnect between volumes of original fiction (she told MacMillan how much she looked forward to working on her next novel after *Chronicles*, calling *The Golden Road* "work more after my own heart") and volumes of revised material (for which she "merely [had] to copy and amplify existing thoughts").[5] Yet the work included in this volume shows us that her stated attitudes about writing and revision were quite selective, obscuring the many instances of repetition and transplantation found in her book-length works of fiction. Moreover, such instances were hardly limited to the items included here: in the first two volumes in The L.M. Montgomery Library, *A Name for Herself* (a selection of so-called miscellaneous pieces) and *A World of Songs* (a selection of fifty poems), I noted several instances of anecdotes, conversations, turns of phrase, and excerpts from these periodical items that reappear in many of her books as well as numerous extracts from her journals that appear in strategically revised form in her 25,000-word celebrity memoir, "The Alpine Path: The Story of My Career." Prior to this, in volume 1 of my critical anthology *The L.M. Montgomery Reader*, I traced the ways that Montgomery repurposed extracts from four essays about the woods published the year she left Prince Edward Island in virtually all her Ontario novels.[6] Not included in the present volume are novel subplots that first appeared in almost identical form as short stories, including a fire at the Burnley house that Emily describes in a letter to her late father in chapter 17 of *Emily of New Moon*, first published as "What Came of a Dare" in 1902; two sequences in chapters 30 to 34 of *Anne of the Island*, first published as "Mrs. Skinner's Story" in 1908 and as "The Deferment of Hester" in 1907; and the subplot in *A Tangled Web* involving the ironically named cousins Big Sam and Little Sam, first published as "A House Divided against Itself" in 1930. I also have not included more than a few samples of early versions of stories that she reworked for book-length story collections or any of the extended excerpts from *Emily of New Moon*, *Emily Climbs*, *Magic for Marigold*, *Anne of Windy Poplars*, and *Anne of Ingleside* that appeared in different form in periodicals prior to or following book publication.[7] In short, while this volume contains a representative sample of instances when Montgomery told the same story twice, it is in no way exhaustive of this facet of her writing practice.[8]

It should be stated at the outset that Montgomery was hardly alone in publishing multiple versions of the same work in periodicals and in books. If we turn to the ten critical editions of early Canadian literary texts besides *Anne of Green Gables* published so far by Broadview Press as one representative sample, only one—Margaret Marshall Saunders's *Beautiful Joe* (1894)—appeared exclusively in book form. Of the remaining nine, Thomas Chandler Haliburton's *The Clockmaker* (1835–1836), James De Mille's *A Strange Manuscript Found in a Copper Cylinder* (1888), Stephen Leacock's *Sunshine Sketches of a Little Town* (1912), and Sara Jeannette Duncan's *The Pool in the Desert* (1903), *The Imperialist* (1904), and *Set in Authority* (1906) had appeared at least in part in periodical form prior to book publication; Isabella Valancy Crawford's *Winona; or, the Foster-Sisters* (1873) and Rosanna Mullins Leprohon's *The Manor House of De Villerai* (1859–1860) had been published exclusively in periodical form; whereas *Tekahionwake: E. Pauline Johnson's Writings on Native North America* is a new collection of periodical writings (some of them previously assembled in book form by Johnson during her lifetime) collected from across her career.[9] And as Wendy Roy has pointed out most recently, Montgomery and her contemporaries Nellie L. McClung and Mazo de la Roche were all "influenced by early-twentieth-century publication, marketing, and reading practices to become heavily invested in the cultural phenomenon of the continuing story" and thus were highly strategic in terms of maximizing their income (to say nothing of their readerships) by publishing their work in serial form as well as in book form.[10]

In addition, as scholarship on the work of some of Montgomery's predecessors and contemporaries has shown, the reasons to revise already published work could be as varied as the authors themselves. In an article focusing on multiple incarnations of Duncan's *The Imperialist*, for instance, Darlene Kelly reveals that the first book version of this novel "contained an astonishing number of revisions" to the two known newspaper serial versions that had preceded it. While some of the changes pertained to the writing style—Duncan "aimed for greater realism, more appealing characters, and sharper political analysis" as she revised—they had also to do with Duncan's access to the cultural milieu she was writing about, given that she had drafted the Ontario-set novel while living in India whereas "the wealth of details added to the last two versions of the text indicates that she became fully informed about political matters [pertaining to Ontario] during her visit to Canada in the autumn of 1903." Carl Spadoni, justifying his choice of copy-text for his critical edition of Leacock's *Sunshine Sketches*, notes that "Leacock conceived of the book as a serialized novel in the same way as nineteenth-century authors such as Dickens and Thackeray serialized their work." Accordingly, because "Leacock did not have an opportunity to proofread the text of each serialized narrative" and had "restructured the novel" for book publication after its serial run, the text of the first book edition reflects his final intentions more closely than the serialized text and is thus a superior choice of copy-text. And while Saunders's *Beautiful Joe* did not appear serially prior to book publication, Keridiana Chez points out that its text was revised considerably in subsequent editions, within and beyond Saunders's lifetime, to meet the perceived needs of shifting reading audiences in North America and the United Kingdom. Moreover, Roy notes that McClung submitted a stand-alone story entitled "Sowing Seeds in Danny" to a writing contest sponsored by an American magazine, and both this story and several more chapters were published individually while McClung continued to work on her book-length manuscript, which was published under the same title as that first story.[11]

Scholarship on these contemporaneous and predecessor authors can shed light on some of the general circumstances under which early Canadian authors revised their own work between periodical publication and book publication. For archival evidence of what these revisions can look like, I turn now to Montgomery's literary successor Alice Munro, the Nobel Prize–winning short story author who acknowledged her debt to Montgomery's work most notably in her afterword to the New Canadian Library edition of *Emily of New Moon*. Munro's fourteen books of short fiction—from *Dance of the Happy Shades* (1968) to *Dear Life* (2012), not counting several more "best of" collections—consist of stories that for the most part saw the light of day in periodicals, most notably in *The New Yorker*, which had a right-of-first-refusal contract with her starting in 1977 and published some sixty short stories by her between 1977 and 2012. As Carol L. Beran suggests in a 1998 article on Munro's work, "Publication by the *New Yorker* brought . . . Munro prestige, money, and a wide audience for her stories," and as such, Munro can serve as a productive contrast with Montgomery, given that both writers had separate but complementary careers as contributors to periodicals and as authors of books.[12] While many of the venues in which Montgomery published her periodical work were aimed at more mainstream audiences than those in which Munro published hers, Montgomery's periodical clients did include prominent magazines that, similar to *The New Yorker* for Munro, offered Montgomery high payment rates and visibility within the trade periodical marketplace: *The Delineator*, *Everybody's Magazine*, and *Good Housekeeping* in New York and *Canadian Home Journal*, *The Canadian Magazine*, and *Everywoman's World* in Toronto.

In their separate investigations into the extensive Alice Munro papers at the University of Calgary archives, Beran, Nadine Fladd, and Helen Hoy come to radically disparate conclusions about the evolution of Munro's stories from periodical to book, showing that the revision process can differ greatly from one project to the next even when the same participants are involved. As Beran reports concerning Munro's 1982 collection *The*

Moons of Jupiter, "Of the five stories that appeared in [*The New Yorker*], four were given to [Munro's Canadian book publisher] directly from the pages of the magazine without further revision," which Beran interprets as evidence of "how satisfied Munro was" with the revision process involving editor Charles ("Chip") McGrath. Munro ran up occasionally against *The New Yorker*'s rather conservative policies regarding coarse language and references to sex and to bodily functions, some of which prompted editorial suggestions that not only cleaned up Munro's language but also in some instances altered character motivation and plot points. Still, Beran points out that not all instances of censorship in *The New Yorker*'s incarnations of these stories were reversed when they appeared in their supposedly final form in Munro's book-length collections. Moreover, Munro "continued to send her editors [at *The New Yorker*] stories containing the types of language and description that she knew they would censor," which Beran sees as an example of "how her vision of her art remained strong in the face of editorial opposition."[13] Thanks to the vast array of drafts and proofs that are part of these Munro papers, Beran is able to piece together the evolution of these stories from submitted draft to periodical publication to book publication, contextualized by ample surviving correspondence between Munro and her editors.

In an article published more recently, Fladd builds on Beran's analysis but zeroes in on the editorial collaboration involving Munro's short story "The Turkey Season," published in *The New Yorker* late in 1980 and included in *The Moons of Jupiter*. Tracing McGrath's creation of a composite of two substantially different typescript versions of the story Munro had submitted to him, Fladd argues that this shared labour becomes an example of what Jerome McGann would call a social text that is created collaboratively between a writer and an editor; more importantly, this story marked "a turning point in Munro's literary aesthetic away from the documentary, and toward indeterminacy." Although she notes that the degree of McGrath's editorial involvement in Munro's work seems to have been limited to this particular short story, Fladd suggests that his hand steered Munro in a new direction as a writer, given that "elements now often considered distinctive to Munro's authorial persona or style have actually been developed in concert with McGrath."[14]

What this shows is that, while the author's name rightly appears as the sole creator of a work of literature, the act of creation is often nurtured, even shaped, by an editor behind the scenes.

Both of these articles follow Hoy's groundbreaking 1989 essay in which she discusses Munro's last-minute reconsideration of the structure and content of the collection that preceded *The Moons of Jupiter*, first advertised as *Rose and Janet* but published as *Who Do You Think You Are?* in fall 1978. As Hoy notes, Munro's epiphany about this collection "meant literally stopping the presses one Monday morning in mid-September while Munro . . . revised, copy-editors proofread, the press rewrote the flap copy, and the printers ordered more paper." Drawing on extensive archival documents and correspondence, Hoy reconstructs the collaborative process involving Munro, her agent, her American editor (who tried unsuccessfully to persuade Munro to transform the collection of linked short stories into a novel), and her Canadian editor, which culminated in Munro asserting her control over her work once she "had finally created the arrangement she felt to be artistically right." In contrast with Beran's observation that four of the five *New Yorker* stories were included unchanged in the manuscript of *The Moons of Jupiter*, suggesting a seamless line between periodical and book incarnations of the same work, in this case, as Hoy remarks, "the collecting of short stories which even hint at connections one with another can entail extensive creative effort by the author, long after the stories themselves have been completed. . . . Even when no revision is necessary, the sequencing of the stories and their consequent interrelationships necessitate difficult artistic decisions."[15] As far as Hoy is concerned, those decisions in terms of content and sequencing can involve fraught conversations with editors over the fine line between art and commerce, but at the end of the day, final decisions need to be made by the author, since it is the author's name—and not the names of agents and editors working with the author—that signs the work and accompanies it into the world.

I bring up these studies of some of Montgomery's literary predecessors, contemporaries, and successors in order to place her writing and editorial processes in context, in terms of what it is possible to determine based on surviving records and what must be left to conjecture. Given that Montgomery discussed her creative work in detail only occasionally in her surviving life writing—she told Ephraim Weber, in response to his question about *Anne of Green Gables* and her writing style, that "I revised and re-wrote and altered words until I nearly bewildered myself," without providing details[16]—it is unfortunate that there are so many gaps in her personal archive. While I am personally grateful that we have access to Montgomery's voluminous journals, two sets of multi-decade correspondence, handwritten manuscripts of most of her books (although those of *Kilmeny* and *Chronicles* are not among them), some contracts and business correspondence, and more than a dozen scrapbooks of published clippings, reading these scholarly contributions about Munro's revision process makes me regret that a wider array of Montgomery's drafts, outlines, typescripts, and correspondence has not survived.[17] The few hints we have about Page's editorial involvement in her early books are to be found in Montgomery's journals, where she is more likely to paraphrase than to quote him, or by comparing surviving handwritten manuscripts to printed texts and conjecturing as to whether discrepancies between versions occurred in the typescript stage or at the proofs stage, two crucial components of a book's production that in Montgomery's case hardly ever survive.[18]

And while few materials pertaining to her short stories and poems survive besides the published versions, Montgomery's numerous scrapbooks—either of pasted clippings or of whole periodical pages sewn together—contain a comprehensive (if not quite complete) repository of her periodical work. Even so, their pages offer inconsistent clues about her processes of writing, revision, and submission. Her earliest scrapbooks include some composition and publication dates written in ink alongside pasted clippings, and the gaps between dates reveal two realities of periodical publication that are not otherwise apparent to readers of her published periodical work: first, Montgomery often had to submit materials to multiple venues before she found homes for them (she later credited her success as a freelancer to the gift of "stick-to-it-iveness"), and second, the interval between submission and acceptance as well as between acceptance and publication could vary considerably from one periodical to the next.[19] Such clues in these scrapbooks about wait times are corroborated by anecdotes Montgomery told Ephraim Weber about her freelance career: for instance, she mentioned in 1906 that she had submitted "The Old South Orchard" first to a New York periodical whose editor acknowledged receipt promptly but waited a full year before declining the submission (it was not published until January 1908), and a few months later she mentioned that *The Youth's Companion*, a highly regarded Boston periodical, currently had four of her poems under consideration, "two of them for over two years."[20] And so, although Montgomery's recording of key dates in her scrapbooks petered out after the first few years of her freelance career, all of these details demonstrate that reading Montgomery's periodical items in chronological order by publication date would be an imperfect way to study her evolving writing style.

Moreover, besides occasionally correcting typographical errors or making minor stylistic corrections in ink in her scrapbooks, Montgomery in a few instances left traces of substantial revision in her scrapbook copies. In Scrapbook 4, for instance, she added a handwritten note to her copy of "The Deferment of Hester" ("Put *Janet* where *Hester* occurs"), but whether this note served as a reminder for herself or as an instruction for a typist is impossible to guess. That is the only change she makes to this copy, even though further revisions would be needed to retrofit this story into *Anne of the Island*. Moreover, the editorial emendations she made in her scrapbook copy of "A Double Surprise," published the same month as *Anne of Green Gables*, suggests that she hoped to publish the story a second time but feared the character of "Aunt Anne" would be too confusing for readers given the exceptional popularity of her recently published first novel, and so she crossed out "Anne" several times and renamed the character "Nan." Looking at these rare substantive interventions in Montgomery's scrapbook copies of her own work for insight into her revision process is complicated by the fact that most of the revisions she makes pertain to name changes only and by the fact that published versions of these revised stories have not yet been found and therefore may never have existed. They also are in marked contrast to several instances in which Montgomery republished short stories years, if not decades, after their first publication, often with only minimal revisions.[21]

In all these instances, the absence of relevant supporting documents makes such investigations speculative rather than definitive. For instance, while no doubt publishers and periodicals at the time of Montgomery's career had their own policies about language and content, as did *The New Yorker* decades later, it is anyone's guess why the short story "The Winning of Lucinda" in *Chronicles of Avonlea* censors a mild expletive (*"You d—d idiot!"*), while the periodical version, published as "A Case of Atavism" in Indianapolis's *The Reader Magazine* seven years earlier, does not (*"You damned idiot!"*): this censoring could have been prompted by Page's editorial policies, Montgomery's awareness of her new position as a minister's wife, or her dread of having to deal with letters from upset members of her substantial fan base.[22] And in one case in which Montgomery narrated a request for revisions from her publisher, she did so in a letter to MacMillan but not in her journal, so the details could easily have been lost given that she likely did not anticipate that this correspondence would be published after her death. The case in question involves her late novel *Anne of Windy Poplars* (1936), which backtracks to Anne's three years as principal of Summerside High School, during which she struggles to be accepted by the indomitable Pringle family, prior to her marriage to Gilbert. As Montgomery reported to MacMillan, there were two snags involving her US publisher, who considered Montgomery's chosen title, "Anne of Windy Willows," "too reminiscent" of Kenneth Grahame's *The Wind in the Willows* (which Montgomery found "very far-fetched") and whose readers had taken issue with two highly similar sequences in which older women tell Anne in great detail how all their relatives died. Montgomery agreed to excise the passages that had been flagged as "too gruesome" (even though many of them are not particularly gruesome) and to change the title to "Anne of Windy Poplars," but due to her UK publisher's difference of opinion about the title and to the decision to create plates from a separate copy of Montgomery's typescript, the UK edition of the book appeared as *Anne of Windy Willows* and included the passages in question.[23] Even so, the UK version of the novel was selected as the "Romantic Book of the Month" for August 1936 by the London *Daily Mirror*, which called the book "a novel which will be enjoyed by all men and women who like fiction packed with incident, drama and romance."[24]

In contrast, Montgomery wrote at length in her journals about the way Page had manipulated her into consenting to the publication of a volume of the leftover *Chronicles* stories, then discarded the revised versions she had sent him for this purpose and, in violation of their agreement, insisted on publishing the versions already in his possession, even though they contained extracts that she had since woven into her subsequent books. "To have a volume of stories come out apparently repeating this material will make me ridiculous," she declared in her journal, and this perceived damage to her literary reputation is part of what prompted her to threaten a lawsuit against her publisher to prevent this book from being published and later to proceed with the lawsuit when Page published the book anyway—as *Further Chronicles of Avonlea* in spring 1920—narrating in her journal every step of this legal battle for posterity.[25] Still, although in this instance Montgomery articulated a concern about textual recycling from one book to another that clearly did not apply when reworking material from periodical to book (judging by the fact that lines from "Our Neighbors at the Tansy Patch" made their way into six of her subsequent books), this stated concern does not explain instances of repetition in books published later. One of these—a reference in *Anne of the Island* to a woman who "wore the same bonnet for eighteen years. Then she got a new one and [her husband] met her on the road and didn't know her," appearing in slightly modified form in *Anne of Ingleside* ("Curtis Ames who met his wife in a new bonnet and didn't know her")—could be explained easily enough as an oversight. But what seems like a far more intentional borrowing involves lines from *Emily Climbs* ("She had a series of brilliant imaginary conversations and thought out so many epigrams that she was agreeably surprised at herself. . . . She was alone but not lonely") that appear in only slightly different form in *Anne of Windy Poplars* ("I was alone but not lonely. I held a series of imaginary conversations with imaginary comrades and thought out so many epigrams that I was agreeably surprised at myself").[26]

And in the case of Montgomery's retrospective accounts of writing *Anne of Green Gables*, the challenge does not involve an absence of supporting documents but the existence of competing ones. Part of the lore surrounding this novel is that she

planned her first book initially as a seven-chapter serial for a
Sunday school periodical, but after feeling creatively energized
by the character in embryo she concluded it was "rather a shame
to waste her on an ephemeral little serial," as she wrote in her
journal and in "The Alpine Path," suggesting that she had come
to this realization after having drafted several chapters of the
planned project. But while these two accounts of the creation
and submission of her first novel are identical in many instances,
where they diverge from each other concerns Montgomery's
stated plans for her manuscript after it was rejected by five
publishers: "some day when I had time I would cut her down
to the seven chapters of my original idea and send her to the
aforesaid Sunday School paper," she wrote in her journal, yet in
"The Alpine Path" these plans include "tak[ing] and reduc[ing]
her to the original seven chapters of her first incarnation." In her
introduction to the Broadview edition of *Anne of Green Gables*,
Cecily Devereux uses the "Alpine Path" comments to support the
theory that Montgomery had intended to end *Anne* as a serial
with chapter 7, "Anne Says Her Prayers," noting that "these
seven chapters are . . . the most 'Sunday Schoolish'" and that
they are "thus perceptible as the body of the text as she had originally intended it." Yet in a 1915 article entitled "How I Began,"
Montgomery complicated this origin story of *Anne* starting out
as a serial by saying the story likely would have fit the orthodox
constraints of a religious publication "if I had had time to go on
with it at once," but crucially, "I did not have time," which suggests that the evolution from serial to book occurred in her mind
prior to her starting to draft the text.[27] And so, even though
the surviving handwritten manuscript of *Anne of Green Gables*
can shed considerable light on Montgomery's writing and revision process—something that Carolyn Strom Collins's recent
manuscript edition of the novel now allows readers to piece
together—competing accounts of Montgomery's shifting intentions regarding this manuscript lead to new forms of speculation
and uncertainty.

While most of the fellow Canadian authors mentioned earlier
intended that their periodical serials should lead to book publication, Montgomery is set apart from them in two key ways.
First, although many of Montgomery's early books were likewise
serialized in periodicals, this serialization occurred *following*

book publication and was arranged by her publishers; as such, any textual differences between her books and these serial versions likely were made without her input or involvement.[28] Second, Montgomery could have continued to revise some of her best stories for inclusion in further collections of linked short fiction, as Munro would do decades later—in fact, given the sales success of *Chronicles of Avonlea*, I am surprised Page did not suggest a repeat effort when Montgomery had no new book ready for 1914[29]—but instead she proved far more selective and strategic in terms of what periodical material she repurposed in her books and how she did so: dialogue in the case of "Aunt Ethelinda's Monument" and "A Chip of the Old Block"; situations in the case of "Our Uncle Wheeler," "A New-Fashioned Flavoring," "Miss Marietta's Jersey," "Tomorrow Comes," and "I Know a Secret"; character and place names in the case of "The Old Chest at Wyther Grange," "Aunt Susanna's Birthday Celebration," and "Our Neighbors at the Tansy Patch"; atmosphere and back story in the case of "The Old South Orchard" and "A Garden of Old Delights"; shifts from written storytelling to oral story-telling (complete with real-time responses from listeners) in the case of "A Pioneer Wooing" and "The Schoolmaster's Bride"; and engaging characters in the case of "The Life-Book of Uncle Jesse," "Aunt Philippa and the Men," "By the Grace of Sarah May," and "Abel and His Great Adventure." Montgomery's attempts to "amplify" these existing stories involved retrofitting specific elements into storylines that centred on new characters and situations, which was no doubt more creatively satisfying to her than the process of transforming "Una" into *Kilmeny* by doubling the length of an already published serial whose overall plot could not be altered.

Reading the stories in this volume now with their eventual novel counterparts in mind reveals complex relationships between multiple texts and solves some lingering mysteries in her well-known novels. Readers of *Anne's House of Dreams* who find Miss Cornelia's rants against all male creatures, while highly entertaining, an odd set of choices for a woman who professes to be keen to get acquainted with the newlywed Anne might understand this character differently knowing that her periodical predecessor, Aunt Philippa, recites many of the same anecdotes about men behaving badly as a well-meaning attempt to comfort young Ursula after her apparently broken engagement and to dissuade her from making the wrong choice of husband. Readers who shared the observation of a reviewer of *The Golden Road* in the London *Bookman* who noted concerning the book's adult male narrator, Beverley King, that "we could not rid ourselves of the impression that it is all told by a girl, instead of by a boy," may feel vindicated by the fact that both "The Old South Orchard" and "A Garden of Old Delights," the precursors to *The Story Girl* and *The Golden Road*, have an adult woman as a retrospective narrator. A careful reading of "Tomorrow Comes" and "I Know a Secret" can uncover the clever ways Montgomery reworked parts of each story into highly similar plot threads in two novels while changing enough details to avoid too much duplication.[30] And as Elizabeth Rollins Epperly notes, comparing *Anne's House of Dreams* to "Abel and His Great Adventure" sheds light on why, in telling the story of a thoughtless summer resident who abandoned her cat when she returned home for the winter, Captain Jim addresses Gilbert as "master," even though the term "really makes no sense with Gilbert (much less Anne)." Given that the narrator of the corresponding short story is a schoolteacher, and given that it is somehow appropriate in several Montgomery texts even for adults to address male school-teachers as "master," Epperly deems it likely that Montgomery drew on this story when writing this part of the novel and forgot to adjust this line of dialogue to account for the fact that the speaker is now addressing a doctor and his wife rather than a schoolteacher.[31]

In addition, tracing the ways Montgomery reused periodi-cal materials in her books can call into question or at least add nuance to the claims she makes in her life writing. Although as I mentioned earlier she had expressed to MacMillan how much she had been looking forward to working on *The Golden Road* after finishing *Chronicles of Avonlea*, the experience of writing that novel in fits and starts in the midst of her new responsibili-ties as a mother and as a minister's wife led to her feeling dis-satisfied with the project: in short, "I have not enjoyed writing it." Perhaps as a consequence of her inability to write this novel without interruption, she ended up reworking at least five peri-odical stories into its plot, and chapter 28, entitled "The Path to Arcady," contains a considerable number of lines lifted from her four woods articles and now attributed to bohemian uncle Blair Stanley, who, so narrator Beverley King claims, "was the only man I have ever known who could, when he so willed, 'talk like a book.'"[32]

As for *Chronicles of Avonlea*, Montgomery may have found its stories "stale" after so many rounds of revision, but a line-by-line comparison of most of the twelve book stories with their initial periodical incarnations shows the kinds of changes she made and the degree to which she revised. To make the story fit the universe she had established in *Anne of Green Gables* and *Anne of Avonlea*, Montgomery switched the locations of these stories to Avonlea and to surrounding settlements in the preceding books (Carmody, Grafton, Spencervale, and White Sands), replaced some characters with those who had appeared briefly (including Mrs. Peter Blewett and Rev. and Mrs. Allan), and rebaptized several characters so that they belonged to established families (those with the surnames Andrews, Gillis, MacPherson, Pye, Sloane, and Spencer). But while she also changed some phrasing and description and in some cases expanded on character development, the plots of the revised versions are identical to those of their earlier periodical incarnations.[33] As for the sequencing of the stories in that collection, Montgomery recorded in a retrospective journal entry dated 1919 that Page had been the one to select the stories to appear in the volume from the longer sample she had sent him, yet the published book reveals that there was some uncertainty about selection and arrangement, even if it is impossible to ascertain to what extent Montgomery was involved in the discussion, what factors informed the deliberation, and who made the final decision.[34]

Moreover, Captain Jim's slip of the tongue when he inexplicably addresses Gilbert as "master" is not the only time that a trace of the earlier periodical version bleeds into the supposedly final version in a book. Thirty years after publishing "The Little Fellow's Photograph," Montgomery decided to recycle this story in *Anne of Windy Poplars*, replacing two adolescent chums on an extended bicycle jaunt in the countryside with twenty-something school principal Anne canvassing for the high school's dramatic club with her student Lewis Allen. Because in the periodical version the boys ask Mr. Armstrong for a meal instead of for a subscription, in the book version, when the "Little Fellow" (now named Teddy) mentions overhearing Anne and Lewis asking his father for something to eat, Anne thinks parenthetically in response, "We didn't but it doesn't matter." When revising "The Matchmaker" for inclusion in *Anne of Ingleside*, Montgomery must have realized that trying to transform widowed busy-body Ellen Churchill into the thirty-something Anne Blythe was starting to strain credibility, especially in the scene in which Mrs. Churchill confronts and berates her brother-in-law Richard Chase, and so in the novel he becomes brother-in-law to Miss Cornelia, who accompanies Anne on her errand to his house and takes over the conversation completely, with the narrator noting that "it was really uncanny . . . the way things helped her out." In spite of these easy fixes, though, a few details from some of these periodical stories ended up overshadowing the corresponding novel text. One mention of "Deland River," the setting of the periodical version of "The Hurrying of Ludovic," made it into the first edition of *Chronicles of Avonlea* and had to be changed to "Grafton" in subsequent printings, and chapter 9 of *Anne's House of Dreams* contains a reference to "Uncle Jim," evidently residue of Uncle Jesse, that never was corrected.[35]

And while most of these examples from Montgomery's writing practices follow a pattern whereby the periodical version is provisional and the book version is "final," there are some notable exceptions to this. After reworking extracts from *Rilla of Ingleside* into "Dog Monday's Vigil" for an anthology of Canadian literature, she evidently attempted to repackage as short stories chapters from her earlier books. Most of the first one hundred pages of the handwritten manuscript of *Anne of Ingleside*, the last book she published in her lifetime, were written on the backs of typescripts that included as return mailing address her home in Norval, where she lived with her family between 1926 and 1935. Titles of these stories include "Anne Says Her Prayers," "Anne Comes to Grief in an Affair of Honour," "An Epoch in Anne's Life," and "A Good Imagination Gone Wrong" (all from *Anne of Green Gables*), "Mr. Harrison's Cow" (from *Anne of Avonlea*), "Encores" (from chapter 14 of *The Story Girl*), "The Parting Tryst" (from *Rilla of Ingleside*), and "As Others See Us" (from *Emily Climbs*).[36] Given that the books from which these type-script stories were excerpted are a mix of those for which she had sold all remaining rights to the Page Company in 1919 and those for which she continued to receive royalties, the fact that none of these stories is believed to have been published indicates that something besides copyright infringement prompted her either to stop submitting these stories to prospective venues or not to submit them at all.[37] But again, the absence of any record of this enterprise except on the backs of her last surviving book-length manuscript means that any explanation is speculative at best and is subject to change depending on what new clues are unearthed in the future.

Still, although in many cases Montgomery tried to rework existing materials into her book-length works of fiction with minimal adjustment, one notable instance of a major revision occurred not between periodical and book versions but between two periodical versions. I mentioned earlier that the version of "The Indecision of Margaret" included in this volume is the revised one appearing in *Maclean's* shortly before the publication of *Anne of the Island*, in which much of the story's plot is incorporated into the novel's story arc involving Anne's frivolous college friend Philippa Gordon, who ends up marrying a minister even after he decides to "take a little mission church down on Patterson Street in the slums." In the initial version of this story, published in 1906 (by which point Montgomery was secretly engaged to Ewan Macdonald, a Presbyterian minister), after Margaret announces to her formidable aunt that she has asked Peter Campbell to marry her, the story concludes as follows:

Aunt Roberta's eyes twinkled. "Young man," she remarked, "you've got the gift of gab, a great thing in your profession. Now, I happen to know you're going to have a call from St. Mary's—"

My eyes grew big. St. Mary's was the richest and most fashionable church in Peter's town.

"My duty," began my affianced, solemnly.

"Your duty isn't altogether to the slums; it's to this poor, frivolous girl who loves you. You've no right to make her a slave to your noble fads. You accept St. Mary's as a blessing of God and give Margaret the comforts she's been accustomed to. Will you?"

"Yes," said Peter, humbly. A moment later he sighed. "I am a weakling."

"So is every man who loves," observed Aunt Roberta, "and woman, too."

Notwithstanding her criticism of me I went up and gave Aunty a grateful kiss. Somehow I think she must have guessed I loved Peter weeks ago.[38]

As with the censoring of the mild expletive in *Chronicles of Avonlea*, it is impossible to determine, given the absence of archival documents or commentary in her life writing, whether the shift in endings between the 1906 version and the 1915 version of "The Indecision of Margaret" was Montgomery's own initiative or a suggestion from an editor at *Maclean's*, even if the latter option seems unlikely. Certainly, the fact that the revised resolution is woven into *Anne of the Island* indicates that Montgomery decided at least to be consistent given how closely to each other the two texts appeared in 1915. If we assume that the revision was her choice, it is worth pondering to what extent it reflects a shift in her thinking about the man who had become her husband in 1911. At the time of their engagement in 1906, Ewan Macdonald had given off the impression of being "a successful young minister ready to climb clerical ladders," as Mary Henley Rubio notes in her biography of Montgomery, in spite of his "competent but mediocre academic career." But by 1915 he had revealed himself to be a minister with little ambition for professional advancement, and so a textual revision that validates a fictional minister's decision to prioritize community need over personal ambition and a female character's choice to marry him anyway may thus reflect "a hopeful version of Montgomery's choice in marriage," as Elizabeth Waterston suggests.[39]

Moreover, while most of the stories in the present volume contain elements that Montgomery reworked into supporting characters and subplots in her novels rather than involving protagonists and major storylines, one story not included here may surprise readers in terms of how central it would be in the corresponding novel. "The Royal Family" tells the story of a schoolteacher named Vere Carleton who writes letters to her mother about her struggles in her work because of the animosity within the community from a domineering family named—you guessed it—the Pringles:

She had felt the antagonism from the first. It had been impossible to get a boarding place in the village. Mrs. Tom Pringle, who had boarded the teachers for twenty years, had suddenly grown tired of "being bothered." Everybody else had some polite excuse. Eventually Vere had to go to Duncan Reed's on the hill, which meant a half mile walk to school every morning. It was not a pleasant boarding house. The Reeds certainly belonged to no royal family from any point of view. They were odd and uncouth. There was no privacy in their household. She had a tiny room over the kitchen which was always hot and full of cooking smells. Her bed had a velley [*sic*] in the middle of it and the cheap mirror distorted her face out of all recognition . . . just as, she felt sure, her personality was distorted in the minds of the Pringle clan. Her only consolation was the view from her window, looking down over the pretty village about which the river looped in silver.

While the published version of this story has not yet been located—it appears in Montgomery's ledger of earnings, indicating that it was published somewhere—most of its typescript pages can be found on the backs of parts of the manuscript of *Pat of Silver Bush*, which suggests that Montgomery wrote the story in the early 1930s. Unlike most of the stories found in this volume, however, this one ended up being repotted into *Anne of Windy Poplars* with little alteration except for Anne's name and the position of high school principal rather than teacher: Vere and Anne meet the same obstacles from the Pringle family members, including from young Jen Pringle, not only in the school but also in the community at large. The only substantial difference is that in "The Royal Family" it is landlord Duncan Reed—whose gossip about the Pringles appears with little modification in the mouths of two female characters in the book—whose great-uncle Andy wrote a diary that Anne finds containing, among other tidbits, a mention of Myrom Pringle and his crew eating Jonas Selkirk while being stranded at sea.[40]

Only the first eleven pages of the typescript survive on the backs of the manuscript to "Pat of Silver Bush," so the excerpt ends in the middle of the scene in which Vere, like Anne in the novel, reassures the two formidable heads of the Pringle clan that she did not send them the diary in an attempt to blackmail them into submission. But while it is unusual even for Montgomery that such a major strand of one of her novels has been lifted from an earlier periodical story, it is not surprising that she turned to an existing short story as a way to help her ease back into the world of Anne fifteen years after completing *Rilla of Ingleside*. As she noted in a journal entry dated 9 March 1935, the day she began brainstorming this new Anne book (omitting any reference to this earlier story), "I had a strange feeling when I sat down to my work. Some interest seemed to return to life. The discovery that I may still be able to work heartens me. So often lately I have been afraid I never could again."[41]

I had hoped to include in this volume the full text of "The Royal Family," especially when I came across a mention of a hitherto unknown Montgomery story entitled "A Family Affair," published in the July 1931 issue of *The Story-Teller*, a London periodical. Unfortunately, when I received a copy of the story in question through my university library's interlibrary loan department, I discovered that the story of this title was, in fact, a reprint of "A House Divided against Itself," featuring precursors to Little Sam and Big Sam from *A Tangled Web*. And so the search for the published version of "The Royal Family" continues.

In the end, what this volume demonstrates is the complexity of Montgomery's self-repetitions, an examination that will continue in later volumes of her collected periodical work. From cannibalization and amplification to transplanting and remixing, these stories and their book-length counterparts reveal Montgomery as a shrewd literary professional whose writing reflects her balancing of her sense of what makes literary art and what is going to appeal to the shifting tastes of a large fiction readership. Reading multiple versions of the same work side by side can thus illuminate Montgomery's process of testing out material in periodical form and perfecting it for her book-length fiction—and sometimes returning to it again even after book publication. As Darlene Kelly states in her work comparing serial and book versions of Duncan's *The Imperialist*, "While collation is sometimes tedious, it can also illuminate in a striking way passages that have been either misread or ignored. Indeed, the study of these variants makes the reader a secret sharer in the creative process, questioning along with Duncan the accuracy of facts, reassessing character, and conceding the greater complexity of issues raised in the book."[42] This can also be said for Montgomery, whose works continue to be read and reread by readers everywhere.

BENJAMIN LEFEBVRE

NOTES

1 As Montgomery indicated in a journal entry dated 1915, Page's contracts had stipulated that she would receive a "beggarly 10% on the wholesale price" rather than "15% on the retail price," the latter percentage corresponding to what she saw as "the ordinary terms offered to any successful author," and she estimated that Page's terms had given her half of what she should have received as a royalty (Montgomery, 26 July 1915, in *LMMCJ*, 1: 202; see also Montgomery, 2 May 1907, in *GGL*, 52; Montgomery, 16 August 1907, in *CJLMM*, 2: 173). She eventually insisted that the five-year clause be removed from her contracts, and after this agreement expired in 1916, she published a book of poems as well as all her remaining books of fiction except one with McClelland, Goodchild, and Stewart (later McClelland and Stewart) in Toronto and the Frederick A. Stokes Company in New York. In her retrospective account of her dealings with Page in a 1929 letter to G.B. MacMillan, she was quite blunt about the Page Company's business methods: "They were *crooks*" (Montgomery to MacMillan, 10 February 1929, in *MDMM*, 141). Copies of Montgomery's contracts for the eight books she published with L.C. Page and Company are housed at Library and Archives Canada (see "Publishing Agreements").

2 For more on *Anne of Green Gables* on North American bestseller lists within the first few years of its publication, see Lefebvre, "Introduction: A Legacy in Review," 12, 41n15.

3 Gerson, "Seven Milestones," 20. In my introduction to volume 3 of *The L.M. Montgomery Reader*, I claimed that *Chronicles of Avonlea* had come about because of the "year of major life changes" that Montgomery had experienced in 1911: the death of the grandmother who had raised her, her departure from her hometown in rural Prince Edward Island, her marriage to Ewan

Macdonald, their honeymoon in England and Scotland, their move to rural Ontario, and the beginnings of her responsibilities as a minister's wife and of her pregnancy with their first child (Lefebvre, "Introduction: A Legacy in Review," 18). In making that claim, I had overlooked a journal entry dated January 1911 that indicates that she had started this revision work several weeks before her grandmother's death (see Montgomery, 17 January 1911, in *CJLMM*, 2: 338).

4 Montgomery, 23 December 1909, in *CJLMM*, 2: 242; Montgomery to MacMillan, 21 May 1909, in *MDMM*, 49; Montgomery, 30 June 1912, in *LMMCJ*, 1: 68; "*Chronicles of Avonlea*," 132–33; "L.M. Montgomery: An Explanation Regarding the Publication of Her Different Books," *Toronto World*, ca. 1912, quoted in Lefebvre, "Introduction: A Life in Print," 10.

5 Montgomery to MacMillan, 20 January 1912, in *MDMM*, 66; Montgomery, 6 January 1910, in *CJLMM*, 2: 248.

6 See Montgomery, "[Seasons in the Woods]"; Lefebvre, Headnote to "[Seasons in the Woods]." These essays had first been published in *The Canadian Magazine* under the titles "Spring in the Woods," "The Woods in Summer," "The Woods in Autumn," and "The Woods in Winter." One instance of transplantation in the material collected in *A Name to Herself* that I previously overlooked is when Cynthia (the narrator of Montgomery's newspaper column, "Around the Table") refers to the experience of "hav[ing] your umbrella turn inside out" as an occasion whereby "I feel convinced of the total depravity of inanimate things," lines that reappear in chapter 25 of *Anne of the Island*, when Anne meets Royal Gardner (*NH*, 162; *AIs*, 218–19). My thanks to Carol Dobson for bringing this omission to my attention. "The Total Depravity of Inanimate Things" is the title of a satirical article, published in 1864, by Katherine Kent Child Walker (1833–1916), American author, and included in *Mark Twain's Library of Humor* (see *NH*, 379n224).

7 In early 1925, Montgomery published in *The Delineator* four stories that she had reworked from parts of *Emily of New Moon* and *Emily Climbs* ("Enter, Emily," "Too Few Cooks," "Night Watch," and "Her Dog Day"), the latter book not published until several months later. The following year, she published in the same periodical four stories about Marigold ("Magic for Marigold," "Lost—a Child's Laughter," "Bobbed Goldilocks," and "Playmate"),

which were followed by four more stories about this character in
1928 and 1929 ("One of Us" and "The Punishment of Billy" in
Canadian Home Journal, "One Clear Call" in *The Household
Magazine*, and "'It'" in *The Chatelaine*), although in "One Clear
Call" the protagonist is named Annabel Page. Montgomery's ledger
of earnings includes mentions of three more stories whose titles
match the titles of additional chapters in *Magic for Marigold* ("A
Counsel of Perfection," "How It Came to Pass," and "Red Ink
or—"), but these stories have not yet been located in periodical
form. Montgomery also revised extracts from two late novels into
two sets of stand-alone stories: eight from *Anne of Windy Poplars*,
published in *The Family Herald and Weekly Star* ("The Man
Who Wouldn't Talk," "The Wedding at Poplar Point," "The Gift
of a Day," "Everybody Is Different," "Miss Much-Afraid," "The
Westcott Elopement," "A Tragic Evening," and "A Day Off"), and
eight from *Anne of Ingleside*, published in *Onward: A Paper for
Young Canadians* (all of them as "Chronicles of Ingleside").

8 There are also numerous instances of repetition between her
journals and her surviving correspondence with G.B. MacMillan of
Scotland and Ephraim Weber of Western Canada. In their volume
of Montgomery's later letters to Weber, Hildi Froese Tiessen and
Paul Gerard Tiessen note that "Montgomery's habit of drawing on
her journal—sometimes word for word—for rather large swaths
of correspondence" invites readers "to examine how she developed
and rehearsed her material for a particular kind of private/public
performance" and "to look at what Montgomery did *not* write to
Weber—and, conversely, at what she wrote to Weber, and did *not*
put down in her journal or in her letters to MacMillan" (Tiessen
and Tiessen, "A Note on the Text," 54, 55).

9 For details on the publication history of Saunders's *Beautiful Joe*,
see Chez, "A Note on the Text." For details on the multiple versions
of the texts by Haliburton, De Mille, Leacock, and Duncan, see
Davies, "A Note on the Text," 43; Burgoyne, "A Note on the
Text," 41; Spadoni, Introduction, lxxiii–lxxxi; Siddall, "A Note on
the Text"; Dean, "A Note on the Text"; Warkentin, "A Note on the
Text." For details on the periodical texts by Crawford, Leprohon,
and Johnson, see Early and Peterman, "A Note on the Text";
Cabajsky, "A Note on the Text"; Fee and Nason, "A Note on the
Text." For details on the competing text versions of *Anne of Green
Gables*, see Devereux, "A Note on the Text."

10 Roy, *The Next Instalment*, 2. For more on nineteenth- and
twentieth-century Canadian authors and the economics of authorship, see Cambron and Gerson, "Literary Authorship"; Davey,
"Economics and the Writer"; Friskney and Gerson, "Writers
and the Market"; Karr, "Popular and Best-Selling Fiction"; Karr,
"Writers and the Market."

11 Kelly, "Rewriting 'The Imperialist,'" 26, 28; Spadoni, Introduction,
lxxvii; Chez, "A Note on the Text," 39; Roy, *The Next Instalment*,
37–40. While conducting research for her critical edition of *The
Imperialist*, Misao Dean discovered a third periodical serialization
of the book in a newspaper called *The Australasian*, published in
the last three months of 1903 (Dean, "A Note on the Text," 39).

12 Beran, "The Luxury of Excellence," 205. Nadine Fladd counts
sixty-two stories that Munro published in *The New Yorker* since
1977 (Fladd, "Alice Munro," 174). According to the website for
The New Yorker (https://newyorker.com), the last story Munro
published in that magazine, "Amundsen," appeared in the
27 August 2012 issue.

13 Beran, "The Luxury of Excellence," 210. For an article connecting
the work of Montgomery to the work of Munro and of Margaret
Laurence, see Beran, "Beautiful Girlhood."

14 Fladd, "Alice Munro," 181, 177.

15 Hoy, "'Rose and Janet,'" 59, 69. For additional studies of Munro's
writing and editing process, see Ware, "The Progress of Writing";
Luft, "Boxed In"; Thacker, *Reading Alice Munro*, 111–96; Lynch,
The One and the Many, 159–81.

16 Montgomery to Weber, 10 September 1908, in *GGL*, 73.

17 A random cluster of letters between Montgomery and the Stokes
Company (mainly typewritten letters she received but also some
handwritten copies of her replies) is part of the L.M. Montgomery
Collection at Archives and Special Collections, University
of Guelph Library (see Montgomery, "Business and Lawsuit
Correspondence"). Several business-related letters (including eleven
from Montgomery's New York agent, Ann Elmo, and dated March
1935 to August 1936) survive on the backs of the manuscript
of *Jane of Lantern Hill*, housed at the Confederation Centre Art
Gallery. These are a small fraction of the letters Montgomery presumably sent or received throughout her fifty-year literary career.

18 In the case of *Anne of Green Gables*, as Cecily Devereux points
out, the "primary variations" between the handwritten manuscript

and the first published edition have to do mainly with the placement of commas and hyphens (Devereux, "A Note on the Text," 48), which suggests that Montgomery's Page novels were not edited substantively by the publisher. In the case of *The Blythes Are Quoted*, which Montgomery completed at the end of her life but which was not published in full until 2009, three undated typescript versions (typed on at least two typewriters) survive but no handwritten manuscript does, and in preparing the text for publication, using what I had judged to be the last of the three typescripts as my copy-text, I corrected typographical errors and regulated some spellings but did not make any substantive changes to Montgomery's text (see Lefebvre, "A Note on the Text").

19 See Montgomery, "Blank Verse? 'Very Blank,' Said Father," 180; Montgomery, "An Autobiographical Sketch," 256; see also *NH*, 281. In the notes to items in this volume and in *A Name for Herself*, I included composition and publication dates whenever Montgomery indicated them in her scrapbook copies (see *NH*, 341, 348–54). Another complication here is Montgomery's handwriting, which is often difficult to decipher: although I am fairly certain that Montgomery indicated that she had written "Miss Marietta's Jersey" in March 1898, it is entirely possible that I have misread the final digit and the actual date is March 1899, even though that would be only four months prior to publication.

20 Montgomery, 8 April 1906, in *GGL*, 41; Montgomery, 21 June 1906, in *GGL*, 43.

21 For instance, the version of "An Afternoon with Mr. Jenkins" appearing in this volume is one of six stories that Montgomery republished in *Girl's Own Paper* between September 1937 and 1940, most of which had first appeared decades earlier: "Elizabeth's Child" in 1904, "A Substitute Journalist" in 1907, "The Little Black Doll" in 1909, "How We Went to the Wedding" in 1913, "The Garden of Spices" in 1918, and "An Afternoon with Mr. Jenkins" in 1933. Two more Montgomery stories—"Janet's Rebellion" and "More Blessed to Give"—are presumed to have been published in this periodical for the first time.

22 *CA*, 152; Montgomery, "A Case of Atavism," 665. I first pointed out this revision in my introduction to a 2009 reprint edition of *A Tangled Web* (see Lefebvre, Introduction, 11, 17n12). For details about Montgomery's experience with fan letters, see Montgomery, "Bits from My Mailbag."

23 In the sequence in which Anne visits a graveyard with Miss
Valentine Courtaloe, the anecdotes appearing in *Windy Willows*
but not in *Windy Poplars* include those involving Miss Valentine's
aunt Cora, who was buried in Summerside despite having spent
her married life in Boston; her absent-minded uncle Jack, who
had "married the wrong woman; but he never let her guess it";
"Cousin Dora's first husband's brother's first wife's first husband" ("I don't know how he came to be buried in *our* plot,
I'm sure"); her cousin Noble Courtaloe, whom the family had
been "a little afraid he was buried alive: he looked so lifelike";
her cousin Ida Courtaloe, who had been "fickle as a breeze"; her
cousin Vernon Courtaloe and Elsie Pringle, who "were to have
been married; but first one thing and then another postponed it,
and finally neither of them wanted it"; Stephen Pringle, who had
died after a fall from a ladder that may have been foul play and
had been buried with his eyes "wide open" because "they couldn't
get [them] closed"; and Helen Avery, who had "died twice—at
least, they thought she died, but she revived when they were laying
her out" (*AWW*, 57–62). In the sequence in which Anne attends a
one-on-one dinner party with Miss Minerva Tomgallon, the
anecdotes appearing in *Windy Willows* but not in *Windy Poplars*
include those involving Miss Tomgallon's great-uncle James, who
"shot himself in the cellar" after "a girl he wished to marry threw
him over"; her brother Arthur, whose bride "just walked out and
never came back" after they quarrelled on their wedding night and
who was rumoured to have agreed to marry him only "because
she couldn't hurt his feelings by saying no, and repented when it
was too late"; a family legend about a dance in her grandparents'
time that had gone too long into the night, at which point "*Satan
entered*"; her great-aunt Ethel, who had "died in the bloom of
life"; her aunt Arabella, who had "hanged herself in that closet"
after she "had been . . . melancholy . . . for quite a time, and finally
she was not invited to a wedding she thought she should have
been, and it preyed on her mind"; and several more besides: "This
one had told her husband a lie, and he had never believed her
again, my dear. That one had all her mourning made in expectation
of her husband's death, and he had disappointed her by getting
well. Oscar Tomgallon had died and come back to life. 'They didn't
want him to, my dear. *That* was the tragedy.' Claude Tomgallon
had shot his son by accident. Edgar Tomgallon had taken the

wrong medicine in the dark, and died in consequence. David
Tomgallon had promised his jealous, dying wife that he would
never marry again, and then *had* married again, and was supposed
to be haunted by the ghost of the jealous Number One. 'His eyes,
my dear—always staring past you at something behind you. People
hated to be in the same room with him. Nobody else ever saw her,
so perhaps it was only his conscience'" (*AWW*, 269–75; ellipses in
original).

24 Montgomery to MacMillan, 27 December 1936, in *MDMM*, 181,
180. In her journals and in her correspondence with Ephraim
Weber, Montgomery mentioned the title change and the *Daily
Mirror* honour but not the revisions to the text. See Montgomery,
11 January 1936, in *SJLMM*, 5: 54; Montgomery, 10 August 1936,
in *SJLMM*, 5: 82; Montgomery to Weber, 18 June 1937, in *AfGG*,
238; Tiessen and Tiessen, in *AfGG*, 238n19; *Daily Mirror*, "'Anne
of Windy Willows.'"

25 Montgomery, 14 February 1920, in *LMMCJ*, 2: 246. For a
retrospective summary of this legal battle, see Montgomery to
MacMillan, 10 February 1929, in *MDMM*, 140–47. The first
edition of *Further Chronicles* appeared with an introduction by
Nathan Haskell Dole, and in spite of Montgomery's ultimately
successful efforts to have the book pulled from circulation in 1928,
it resurfaced in the 1950s and remains in print. For more on this
book, see Lefebvre, "Introduction: A Legacy in Review," 26–27.

26 *AIn*, 300; *AIs*, 248; *EC*, 145; *AWP*, 28. Incidentally, the line
in *Anne of the Island* about the man who didn't recognize
his wife because of her new bonnet, spoken by Mrs. Skinner,
does not appear in the stand-alone short story that precedes it
(see Montgomery, "Mrs. Skinner's Story," 268).

27 Montgomery, 16 August 1907, in *CJLMM*, 2: 172–73; *NH*,
289–90, 294–95; Devereux, Introduction, 16; Montgomery, "How
I Began," 146.

28 For details about the known periodical serializations of *Anne of
Green Gables*, *Anne of Avonlea*, *Kilmeny of the Orchard*, *The
Story Girl*, and *The Blue Castle*, see Roy, *The Next Instalment*,
124–37, 154–55.

29 An ad by the Page Company appearing in several newspapers in
mid-1915 and announcing the publication of Montgomery's seventh book, *Anne of the Island*, provides concrete sales figures for
the six books that preceded it. These figures show a steady decline

that makes sense in terms of the relative length of time each book
had been out and the fact that *Anne of Green Gables* remained her
strongest-selling book by far: "310th thousand" for *Anne of Green
Gables* (1908), "109th thousand" for *Anne of Avonlea* (1909),
"45th thousand" for *Kilmeny of the Orchard* (1910) and for *The
Story Girl* (1911), "33rd thousand" for *Chronicles of Avonlea*
(1912), and "27th thousand" for *The Golden Road* (1913) (see
Dallas Morning News, "Published Today").

30 *"The Golden Road,"* 150. While the general circumstance in
"Tomorrow Comes" concerning a young girl who lives with her
tyrannical grandmother and discovers that her father is alive after
all certainly echoes the main plot of *Jane of Lantern Hill*, the text
of this story appears with minimal revision as the resolution of
the Little Elizabeth storyline in *Anne of Windy Poplars*. Although
in the novel Anne intervenes by writing to Elizabeth's father and
urging him to take responsibility for the daughter he has never
acknowledged since his wife died in childbirth, the dialogue and
much of the description of Little Elizabeth's final scene are taken
straight out of this short story—as is the final scene in *Jane* in
which Jane wakes up as she is recovering from pneumonia and
overhears scraps of a conversation between her estranged parents
(see *AWP*, 283–94; *JLH*, 293–97). And while the plot of "I Know a
Secret" is woven into *Anne of Ingleside*, the title phrase is replaced
by "*I* know something you don't know"—most likely because
a mean girl who manipulates the protagonist with the phrase "I
know a secret" already appears in chapter 5 of *Jane of Lantern
Hill* (*AIn*, 210–28; *JLH*, 32–34).

31 Epperly, *The Fragrance of Sweet-Grass*, 255n2; *AHD*, 88. In
Kilmeny of the Orchard, schoolteacher Eric Marshall is addressed
as "Master" by Mr. and Mrs. Williamson (who call each other
"Mother" and "Father" despite having no living children), at
whose house he boards (*KO*, 22, 41–52).

32 Montgomery, 21 May 1913, in *LMMCJ*, 1: 100; *GR*, 324;
Lefebvre, Headnote to "[Seasons in the Woods]," 74. Periodical
stories appearing in revised form in *The Golden Road* include
"Polly Patterson's Autograph Square," published in 1904 and
reworked for chapter 23, in which Cecily, accompanied by narrator Beverley, requests another donation from local curmudgeon
Mr. Campbell; "Paul, Shy Man," published in 1907 and reworked
for chapter 25, in which an adult Sara Stanley narrates in written

form the story of Jasper Dale; "A Will, a Way and a Woman,"
published in 1908 and reworked into a story Sara Stanley narrates
orally in chapter 2; and "The Locket That Was Baked," published
in 1908 and reworked into a short story Peter Craig contributes
to *Our Magazine* in chapter 20. I also note the existence of "Love
Story of an Awkward Man," a short story published in 1905 and
describing a character named Cuthbert Martin, who is similar to
Jasper Dale but whose plot wasn't retained for the novel.

33 Of the twelve stories in *Chronicles of Avonlea*, the initial periodical version of "Old Lady Lloyd" has not yet been found. The copy
of Montgomery's story "The Education of Sally" in Scrapbook 4
shows that in this case, the process of readying this story for
republication in book form involved correcting character names
("Sally" with "Betty") and place names ("Glenellyn" and "Gray
Gables" with "Glenby" and "The Maples") in ink and crossing
out a few extraneous sentences; a version with these corrections
appears as "The Education of Betty" in *Further Chronicles of
Avonlea*, but a third version, still with Sally as the name of the title
character and the locations called "Glenellyn" and "Owlwood,"
appeared in *The Canadian Courier* in 1913. A more detailed
comparison of the stories appearing in *Chronicles* and *Further
Chronicles* and their periodical antecedents will be part of a future
study.

34 Montgomery, 19 January 1919, in *CJLMM*, 2: 91. On the
title page of the first published edition, the title "Chronicles of
Avonlea" is followed by an exceedingly long explanatory sub-
title that connects the text to Anne and lists each of the stories
by title: "In which Anne Shirley of Green Gables and Avonlea
plays some part, and which have to do with other personalities and events, including The Hurrying of Ludovic, Old Lady
Lloyd, The Training of Felix ['Each in His Own Tongue'], Little
Joscelyn, The Winning of Lucinda, Old Man Shaw's Girl, Aunt
Olivia's Beau, The Quarantine at Alexander Abraham's, Pa Sloane's
Purchase, The Courting of Prissy Strong, The Miracle at Carmody,
and finally The End of a Quarrel" (*CA*, title page). Yet an ad for
the book appearing in this edition's end matter lists the "other
personalities and events" as "including The Purchase of Sloane,
The Baby Which Came to Jane, The Mystery of Her Father's
Daughter and of Tannis of the Flats, The Promise of Lucy Ellen,
The Beau and Aunt Olivia, The Deferment of Hester, and finally

of The Hurrying of Ludovic" (*CA*, n.pag.). Of the eight stories in this second list, "Pa Sloane's Purchase," "Aunt Olivia's Beau," and "The Hurrying of Ludovic" are the only three to make it into the final selection, whereas "Jane's Baby," "Her Father's Daughter," and "Tannis of the Flats" ended up appearing in *Further Chronicles of Avonlea* and "The Promise of Lucy Ellen" and "The Deferment of Hester" did not appear in either volume.

35 *AWP*, 152; *AIn*, 111; *CA*, 5; *AHD*, 82; ellipsis in original. My thanks to Bernadeta Milewski for reminding me of the reference to "Uncle Jim" as I was finishing up a draft of this afterword. It is also worth pointing out that, although "The Matchmaker" was published in 1919, copies of scattered pages of its typescript are found on the backs of part of the manuscript of *Anne of Windy Poplars*, pointing to the possibility that Montgomery had attempted to republish this story at some point in the 1930s.

36 Chapter 4 of *Emily Climbs* is in fact entitled "'As Ithers See Us,'" alluding to Robert Burns's poem "To a Louse": "O wad some Power the giftie gie us / To see oursels as ithers see us!"

37 Two excerpts from Montgomery's books that were reprinted in Montgomery's lifetime (besides "Dog Monday's Vigil") appeared most likely by arrangement with her publishers rather than with her: "Anne to the Rescue," appearing in *Selected Stories from Canadian Prose* in 1929 (for which the Page Company is credited as giving permission), and an excerpt from the first few chapters of *Emily of New Moon*, appearing in *The Voice of Canada: Canadian Prose and Poetry* in 1926.

38 *AIs*, 231; Montgomery, "The Indecision of Margaret," 165.

39 Rubio, *Lucy Maud Montgomery*, 123; Waterston, *Magic Island*, 74.

40 One diary entry in this short story is omitted from the corresponding scene in the novel: "Old Matilda Pringle has a new set of teeth and a new fur coat. . . . Now if she could get a new set of branes [*sic*] she would do very well for awhile."

41 Montgomery, 9 March 1935, in *SJLMM*, 4: 357.

42 Kelly, "Rewriting 'The Imperialist,'" 35.

Notes

ABBREVIATIONS

In addition to the abbreviations to texts by L.M. Montgomery listed at the beginning of this book, the notes rely on the following for secondary sources:

AHDI   *The American Heritage Dictionary of Idioms* (2nd ed.), by Christine Ammer
KJV   *The Bible: Authorized King James Version*
ODP   *Oxford Dictionary of Proverbs* (6th ed.), by Jennifer Speake
OED   *Oxford English Dictionary* at https://oed.com

OUR UNCLE WHEELER

Golden Days for Boys and Girls (Philadelphia), 22 January 1898, 145–46. Scrapbook 7 ("Written Sept. 1897 / Published Jan. 1898 / In 'Golden Days'"). Also in Montgomery, *Anne of Green Gables*, edited by Devereux, 335–44.

3 HEADNOTE. Montgomery, 27 January 1911, in *CJLMM*, 2: 355; Devereux, Headnote to "Our Uncle Wheeler," 335.

4 A CAT ON HOT BRICKS. "In a state of anxiety, agitation, or restlessness" (*OED*, s.v. "hot brick, *n.*"), a popular saying in the nineteenth century.

TOM, DICK OR HARRY. This expression, "used to refer to any average men, taken at random," originates in the mid-eighteenth century (*OED*, s.v. "Tom, *n.¹*"). See *NH*, 122, 215, 371n138.

6 DUFFER. This nineteenth-century British colloquialism refers to "a person who is, or proves to be, without practical ability or capacity in a particular occupation or undertaking; an incompetent, inefficient, or useless person; (also) a person lacking in spirit or courage. Also more generally: a stupid or foolish person" (*OED*, s.v. "duffer, *n.*²").

LAMMED. Colloquial term meaning "to beat soundly; to thrash; to 'whack'" (*OED*, s.v. "lam, *v.*").

7 SCRAPE. This early eighteenth-century term, referring to "an embarrassing or awkward predicament or situation, usually one into which a person is brought by [their] own imprudence and thoughtlessness" (*OED*, s.v. "scrape, *n.*¹"), recurs in *Anne of Green Gables* and its sequels.

10 CAPITAL. Used here in the sense, now dated, of "excellent, outstanding, first-rate [and] frequently as an exclamation of approval" (*OED*, s.v. "capital, *adj.* and *n.*²").

RHEUMATISM. "Pain or stiffness in joints, muscles, or related components of the musculoskeletal system; an attack or instance of this" (*OED*, s.v. "rheumatism, *n.*"). In *Anne of the Island*, twenty-year-old Anne predicts rain because "I've rheumatism in my leg," but Aunt Jamesina cautions her that "anybody is liable to rheumatism in her legs" but that "when you get rheumatism in your soul you might as well go and pick out your coffin" (*AIs*, 215). In *Rilla of Ingleside*, this condition is associated with getting older: Anne, now in her late forties, claims to have "an ache" in an ankle "when the wind is east. I won't admit that it is rheumatism, but it *does* ache" (*RI*, 8–9).

TOUSING-UP. The transitive verb "to touse," now rare, means "to pull roughly about; to drag or push about; to handle roughly" (*OED*, s.v. "touse, *v.*").

11 BEARD THE LION IN HIS DEN. "Confront a danger, take a risk," a proverb whose origins are in 1 Samuel 17:35 and Daniel 6:16–24 (*KJV*) (*AHDI*, s.v. "beard the lion").

SCREWED UP OUR COURAGE. Variant of "pluck up one's courage," meaning "forc[ing] oneself to overcome fear or timidity" (*AHDI*, s.v. "pluck up one's courage").

BEAT ABOUT THE BUSH. This expression, meaning to "approach indirectly, in a roundabout way, or too cautiously," originates in the sixteenth century (*AHDI*, s.v. "beat around the bush").

12 A TWENTY-DOLLAR BILL. This amount of money in 1914 (the earliest recorded consumer price index on the Bank of Canada's online inflation calculator) would be worth over $465 in 2021.
A BRICK. "A person regarded as decent, generous, helpful, or reliable" (*OED*, s.v. "brick, *n.¹* and *adj.¹*"). Sally Jane uses this term in reference to her aunts in "An Afternoon with Mr. Jenkins" later in this volume.

A NEW-FASHIONED FLAVORING

Golden Days for Boys and Girls (Philadelphia), 27 August 1898, 641–42. Scrapbook 2 ("Written July 1897 / Published Aug. 1898 / In 'Golden Days'"). Also in Montgomery, *Anne of Green Gables*, edited by Devereux, 344–56.

13 HEADNOTE. Montgomery, 27 January 1911, in *CJLMM*, 2: 355; Rubio and Waterston, in *CJLMM*, 1: 231n1; "Author Tells How He Wrote His Story," 34; Wilmshurst, "Cooking with L.M. Montgomery," 48; see also *GR*, 67–89.
SCRAPES. See the note to page 7 ("scrape"), above.

14 THE HOUSE BURNED TO THE GROUND. In chapter 12 of *The Story Girl*, Aunt Janet makes a similar declaration at the prospect of leaving the children unsupervised for a week: "We'd come home and find them all sick, and the house burned down" (*SG*, 125).

15 FAIRIES AND THREE WISHES. Edmund refers here to numerous folktales from around the world in which fairies offer mortal humans three wishes; these include "The Three Wishes," by Joseph Jacobs (1854–1916), Australian folklorist.

17 THE PHILISTINES BE UPON THEE. From Judges 16:9 (*KJV*): "And [Delilah] said unto him, The Philistines *be* upon thee, Samson." In her annotation of this story in her critical edition of *Anne of Green Gables*, Cecily Devereux notes that the term "philistine," used in this Biblical passage to refer to enemies of the Israelites, "has come to mean a person who is ignorant and uncultured" and points to similar phrasing in *Far from the Madding Crowd* (1874), a novel by Thomas Hardy (1840–1928), British novelist. See Devereux, in *Anne of Green Gables*, edited by Devereux, 348n1.
BEARD THE LION IN HIS DEN. See the note to page 11, above.

19 AN EPICURE. Someone with a refined taste for food and drink, known today as a "foodie."

QUINCE. Small yellow fruit similar to apples and pears.

INFANT TERRIBLE. "Enfant terrible," French for "terrible child."

20 COCOANUT. Archaic spelling of "coconut."

'CHARGE. . . . WE'LL WIN THE DAY.' Possibly an allusion to "We'll Win the Day," a nineteenth-century temperance song.

WITH FEAR AND TREMBLING. From Philippians 2:12 (*KJV*): "Wherefore, my beloved, as ye have always obeyed, . . . work out your own salvation with fear and trembling."

SILENCE TO BE GOLDEN. From the nineteenth-century proverbial phrase "Silence is golden," from the older proverb "Speech is silver and silence is golden," which suggests that sometimes saying nothing is preferable to or a greater virtue than speaking (*AHDI*, s.v. "silence is golden").

21 ANODYNE LINIMENT. Anodyne refers to "a medicine or drug which alleviates pain" (*OED*, s.v. "anodyne, *adj.* and *n.*"), and a liniment is an oil-based liquid usually used on the exterior of the body, as opposed to one that is ingested. A more recent example of a liniment is Vicks Vap-o-Rub.

22 ACCIDENTS WILL HAPPEN. Early eighteenth-century proverb (*ODP*, s.v. "Accidents will happen [in the best-regulated families]").

FEED THAT LINIMENT CAKE TO THE PIG. In the corresponding scene in *Anne of Green Gables*, Marilla can't help but make a dig at her French Canadian hired boy: "Well, you'd better go and give that cake to the pigs. . . . It isn't fit for any human to eat, not even Jerry Buote" (*AGG*, 247).

24 LET BYGONES BE BYGONES. Seventeenth-century expression, referring to an invitation to leave past mistakes in the past (*AHDI*, s.v. "let bygones be bygones").

A BRICK. See the note to page 12, above.

REPENT IN SACKCLOTH AND ASHES. "Mourning or penitence, [from] the ancient Hebrew custom of indicating humility before God by wearing a coarse cloth, normally used to make sacks, and dusting oneself with ashes" (*AHDI*, s.v. "sackcloth and ashes"). See Esther 4:1, Daniel 9:3, and Matthew 11:21 (*KJV*).

'LONG LIVE ANODYNE LINIMENT!' An allusion to the royal proclamation "The King is dead; long live the King," whose origins are in fifteenth-century France.

MISS MARIETTA'S JERSEY

The Household (Boston), July 1899, 5–6. Scrapbook 2 ("Written March 1898 / Published July 1899 / In 'Household'"). Also in *Farm, Field, and Fireside* (Chicago), 29 July 1899, 656–57.

25 HEADNOTE. Chapter 1 of *Anne of Avonlea* is entitled "An Irate Neighbour." The episode that originates in this story appears in chapter 2, "Selling in Haste and Repenting at Leisure," an allusion to "marry in haste and repent at leisure," a proverbial saying whose origins can be traced to the seventeenth century (*ODP*, s.v. "marry in haste and repent at leisure").

SIBILANT. Used here in the sense of "making a hissing or whistling sound" (*OED*, s.v. "sibilant, *adj.* and *n.*").

NOBODY EVER THOUGHT OF HER AS "HIRED HELP." Compare this statement here to *Magic for Marigold*, in which Salome Silversides "isn't really a servant," according to young Marigold, because "she is related to us" (*MM*, 147), or to *Anne of Windy Poplars*, in which Rebecca Dew "isn't a servant" but "a far-off cousin" of Aunt Kate's late husband (*AWP*, 7).

28 FRACASES. Plural form of "fracas," French for "a disturbance, noisy quarrel, 'row,' [or] uproar" (*OED*, s.v. "fracas, *n.*"). In *Rainbow Valley*, Miss Cornelia refers to the Second Boer War of 1899–1902 as "that South African fracas" (*RV*, 74).

31 SCRAPE. See the note to page 7, above.

32 CRIMPS. Used here in the sense of "an artificially waved or curled section of a person's hair" (*OED*, s.v. "crimp, *n.*³").

THE OLD CHEST AT WYTHER GRANGE

Waverley Magazine (Boston), 19 September 1903, 185–86. Scrapbook 9. Also in Montgomery, *Among the Shadows*, 167–80.

35 HEADNOTE. Montgomery, 23 May 1911, in *CJLMM*, 2: 406. Chapter 22 of *Emily of New Moon* is entitled "Wyther Grange."

36 PEREGRINATIONS. Used here in the sense of "travels; ramblings; random movements" (*OED*, s.v. "peregrination, *n.*").

37 A SENTIMENTAL, FANCIFUL CREATURE. In *The Story Girl*, Aunt Janet apparently has a similar opinion of Rachel Ward, whose blue chest has been under her roof for over fifty years: according to her daughter Felicity, "Mother says she was awful sentimental and romantic" (*SG*, 128).

39 PUFFED SLEEVES. In *Anne of Green Gables*, eleven-year-old Anne longs for a dress with puffed sleeves, but unfortunately for her, Marilla does not believe in "pampering vanity" or in wasting material on such "ridiculous-looking things" (*AGG*, 110); in chapter 25, Matthew conspires with Mrs. Lynde to give Anne a dress with puffed sleeves for Christmas. In her journal, Montgomery recorded that this aspect of the story was "an echo of my old childish longing after 'bangs'" (Montgomery, 27 January 1911, in *CJLMM*, 2: 351).

    DAMASK. Used here in the sense of "a rich silk fabric woven with elaborate designs and figures, often of a variety of colours" (*OED*, s.v. "damask, *n.* and *adj.*").

42 BADINAGE. "Humorous, witty, or trifling discourse; banter; frivolous or light-hearted raillery" (*OED*, s.v. "badinage, *n.*").

AUNT ETHELINDA'S MONUMENT

The Christian Advocate (New York), 1 December 1904, 1940–41.

45 HEADNOTE. *AIs*, 107, 236.

    ELSBETH. Scottish variation of Elizabeth (see Satran and Rosenkrantz, *The Baby Name Bible*, 92).

46 "IN A KILTER." Used here in the sense of being "out of kilter," meaning "not properly adjusted, not working well, out of order" (*AHDI*, s.v. "out of kilter").

47 EIGHTY DOLLARS . . . ONE HUNDRED. These amounts of money in 1914 (the earliest recorded consumer price index on the Bank of Canada's online inflation calculator) would be worth over $1,860 and over $2,300 in 2021.

49 CYRILLA POTTER. In chapter 4 of *Emily Climbs*, Emily unwittingly eavesdrops—while trapped in a boot closet wearing an outfit she is embarrassed to be seen in—on a conversation between two neighbourhood gossips, one of whom is named Ann Cyrilla Potter (*EC*, 59–66).

50 I'D AS LIEF NOT. "I had rather not," "lief" being used here as a past subjunctive in the sense of gladly or willingly (*OED*, s.v. "lief, *adj.* [and *n.*] and *adv.*").

51 ACTIONS SPEAK LOUDER THAN WORDS. Although this proverb, meaning "what one does is more important than what one says," appears in numerous languages, this version dates from the 1730s (*AHDI*, s.v. "actions speak louder than words").

SIXTY DOLLARS. This amount of money in 1914 (the earliest recorded consumer price index on the Bank of Canada's online inflation calculator) would be worth nearly $1,400 in 2021.

AUNT SUSANNA'S BIRTHDAY CELEBRATION

New Idea Woman's Magazine (New York), February 1905, 30–31. Scrapbook 11. Also in Montgomery, *Across the Miles*, 155–62.

54 MOSSEL. Obsolete variant of "morsel."

PRINK. Used here in the sense of "to make tidy, spruce, or smart; to dress up, deck out, adorn" (*OED*, s.v. "prink, *v.*²"). See also *NH*, 145, 375n184.

56 PURPLE AND FINE LINEN. From Luke 16:19 (*KJV*).

SACKCLOTH AND ASHES. See the note to page 24 ("repent in sackcloth and ashes"), above.

KLONDIKE. Following the discovery of gold in 1896 in what is now Yukon Territory, thousands of budding prospectors (most of whom were American) headed to the Klondike between 1897 and 1899 to try their luck.

THE HURRYING OF LUDOVIC

The Canadian Magazine (Toronto), May 1905, 67–71. Also, in revised form, in *CA*, 1–17.

59 'DE TROP.' French for "too much" (in the more figurative sense of excessive), the latter word rhyming with "go," not with "stop."

DILATORY. "Tending to cause delay; made for the purpose of gaining time or deferring decision or action" (*OED*, s.v. "dilatory, *adj.*¹ and *n.*").

A BROWN STUDY. "A state of mental abstraction or musing" (*OED*, s.v. "brown study").

BOSCAGE. "A mass of growing trees or shrubs; a thicket, grove; woody undergrowth; sylvan scenery" (*OED*, s.v. "boscage | boskage").

TUFT OF IMPERIAL. "A small pointed beard growing beneath the lower lip" (*OED*, s.v. "imperial").

60 CHRISTIAN SCIENCE. A religious movement started in New England by Mary Baker Eddy (1821–1910), who believed that faith alone could cure illness and suffering. Her book *Science and Health with Key to the Scriptures* was published in 1875.

BATTENBURG LACE. Properly, Battenberg lace, named after Prince Henry of Battenberg (1858–1896), a son-in-law of Queen Victoria (1819–1901). This kind of lace blends machine-made tape and handmade stitches.

JUNO-LIKE FASHION. Resembling Juno, a Roman goddess who was believed to preside over the lives of women. See Donald L. Wasson, "Juno," World History Encyclopedia, 8 April 2015, https://www.worldhistory.org/Juno/.

61 SERE. "Dry, withered," sometimes in a figurative sense (*OED*, s.v. "sere | sear, *adj.*^{1}").

62 HELPED THE LAME DOG CANNILY OVER THE STILE. "To come to the aid of someone in need," a seventeenth-century saying (*OED*, s.v. "dog, *n.*^{1}").

NOTHING VENTURE, NOTHING WIN. Variation on "nothing ventured, nothing gained," a seventeenth-century adage meaning "one must take risks to achieve something" (*AHDI*, s.v. "nothing ventured, nothing gained").

64 EARLY SETTLERS HAD A PASSION FOR SOLITUDE. Compare this to the mention that Green Gables had been "built at the furthest edge" of the Cuthbert property and was "barely visible from the main road" (*AGG*, 4).

THE LITTLE FELLOW'S PHOTOGRAPH

The Classmate (Cincinnati), 8 September 1906, 281–82. Scrapbook 5.

67 POT LUCK. "One's luck or chance with regard to what may be in the pot (i.e., cooked and available to eat), used originally and chiefly in reference to a person's accepting another's hospitality at a meal without any special preparation having been made" (*OED*, s.v. "potluck, *n.*").

68 WHEN A MAN'S BARNS ARE BIGGER THAN HIS HOUSE. The narrator of "The Quarantine at Alexander Abraham's," a story appearing in *Chronicles of Avonlea*, makes a similar observation: "My father always said that when a man's barns were bigger than his house it was a sign that his income exceeded his expenditure" (*CA*, 207).

75 MARY GARDINER. In *Pat of Silver Bush* and *Mistress Pat*, Mary Gardiner is the married name of Pat's mother. This name is retained in the reworked version of this story in *Anne of Windy Poplars*, published a year after *Mistress Pat* (*AWP*, 161).

THE OLD SOUTH ORCHARD

The Outing Magazine (Deposit, NY), January 1908, 413–16.
Scrapbook 4.

76 HEADNOTE. Montgomery to Weber, 8 April 1906, in *GGL*, 41.

77 BIRTHTREE. Prior to developing the notion of birth trees for King family members in this story and in *The Story Girl*, Montgomery had included it in a 1901 sketch entitled "Half an Hour with Canadian Mothers" (*NH*, 193–96).

"UNCLE STEPHEN'S AVENUE." The description here is similar to the narrator's description of "the 'Avenue'" in *Anne of Green Gables*, "a stretch of road four or five hundred yards long, completely arched over with huge, wide-spreading apple-trees, planted years ago by an eccentric old farmer" (*AGG*, 25). Although "a double row of apple trees, running down the western side of the orchard," appears in *The Story Girl*, it is renamed "Uncle Stephen's Walk" (*SG*, 25).

78 DAGUERREOTYPE. "One of the earliest photographic processes, first published by Daguerre of Paris in 1839, in which the impression was taken upon a silver plate sensitized by iodine, and then developed by exposure to the vapour of mercury" (*OED*, s.v. "daguerreotype, *n.*").

"WHEN MY SHIP COMES IN." Mid-nineteenth-century idiom meaning "when one has made one's fortune," which "alludes to ships returning from far-off places with a cargo of valuables" (*AHDI*, s.v. "when one's ship comes in").

81 THE WELL OF URDA. In Norse mythology, the Well of Urd (sometimes spelled Urda), representing fate, is one of several springs at the roots of the Yggdrasil, an ash tree that connects the various realms of humans and divine beings.

PONCE DE LEON'S FOUNTAIN OF YOUTH. The legend of Juan Ponce de León (ca. 1474–1521), Spanish explorer, searching for a fountain of youth that would restore youth and vitality to those who drink or bathe in its waters began shortly after his death and gained cultural prominence through literature and art starting in the nineteenth century.

83 PLAYING "IVANHOE." In a 1919 essay, Montgomery mentioned Sir Walter Scott's historical novel *Ivanhoe* (1820), set in twelfth-century England, as one of several books she had read as a child (Montgomery, "The Gay Days of Old," 167).

THE LIFE-BOOK OF UNCLE JESSE

The Housekeeper (Minneapolis), August 1909, 8–9. Scrapbook 12.
Also in Montgomery, *Along the Shore*, 33–47.

84 HEADNOTE. Campbell, "'A Window Looking Seaward,'" 312n28;
Epperly, *The Fragrance of Sweet-Grass*, 86.

85 THE PINK OF NEATNESS. In this context, "pink" means "the most
excellent example of something; the embodiment or model of a
particular quality" (*OED*, s.v. "pink, *n.⁵* and *adj.²*").

86 GOODS AND CHATTELS. "A comprehensive phrase for all kinds of
personal property" (*OED*, s.v. "chattel, *n.*").

"FAERIE LANDS FORLORN." From "Ode to a Nightingale," a
poem by John Keats (1795–1821), English poet.

87 THE GODS ON HIGH OLYMPUS. Olympus, the highest mountain
in Greece, is according to Greek mythology the home of the
twelve Greek gods.

PHIZ. An archaic and colloquial term meaning "a face or facial
expression" (*OED*, s.v. "phiz, *n.*").

"UNHAPPY, FAR-OFF THINGS." From "The Solitary Reaper," a
poem by William Wordsworth (1770–1850), English poet.

89 THE MILK OF HUMAN KINDNESS. From *Macbeth*, a play by
William Shakespeare (ca. 1564–1916), English playwright and
poet.

THE WISDOM OF THE SERPENT. The depiction of a snake as
wise or cunning can be traced back to chapter 3 of the Book of
Genesis (*KJV*), part of the creation story of Adam and Eve. In
Matthew 10:16 (*KJV*), Jesus instructs his twelve apostles to be
"wise as serpents, and harmless as doves."

INFIDEL. While this term has historically been used within
Christianity to refer to people with faith commitments outside
this religion, Montgomery typically uses it to refer to people
who reject orthodox Christian tenets about the divine or
the afterlife or who embrace unorthodox thinking. In *Emily
of New Moon*, Dr. Burnley is considered an infidel because
he rejects the existence of God, whereas his daughter, Ilse,
is labelled an infidel because she apparently spells the name
"God" with a lowercase g in dictations at school (*ENM*, 77, 89).
In *Emily's Quest*, Aunt Ruth accuses Dean Priest of being an
infidel because "he doesn't believe what *we* believe!" (*EQ*, 83),
whereas in *A Tangled Web*, Hugh Dark is reputed to be

an infidel because he owns copies of the work of Robert G. Ingersoll (1833–1899), an American lawyer and orator who attacked standard doctrines of Christian faith and promoted the idea of agnosticism (*TW*, 28).

RHEUMATIZ. British and American regionalism referring to rheumatism; see the note to page 10 ("rheumatism"), above.

WHETHER IN THE BODY OR OUT OF THE BODY. From 2 Corinthians 12:3 (*KJV*): "And I knew such a man, (whether in the body, or out of the body, I cannot tell: God knoweth)."

91 STANCHLY. An alternative spelling of "staunchly," in the sense of "standing firm and true to one's principles or purpose" or "showing determination or resolution" (*OED*, s.v. "staunch | stanch, *adj.*").

ROBERT KENNEDY. In *Jane of Lantern Hill*, Jane's grandmother's late husband was named Robert Kennedy (*JLH*, 3).

92 THE FLYING DUTCHMAN. A ship that was wrecked during a storm in 1641 after its captain, Hendrick van der Decken, refused to turn back. According to nautical legend, subsequent sightings of this ghost ship, although possibly an optical illusion, are believed to be a warning of doom. This legend was reworked into an 1843 opera entitled *The Flying Dutchman* by Richard Wagner (1813–1883), German composer and librettist.

MALAY. "A member of a people chiefly inhabiting Malaysia, Brunei, and parts of Indonesia, and characteristically speaking the Malay language" (*OED*, s.v. "Malay, *n.* and *adj.*").

A GARDEN OF OLD DELIGHTS

The Canadian Magazine (Toronto), June 1910, 154–60. Scrapbook 4.
95 HEADNOTE. *GR*, 37; *EC*, 160–61.

THAT WISE OLD EDEN STORY. From Genesis 1–3 (*KJV*).

97 THE FITNESS OF THINGS. Popular phrase meaning "what is fitting or appropriate" that can be traced to the works of Samuel Clarke (1626–1701), English nonconformist minister and Biblical scholar who in his writings referred to "the eternal reason of things" but frequently used "fitness" as a synonym for "reason" (*OED*, "fitness, *n.*"). In chapter 7 of *Anne of Green Gables*, the narrator mentions that Marilla possesses "the glimmerings of a sense of humour—which is simply another name for a sense of the fitness of things" (*AGG*, 72–73).

APHIS. "A family of minute insects, also called *plant-lice*, which are very destructive to vegetation" (*OED*, s.v. "aphis, *n.*").

98 BLEEDING HEARTS. *Lamprocapnos spectabilis*, a plant with heart-shaped flowers.

SWEET WILLIAM. "A species of pink, *Dianthus barbatus*, cultivated in numerous varieties, bearing closely-clustered flowers of various shades of white and red, usually variegated or particoloured" (*OED*, s.v. "sweet-william, *n.*"). *NH*, 194, 385n4.

BRIDE'S BOUQUET. *Poranopsis paniculata*, also known as "Christmas Vine" and "Snow Creeper," a climbing vine of green leaves with thick clusters of white flowers.

BUTTER-AND-EGGS. *Linaria vulgaris*, a species of toadflax whose flowers are similar to those of a snapdragon.

ADAM-AND-EVE. *Aplectrum hyemale*, a type of orchid.

BOUNCING BETS. Properly, Bouncing Bess (*Saponaria officinalis*), also called "soapwort," a plant with clusters of pink or white flowers whose petals are shaped in a way that resembles a Maltese cross. Many of these flower names appear in Montgomery's first "Around the Table" column (*NH*, 78, 359n14).

100 "THE LOST DIAMOND." In chapter 7 of *Emily of New Moon*, Cousin Jimmy tells Emily about a visiting ancestor from half a century earlier who lost her diamond ring somewhere on the grounds of New Moon Farm (*ENM*, 77–78). Although Emily immediately "made up her mind that she would find the Lost Diamond" (*ENM*, 78), she stumbles upon it only as an adult, in chapter 18 of *Emily's Quest* (*EQ*, 191–93).

103 CANTERBURY-BELLS. *Campanula medium*, a plant with long flower stalks and bell-shaped flowers.

104 SOUTHERNWOOD. *Artemisia abrotanum*, a type of flowering plant in the sunflower family; "apple-ringie" and "boy's love" are among several common names for it.

A PIONEER WOOING

The Canadian Courier (Toronto), 20 May 1911, 8, 26–28. Also, in earlier form, in *The Farm and Fireside* (Springfield, OH), 15 September 1903, 14–15. Scrapbook 3.

107 HEADNOTE. *SG*, 71–72; Montgomery, 23 May 1911, in *CJLMM*, 2: 404. For more on the historical genesis of this story, see

Montgomery, 23 May 1911, in *CJLMM*, 2: 405; Montgomery to MacMillan, 5 June 1905, in *MDMM*, 9–10; Montgomery, 2 June 1931, in *LMMCJ*, 5: 160–61, 166–67; *NH*, 238–39, 392nn24–28.

108 "ANNIE LAURIE." Scottish song based on a poem attributed to William Douglas (1682?–1748), with music added and lyrics modified by Alicia Ann Spottiswoode (1810–1900), also known as Lady John Scott, in the 1830s. The phrase "Her face it is the fairest that e'er the sun shone on" appears in the second of three stanzas in the Spottiswoode version.

REELS AND STRATHSPEYS. These Scottish dances are similar to each other, except that a strathspey is performed more slowly than a reel; a reel tends to involve at least four dancers, whereas a strathspey usually consists of two or four dancers.

111 GROG. Alcohol (usually liquor), sometimes mixed with water.

ALL WAS FAIR IN LOVE AND WAR. "Any conduct is permissible in certain circumstances," an idiom whose usage dates to the sixteenth century (*AHDI*, s.v. "all's fair in love and war").

112 UNITED EMPIRE LOYALISTS . . . THE AMERICAN WAR OF INDEPENDENCE. Also known as the American Revolutionary War, which was fought from 1775 to 1783 and resulted in American independence from British rule. United Empire Loyalists were people who lived in the United States and whose allegiance was with Great Britain during this war.

115 HAIR THAT LAY IN SKEINS. Hair that is dressed to resemble a skein, which is "a quantity of thread or yarn, wound to a certain length upon a reel, and usually put up in a kind of loose knot" (*OED*, s.v. "skein, *n.*^{1}").

116 THE DUST UNDER HER FEET. From Mark 6:11 (*KJV*): "And whosoever shall not receive you, nor hear you, when ye depart thence, shake off the dust under your feet for a testimony against them."

A FAIR EXCHANGE IS NO ROBBERY. "If something is swapped for another thing of equal value that is a reasonable exchange" (*ODP*, s.v. "A fair exchange is no robbery").

BRAW. Scottish term meaning "brave," in the sense of "finely-dressed; splendid, showy" or "worthy, excellent, capital, fine" (*OED*, s.v. "braw, *adj.* [and *adv.*] and *n.*").

ABUNE. A variation on "aboon," which in Scots and British dialect means "above."

A CHIP OF THE OLD BLOCK

The Canadian Courier (Toronto), 8 February 1913, 8, 21–22. Also, in earlier form, in *Springfield (MA) Republican*, 6 January 1907, 22. Scrapbook 8.

119 HEADNOTE. *RV*, 175. The expression "chip off the old block," "with its analogy to a chip of stone or wood that closely resembles the larger block it was cut from," had appeared by the seventeenth century (*AHDI*, s.v. "chip off the old block").

120 THE CAT'S GOT MARY'S TONGUE. Reference to a mid-nineteenth-century idiom used as "a comment made when someone is unaccountably or unusually quiet," often "used mainly with a child who did something wrong and refused to answer any questions" (*AHDI*, s.v. "cat got one's tongue").

CUMBERER OF THE GROUND. Used here in the sense of someone who is useless. In a New Testament parable about a man with a fig tree that bears no fruit, the man in question is reported to have ordered it cut: "Why cumbereth it the ground?" See Luke 13:7 (*KJV*).

122 CARMODY. In the Anne books, this larger settlement a short distance from Avonlea is the location of several stores (including the one in which Matthew Cuthbert tries to buy Anne a dress with puffed sleeves), a doctor, and a train station, and Anne's friends Priscilla Grant and Ruby Gillis both teach there a year.

BEARD THE LION IN HIS DEN. See the note to page 11, above.

MR. BENTLEY. In *Anne of Green Gables*, a minister by this name fails to capture Anne's attention while preaching and eventually resigns after eighteen years of service in Avonlea (*AGG*, 115, 235–36). In *The Blue Castle*, a Presbyterian minister is named Mr. Bently (*BC*, 108).

123 DISCRETION IS THE BETTER PART OF VALOUR. Properly, "The better part of valour is discretion," a line spoken by Falstaff in *1 Henry IV* (1598), a play by Shakespeare.

MRS. PETER SLOANE. A minor character in *Anne of Avonlea* "who had a habit of sighing over everything and even finished off her jokes that way" (*AA*, 332); she returns briefly—again with a sigh—in *Anne of the Island*, and in spite of her stated hope that Anne's strength will not fail her during her undergraduate studies, it is she who dies within the year (*AIs*, 15, 103).

HER CHIN GAVE THE WORLD ASSURANCE OF A CHIN. An allusion to *Hamlet* (1623), a play by Shakespeare ("To give the world assurance of a man"). Eric Marshall in chapter 1 of *Kilmeny of the Orchard* and Jim Wilcox in part 1 of *Anne of Windy Poplars* are likewise known for having "a chin that gave the world assurance of a chin" (*KO*, 4; *AWP*, 135).

TARTAR. Used here in the sense of "one hard to beat or surpass in skill" or a bully (*OED*, s.v. "Tartar | Tatar, *n.*² and *adj.*").

THE INDECISION OF MARGARET

Maclean's Magazine (Toronto), January 1915, 9–11, 90–92. Scrapbook 11. Also, in earlier form, in *Gunter's Magazine* (New York), September 1906, 156–65. Scrapbook 4.

127 PROVIDENCE. Theological term referring to the intervention of God in the world. In chapter 6 of *Anne of Green Gables*, Mrs. Spencer "call[s] it positively providential" that Marilla wants to return Anne to the orphanage given that their neighbour Mrs. Blewett wants domestic help for her large family, but the narrator adds that "Marilla did not look as if she thought Providence had much to do with the matter" (*AGG*, 63). Later, commenting on Mrs. Spencer's mistake in bringing back a girl from the orphanage for them instead of the boy they had asked for, Matthew proclaims that "it was Providence, because the Almighty saw we needed her, I reckon" (*AGG*, 385).

TWENTY-FIVE IS THE FIRST CORNER. The age after which a woman was perceived as less likely to marry. In chapter 2 of *Anne's House of Dreams*, Avonlea gossip Mrs. Harmon Andrews uses this expression as a way to make a dig at Anne's age on the eve of her wedding: "When I was a girl twenty-five was the first corner" (*AHD*, 13).

A LIFE INTEREST IN EVERYTHING. Presumably, Aunt Roberta inherited her property and assets according to a will that stipulated that she could not bequest any of it to someone of her choosing at her own death. Although the story does not state conclusively that Aunt Roberta has been married, her comments about women and marriage suggest she must be, so the will in question would be that of her (presumed) late husband.

128 PREDESTINATION AND FREE-WILL. Predestination is a religious belief that the salvation of humans is predetermined by God

regardless of a person's actions, whereas "free will" in this context is the belief that salvation is determined by individuals' actions while on earth. Although Montgomery scorned the notion of predestination as a teenager, her husband later became convinced that he was not among the "elect"—a stance that complicated his career as a Presbyterian minister, to say the least. See Rubio, *Lucy Maud Montgomery*, 19, 63, 212.

    MY EYES WERE GREY; THEY ARE GREEN SOMETIMES. In this, Margaret has much in common with Anne, whose eyes, the narrator reveals in *Anne of Green Gables*, "looked green in some lights and moods and gray in others" (*AGG*, 16).

129 HIS HAIR WAS BRICK RED. Peter Campbell's equivalent in *Anne of the Island*, Jonas Blake, has "tow-colour" hair (*AIs*, 210), meaning the colour of fibres of flax or hemp.

    TOUSLY. "Characterized by being tousled or dishevelled" (*OED*, s.v. "tously, *adj.*").

130 FLESH POTS. Luxuries. See Exodus 16:3 (*KJV*).

132 NICENESS FAIRLY EXHALED FROM HIM. This sentence appears in Philippa Gordon's description of Jonas Blake in *Anne of the Island* (*AIs*, 211) and again in "Aunt Cynthia's Persian Cat," the first story in *Further Chronicles of Avonlea* (*FCA*, 19).

136 TO GREENLAND'S ICY MOUNTAINS. "From Greenland's Icy Mountains," a 1819 hymn with lyrics by Reginald Heber, beginning with the following couplet: "From Greenland's Icy Mountains, / From India's coral strand." In chapter 9 of *Jane of Lantern Hill*, Jane experiences "a thrill" when hearing this hymn at church: "There was something fascinating about coral strands and icy mountains" (*JLH*, 64).

AUNT PHILIPPA AND THE MEN

The Red Book Magazine (Chicago), January 1915, 518–24. Scrapbook 4. Also in Montgomery, *At the Altar*, 1–16.

140 HEADNOTE. Epperly, *The Fragrance of Sweet-Grass*, 88; Lefebvre, "Introduction: A Life in Print," 22, 28n52. "Miss Cornelia Makes a Call" and "Miss Cornelia's Startling Announcement" were included in French's anthology under "Humorous" (along with instructions on how to dramatize these excerpts as a two-person play), whereas "A Disappointment" and "Captain Jim's Enjoyment," paragraph-long excerpts from

the same novel, were the sole selections under "Short Encore Pieces." Montgomery's poem "Off to the Fishing Ground," first published in 1904, also appears in this volume. French referred to Montgomery as "the Jane Austen of Canada" in a 1914 article and as "the Jane Austen of Canadian Literature" in a 1921 newspaper piece, but when a reworked version of the 1914 article appeared in *Highwaters of Canadian Literature* (1924), which he co-wrote with J.D. Logan, the connection with Austen was omitted. See French, "Canada's Jane Austen"; French, "Rilla, Daughter of 'Anne'"; Logan and French, *Highwaters of Canadian Literature*, 298–302.

141 A HOWLING WILDERNESS. From Deuteronomy 32:10 (*KJV*): "He found him in a desert land, and in the waste howling wilderness." In *Anne of the Island*, Anne is relieved to see her old friend Priscilla Grant again: "What a comfort one familiar face is in a howling wilderness of strangers!" (*AIs*, 26).

143 THE IRON THAT FLOATED. In 2 Kings 6:1–7 (*KJV*), the prophet Elisha miraculously makes an iron axe head float after it is dropped in the Jordan river.

145 JOSEPH . . . HIS COAT IS OF MANY COLORS. In Genesis 37:3 (*KJV*), Jacob, grandson of Abraham, gives "a coat of many colours" to his youngest and favourite son, Joseph, to the great consternation of Joseph's eleven brothers.

147 'FAVOR IS DECEITFUL AND BEAUTY IS VAIN.' From Proverbs 31:30 (*KJV*): "Favour *is* deceitful, and beauty *is* vain: *but* a woman *that* feareth the Lord, she shall be praised."

148 NEITHER TRUTH NOR CONSTANCY. This phrase appears in an essay on the Holy Ghost (translated in English by William Hazlitt) by Martin Luther (1483–1546), German theologian.

150 A WOLF IN SHEEP'S CLOTHING. "An enemy disguised as a friend," an idiomatic phrase from "the ancient fable about a wolf that dresses up in the skin of a sheep and sneaks up on a flock" (*AHDI*, s.v. "wolf in sheep's clothing").

BY THE GRACE OF SARAH MAY

Maclean's Magazine (Toronto), August 1916, 27–28. Scrapbook 11. Also, in earlier form and as "By the Grace of Sarah Maud," in *Modern Women* (Boston), June 1905, 4–5. Scrapbook 9.

152 HEADNOTE. Gammel, *Looking for Anne*, 215, 216.

154 THE WRECK OF ALL THINGS. From *Scenes and Incidents in the Life of the Apostle Paul* (1869), a book of theological essays by Albert Barnes (1798–1870), American theologian.

155 ARCADY. A bucolic paradise. Chapter 28 of *The Golden Road* is entitled "The Path to Arcady."

BEGONE, DULL CARE. Title of a seventeenth-century song.

DAFF THE WORLD . . . ASIDE. Properly, "daft the world aside." From *1 Henry IV*, a play by Shakespeare. In this context, to "daff" means "to put or turn aside, to thrust aside" (*OED*, s.v. "daff, *v.*²"). In chapter 17 of *Anne of Avonlea*, Anne suggests to Marilla that they "shut Green Gables up and spend the whole day at the shore, daffing the world aside" (*AA*, 195), but not surprisingly, Marilla declines.

NO SORROW ICE CREAM COULD NOT CURE. In chapter 25 of *Anne of Avonlea*, the narrator states that "Davy had no sorrows plum jam could not cure" (*AA*, 289).

156 SAVVY. As a transitive verb, this means "to know or understand (something)" (*OED*, s.v. "savvy, *v.*").

158 THE END OF ALL THINGS. From 1 Peter 4:7 (*KJV*): "But the end of all things is at hand: be ye therefore sober, and watch unto prayer."

ABEL AND HIS GREAT ADVENTURE

The Canadian Magazine (Toronto), February 1917, 355–63. Scrapbook 4. Also in Montgomery, *The Doctor's Sweetheart and Other Stories*, 124–39.

159 HEADNOTE. Epperly, *The Fragrance of Sweet-Grass*, 255n2; Wiggins, *L.M. Montgomery*, 157.

160 GARRULOUS. The act of being fond of talking.

161 LOMBARDY POPLARS. A Lombardy is "a columnar variety of poplar," and the *OED* includes as an example an extract from Montgomery's *Anne's House of Dreams*: "The Lombardies down the lane, tall and sombre" (*OED*, s.v. "Lombardy, *n.*"; see *AHD*, 58). Like Abel in this story, Captain Jim refers to Lombardies as "the trees of princesses" (*AHD*, 58).

TOM, DICK AND HARRY. See the note to page 4 ("Tom, Dick or Harry"), above.

162 'WITHOUT MONEY AND WITHOUT PRICE.' From Isaiah 55:1 (*KJV*).

IF YOU CAN SIT IN SILENCE WITH A PERSON FOR HALF AN HOUR. In *The Blue Castle*, this idea is attributed to Valancy's favourite writer, John Foster: "If you can sit in silence with a person for half an hour and yet be entirely comfortable, you and that person can be friends. If you cannot, friends you'll never be and you need not waste time in trying" (*BC*, 157).

163 CAPTAIN KIDD. Named after William Kidd (ca. 1645–1701), a Scottish privateer whose exploits as a pirate led to him being hanged.

164 MEEK AS MOSES. Mild-mannered or humble, an allusion to Numbers 12:3 (*KJV*): "Now the man Moses *was* very meek."

LONG IN THE LAND. From Exodus 20:12 (*KJV*): "Honour thy father and thy mother: that thy days may be long upon the land."

165 DOG-DAYS. "Hot, sultry summer weather; also, a period of stagnation" (*AHDI*, s.v. "dog days").

166 BIRDS OF A FEATHER. Short form of "Birds of a feather flock together," a sixteenth-century expression referring to people of similar backgrounds or interests (*AHDI*, s.v. "birds of a feather [flock together]").

EFFULGENT. Resplendent or radiant (*OED*, s.v. "effulgent, *adj.*").

168 TENNYSON SPOKE TRUTH WHEN HE SAID THAT. Rea Wilmshurst suggests that the reference to Tennyson that appears in the corresponding scene in *Anne's House of Dreams* (see *AHD*, 150) alludes to his poem "In Memoriam," specifically the line "He thinks he was not made to die" (Wilmshurst, "L.M. Montgomery's Use of Quotations and Allusions," 27).

VALE OF TEARS. The trials and sorrows of earthly life, a term found frequently in poems and hymns. In *Anne of Avonlea*, Anne and Diana request a donation from Eliza Andrews, who, the narrator notes, "was one of those people who give you the impression that life is indeed a vale of tears, and that a smile, never to speak of a laugh, is a waste of nervous energy truly reprehensible" (*AA*, 56).

'BEYOND THE BOURNE OF SUNSET.' Given that this quotation appears as "to sail beyond the bourne of sunset" in *Anne's House of Dreams* (*AHD*, 63), this is likely a misquotation of "To sail beyond the sunset," from Tennyson's poem "Ulysses." A second reference to this poem, this time identifying it by name, appears later in that novel (*AHD*, 91). The quotation "the bourne of sunset" appears in *Kilmeny of the Orchard* (*KO*, 63), whereas Montgomery's nature essay "Spring in the Woods" has the phrase "the far bourne of sunset" without quotation marks (Montgomery, "[Seasons of the Woods]," 76).

THE SCHOOLMASTER'S BRIDE

Everywoman's World (Toronto), July 1917, 5, 43.

173 HEADNOTE. *AHD*, 48–52; Montgomery, 29 November 1915, in *LMMCJ*, 1: 208.

174 RECKING. Used here in the obsolete sense of concerned or worried.

LINDSAY. Also the Prince Edward Island setting of *Kilmeny of the Orchard* (*KO*, 20).

I LOVED HIM AS DAVID LOVED JONATHAN. MY SOUL WAS KNIT TO HIS. From 1 Samuel 18:1 (*KJV*): "And it came to pass . . . that the soul of Jonathan was knit with the soul of David, and Jonathan loved him as his own soul."

BYRON AND SCOTT AND WORDSWORTH, SHELLEY AND KEATS. George Gordon, Lord Byron (1788–1824), English poet; Sir Walter Scott (1771–1832), Scottish novelist and poet; William Wordsworth (1770–1850), English poet; Percy Bysshe Shelley (1792–1822), English poet; John Keats (1795–1821), English poet. Montgomery identified Byron and Scott as her favourite poets in a 1914 journal entry (Montgomery, 15 April 1914, in *LMMCJ*, 1: 154), and allusions to the work of all five of these poets are peppered throughout her fiction.

MRS. HEMANS. Felicia Hemans (1793–1835), English poet whose work Montgomery reread in late 1914 (Montgomery, 19 December 1914, in *LMMCJ*, 1: 174–75).

176 RABBLE. Obsolete term referring to "a kind of shovel or rake used by charcoal burners to remove the covering from a burned pile" (*OED*, s.v. "rabble, *n.*²").

178 COUNT THE DAYS LIKE SILVER BEADS ON A ROSARY. In chapter 18 of *Anne's House of Dreams*, Anne is "counting her days like silver beads on a rosary" (*AHD*, 164), an oblique reference to the advanced stages of pregnancy.

AS A SEA-FOG STEALING LANDWARD. This phrase is used in slightly different form in *Anne's House of Dreams* to describe the beginnings of Anne's worry after the birth of her daughter

Joyce, who lives only a day: "Then, as subtly, and coldly, and remorselessly as a sea-fog stealing landward, fear crept into her heart" (*AHD*, 175).

RAVENING. Used here in the figurative sense of "to rage *with* hunger" (*OED*, s.v. "raven, *v.*").

179 AN HOUR IN WHICH A MAN MIGHT BE HAPPY ALL HIS LIFE. "There is an hour wherein a man might be happy all his life could he but find it," a saying attributed to George Herbert (1593–1633), Welsh-born English poet and theologian. In chapter 8 of *The Blue Castle*, Valancy reflects during a sleepless night on the fact that she has "never had one wholly happy hour in my life. . . . I remember reading somewhere once that there is an hour in which a woman might be happy all her life if she could find it" (*BC*, 56).

OUR NEIGHBORS AT THE TANSY PATCH

Canadian Home Journal (Toronto), August 1918, 7, 18, 38–39. Also in Montgomery, *After Many Years*, 89–106.

182 HEADNOTE. *Canadian Home Journal*, Contents, 3.

183 SALOME. A servant named Salome Silversides also appears in *Magic for Marigold*.

SKINAMULINX. A regional colloquialism, with multiple spellings, referring to a skinny person (*OED*, s.v. "skinnymalink, *n.*").

I WOT NOT. "I know not," "wot" being a Scottish dialect variant of the transitive verb "to wit," meaning "to know" (*OED*, s.v. "wit, *v.*^{1}").

SORROWED AS ONE WITHOUT HOPE. The phrase "that I may not sorrow as one without hope" appears in a prayer entitled "Against Sorrow without Hope," part of *The Christian's Manual of Faith and Devotion*, a second edition of which appeared in 1818.

184 CAPTAIN KIDD. See the note to page 163, above.

185 THE DIVINE AFFLATUS. "The communication of supernatural or spiritual knowledge; divine impulse; inspiration, *esp.* poetic inspiration" (*OED*, s.v. "afflatus, *n.*").

186 RHEUMATISM. See the note to page 10, above.

187 WHEN STONES BLEED. From the expression "You cannot get blood from a stone," meaning "it is hopeless to try extorting money, etc., from those who have none," which can be traced

to Charles Dickens's 1850 novel *David Copperfield* (*ODP*, s.v. "You cannot get blood from a stone").

PECKS. Used here in the sense of "a considerable quantity or number; a great deal, a heap, a lot" (*OED*, s.v. "peck, *n.*¹").

188 YOU BLATANT BEAST! YOU PUTRID PUP! These are among the insults spoken by Norman Douglas after Mr. Pryor makes a palpably pacifist prayer at a church meeting in chapter 20 of *Rilla of Ingleside* (*RI*, 236).

189 HOW SHOULD I KNOW WHERE YOU ARE GOING, GOSLING? Roaring Abel Gay asks a similar question of a minister in chapter 19 of *The Blue Castle* (*BC*, 139).

GRANNY ROUTED AN AUTOMOBILE. This incident occurs again, with some new "maledictions," in chapter 12 of *Magic for Marigold* (*MM*, 188).

190 A NEST OF FIVE EGGS. In chapter 16 of *Rilla of Ingleside*, Susan Baker tells this same anecdote, this time about a Mrs. MacAllister who "was well-known to be a heedless creature" (*RI*, 184).

191 THE RETURNED SOLDIERS OF THE BOER WAR. The First Boer War had been fought from December 1880 to March 1881, the Second Boer War between October 1899 and May 1902. In one of her "Around the Table" columns appearing in the *Halifax Daily Echo* in 1901, a character refers to the day "the first contingent came home," referring to soldiers returning to Canada in December 1900 (*NH*, 84, 362n41).

"CANADA, LIKE A MAIDEN, WELCOMES BACK HER SONS." In chapter 8 of *Emily Climbs*, Perry Miller also writes a poem with this contradictory line (a maiden by definition is unmarried and has no children), which a secondary character deems to be "a scream" (*EC*, 117).

SYLPH-LIKE. The term "sylph" refers to "one of a race of beings or spirits supposed to inhabit the air" but can be applied also "to a graceful woman or girl; usually with implication of slender figure and light airy movement" (*OED*, s.v. "sylph, *n.*").

192 YOU OUGHT TO BITE HER OFTENER. This exchange occurs again in chapter 12 of *Magic for Marigold*, except there T.B. bites Granny after "she smacked Aunt Lily" (*MM*, 186).

"MEMOIR OF SUSANNA B. MORTON." Possibly an echo of John A. Clark's *The Young Disciple; or, A Memoir of Anzonetta R. Peters* (1837), which, according to her account in "The Alpine Path," Montgomery had loved as a child (*NH*, 271–72, 402n128).

I WON'T BE PRAYED FOR. Ilse Burnley has an identical reaction to this idea in chapter 11 of *Emily of New Moon* (*ENM*, 119).

193 ANTS . . . DURNED INT'RESTING. Mary Vance repeats most of this speech in chapter 8 of *Rainbow Valley* (*RV*, 84–85).

"MEMORIES OF OTHER DAYS." In 1936, Montgomery published an essay entitled "Memories of Childhood Days" that she was particularly proud of: "It seems to me that, in one happy moment of inspiration I captured the very essence of P.E. Islandism" (Montgomery, 9 April 1936, in *SJLMM*, 5: 60).

194 MIX UP CAKES IN THE WASH-PAN. In chapter 12 of *Rainbow Valley*, Susan Baker dismisses a neighbour's disparaging comment about another neighbour's poor housekeeping skills and is tempted to retort, "Every one knows that *you* have been seen mixing up cakes in the kitchen wash-pan" (*RV*, 124).

CANNIBAL ISLANDS. Now Fiji, an island nation in the South Pacific Ocean.

PALMY DAYS. Figurative term meaning past times that were "triumphant, flourishing, successful" (*OED*, s.v. "palmy, *adj.*").

THE BILL OF FARE. A menu of dishes, either at a banquet or at a restaurant.

195 DAMASK. See the note to page 39, above.

196 MY HEART IS KNIT TO HIS. A reference to the Biblical story of David and Jonathan. See the note to page 174 ("I loved him as David loved Jonathan. My soul was knit to his"), above.

THE MATCHMAKER

Canadian Home Journal (Toronto), September 1919, 7, 46–49. Also in Montgomery, *After Many Years*, 107–24.

197 HEADNOTE. *AIn*, 97, 102. Ludovic Speed and Theodora Dix appear in "The Hurrying of Ludovic," the lead story in *Chronicles of Avonlea* whose first incarnation appears earlier in this volume; Stephen Clark and Prissy Strong (referred to erroneously in *Anne of Ingleside* as Prissie Gardner) appear in "The Courting of Prissy Strong," also in *Chronicles of Avonlea*; Janet Sweet and John Douglas appear in chapters 31 to 34 of *Anne of the Island*; and the last three couples are featured at different times in *Anne of Windy Poplars*.

199 FOUR HUNDRED. According to the Bank of Canada's online inflation calculator, this amount of money in 1919 would be worth nearly $6,000 in 2021.

'THE LORD GAVE AND THE LORD TAKETH AWAY.' From Job 1:21 (*KJV*): "the Lord gave, and the Lord hath taken away." In chapter 19 of *Anne's House of Dreams*, Miss Cornelia says a slightly different version of this quotation to Anne as a form of condolence when Joyce, Anne's baby daughter, dies shortly after birth (*AHD*, 176).

200 NEURALGIA. "Pain, typically stabbing or burning, in the area served by a nerve; (also) an instance, type, or case of this" (*OED*, s.v. "neuralgia").

RHEUMATISM. See the note to page 10, above.

BY HOOK OR BY CROOK. By any means, an idiom whose origins are open to dispute.

SHEEP'S EYES. "To look lovingly, amorously, or longingly at" a person (*OED*, s.v. "sheep's eye(s), *n.*"). In chapter 1 of *Rilla of Ingleside*, Miss Cornelia annoys Susan by suggesting that "Jerry Meredith is making sheep's eyes at Nan" (*RI*, 8).

203 I COULDN'T ASK THE MINISTER TO A DANCE. In some Christian denominations, ministers and their family members are prohibited from dancing, even when members of the congregation are not. In chapter 4 of *Rilla of Ingleside*, Rilla's friends the Merediths are not permitted to dance at a party because their father is a minister (*RI*, 23–24).

204 LOVER'S LANE. Montgomery used this place name—based on a stretch of woods near her home in Cavendish—in a 1903 poem (see *WS*, 13–14), in *Anne of Green Gables* and its sequels, and in *The Blue Castle*. See also *NH*, 410n196. The Cavendish stretch of woods in question is a delightful spot, and I highly recommend it to anyone visiting Montgomery locations in Prince Edward Island.

205 THE WIND IS EAST. See the note to page 10 ("rheumatism"), above. In literary texts, an east wind can symbolize change, mischief, trouble, foreboding, or evil.

207 THE OLD NICK. "A humorous or familiar name for: the Devil" from the mid-seventeenth century onward (*OED*, s.v. "Old Nick, *n.*").

SNOW PUDDING. A dessert consisting of unflavoured gelatin, lemon zest, lemon juice, and egg whites.

A FAMILIAR. Although as a noun this word can be understood as referring to "a spirit, often taking the form of an animal, which obeys and assists a witch or other person," in this context it refers to a domesticated animal "accustomed to the company of humans" (*OED*, s.v. "familiar, *n.*, *adj.*, and *adv.*").

LUCIFER. Although this term was once synonymous with Satan, the *OED* also defines it as "the morning star; the planet Venus when she appears in the sky before sunrise" (*OED*, s.v. "Lucifer, *n.*"). In *Magic for Marigold*, Old Grandmother's cat is named Lucifer (*MM*, 3).

GIVES THE WORLD ASSURANCE OF A CAT. See the note to page 123 ("her chin gave the world assurance of a chin"), above.

208 LORETTA. A continuity error involving Mrs. Churchill's late sister, who is named Lisette earlier in the story; this error is corrected in the corresponding scene in *Anne of Ingleside* (*AIn*, 113).

209 TOM, DICK OR HARRY. See the note to page 4, above.

MY STAR, WHO . . . IS FIT TO SHINE IN THE PALACES OF KINGS. This phrase, which appears in the corresponding scene in *Anne of Ingleside* (*AIn*, 114), is also used by Dean Priest to describe Emily Byrd Starr, whom he nicknames Star, in chapter 9 of *Emily's Quest* (*EQ*, 96).

210 'A MAN SHALL LEAVE FATHER AND MOTHER AND CLEAVE UNTO HIS WIFE.' From Genesis 2:24 (*KJV*): "Therefore shall a man leave his father and his mother, and shall cleave unto his wife: and they shall be one flesh."

TOMORROW COMES

Canadian Home Journal (Toronto), July 1934, 12–13, 32–34, 59. Also in Montgomery, *After Many Years*, 239–56.

212 HEADNOTE. Epperly, "Approaching the L.M. Montgomery Manuscripts," 80.

BARTIBOG. In *Jane of Lantern Hill*, Bartibog is a train station in New Brunswick (*JLH*, 229).

213 TIMOTHY SALT. Montgomery would repurpose this name for a character in *Jane of Lantern Hill*, an elderly gentleman who "told [Jane] tales of old disaster on the sea, fading old legends of dune and headland, old romances of the North Shore that were like misty wraiths" (*JLH*, 144–45).

MARTHA MONKMAN. This name is retained for the "woman" of Little Elizabeth's great-grandmother, Mrs. Campbell, in *Anne of Windy Poplars* (*AWP*, 25).

216 TILLYTUCK. In *Mistress Pat*, published a year after this story, the Gardiners' hired man is named Josiah Tillytuck (*MP*, 24).

219 SKEESICKS. American slang term for a child that means a rascal or a rogue when referring to an adult.

221 "PUT THE KIBOSH ON IT." Put a stop to something.

"THE LITTLE HILLS REJOICE ON EVERY SIDE." From Psalm 65:12 (*KJV*).

222 A CERTAIN MRS. THOMPSON. In *Anne of Windy Poplars*, Anne takes Little Elizabeth to see "a certain Mrs. Thompson," who in that version is "convenor of the refreshment committee of the Ladies' Aid" (*AWP*, 287).

I KNOW A SECRET

Good Housekeeping (New York), August 1935, 22–25, 137–39. Also in Montgomery, *The Doctor's Sweetheart and Other Stories*, 175–90.

227 BARTIBOG. See the note to page 212, above.

228 AS MEAN AS SECOND SKIMMINGS. This expression means someone who is stingy or exceedingly frugal to the point of rudeness and refers "to the process of skimming cream from milk, normally done once" (Devereux, in Montgomery, *Anne of Green Gables*, edited by Devereux, 276n1).

ONE APPLE A DAY—"TO KEEP THE DOCTOR AWAY." Proverb from the seventeenth century: "A small preventive treatment wards off serious problems" (*AHDI*, s.v. "apple a day").

229 POOR AS CHURCH MICE. "Having little or no wealth and few possessions," an expression that originates in the seventeenth century (*AHDI*, s.v. "poor as a churchmouse").

230 THROUGH THE LOOKING GLASS LIKE ALICE. An allusion to the sequel to Lewis Carroll's *Alice's Adventures in Wonderland*, entitled *Through the Looking Glass and What Alice Found There*, published in 1871. In chapter 4 of *Jane of Lantern Hill*, the narrator reveals that Jane once "longed to get into the looking-glass as *Alice* did" (*JLH*, 30).

JANE LOVED THE MOON. In *Jane of Lantern Hill*, Jane's dreams about the moon replace her attempts to "get into the looking-glass world" (*JLH*, 30).

232 CROSS YOUR HEART AND HOPE TO DIE. An expression meaning "I swear that I am telling the truth," one that is "most often uttered by children" and first recorded in 1908 (*AHDI*, s.v. "cross my heart and hope to die").

235 "I SAW A SHIP A-SAILING . . . PRETTY THINGS FOR ME." From a nineteenth-century nursery rhyme.

THEIR SHIP WOULD COME IN. See the note to page 78 ("when my ship comes in"), above.

237 THE CHEESE. Nineteenth-century term meaning "something first-rate, genuine, or exemplary" (*OED*, s.v. "cheese, *n.*²").

239 RIGMAROLE. In this context, an illogical explanation or story.

RETRIBUTION

Undated typescript. In Montgomery, "Road to Yesterday—Typed Copies of Some of the Stories, n.d.," XZ1 MS A098004, L.M. Montgomery Collection, Archival and Special Collections, University of Guelph Library. Also, in substantially revised form, in *BQ*, 96–113.

241 HEADNOTE. The typescripts for this short story and for the stories "A Commonplace Woman," "A Dream Comes True," "The Reconciliation," "The Pot and the Kettle," and "Penelope Struts Her Theories" are housed in a folder pertaining to *The Road to Yesterday*, a heavily abridged edition of *The Blythes Are Quoted*, even though these copies precede the revisions Montgomery made to include these stories in her final book; all but "The Reconciliation" include her Toronto mailing address.

242 CEYLON . . . SINGAPORE . . . MANDALAY. Places in Southeast Asia that were or were in British colonies when Montgomery wrote this story: Ceylon, now Sri Lanka; Singapore, a sovereign island city-state; and Mandalay, a city in Myanmar (also known as Burma).

AN AFTERNOON WITH MR. JENKINS

Girl's Own Paper (London), November 1939, 58, 61, 79–82. Also, in earlier form, in *The Family Herald and Weekly Star* (Montreal), 2 August 1933, 17, 20, and in revised form in *BQ*, 75–87. Scrapbook 5.

247 MRS. METHUSALEH. Methusaleh is a male Biblical figure whose name is more commonly spelled "Methuselah" and whose lifespan of 969 years makes him the oldest person recorded

in the Bible, and while his descendants are listed, his wife is unidentified; see Genesis 5:21–27 (*KJV*). In *Jane of Lantern Hill*, Jane's father has a vague ambition to write an epic poem on the life of Methuselah, but he never completes it (*JLH*, 147, 162, 296).

248 POCKET MONEY. Spending money, including that given to a child; the term is more in keeping with a British setting, compared to "allowance," used more commonly in the US (see *OED*, s.v. "pocket money, *n.*").

251 BRICKS. See the note to page 12 ("a brick"), above.

252 SEVENTH HEAVEN OF DELIGHT. "A place or state of supreme bliss"; "ecstatically happy" (*OED*, s.v. "seventh heaven, *n.*").

253 HARD WORDS BREAK NO BONES. Mid-fifteenth-century proverb (*ODP*, s.v. "Hard words break no bones").

APPENDIX: DOG MONDAY'S VIGIL

By Lucy Maud Montgomery. In *Our Canadian Literature: Representative Prose and Verse*, chosen by Albert Durrant Watson and Lorne Albert Pierce, third edition (Toronto: The Ryerson Press, 1923), 381–88. Adapted from chapters 2, 6, 8, 10, 11, 21, 22, 29, and 35 of *Rilla of Ingleside*.

255 HEADNOTE. *RI*, 18–19; Noomé, "The Nature of the Beast," 204; Montgomery, 23 November 1921, in *LMMCJ*, 2: 350; Roy, *The Next Instalment*, 147.

DOG MONDAY. "Variation on 'Man Friday,' a character in the novel *Robinson Crusoe* (1719), by Daniel Defoe, a term also used to refer to a male servant or assistant" (Lefebvre and McKenzie, Glossary, 363).

256 VALCARTIER. "Valcartier, Quebec, located 25 miles north of Quebec City, where a training camp for the first contingent of Canadian volunteer soldiers was built in August 1914" (Lefebvre and McKenzie, Glossary, 385).

257 COURCELLETTE. Properly, the Battle of Courcelette (France), fought in September 1916.

Bibliography

Ammer, Christine. *The American Heritage Dictionary of Idioms.*
2nd ed. Boston: Houghton Mifflin Harcourt, 2013.
"Author Tells How He Wrote His Story." In Lefebvre, *The L.M.
Montgomery Reader*, 1: 33–34. Previously in *Boston Journal*,
21 November 1908, 6.
Beran, Carol L. "Beautiful Girlhood, a Double Life: Lucy Maud
Montgomery, Margaret Laurence, and Alice Munro." *American
Review of Canadian Studies* 45, no. 2 (2015): 148–60.
———. "The Luxury of Excellence: Alice Munro in the *New Yorker*."
Essays on Canadian Writing 66 (Winter 1998): 204–31.
The Bible: Authorized King James Version. Oxford: Oxford University
Press, 2008. Oxford World's Classics.
Burgoyne, Daniel. "A Note on the Text." In De Mille, *A Strange
Manuscript Found in a Copper Cylinder*, 41–42.
Cabajsky, Andrea. "A Note on the Text." In Leprohon, *The Manor
House of De Villerai*, 37–41.
Cambron, Micheline, and Carole Gerson. "Literary Authorship." In
Lamonde, Fleming, and Black, *History of the Book in Canada*,
2: 119–34.
Campbell, Claire E. "'A Window Looking Seaward': Finding
Environmental History in the Writing of L.M. Montgomery." In *The
Greater Gulf: Essays on the Environmental History of the Gulf of
St. Lawrence*, edited by Claire E. Campbell, Edward MacDonald,
and Brian Payne, 283–318. Montreal and Kingston: McGill-Queen's
University Press, 2019.
Canadian Home Journal (Toronto). Contents. July 1918, 3.

Chez, Keridiana. "A Note on the Text." In Saunders, *Beautiful Joe*, 39–40.

"*Chronicles of Avonlea*." In Lefebvre, *The L.M. Montgomery Reader*, 3: 115–38.

Collins, Carolyn Strom, comp. and ed. *An Annotated Bibliography of L.M. Montgomery's Stories and Poems*. Charlottetown: L.M. Montgomery Institute, 2016.

———. Introduction to Montgomery, *Anne of Green Gables: The Original Manuscript*, 1–16.

Crawford, Isabella Valancy. *Winona; or, The Foster-Sisters*. 1873. Edited by Len Early and Michael A. Peterman. Peterborough: Broadview Editions, 2007.

Daily Mirror (London). "'Anne of Windy Willows' Is Our August Romantic Book of the Month." 31 July 1936, 12.

Dallas Morning News. "Published Today: From Page's List." 2 August 1915, 4.

Davey, Frank. "Economics and the Writer." In Gerson and Michon, *History of the Book in Canada*, 3: 103–13.

Davies, Richard A. "A Note on the Text." In Haliburton, *The Clockmaker*, 43–46.

Dean, Misao. "A Note on the Text." In Duncan, *The Imperialist*, 39–40.

De Mille, James. *A Strange Manuscript Found in a Copper Cylinder*. 1888. Edited by Daniel Burgoyne. Peterborough: Broadview Editions, 2011.

Devereux, Cecily. Headnote to "Our Uncle Wheeler," by L.M. Montgomery. In Montgomery, *Anne of Green Gables*, edited by Devereux, 335.

———. Introduction to Montgomery, *Anne of Green Gables*, edited by Devereux, 12–38.

———. "A Note on the Text." In Montgomery, *Anne of Green Gables*, edited by Devereux, 42–50.

Dole, Nathan Haskell. "Introduction to *Further Chronicles of Avonlea*, by L.M. Montgomery." In Lefebvre, *The L.M. Montgomery Reader*, 1: 169–73. Previously in Montgomery, *Further Chronicles of Avonlea*, v–xi.

Duncan, Sara Jeannette. *The Imperialist*. 1904. Edited by Misao Dean. Peterborough: Broadview Editions, 2005.

———. *The Pool in the Desert*. 1903. Edited by Gillian Siddall. Peterborough: Broadview Literary Texts, 2001.

————. *Set in Authority*. 1906. Edited by Germaine Warkentin. Peterborough: Broadview Literary Texts, 1996.

Early, Len, and Michael A. Peterman. "A Note on the Text." In Crawford, *Winona*, 65–68.

Epperly, Elizabeth Rollins. "Approaching the Montgomery Manuscripts." In *Harvesting Thistles: The Textual Garden of L.M. Montgomery; Essays on Her Novels and Journals*, edited by Mary Henley Rubio, 74–83. Guelph: Canadian Children's Press, 1994.

————. *The Fragrance of Sweet-Grass: L.M. Montgomery's Heroines and the Pursuit of Romance*. 1992. Toronto: University of Toronto Press, 2014.

————. "L.M. Montgomery's Manuscript Revisions." In Lefebvre, *The L.M. Montgomery Reader*, 2: 228–35. Previously in *Atlantis* 20, no. 1 (Fall–Winter 1995): 149–55.

Fee, Margery, and Dory Nason. "A Note on the Text." In Johnson, *Tekahionwake*, 33–34.

Fladd, Nadine. "Alice Munro, Charles McGrath, and the Shaping of 'The Turkey Season.'" *American Review of Canadian Studies* 45, no. 2 (2015): 174–86.

French, Donald Graham. "Canada's Jane Austen." *The School* (Toronto), December 1914, 268–70.

————. "Rilla, Daughter of 'Anne.'" *Globe* (Toronto), 8 October 1921, 19.

————, comp. and ed. *Standard Canadian Reciter: A Book of the Best Readings and Recitations from Canadian Literature*. Toronto: McClelland and Stewart, 1921.

Friskney, Janet B., and Carole Gerson. "Writers and the Market for Fiction and Literature." In Gerson and Michon, *History of the Book in Canada*, 3: 131–38.

Gammel, Irene. *Looking for Anne: How Lucy Maud Montgomery Dreamed Up a Literary Classic*. 2008. Toronto: Key Porter Books, 2009.

Gerson, Carole. "Seven Milestones: How *Anne of Green Gables* Became a Canadian Icon." In *Anne's World: A New Century of Anne of Green Gables*, edited by Irene Gammel and Benjamin Lefebvre, 17–34. Toronto: University of Toronto Press, 2010.

Gerson, Carole, and Jacques Michon, eds. *History of the Book in Canada*, Volume 3: *1918–1980*. Toronto: University of Toronto Press, 2007.

"*The Golden Road.*" In Lefebvre, *The L.M. Montgomery Reader*, 3: 139–54.

Haliburton, Thomas Chandler. *The Clockmaker; or The Sayings and Doings of Samuel Slick, of Slickville.* 1835–1836. Edited by Richard A. Davies. Peterborough: Broadview Editions, 2014.

Hoy, Helen. "'Rose and Janet': Alice Munro's Metafiction." *Canadian Literature* 121 (Summer 1989): 59–83.

Johnson, E. Pauline. *Tekahionwake: E. Pauline Johnson's Writings on Native North America.* Edited by Margery Fee and Dory Nason. Peterborough: Broadview Editions, 2016.

Karr, Clarence. *Authors and Audiences: Popular Canadian Fiction in the Early Twentieth Century.* Montreal and Kingston: McGill-Queen's University Press, 2000.

———. "Popular and Best-Selling Fiction." In Lamonde, Fleming, and Black, *History of the Book in Canada*, 2: 396–401.

———. "Writers and the Market for Non-fiction." In Gerson and Michon, *History of the Book in Canada*, 3: 138–42.

Kelly, Darlene. "Rewriting 'The Imperialist': Duncan's Revisions." *Canadian Literature* 121 (Summer 1989): 26–38.

Lamonde, Yvan, Patricia Lockhart Fleming, and Fiona A. Black, eds. *History of the Book in Canada*, Volume 2: *1840–1918*. Toronto: University of Toronto Press, 2005.

Leacock, Stephen. *Sunshine Sketches of a Little Town.* 1912. Edited by Carl Spadoni. Peterborough: Broadview Literary Texts, 2002.

Lefebvre, Benjamin. Afterword to Montgomery, *A World of Songs*, 105–20.

———. Headnote to "[Seasons in the Woods]," by L.M. Montgomery. In Lefebvre, *The L.M. Montgomery Reader*, 1: 73–74.

———. Introduction to *A Tangled Web*, by Lucy Maud Montgomery, 9–18. Toronto: Dundurn Press, 2009. Voyageur Classics: Books That Explore Canada.

———. "Introduction: A Legacy in Review." In Lefebvre, *The L.M. Montgomery Reader*, 3: 3–48.

———. "Introduction: A Life in Print." In Lefebvre, *The L.M. Montgomery Reader*, 1: 3–28.

———, ed. *The L.M. Montgomery Reader*, Volume 1: *A Life in Print*; Volume 2: *A Critical Heritage*; Volume 3: *A Legacy in Review*. Toronto: University of Toronto Press, 2013, 2014, 2015.

———. "A Note on the Text." In Montgomery, *The Blythes Are Quoted*, 521–22.

Lefebvre, Benjamin, and Andrea McKenzie. Glossary. In *Rilla of Ingleside*, by L.M. Montgomery, edited by Benjamin Lefebvre and Andrea McKenzie, 354–87. Toronto: Viking Canada, 2010.

Leprohon, Rosanna Mullins. *The Manor House of De Villerai: A Tale of Canada under the French Dominion. 1859–1860.* Edited by Andrea Cabajsky. Peterborough: Broadview Editions, 2015.

Logan, J.D., and Donald G. French. *Highways of Canadian Literature.* Toronto: McClelland and Stewart, 1924.

Luft, Joanna. "Boxed In: Alice Munro's 'Wenlock Edge' and *Sir Gawain and the Green Knight*." *Studies in Canadian Literature / Études en littérature canadienne* 35, no. 1 (2010): 103–26.

Lynch, Gerald. *The One and the Many: English-Canadian Short Story Cycles.* Toronto: University of Toronto Press, 2001.

Montgomery, L.M. *Across the Miles: Tales of Correspondence.* Edited by Rea Wilmshurst. Toronto: McClelland and Stewart, 1995.

———. *After Green Gables: L.M. Montgomery's Letters to Ephraim Weber, 1916–1941.* Edited by Hildi Froese Tiessen and Paul Gerard Tiessen. Toronto: University of Toronto Press, 2006.

———. *After Many Days: Tales of Time Passed.* Edited by Rea Wilmshurst. Toronto: McClelland and Stewart, 1991.

———. *After Many Years.* Edited by Carolyn Strom Collins and Christy Woster. Halifax: Nimbus Publishing, 2017.

———. *Against the Odds: Tales of Achievement.* Edited by Rea Wilmshurst. Toronto: McClelland and Stewart, 1993.

———. *Akin to Anne: Tales of Other Orphans.* Edited by Rea Wilmshurst. Toronto: McClelland and Stewart, 1988.

———. *Along the Shore: Tales by the Sea.* Edited by Rea Wilmshurst. Toronto: McClelland and Stewart, 1989.

———. *Among the Shadows: Tales from the Darker Side.* Edited by Rea Wilmshurst. Toronto: McClelland and Stewart, 1990.

———. *Anne of Avonlea.* Boston: L.C. Page and Company, 1909.

———. "Anne of Green Gables." MS. CM 67.5.1, Confederation Centre Art Gallery, Charlottetown.

———. *Anne of Green Gables.* Boston: L.C. Page and Company, 1908.

———. *Anne of Green Gables.* 1908. Edited by Cecily Devereux. Peterborough: Broadview Editions, 2004.

———. *Anne of Green Gables: The Original Manuscript.* Edited by Carolyn Strom Collins. Halifax: Nimbus Publishing, 2019.

———. "Anne of Ingleside." MS. CM 67.5.4, Confederation Centre Art Gallery, Charlottetown.

———. *Anne of Ingleside*. Toronto: McClelland and Stewart, 1939.

———. *Anne of the Island*. Boston: The Page Company, 1915.

———. "Anne of Windy Poplars." MS. CM 67.5.7, Confederation Centre Art Gallery, Charlottetown.

———. *Anne of Windy Poplars*. Toronto: McClelland and Stewart, 1936.

———. *Anne of Windy Willows*. London: George G. Harrap and Company, 1936.

———. *Anne's House of Dreams*. Toronto: McClelland, Goodchild, and Stewart, 1917.

———. "Anne to the Rescue." In *Selected Stories from Canadian Prose*, 255–68. Toronto: The Macmillan Company of Canada, 1929.

———. *Around the Hearth: Tales of Home and Family*. Edited by Joanne Lebold. Originally selected by Rea Wilmshurst. Halifax: Nimbus Publishing, 2022.

———. *At the Altar: Matrimonial Tales*. Edited by Rea Wilmshurst. Toronto: McClelland and Stewart, 1994.

———. "Aunt Olivia's Beau." *The Designer* (New York), June 1905, 196–200. Also, in revised form, in Montgomery, *Chronicles of Avonlea*, 176–201.

———. "An Autobiographical Sketch." In Lefebvre, *The L.M. Montgomery Reader*, 1: 254–59. Previously in *Ontario Library Review* 13, no. 3 (February 1929): 94–96.

———. "An Autumn Evening." *The Youth's Companion* (Boston), 29 November 1906, 614. Also, signed Lucy Maud Montgomery, in Watson and Pierce, *Our Canadian Literature*, 155–56.

———. "Bits from My Mailbag." In Lefebvre, *The L.M. Montgomery Reader*, 1: 185–88. Previously in *Manitoba Free Press* (Winnipeg), 9 December 1922, Christmas Book Section, 5.

———. "Blank Verse? 'Very Blank,' Said Father." In Lefebvre, *The L.M. Montgomery Reader*, 1: 180–81. Previously in *Winnipeg Evening Tribune*, 3 December 1921, Magazine Section, 3.

———. *The Blue Castle*. Toronto: McClelland and Stewart, 1926.

———. *The Blythes Are Quoted*. Edited by Benjamin Lefebvre. Toronto: Viking Canada, 2009.

———. "Bobbed Goldilocks." *The Delineator* (New York), July 1926, 10, 70–71.

———. "Book Price Record Book, 1908–1942." XZ1 MS A098043, L.M. Montgomery Collection, Archival and Special Collections, University of Guelph Library.

————. "Business and Lawsuit Correspondence Including Much on Movie Contracts, 1928–1940, 1973." XZ1 MS A098011, L.M. Montgomery Collection, Archival and Special Collections, University of Guelph Library.

————. "Captain Jim's Enjoyment." In French, *Standard Canadian Reciter*, 259.

————. "A Case of Atavism." *The Reader Magazine* (Indianapolis), November 1905, 658–66. Also, in revised form and as "The Winning of Lucinda," in Montgomery, *Chronicles of Avonlea*, 135–55.

————. *Christmas with Anne and Other Holiday Stories*. Edited by Rea Wilmshurst. Toronto: McClelland and Stewart, 1995.

————. *Chronicles of Avonlea*. Boston: L.C. Page and Company, 1912.

————. "Chronicles of Ingleside." *Onward: A Paper for Young Canadians* (Toronto), 10 September 1939, 577–79, 591; 17 September 1939, 596–97, 602–3; 24 September 1939, 612–13, 619, 623; 1 October 1939, 625–28, 638–39; 8 October 1939, 644–45, 655; 15 October 1939, 662–63; 22 October 1939, 674–75, 687; 29 October 1939, 698–99, 702–3.

————. *The Complete Journals of L.M. Montgomery: The PEI Years, 1889–1900*. Edited by Mary Henley Rubio and Elizabeth Hillman Waterston. Toronto: Oxford University Press, 2012.

————. *The Complete Journals of L.M. Montgomery: The PEI Years, 1901–1911*. Edited by Mary Henley Rubio and Elizabeth Hillman Waterston. Toronto: Oxford University Press, 2013.

————. "The Courting of Prissy Strong." *The Housewife* (New York), July 1909, 12–13. Also, in revised form, in Montgomery, *Chronicles of Avonlea*, 246–64.

————. "A Day Off." *The Family Herald and Weekly Star* (Montreal), 1 July 1936, 20–21.

————. "The Deferment of Hester." *The Blue Book Magazine* (Chicago), July 1907, 625–31.

————. "A Disappointment." In French, *Standard Canadian Reciter*, 41.

————. *The Doctor's Sweetheart and Other Stories*. Selected by Catherine McLay. Toronto: McGraw-Hill Ryerson, 1979.

————. "A Double Surprise." *The Blue Book Magazine* (Chicago), June 1908, 341–46.

————. "Each in His Own Tongue." *The Delineator* (New York), October 1910, 247, 324–28. Also, in revised form, in Montgomery, *Chronicles of Avonlea*, 78–115.

———. "The Education of Sally." *Gunter's Magazine* (New York), April 1906, 297–306. Also, in revised form, in *The Canadian Courier* (Toronto), 21 June 1913, 9–10, 25–26. Also, in revised form and as "The Education of Betty," in Montgomery, *Further Chronicles of Avonlea*, 188–214.

———. "Elizabeth's Child." *Young People* (Philadelphia), 17 December 1904, 407–8. Also in *Girl's Own Paper* (London), December 1937, 99–104.

———. *Emily Climbs*. Toronto: McClelland and Stewart, 1925.

———. *Emily of New Moon*. Toronto: McClelland and Stewart, 1923.

———. "Emily of New Moon." In *The Voice of Canada: Canadian Prose and Poetry*, selected by A.M. Stephen, 97–100. Toronto: J.M. Dent, 1926.

———. *Emily's Quest*. Toronto: McClelland and Stewart, 1927.

———. "The End of a Quarrel." *American Agriculturist* (New York), 20 July 1907, 56, 58–59. Also, in revised form, in Montgomery, *Chronicles of Avonlea*, 288–306.

———. "Enter, Emily." *The Delineator* (New York), January 1925, 10–11, 56–57.

———. "Everybody Is Different." *The Family Herald and Weekly Star* (Montreal), 27 May 1936, 20–21.

———. *Further Chronicles of Avonlea*. Boston: The Page Company, 1920.

———. "The Garden of Spices." *Maclean's Magazine* (Toronto), March 1918, 28–30, 93, 95–96, 98–100. Also in *Girl's Own Paper* (London), September 1937, 529–35, 537. Also in Montgomery, *The Doctor's Sweetheart and Other Stories*, 140–59.

———. "The Gay Days of Old." In Lefebvre, *The L.M. Montgomery Reader*, 1: 163–68. Previously in *Farmers' Magazine* (Toronto), 15 December 1919, 18, 46.

———. "The Gift of a Day." *The Family Herald and Weekly Star* (Montreal), 20 May 1936, 20–21, 30.

———. "The Girls of Silver Bush." MS. CM 78.5.6, Confederation Centre Art Gallery, Charlottetown.

———. *The Golden Road*. Boston: L.C. Page and Company, 1913.

———. *The Green Gables Letters from L.M. Montgomery to Ephraim Weber, 1905–1909*. Edited by Wilfrid Eggleston. Toronto: The Ryerson Press, 1960.

———. "Her Dog Day." *The Delineator* (New York), April 1925, 10, 80–83.

———. "Her Father's Daughter." *The Christian Endeavor World* (Boston), 26 December 1907, 269, 275–77. Also, in revised form, in Montgomery, *Further Chronicles of Avonlea*, 38–69.

———. "A House Divided against Itself." *Canadian Home Journal* (Toronto), March 1930, 3–5, 70, 72. Also, as "A Family Affair," in *The Story-Teller* (London), July 1931, 538–46. Also in Montgomery, *Along the Shore*, 275–95.

———. "How I Began." In Lefebvre, *The L.M. Montgomery Reader*, 1: 144–47. Previously in *The Canadian Bookman* (Toronto), 1 April 1915, 6–7.

———. "How I Began to Write." In Lefebvre, *The L.M. Montgomery Reader*, 1: 67–72. Previously in *Globe* (Toronto), 7 January 1911, 10.

———. "How We Went to the Wedding." *The Housewife* (New York), April 1913, 3–5, 31; May 1913, 12–13, 28. Also, in revised form, in *Girl's Own Paper* (London), October 1938, 11–21.

———. "The Indecision of Margaret." *Gunter's Magazine* (New York), September 1906, 156–65.

———. "'It.'" *The Chatelaine* (Toronto), April 1929, 21, 56, 58.

———. "Jane of Lantern Hill." MS. CM 67.5.3, Confederation Centre Art Gallery, Charlottetown.

———. *Jane of Lantern Hill*. Toronto: McClelland and Stewart, 1937.

———. "Jane's Baby." *The Christian Endeavor World* (Boston), 20 December 1906, 249, 260–61. Also, in revised form, in Montgomery, *Further Chronicles of Avonlea*, 70–88.

———. "Janet's Rebellion." *Girl's Own Paper* (London), December 1938, 117–20. Also in Montgomery, *After Many Years*, 275–81.

———. *Kilmeny of the Orchard*. Boston: L.C. Page and Company, 1910.

———. "The Little Black Doll." *Zion's Herald* (Boston), 11 August 1909, 1012–13. Also in *Girl's Own Paper* (London), January 1939, 207–10. Also in Montgomery, *Akin to Anne*, 165–75.

———. "Little Joscelyn." *The Christian Endeavor World* (Boston), 1 September 1904, 988–89. Also, in revised form, in Montgomery, *Chronicles of Avonlea*, 116–34.

———. *L.M. Montgomery's Complete Journals: The Ontario Years, 1911–1917*. Edited by Jen Rubio. N.p.: Rock's Mills Press, 2016.

———. *L.M. Montgomery's Complete Journals: The Ontario Years, 1918–1921*. Edited by Jen Rubio. N.p.: Rock's Mills Press, 2017.

———. *L.M. Montgomery's Complete Journals: The Ontario Years, 1930–1933*. Edited by Jen Rubio. N.p.: Rock's Mills Press, 2019.

———. "The Locket That Was Baked." *The Congregationalist and Christian World* (Boston), 7 March 1908, 318.

———. "Lost—a Child's Laughter." *The Delineator* (New York), June 1926, 15, 68, 70.

———. "Love Story of an Awkward Man." *Springfield (MA) Sunday Republican*, 25 June 1905, 22.

———. "Magic for Marigold." *The Delineator* (New York), May 1926, 10–11, 82, 85.

———. *Magic for Marigold*. Toronto: McClelland and Stewart, 1929.

———. "The Man Who Wouldn't Talk." *The Family Herald and Weekly Star* (Montreal), 6 May 1936, 22–23, 30.

———. "Memories of Childhood Days." In Lefebvre, *The L.M. Montgomery Reader*, 1: 341–42. Previously in *The Maritime Advocate and Busy East* (Sackville, NB), May–June 1936, 35.

———. "The Miracle at Mayfield." *The Christian Endeavor World* (Boston), 28 October 1909, 69–70. Also, in revised form and as "The Miracle at Carmody," in Montgomery, *Chronicles of Avonlea*, 265–87.

———. "Miss Cornelia Makes a Call." In French, *Standard Canadian Reciter*, 115–27.

———. "Miss Cornelia's Startling Announcement." In French, *Standard Canadian Reciter*, 128–33.

———. "Miss Much-Afraid." *The Family Herald and Weekly Star* (Montreal), 3 June 1936, 20–21.

———. *Mistress Pat: A Novel of Silver Bush*. Toronto: McClelland and Stewart, 1935.

———. "More Blessed to Give." *Girl's Own Paper* (London), December 1939, 125–28. Also in Montgomery, *After Many Years*, 283–90.

———. "Mrs. Skinner's Story." *The Westminster* (Toronto), October 1907, 255–58.

———. *My Dear Mr. M: Letters to G.B. MacMillan from L.M. Montgomery*. Edited by Francis W.P. Bolger and Elizabeth R. Epperly. Toronto: McGraw-Hill Ryerson, 1980.

———. *A Name for Herself: Selected Writings, 1891–1917*. Edited by Benjamin Lefebvre. Toronto: University of Toronto Press, 2018. The L.M. Montgomery Library.

———. "Night Watch." *The Delineator* (New York), March 1925, 10–11, 96–97.

———. "Novel Writing Notes." In Lefebvre, *The L.M. Montgomery Reader*, 1: 197–98. Previously in *The Editor: The Journal of Information for Literary Workers* (Highland Falls, NY), 17 November 1923, 53–54.

———. "Off to the Fishing Ground." *The Youth's Companion* (Boston), 3 November 1904, 556. Also in French, *Standard Canadian Reciter*, 149–50.

———. "Ol' Man Reeves' Girl." *The Farm and Fireside* (Springfield, OH), 15 June 1905, 14–15. Also, in revised form and as "Old Man Shaw's Girl," in Montgomery, *Chronicles of Avonlea*, 156–75.

———. "One Clear Call." *The Household Magazine* (Topeka, KS), August 1928, 6–7, 21.

———. "One of Us." *Canadian Home Journal* (Toronto), February 1928, 8–9, 54.

———. "On the Hills." *Zion's Herald* (Boston), 6 October 1909, 1265. Also, signed Lucy Maud Montgomery, in Watson and Pierce, *Our Canadian Literature*, 156–57.

———. "Pa Rudge's Purchase." *The Christian Endeavor World* (Boston), 22 February 1906, 421–22. Also, in revised form and as "Pa Sloane's Purchase," in Montgomery, *Chronicles of Avonlea*, 232–45.

———. "Pat of Silver Bush." MS. CM 78.5.4, Confederation Centre Art Gallery, Charlottetown.

———. *Pat of Silver Bush*. Toronto: McClelland and Stewart, 1933.

———. "Paul, Shy Man." *The Housekeeper* (Minneapolis), March 1907, 5–6, 39.

———. "Playmate." *The Delineator* (Toronto), August 1926, 15, 66.

———. "Polly Patterson's Autograph Square." *Zion's Herald* (Boston), 3 February 1904, 146–47.

———. "The Promise of Lucy Ellen." *The Delineator* (New York), February 1904, 268–71. Also in *The Canadian Courier* (Toronto), 3 May 1913, 8–9, 25. Also in Montgomery, *The Doctor's Sweetheart and Other Stories*, 58–66.

———. "The Punishment of Billy." *Canadian Home Journal* (Toronto), February 1929, 16–17, 77.

———. "The Quarantine at Alexander Abraham's." *Everybody's Magazine* (New York), April 1907, 495–503. Also, in revised form, in Montgomery, *Chronicles of Avonlea*, 202–31.

———. *Rainbow Valley*. Toronto: McClelland and Stewart, 1919.

———. *Readying Rilla: L.M. Montgomery's Reworking of* Rilla of Ingleside. Edited by Elizabeth Waterston and Kate Waterston. N.p.: Rock's Mills Press, 2016.

———. *Rilla of Ingleside.* Toronto: McClelland and Stewart, 1921.

———. "Road to Yesterday—Typed Copies of Some of the Stories, n.d." XZ1 MS A098004, L.M. Montgomery Collection, Archival and Special Collections, University of Guelph Library.

———. *The Road to Yesterday.* Toronto: McGraw-Hill Ryerson, 1974.

———, comp. Scrapbooks 1–12. PEI.OXZ PS 8525.068 A16 1981, University Archives and Special Collections, University of Prince Edward Island Library.

———. "[Seasons in the Woods]." In Lefebvre, *The L.M. Montgomery Reader,* 1: 73–97.

———. *The Selected Journals of L.M. Montgomery,* Volume 4: *1929–1935;* Volume 5: *1935–1942.* Edited by Mary Rubio and Elizabeth Waterston. Toronto: Oxford University Press, 1998, 2004.

———. "Spring in the Woods." *The Canadian Magazine* (Toronto), May 1911, 59–62.

———. *The Story Girl.* Boston: L.C. Page and Company, 1911.

———. "A Substitute Journalist." *Forward* (Philadelphia), 9 March 1907, 73–74. Also in *Girl's Own Paper* (London), September 1940, 485–88. Also in Montgomery, *Against the Odds,* 217–27.

———. *A Tangled Web.* Toronto: McClelland and Stewart, 1931.

———. "Tannis of the Flats." *The Criterion* (New York), April 1904, 11–15. Also in *The Canadian Magazine* (Toronto), January 1914, 275–82. Also, in revised form, in Montgomery, *Further Chronicles of Avonlea,* 280–301.

———. "Too Few Cooks." *The Delineator* (New York), February 1925, 10, 78, 81–82.

———. "A Tragic Evening." *The Family Herald and Weekly Star* (Montreal), 24 June 1936, 20–21.

———. "Una of the Garden." *The Housekeeper* (Minneapolis), December 1908, 7, 18; January 1909, 11–12; February 1909, 8–9, 16; March 1909, 7, 17; April 1909, 8–9, 32.

———. *Una of the Garden.* Edited by Donna J. Campbell and Simon Lloyd. N.p.: L.M. Montgomery Institute, 2010.

———. *The Watchman and Other Poems.* Toronto: McClelland, Goodchild, and Stewart, 1916.

———. "The Wedding at Poplar Point." *The Family Herald and Weekly Star* (Montreal), 13 May 1936, 22–23, 30.

———. "The Westcott Elopement." *The Family Herald and Weekly Star* (Montreal), 10 June 1936, 20–21.

———. "What Came of a Dare." *The Designer* (New York), May 1902, 94–95.

———. "A Will, a Way and a Woman." *American Agriculturist* (Springfield, MA), 15 August 1908, 136; 22 August 1908, 157–58.

———. "The Woods in Autumn." *The Canadian Magazine* (Toronto), October 1911, 574–77.

———. "The Woods in Summer." *The Canadian Magazine* (Toronto), September 1911, 399–402.

———. "The Woods in Winter." *The Canadian Magazine* (Toronto), December 1911, 162–64.

———. *A World of Songs: Selected Poems, 1894–1921.* Edited by Benjamin Lefebvre. Toronto: University of Toronto Press, 2019. The L.M. Montgomery Library.

Munro, Alice. Afterword to *Emily of New Moon*, by L.M. Montgomery, 357–61. Toronto: McClelland and Stewart, 1989. New Canadian Library.

———. "Amundsen." *The New Yorker*, 27 August 2012, 58–69.

———. *Dance of the Happy Shades.* Toronto: The Ryerson Press, 1968.

———. *Dear Life.* Toronto: McClelland and Stewart, 2012.

———. *The Moons of Jupiter.* Toronto: Macmillan of Canada, 1982.

———. *Who Do You Think You Are?* Toronto: Macmillan of Canada, 1978.

Noomé, Idette. "The Nature of the Beast: Pets and People in L.M. Montgomery's Fiction." In *L.M. Montgomery and the Matter of Nature(s)*, edited by Rita Bode and Jean Mitchell, 198–211, 245–49. Montreal and Kingston: McGill-Queen's University Press, 2018.

"Publishing Agreements." 1907–1919. MG30-D342, R2434-1-2-E, Lucy Maud Montgomery Collection, Library and Archives Canada.

Roy, Wendy. *The Next Instalment: Serials, Sequels, and Adaptations of Nellie L. McClung, L.M. Montgomery, and Mazo de la Roche.* Waterloo: Wilfrid Laurier University Press, 2019.

Rubio, Mary Henley. *Lucy Maud Montgomery: The Gift of Wings.* N.p.: Doubleday Canada, 2008.

Russell, Ruth Weber, D.W. Russell, and Rea Wilmshurst. *Lucy Maud Montgomery: A Preliminary Bibliography.* Waterloo: University of Waterloo Library, 1986. University of Waterloo Library Bibliography 13.

Satran, Pamela Redmond, and Linda Rosenkrantz. *The Baby Name Bible: The Ultimate Guide by America's Baby-Naming Experts.* New York: St. Martin's Griffin, 2007.

Saunders, Margaret Marshall. *Beautiful Joe.* 1894. Edited by Keridiana Chez. Peterborough: Broadview Editions, 2015.

Siddall, Gillian. "A Note on the Text." In Duncan, *The Pool in the Desert,* 21–22.

Spadoni, Carl. Introduction to Leacock, *Sunshine Sketches of a Little Town,* vii–lxxxi.

Speake, Jennifer. *Oxford Dictionary of Proverbs.* 6th ed. Oxford: Oxford University Press, 2015.

Thacker, Robert. *Reading Alice Munro, 1973–2013.* Calgary: University of Calgary Press, 2016.

Tiessen, Hildi Froese, and Paul Gerard Tiessen. "A Note on the Text." In Montgomery, *After Green Gables,* 53–55.

Ware, Tracy. "The Progress of Writing in Alice Munro's 'The Office.'" *Studies in Canadian Literature / Études en littérature canadienne* 44, no. 2 (2019): 271–92.

Warkentin, Germaine. "A Note on the Text." In Duncan, *Set in Authority,* 324–27.

Waterston, Elizabeth. "L.M. Montgomery's Creative Path to Publication." In Montgomery, *Readying Rilla,* v–xvi.

———. *Magic Island: The Fictions of L.M. Montgomery.* Toronto: Oxford University Press, 2008.

Watson, Albert Durrant, and Lorne Albert Pierce, chosen by. *Our Canadian Literature: Representative Prose and Verse.* 3rd ed. Toronto: The Ryerson Press, 1923.

Wiggins, Genevieve. *L.M. Montgomery.* New York: Twayne Publishers, 1992. Twayne's World Authors Series 834.

Wilmshurst, Rea. "Cooking with L.M. Montgomery." *Canadian Children's Literature / Littérature canadienne pour la jeunesse* 37 (1985): 47–52.

———. "Finding L.M. Montgomery's Short Stories." In Lefebvre, *The L.M. Montgomery Reader,* 2: 223–27. Previously as Afterword to Montgomery, *Across the Miles,* 255–60.

———. "L.M. Montgomery's Use of Quotations and Allusions in the 'Anne' Books." *Canadian Children's Literature / Littérature canadienne pour la jeunesse* 56 (1989): 15–45.

———. "Quotations and Allusions in L.M. Montgomery's Other Novels." Toronto: N.p., 1990.